Dance and Modernism in Irish and German Literature and Culture

Dance and Modernism in Irish and German Literature and Culture

Connections in Motion

Edited by Sabine Egger, Catherine E. Foley, and Margaret Mills Harper

LEXINGTON BOOKS
Lanham • Boulder • New York •London

Published by Lexington Books
An imprint of The Rowman & Littlefield Publishing Group, Inc.
4501 Forbes Blvd., Ste. 200, Lanham, MD 20706
www.rowman.com

6 Tinworth Street, London SE11 5AL, United Kingdom

British Library Cataloguing in Publication Information Available

Library of Congress Cataloging-in-Publication Data

Names: Egger, Sabine, editor. | Foley, Catherine E., editor. | Harper, Margaret Mills, 1957- editor. | International Conference in Irish-German Studies (16th : 2016 : University of Limerick)
Title: Dance and modernism in Irish and German literature and culture : connections in motion / edited by Sabine Egger, Catherine E. Foley, and Margaret Mills Harper.
Description: Lanham : Lexington Books, [2020] | "This volume is derived from ideas explored at the interdisciplinary conference 'Connections in Motion: Dance in Irish and German Literature, Film and Culture,' held at the University of Limerick in November 2016"— Introduction. | Includes bibliographical references and index. | Summary: "This collection of essays by dancers, scholars of ethnochoreology, dance studies, drama studies, cultural studies, literature, and architecture explores Irish-German connections through dance in choreographic processes and on stage, in literary texts, photography, dance documentation, film, and architecture since the 1920s"— Provided by publisher.
Identifiers: LCCN 2019045692 (print) | LCCN 2019045693 (ebook) | ISBN 9781498594264 (cloth) | ISBN 9781498594288 (pbk)
ISBN 9781498594271 (epub)
Subjects: LCSH: Modern dance—Ireland. | Modern dance—Germany. | Literature and dance—Ireland. | Literature and dance—Germany. | Modernism (Aesthetics)—Ireland. | Modernism (Aesthetics)—Germany. | Ireland—Relations—Germany. | Germany—Relations—Ireland.
Classification: LCC GV1646.I8 D36 2020 (print) | LCC GV1646.I8 (ebook) | DDC 793.3/19415—dc23
LC record available at https://lccn.loc.gov/2019045692
LC ebook record available at https://lccn.loc.gov/2019045693

∞™ The paper used in this publication meets the minimum requirements of American National Standard for Information Sciences—Permanence of Paper for Printed Library Materials, ANSI/NISO Z39.48-1992.

Contents

PART II

Figures

Introduction

This volume is derived from ideas explored at the interdisciplinary conference "Connections in Motion: Dance in Irish and German Literature, Film and Culture," held at the University of Limerick in November 2016 (http://www.ictstudies.eu/news-events/ or http://ulsites.ul.ie/irishgerman/). The event brought together dancers and scholars of ethnochoreology, dance studies, drama studies, cultural studies, literature, and architecture, who explored Irish-German connections through dance in choreographic processes and on stage, in literary texts, photography, dance documentation, film, and architecture from the 1920s to today. Taking the findings of the conference as a starting point, the chapters included in this volume discuss modernism, with a specific focus on modern dance, and its impact on different art forms and discourses in Irish and German culture. Within this framework, dance is regarded both as a motif and a specific form of spatial movement, which allows for the transgression of medial and disciplinary boundaries as well as gender, social, or cultural differences. The interdisciplinary focus on dance as a form of movement, trace (Derrida), or mode of transgression (Foucault), thus opens new perspectives on several areas of Irish and German Studies.

The volume consists of two parts, Part I focusing on Irish-German cultural connections made through dance, and Part II exploring the role of dance in Irish and German literature, visual art, and architecture.

BACKGROUND AND STRUCTURE

Modern Dance, understood as a *Gesamtkunstwerk*, influenced, and was influenced by, other art forms, including architecture and industrial design in the early twentieth century; it fundamentally changed perceptions of space and movement to the present. Gestural movement, choreography, and corporeality took a central role on stage, in literature, visual media, and the design of buildings, a shift that still finds its reflection in contemporary culture. In the Irish context, this shift is of particular interest with regard to the leading role of Irish modernist literature internationally; the significance of Irish traditional dance and culture as identity markers; and their relationship to ballet, contemporary dance, and other expressions of culture for Irish as well as international audiences.

Part I of the volume looks at direct influences and contact points between modernism in German-speaking countries and Ireland, including the significance of such "connections in motion" until the present. "Emergency Dublin" became a safe haven for ex-pat Bohemians fleeing WWII in the 1930s and 1940s and a space of exchange among writers, directors, architects, and artists such as the German-Irish dancer Erina Brady. Emigrants brought ideas of movement and space popular in the German-speaking countries of the time to Ireland, where these took on new directions in the Irish context, and vice versa. Examples include the influence of Dalcroze Eurhythmics, the movement choirs of Rudolf von Laban, and the work of Mary Wigman on plays at the Abbey Theatre or on physical education in Ireland. Other connections explored in Part I include European and Gaelic connections in classical music and dance, and Irish-German intellectual inheritances. These connections influenced ideas on dance as well as views on corporeality, dance documentation for archival purposes, dance research, and choreographic processes.

In chapter 1, Gisela Holfter examines the role of German-speaking immigrants to Ireland in the 1930s and 1940s, focusing on intermediaries of modernity including the physicist Edwin Schrödinger and the modern dancer Erina Brady. Holfter discusses how Germany played a considerable role in the development of both modern dance and modern physics, and she explores the impact that they both had on Ireland through these intermediaries. Chapter 2, by Deirdre Mulrooney, examines documentary and contextual evidence to support the theory that the 1940s Irish-German modern dance pioneer Erina Brady was a disciple of Mary Wigman, the inventor of *Ausdruckstanz* or Expressionist Dance. Mulrooney compares the pioneering work of Brady in spreading Wigman's *Ausdruckstanz* in Dublin with that of Hanya Holm in the United States, and argues that Brady laid the foundation for today's thriving contemporary dance scene in twenty-first-century Ireland.

Chapter 3, by Ruth Fleischmann, sketches the life-long artistic collaboration between Aloys Fleischmann, the Irish composer, music professor, and scholar of German parentage, and Joan Moriarty, choreographer and founder of professional ballet in Ireland, from 1947 to 1992. Fleischmann explores a duality of cultural influence on these artists as they sought to develop an

Irish classical art in both music and ballet in Ireland, but also influenced by Ireland's Gaelic cultural heritage. In chapter 4, Catherine E. Foley examines the emergence of archives in the Western world, and the notion of collecting music and dance practices for museums and archives, as part of a wider European enterprise going back to the eighteenth century and, in particular, to the German philosopher, theologian, poet, and literary critic Johann Gottfried Herder (1744–1803). She reflects on Irish-German connections and intellectual inheritances as manifested in her education, early training, and early professional self as a collector of Irish traditional music, song, and dance, ethnochoreologist, and ethnomusicologist, and focuses on the Irish traditional step-dance collection. Foley recounts how she applied Labanotation, the movement documentation system invented in 1928 by Rudolf Laban, one of the founders of European modern dance, to document and analyze Irish traditional step-dancing for archival and research purposes in the 1980s.

Chapter 5, by Irish-born German choreographer Marguerite Donlon, examines the process of choreographing the work "Somewhere Between Remembering and Forgetting," based on Brendan Kennelly's poem "The Man Made of Rain," for Stuttgart Ballet, Germany, in 2002. In exploring her dance trajectory from her early training in Irish dancing and ballet in Longford, Ireland, to her professional career as a ballet dancer and choreographer, Donlon reveals her choreographic process, including the influences, impulses, and collaborations on which she drew to choreograph this work. In chapter 6, Finola Cronin reflects on the work and choreographic process of German choreographer Pina Bausch, director of Tanztheater Wuppertal and, in particular, Bausch's use of the *Aufgaben* (tasks) phase, a rehearsal method in which she asked her ensemble members, drawn from a range of nationalities, to mine ideas from their diverse cultures. As a member of Bausch's ensemble from 1985 to 1994, Cronin reflects on how she "found Ireland" through the *Aufgaben* phase, which she argues was the result of embodied research formed into composition.

Chapters in Part II explore the significance of modernism as a movement with dance occupying a key position, in Irish and German literature, drama, photography, film, and architecture from the beginning of the twentieth century to the present. The focal point of this section is the legacy of modernism in the form of dance and gestural movement crossing cultural, social, disciplinary, and medial limits, with transgression understood here as any performative practice crossing cultural and other boundaries (in Foucaultian terms), or, alternatively, as a trace or motion of deferment (as conceived by Derrida). While individual chapters in this section focus on either Irish or German examples, parallels and points of connection between both become apparent in the course of the section, also in the light of findings from Part I.

At the same time, Part II explores ways in which dance and literature, dance and architecture, or dance and photography, as very different forms of artistic expression, can enter into intermedial encounters. Apart from dance as a motif or metaphor, chapters in this section look at the way literature and other forms of expression incorporate dance as another medial form of expression. This connection poses particular challenges, since dance and literature, or dance and architecture at first sight appear to be medial antagonists, dance being kinetic and multi-medial, while literature—as the written word on the page—or buildings seem rather static, and, in the case of literature or photography, two dimensional.

The first chapter of this section, chapter 7, by Susan Jones, examines Samuel Beckett's connections to the aesthetics of dance, focusing particularly on Beckett's one "dance" play, *Quadrat I and II* (1981). This strange work for television bears uncanny resemblances to the work of Bauhaus choreographer and director Oskar Schlemmer, whose own career in art began in Stuttgart in the early twentieth century. Beckett's innovative modernist aesthetic for television echoes the formal design and choreographic drive of Schlemmer's *Raumtanz* (1926), one of the *Bauhaus Dances*. Jones shows how Beckett responded to Schlemmer's blueprint, converting Schlemmer's formalist structure into an exploration of affectless propulsion in which the body moves repeatedly and mechanically through geometricized pathways, suggesting a far more menacing, Dantean journey. Furthermore, Jones argues, rather than representing an outlier in Beckett's canon, *Quad* in many ways develops from experiments with corporeal movement encountered in the shorter prose of the 1960s and 1970s. In chapter 8, Siobhán Purcell argues for another influence of dance on literature in her claim that received narratives of Lucia Joyce as a dancer, as well as her fictionalization within a number of works by both her father James Joyce and Samuel Beckett, belie her importance as an innovator and artist in her own right. In works like Joyce's *Pomes Penyeach* and *Finnegans Wake* and Beckett's *Dream of Fair to Middling Women* and *More Pricks than Kicks*, representations of Lucia Joyce tacitly undermine the contributions of female, queer, and disabled voices in the 1930s. In excavating her involvement in those works and the distortion of her memory, Purcell traces the significance of dance to the modernist impulse and aims to recover a sliver of European modernism in the 1930s.

Chapter 9 focuses on another Irish modernist writer, W. B. Yeats. Margaret Mills Harper offers a rereading of figures of dancers, a common motif in Yeats's poetry and drama, using ideational structures from the "system" of *A Vision*, the philosophic book written from materials generated by Yeats and his wife George (née Hyde Lees) through automatic writing and other occult experiments. Harper argues that the figures of dancers in several of

Yeats's most well-known poems, characterized by ambiguities of gender and sexuality, can be seen, if read through principles of *A Vision*, to represent changing and unsettled states of being. In chapter 10, Lucia Ruprecht shows how modernist poetics of dance have been taken further in contemporary, postmodernist writing and performance. In the work of German writers and artists discussed by Ruprecht—Anne Juren, Martina Hefter, Monika Rinck, and Philipp Gehmacher—dance tends to be experienced by a (non-fixed) subject rather than regarded and made to mean as object. Ruprecht's chapter explores a biographically informed focus on movement beyond established choreographic modes in these examples of contemporary poetry and dance. Looking at poetic concepts and poetological movement, Ruprecht delineates modes of artistic research in writing and performance. Saying or dancing "I" is shown here to take place within structures of address that establish forms of profound relationality. Approached with reference to Adriana Cavarero and Judith Butler, this relationality brings about accounts of a self that acts ethically, even though it must remain inaccessible to itself.

Sabine Egger's comparative analysis of transgressive dance in autobiographical texts by Johannes Bobrowski (1917–1965) and Katja Petrowskaja (born 1970) in chapter 11 highlight how perceptions of ethics and identity can be (de)stabilized through a poetics of memory working with dance on a number of levels, and how such a poetics may be situated in specific cultural and generational contexts. Both writers address the question of how to remember the Second World War and the Holocaust as key events for German literature from the second half of the twentieth century to the present. Both employ dance as a carnivalesque mode of transgression or deconstruction, drawing on Eastern European Hasidic traditions of dance and music, and on modern dance forms. However, in contrast to Bobrowski's "Der Tänzer Malige" (The Dancer Malige, 1965), which engages with the topic from a perpetrator or contemporary witness perspective, Petrowskaja's *Vielleicht Esther* (Maybe Esther, 2014) reflects on the author's Jewish family history from the viewpoint of a third-generation victim. Furthermore, Petrowskaja's postmodernist approach to the subject's physical movement and memory distinguishes her poetics from Bobrowski's balancing act between realism and modernism. Joseph Twist's contribution in chapter 12 adds an awareness of both the energy and violence inherent in the destabilizing potential of dance in contemporary writing with a focus on Turkish-German literature, as well as intercultural and gender issues. The short stories "Libidoökonomie" (Libido Economy) and "Der Kranich auf dem Kiesel in der Pfütze" (The Crane on the Pebble in the Puddle), published in Feridun Zaimoglu's 2004 collection of stories, rediscover the radical potential of belly and dervish dances in view of our understanding of identity and subjectivity in the postmodern age. In "Libidoökonomie," belly dance plays a role in undermining the violence of identity formation within the Self-Other binary, as it disrupts the defining power of the male gaze and ultimately unveils no hidden truth. In "Der Kranich," an Alevi-Bektaşi *semah* ritual points toward a similarly non-appropriative openness, but in this instance toward the divine. Both dances imply an idea of subjectivity with a radically transformative potential, Twist argues. They convey a sense of self that is decentered and destabilized rather than being presumed to be unitary and sovereign over itself and others, challenging modernist views of dance and dancers that operate within the confines of a system of binary opposites, striving toward unity.

To conclude this survey of dance in modernist and postmodernist Irish and German literature and culture, Jan Frohburg and Tanja Poppelreuter's chapter 13, on the interrelation of dance and architecture in the work of the German-American architect Ludwig Mies van der Rohe, brings us back to the modernist idea of free movement and unity as a starting point of this volume. Their exploration of movement and space from a different disciplinary perspective illuminates the complex links between various art forms and ideals of social life and the emergence of a "New Man" at the beginning of the twentieth century. Frohburg and Poppelreuter show how the work of Mies, widely regarded as one of the pioneers of modernist architecture, was partly inspired by a number of groundbreaking dance performances at *Gartenstadt Hellerau* near Dresden, Germany, in 1913, organized by the Jaques-Dalcroze Institute, which had a far-reaching impact on a variety of avant-garde artists at the time.

We would like to acknowledge and take the opportunity to thank the following institutions and funding agencies that have supported this project, from the conference at the Irish World Academy of Music and Dance, University of Limerick, in November 2016, co-organized by Sabine Egger, Catherine E. Foley, Jan Frohburg, Margaret Mills Harper, and Gisela Holfter, to the present volume: the Goethe Institute, Ireland; the German Academic Exchange Service; the German Embassy, Dublin; the Institute for Irish Studies and the Research and Graduate School at Mary Immaculate College; the Irish World Academy of Music and Dance; the National Dance Archive of Ireland; and the School of English, Irish, and Communication, University of Limerick. Special thanks go to Gisela Holfter, Joint Director of the Centre for Irish-German Studies (University of Limerick), which co-hosted the conference in 2016, together with the Irish World Academy of Music and Dance, the National Dance Archive of Ireland, and the Irish Centre for Transnational Studies. We also wish to thank Mayuri Goswami for her assistance in formatting this volume and Sarah Scarborough, who compiled the index.

PART I

Chapter One

Modernism, Migration, and Irish-German Connections in the 1930s and 1940s

The Impact of Modern Physics and Dance on Ireland

Gisela Holfter

Modernism is notoriously difficult to define (recent scholarship states that "(t)here is no such thing as modernity, only multiple modernities."[1] A number of features of modernity as defined by Michel Foucault, however, can be utilized to characterize this category as a phenomenon which is marked by developments such as a questioning or rejection of tradition; the prioritization of individualism, freedom, faith in inevitable social, scientific and technological progress, rationalization and professionalization.[2] My interest is to look at modernity and migration in the context of Irish-German relations, focusing on the role of particular German-speaking immigrants to Ireland in the 1930s and 1940s and to what extent we can find examples of intermediaries of modernity coming to Ireland.

Migrants as agents of change have a history as long as humanity. In the Irish-German context, this can be traced back to the hugely influential Irish missionaries on the Continent. Unsurprisingly, this impact of migrants continues throughout time, for example with Lola Montez,[3] who influenced King Ludwig I of Bavaria (and who contributed to his downfall) or William Mulvany,[4] who modernized coal mining in the Ruhr area. German influence on the modernization of Ireland has also long been recognized, an often-quoted example being the electrification scheme including the building of the hydroelectric power station in Ardnacrusha by Siemens-Schuckert 1925–1929. In the following, I want to concentrate on two different and quite disparate areas—science and dance. One could argue that, by doing so, to some extent I am following the example of the Irish Taoiseach of the time, Éamon de Valera, who wanted to establish a Dublin Institute for Advanced Studies with two main areas not closely related—Physics and the Irish language. With an eye to this Institute's Physics department, I will give examples of how Ireland benefited from its small intake of German-speaking refugees, and then in a second step focus on dance, not only in the Republic of Ireland but also in Northern Ireland. In the first decades of the twentieth century, there had been completely new and exciting developments in both physics and dance. Physics underwent "the greatest scientific revolution since Newton"[5] thanks to quantum mechanics (generally associated with Max Planck, Niels Bohr, Werner Heisenberg, Erwin Schrödinger, Max Born, Albert Einstein, Paul Dirac, and Arnold Sommerfeld) which, together with Albert Einstein's relativity theory, forms what is generally still understood as "modern physics" today. Likewise, the twenties "saw the gradual formation and definition of Modern Dance in Europe,"[6] a movement mainly associated with names such as Émile Jaques-Dalcroze, Rudolf Laban, Kurt Jooss, and Mary Wigman. Wigman expressed their sense of mission and importance in the context of the first Dancers' Congress in Magdeburg in May 1927 (attended also by Laban and Jooss) with a forceful statement: "Our dance is born of our age and its spirit: it has the stamp of our time as no other art form has. I wish that our contemporaries would become fully aware of their responsibilities toward their own and most alive creation, the modern dance."[7] Different though the two areas of dance and physics were, each in a sense symbolized the changing times, and their proponents believed in their special importance in terms of embodying a hugely significant transformation.

Germany played a considerable role in the development of both modern dance and modern physics, though it should be remembered that each was strongly transnational in outlook and impact. But how does Ireland fit into this picture? It had no hand in either modern physics or modern dance at that point, and for the time period we concentrate on here, it has long been seen as an example of Plato's Cave, removed from all important political (and cultural) events and isolated.[8] While this has been challenged with regard to some areas,[9] even an excellent study such as Clair Wills' *That Neutral Country—A Cultural History of Ireland during the Second World War* seems to present only a limited impression of what was happening in Ireland at that time. Of all the "agents for change" which will be named in the following, only Erwin Schrödinger is mentioned by her, and only in passing.[10] However, her account is very illuminating of the situation of Irish and migrant British writers such as T.H. White and specifically the impact of the influx of artists to Ireland, most importantly the White Stag Group.[11]

In the following I hope to make clear that thanks to the German-speaking refugees and migrants who came to Ireland in the 1930s and 1940s, new and modern developments found their way to Ireland in areas such as science and dance. Furthermore, I will argue that there was already considerable interest in and awareness of these modern developments in Ireland, at least among some people, including academics, politicians, and journalists: although the impact in both areas has long been overlooked, it can be found if one goes back to contemporary sources of the time. The seed did not always go on to flower, but there was more awareness and interest than has been previously acknowledged. "The fact that we are one of the nations turned to for sanctuary in itself makes us proud, but later on, when the influence of such men as these is fully felt, we will be not so much proud but grateful."[12]

According to Norman Bentwich, writing in the 1950s, the "idea of a haven for exiled scholars" was a motive for the creation of the Dublin Institute for Advanced Studies (DIAS).[13] Although at the time there was at least occasional appreciation in Ireland of the country's status as a destination for refugee scholars, as shown by the excerpt quoted above from an *Irish Times* article from April 1940 (which referred to lectures by different refugee scholars), this was mainly forgotten for many decades afterwards. The driving force behind the Dublin Institute for Advanced Studies was, as mentioned, the Irish Taoiseach, Éamon de Valera. In its early stages, the establishment was controversial. Michael Tierney, a later president of University College Dublin, argued that "nobody really likes this combination of mathematical physics and Celtic studies except the Taoiseach himself. It is his own idea and nobody else [. . .] likes it or wants it."[14] That the research institute became a success was thanks to the people running it, not only Erwin Schrödinger but also Walter Heitler (a refugee scholar who emigrated to Bristol in 1933 and who had been regarded by de Valera and Whittaker from the beginning as a promising combination with Schrödinger—he came to Dublin in 1941) as well as other German émigré academics and their international outlook. De Valera wanted to accelerate scientific research in Ireland focusing on subjects particularly close to his heart (mathematics / physics and the study of Irish) and saw Albert Einstein's new professional domain, the Institute for Advanced Study in Princeton, founded in 1930, as a model for the planned Dublin Institute for Advanced Studies (DIAS). Together with Edmund Whittaker, he was on the lookout for international leaders in the sciences, and as Max Born and Albert Einstein were already committed elsewhere, they approached Erwin Schrödinger—in a manner worthy of a spy thriller, according to the recollections of Anny Schrödinger. Erwin Schrödinger did come, and continues to capture the imagination, not only for academic but also for personal reasons, especially due to his rather unconventional family life. His colleague and fellow Nobel Prize winner Max Born described him in glowing terms: "His private life seemed strange to bourgeois people like us. But all this did not matter. He was a most lovable person, independent, amusing, temperamental, kind and generous, and he had a most perfect and efficient brain."[15] Schrödinger, born in Vienna in 1887, was one of the great names in physics of the twentieth century, especially after his 1926 publications on wave mechanics, for which he was awarded the Nobel Prize in 1933, together with Paul Dirac, a British physicist in Cambridge. Schrödinger had succeeded Max Planck in Berlin in 1927 but left for Oxford in 1933 when a British scientist offered positions to the most promising young German scientists suffering under the Nazi regime. Schrödinger himself was not under threat, but had no time for Hitler's policies. Living in an extra-marital relationship with Hilde March, Schrödinger arranged for Hilde's husband Arthur March to come to Oxford as well, and in May 1934 Schrödinger's and Hilde's daughter was born there, to be brought up by her mother and Schrödinger's wife Anny (who largely tolerated Erwin's affairs). Schrödinger came to Dublin in October 1939, after an interim period in Graz, Austria, brought to a close by the *Anschluss*, and Belgium. Together with Walter Heitler, Schrödinger organized international colloquiums and seminars with speakers such as Paul Peter Ewald (a refugee physicist in Belfast), Max Born (who had found a position in Edinburgh) and Paul Dirac. Accordingly, the DIAS, and indeed Ireland, became an internationally known center for research work in physics. There was considerable flexibility and the impact went beyond physics. For example, Schrödinger's lectures on "What is life?" in Dublin in 1943 were attended by some 400 listeners, the audience comprising not only many Irish academics and students but also the interested public (as well as de Valera, of course). It was even remarked upon by the American magazine *Time*: "Only in the precarious peace of Eire could Europe today provide such a spectacle. At Dublin's Trinity College last month crowds were turned away from a jam-packed scientific lecture. Cabinet ministers, diplomats, scholars and socialites loudly applauded a slight, Vienna-born professor of physics."[16]

These lectures were published a year later as a book which sold more than 100,000 copies and became one of the most influential scientific publications of the twentieth century.[17] A number of other refugee scientists who came to Ireland fall outside the scope of this article, but brief reference should be made to one who was involved in a number of modern developments and not only knew the "movers and shakers" personally, but helped bring them together. Ludwig Hopf did his PhD in Munich with Arnold Sommerfeld and became Albert Einstein's first assistant. Not only a brilliant mathematician and pedagogue, he had an astounding range of interests and abilities: he was a keen follower of C.G. Jung's ideas and introduced Jung and Einstein to each other in his house; he also explained aspects of relativity to Max Brod and Franz Kafka in Prague,[18] and was friends with artists such as Franz Marc and Max Unold.[19] Had it not been for his untimely death half a year after his arrival in Dublin, aged only fifty-five, he might have played a similar role in Ireland.

DANCE

Modern Dance was first taught in Ireland by a pupil of Mary Wigman, Erina Brady (1891–1961).[20] Daughter of a German mother and an Irish father, like most of the refugees escaping Hitler, she came to Ireland in the late 1930s. Unlike the refugees, she was not chiefly seeking safety but was on a private and professional mission. Brady's work has long been overlooked, but its importance has been acknowledged in recent years both by former pupils such as Jacqueline Robinson (who went on to be a key figure of modern dance in France and founder of L'Atelier de la Danse in Paris in 1955),[21] and by Irish scholars.[22] Brady's dance classes had a most unusual mix of pupils in wartime years, including children of the German envoy in Ireland, Eduard Hempel, as well as the son of John Betjeman. We should also remember that Erina Brady was supported in her endeavors to bring modern dance to Ireland by a number of German-speaking refugees, such as Eva Bieler (whose husband Ludwig Bieler was instrumental in cataloguing and building up a collection of medieval Hiberno-Latin manuscripts in Dublin), Lotte Sachs (whose husband Hans Sachs, formerly a leading cancer researcher in Germany, was a specialist in blood groups) and John Hennig, who had actually met Mary Wigman in Germany.[23]

Apart from Brady, early contacts with modern dance in Ireland were provided by visiting companies, most prominently that of Kurt Jooss (1901–1979).[24] A pupil of Rudolf Laban, Jooss very quickly found his own style and became the founder of the *Neue Tanzschule* in 1926. Jooss was also the co-founder of the Folkwang School in Essen, an endeavor that was parallel in spirit to the Bauhaus in Weimar and later Dessau, as Partsch-Bergson points out[25]—with two divisions, one the School for Expressive Arts (including music, dance, and speech), of which Jooss was in charge, the other the School for Design. When pressurized to let go of his Jewish dancers and collaborators after the Nazis came to power in 1933, he chose exile instead. This was in marked contrast to Rudolf Laban (1879–1958), whose role in the Third Reich up to 1937 (characterized by close cooperation until 1936 and including the preparation of a huge dance performance for the 1936 Olympics in Berlin) has been increasingly exposed as very problematic,[26] something that is still often not acknowledged among his pupils and by modern dancers. Susanne Franco argues that the "transmission of Laban's vision of dance and of his career still suffers from a binary opposing his pupils' personal memories (both bodily and oral) to historical analyses performed by scholars in the archive."[27] With Kurt Jooss there is far less ambiguity, and his impact continued after his death, [28] though arguably less strongly than Laban's influence.

Jooss came to Dublin twice in 1939 to perform to great acclaim, among other pieces, a pacifist ballet, *The Green Table*. Jooss's dance group at the time included two Irish dancers, Monica Johnson and David Grey (even though this was rarely mentioned in Irish media reports). *The Green Table*, created in 1932, had won first prize at the international competition for new choreography "Concours international de chorégraphie" held by the Archives Internationales de la Danse in Paris in 1932. It was a strong anti-war statement which "catapulted him to instant world fame."[29]

His visit to Dublin in March 1939 was met by enthusiastic reviews. The *Evening Herald* wrote: "On the whole, no work has ever been presented in Dublin during recent years which has aroused so much interest among the public as the Ballets Jooss,"[30] while the *Irish Press* declared "The Revolt is Essence of Ballets Jooss."[31] The company's return in November 1939 was already newsworthy in October,[32] and the actual performances were hailed as "The Ballet at its Best"[33] by the *Irish Independent*. The positive reception continued the following year. On 12 April 1940, the readers of the *Irish Press* were alerted that Kurt Jooss was to give a fortnight's course on Movement and Dancing, beginning ten days later. There is no doubt that the performances by the German dancer and choreographer and his ensemble had left a deep impression, as becomes clear in subsequent news coverage: "The striking success of the Ballets Jooss when in Dublin last November should ensure the success of the course and the lectures, because the art of dancing as taught by him in the Jooss Leeder School of Dance at Dartington Hall, London, has created profound interest in every artistic circle in Dublin."[34]

Jooss and his dancers continued to perform in Ireland after the war: he returned to Dublin in May 1953, still highly acclaimed.[35]

> The time was ripe,
> and the place was right,
> for dance in Belfast[36]

Most of this article has concentrated on Éire. I want to present at least a brief look at the part of Ireland that remained part of the United Kingdom. For Northern Ireland there has been a greater awareness of the cultural input and impact of refugees. As mentioned, Paul Peter Ewald was closely aligned to the Dublin Institute for Advanced Studies. In terms of music and art, the influence of people such as musician Heinz Hammerschlag, artists Alice Berger and Clara Ewald (Paul Peter Ewald's mother who incidentally was very friendly with the Schrödingers) played a considerable role in cultural life. Guy Woodward argues in his study *Culture, Northern Ireland, and the Second World War*: "Somewhat perversely, the Second World War created conditions in which visual artists in Northern Ireland could flourish. The unprecedented influx of foreign troops and refugees brought many new cultural modes and traditions to the province."[37] He singles out Alice Berger, of whom Diarmuid Kennedy said that she was of "inestimable value to the progress of art in Northern Ireland."[38]

In terms of dance, the greatest impact was to come not from an exile who had managed to flee Nazi Germany before the war, but from someone who had survived the horrors of the concentration camp: Helen Lewis. Born in 1916 as Helena Katz in Trutnov, Bohemia, she was passionate about dance from a young age. In the mid-1930s she had had a romance with the man she was to marry in 1947, Harry Lewis. They both came from the same small town in Bohemia, Trautenau, in the Sudetenland. However, Harry and Helena broke up after about a year over her love for dance. Harry did not dislike dance itself but rather Helena's fervor and passion for it.[39] Helena, however, was devoted to it and finished a three-year training program. Her teacher in Prague, Milca Mayerova, had studied in Germany with Rudolf von Laban.[40] While in Prague, Helena married Paul Hermann. She also taught as an assistant to Milca Mayerova and in this role she had opportunities to do some choreography. Hitler's invasion of Czechoslovakia changed life radically. In 1942, the couple was deported to the concentration camp in Terezin and, in 1944, to Auschwitz where they were separated. Paul was murdered but Helen survived. Renewed contact with Harry Lewis, who had found refuge in Belfast, led to their wedding in Prague in 1947, and Helen moved with Harry to Northern Ireland that year. After some years raising a young family and finding her way in the new environment, Helen Lewis increasingly returned to her earliest passion, dance. In 1956, she was invited to choreograph a school ballet production set to Czech composer Bedřich Smetana's *The Bartered Bride* and Dvořák's *The Golden Spinning Wheel*. For Lewis, Laban was her main inspiration and guiding light: for her he was "the first and greatest founder of modern dance in Europe. [. . .] In dance, Laban is supreme. I was lucky enough to meet him once in postwar London on a summer course."[41]

Later, in 1962, she founded the Belfast Modern Dance Group, and former pupils of the group such as Philip Johnston and Jane Mooney subsequently carved out careers as international performers or teachers. But her impact went beyond dance: she also captured the literary imagination of Northern Irish writers. Novelist Jennifer Johnston provided the foreword to Lewis's 1992 autobiography *A Time to Speak*, and Belfast writer Michael Longley dedicated his poem "A Linen Handkerchief" to Helen, evoking the impact she and her husband Harry Lewis had on Northern Irish society, culture, and arts:

A Linen Handkerchief

for Helen Lewis

Northern Bohemia's flax fields and the flax fields
Of Northern Ireland, the linen industry, brought Harry,
Trader in linen handkerchiefs, to Belfast, and then
After Terezin and widowhood and Auschwitz, you.

Odysseus as a girl, your sail a linen handkerchief
On which he embroidered and unpicked hundreds of names
All through the war, but in one corner the flowers
Encircling your initials never came undone.[42]

Helen Lewis's book *A Time to Speak*, about her experiences before and during the war, was published in 1992 (an Italian translation, *Il tempo di parlare*, came out in 1996). Her death at the end of 2009 was mourned not only in Northern Ireland,[43] where she was described as "an inspirational figure, a life force, a dancer to the very core of her being," Great Britain ("Her extraordinary gifts as a teacher are remembered by generations of dancers who continue to teach her work throughout the world"),[44] and the Republic of Ireland, but was even commemorated in Italy.[45] In 2017, an Ulster History Circle blue plaque in her memory was unveiled at the Crescent Arts Centre in south Belfast.[46]

The developments outlined here present only a small part of the impact of the small number of refugees who managed to come to Ireland. Other areas were, for example, industrial developments in the Irish periphery in places such as Castlebar, Longford, Galway, and Carrick-on-Suir. Likewise, in Northern Ireland the newly founded factories and new enterprises that were brought in by refugees contributed considerably to the economic landscape. They contributed in so many other ways, culturally, academically, and, in religious terms, with helping to establish the Progressive Jewish community in Dublin.

The refugees and immigrants mentioned above remind us of the contributions of the outsiders—not only in Ireland, as chosen here for this study, but in every country, and of the value of accepting strangers. But we also need to remember that in many different areas, here exemplified by dance and physics, and in such a seemingly isolated place and desolate time as Ireland in the 1930s and 1940s, there was awareness of, interest in, and support for modern developments—and the influence of these outsiders has had considerable ongoing impact, in Ireland (including Northern Ireland) and internationally.

NOTES

1. Carl R. Trueman, "John Owen and Modernity: Reflections on Historiography, Modernity and the Self," in *John Owen between Orthodoxy and Modernity*, ed. Willem van Vlastuin and Kelly M. Kapic (Leiden/Boston: Brill, 2019), 36.

2. Michel Foucault, *Discipline and Punish: The Birth of the Prison*, trans. Alan Sheridan (Harmondsworth: Penguin 1979), 170–177.

3. Cf. Bruce Seymour, *Lola Montez: A Life* (New Haven, CT: Yale University Press, 1996).

4. Cf. John J. O'Sullivan, *Breaking Ground: The Story of William T. Mulvany* (Cork: Mercier, 2004).

5. "Rise of quantum theory and other highlights, 1920–29." *Science News* 181, no. 6 (March 2012): 22.

6. Isa Partsch-Bergsohn, *Modern Dance in Germany and the United States: Crosscurrents and Influences* (Abingdon: Routledge, 2011), 49.

7. Magdeburg daily paper, published 15 May 1927, see Partsch-Bergsohn, *Modern Dance*, 40.

8. Cf. F. S. L. Lyons. *Ireland since the Famine* (London: Fontana, 1971), 551–558.

9. See for example Bryce Evans, *Ireland during the Second World War —Farewell to Plato's Cave* (Manchester: Manchester University Press, 2014).

10. Clair Wills, *That Neutral Country—A Cultural History of Ireland during the Second World War* (London: Faber and Faber, 2007), 207.

11. See Róisín Kennedy, "Experimentalism or Mere Chaos? The White Stag Group and the Reception of Subjective Art in Ireland," in *Irish Modernism—Origins, Contexts, Publics*, eds. Edwina Keown and Carol Taaffe (Bern and Oxford: Peter Lang, 2009), 179–194.

12. "Special Lectures," *Irish Times*, 15 April 1940. The full quote is as follows and shows the range of topics covered by these lectures alone: "Arrangements have been made whereby two series of special lectures will be given by distinguished Continental professors, refugee scholars, who are obtaining in Ireland the opportunity denied to them in their native countries. As we remarked earlier in the year, when Professor Erwin Schrödinger delivered lectures on wave mechanics, the fact that we are one of the nations turned to for sanctuary in itself makes us proud, but later on, when the influence of such men as these is fully felt, we will be not so much proud but grateful. Of the new series, one is to be given by Dr. Victor Ehrenberg. He has already commenced Seminars on "Social Life as illustrated by old Attic Comedy," and will deliver a number of lectures on "The origins of European History" comemncing [sic] on Wednesday. The other guest lecturer is Dr. Ludwig Bieler, who will deliver general lectures on Thursdays from 4 to 5 p.m., and Seminars Fridays from 3 to 5 on

the subject, "The relations between the Irish, English and Continental writing in the Middle Ages." All these lectures are open to the general public."

13. Norman Bentwich, *The Rescue and Achievement of Refugee Scholars* (The Hague: M. Nijhoff 1953), 53.

14. Seanad Éireann debate, 15 May 1940, Institute for Advanced Studies Bill, 1939—Second Stage, accessed 20 May 2019, https://www.oireachtas.ie/en/debates/debate/seanad/1940-05-15/3/?highlight%5B0%5D=taoiseach&highlight%5B1%5D=himself&highlight%5B2%5D=his&highlight%5B3%5D=own&highlight%5B4%5D=idea&highlight%5B5%5D=nobody&highlight%5B6%5D=else.

15. Max Born, *My Life* (London: Taylor & Francis, 1978), 270.

16. "Science," *Time Magazine*, 5 April 1943.

17. *What is Life* subsequently inspired James D. Watson, Francis Crick, and Maurice Wilkins in their work on the structure of DNA. On this and more detail on the refugee scholars in Ireland see also Gisela Holfter and Horst Dickel, *An Irish Sanctuary—German-speaking Refugees in Ireland 1933–1945* (Berlin and Boston: de Gruyter, 2017).

18. See Reiner Stach, *Kafka: Die frühen Jahre* (Frankfurt am Main: S. Fischer, 2016), 569.

19. Thanks to Ludwig Hopf's great-grandson Michael Hopf in Australia.

20. See Deirdre Mulrooney's contribution to this volume.

21. Jacqueline Robinson, "Modern Dance in Dublin in the 1940s (yes, there was . . .)," unpublished manuscript, Dance Ireland archive, 1999.

22. See Aoife McGrath, *Dance Theatre in Ireland* (London: Palgrave Macmillan, 2013), 52–62 and especially Deirdre Mulrooney—see her collection of key figures in Irish dance, *Irish Moves—an Illustrated History of Dance and Physical Theatre in Ireland* (Dublin: The Liffey Press, 2006) and also her excellent work in promoting the work of Erina Brady with her films *1943: A Dance Odyssey* (2013) and *Dance Emergency* (2014), as well as articles and lectures.

23. Cf. Holfter and Dickel, *An Irish Sanctuary*, 266.

24. Both Mulrooney in *Irish Moves* and Aoife McGrath in *Dance Theatre in Ireland* focus on Jooss's performances in the 1950s; McGrath points out how important his and other visiting dance productions were for Ireland in the 1950s and 1960s (see McGrath, op. cit., 63 and see also Carolyn Swift, *Stage by Stage* (Dublin: Poolbeg, 1985). Swift also briefly mentions one performance in 1939 (1985, 81).

25. See Partsch-Bergsohn, *Modern Dance*, 43–47.

26. See Lilian Karina and Marion Kant, *Tanz unterm Hakenkreuz* (Berlin: Henschel, 1996). An English translation appeared seven years later: *Hitler's Dancers: German Modern Dance and the Third Reich* (New York, NY: Berghan Books, 2003), Laure Guilbert, *Danser avec le IIIe Reich–Les danseurs modernes sous le nazisme* (Brussels: Editions Complexe, 2000). Thanks also to Laure Guilbert for sharing with me her paper "Dance in British Exile—a comparative study of Kurt Jooss and Rudolf von Laban's paths and networks" presented at the conference "Marginalität und Zentralität" of the Gesellschaft für Exilforschung in Aberystwyth in July 2016. On Laban see also Christine Dickson, "Dance Under the Swastika: Rudolf von Laban's

Influence on Nazi Power," accessed 14 May 2019, http://www.cornish.edu/dance/writing/dance_under_the_swastika_rudolf_von_labans_influence_on_nazi_power/.

27. Susanne Franco, "The Motion of Memory, the Question of History: Recreating Rudolf Laban's Choreographic Legacy," in *The Oxford Handbook of Dance and Reenactment*, Mark Franco, ed. (Oxford: Oxford University Press, 2017), 147.

28. "History may prove Jooss, after all, to be the key figure in dance Expressionism. He is, after all, more than the choreographer of ''The Green Table.'' This exhibition of photographs and documents organized by Anna Markard, Jooss's daughter, for the 1981 ''Danza Europa'' festival in Venice, tells us that his principles are alive enough to constitute a heritage still valid for young choreographers to draw upon." Anna Kisselgoff, "Dance View—How Much Does Dance Owe to Jooss?" *New York Times*, 11 July 1982, accessed 10 May 2019, https://www.nytimes.com/1982/07/11/arts/dance-view-how-much-does-dance-owe-to-jooss.html.

29. Suzanne K. Walther, *The Dance of Death—Kurt Jooss and the Weimar Years* (Chur: Harwood Academic Publishers, 1994), xv.

30. *Evening Herald*, 24 March 1939 (where it was also mentioned that London was at first slow to understand the performance, then Milan went wild about it, as did New York, and on seeing it again at the Old Vic, London realised its merits).

31. *Irish Press,* 28 March 1939.

32. See *Evening Herald*, 18 October 1939, "The Ballets Jooss . . . is paying a return visit to Dublin and will appear at the Gaiety Theatre during the week of 6 November. They will present a repertory of their most successful ballets, including two new productions for Dublin: 'Chronica,' a dance drama in 3 acts, and 'The Prodigal Son,' a dance legend in 6 scenes."

33. *Irish Independent*, 7 November 1939.

34. *Irish Independent*, 17 April 1940.

35. See *Evening Herald*, 20 April 1953 about the performance of the Green Table: "a grimly satirical indictment of war between the nations, as true now as it was then [in 1932]—and still terrifyingly impressive."

36. Helen Lewis, "An Irish Epilogue," *Irish Pages* 1, no. 1, Inaugural Issue: Belfast in Europe (Spring, 2002), 29.

37. Guy Woodward, *Culture, Northern Ireland, and the Second World War* (Oxford: Oxford University Press 2015), 131.

38. Diarmuid Kennedy, "The Legend who lived in lost Belfast," *Belfast Telegraph*, 5 April 2007.

39. Helen Lewis, *A Time to Speak* (Belfast: Blackstaff, 1992), 2.

40. Lewis, *A Time to Speak*, 3.

41. Lewis, Irish Epilogue, 26.

42. Michael Longley, "A Linen Handkerchief," in *Weather in Japan* (London: Jonathan Cape, 2000), 254. Longley dedicated a number of poems to Helen Lewis, maybe most poignantly "Helen," recalling her time in the concentration camp. Thanks to Michael Longley for permission to reprint his poem.

43. Lesley-Anne Henry, "Survivor of Auschwitz death camp Helen Lewis dies at 93," *Belfast Telegraph*, 2 January 2010.

44. Richard Johnston, "Helen Lewis obituary," *The Guardian*, 17 March 2010. See also "Belfast Auschwitz survivor Helen Lewis dies aged 93," *BBC*, 1 January 2010 and "Helen Lewis Obituary," *The Telegraph*, 15 January 2010.

45. Morta Helen Lewis, ballerina sopravvissuta all'Olocausto, 16 January 2010, accessed 23 May 2019, http://www.liberoquotidiano.it/news/home/328940/morta-helen-lewis-ballerina-sopravvissuta-all-olocausto.html.

46. "Helen Lewis: Belfast plaque for Holocaust survivor," *BBC*, 27 January 2017, accessed 23 May 2019, https://www.bbc.com/news/uk-northern-ireland-38763249.

BIBLIOGRAPHY

Bentwich, Norman. *The Rescue and Achievement of Refugee Scholars*. The Hague: M. Nijhoff, 1953.

Born, Max. *My Life*. London: Taylor & Francis, 1978.

Dickson, Christine. "Dance Under the Swastika: Rudolf von Laban's Influence on Nazi Power." Accessed 14 May 2019. http://www.cornish.edu/dance/writing/dance_under_the_swastika_rudolf_von_labans_influence_on_nazi_power/.

Evans, Bryce. *Ireland during the Second World War—Farewell to Plato's Cave*. Manchester: Manchester University Press, 2014.

Foucault, Michel. *Discipline and Punish: The Birth of the Prison*. Translated by Alan Sheridan. Harmondsworth: Penguin, 1979.

Franco, Susanne. "The Motion of Memory, the Question of History: Recreating Rudolf Laban's Choreographic Legacy." In *The Oxford Handbook of Dance and Reenactment*, edited by Mark Franco, 143–164. Oxford: Oxford University Press, 2017.

Guilbert, Laure. *Danser avec le IIIe Reich—Les danseurs modernes sous le nazisme*. Brussels: Editions Complexe, 2000.

Henry, Lesley-Anne. "Survivor of Auschwitz Death Camp Helen Lewis Dies at 93." *Belfast Telegraph*, 2 January 2010.

Holfter, Gisela, and Horst Dickel. *An Irish Sanctuary—German-speaking Refugees in Ireland 1933–1945*. Berlin/Boston: de Gruyter, 2017.

Johnston, Richard. "Helen Lewis Obituary." *The Guardian*, 17 March 2010.

Karina, Lilian, and Marion Kant. *Tanz unterm Hakenkreuz*. Berlin: Henschel, 1996.

Kennedy, Diarmuid. "The Legend who lived in lost Belfast." *Belfast Telegraph*, 5 April 2007.

Kennedy, Róisín. "Experimentalism or Mere Chaos? The White Stag Group and the Reception of Subjective Art in Ireland." In *Irish Modernism—Origins, Contexts, Publics*, edited by Edwina Keown and Carol Taaffe, 179–194. Bern/Oxford: Peter Lang, 2009.

Kisselgoff, Anna. "Dance View—How Much Does Dance Owe to Jooss?" *New York Times*, 11 July 1982.

Lewis, Helen. *A Time to Speak*. Belfast: Blackstaff, 1992.

———. "An Irish Epilogue." *Irish Pages* 1, no. 1 (Spring 2002): 25–30.

Longley, Michael. *Weather in Japan*. London: Jonathan Cape, 2000.

Lyons, F.S.L. *Ireland since the Famine*. London: Fontana, 1971.
McGrath, Aoife. *Dance Theatre in Ireland.* London: Palgrave Macmillan, 2013.
Mulrooney, Deirdre. *Irish Moves—An Illustrated History of Dance and Physical Theatre in Ireland*. Dublin: The Liffey Press, 2006.
O'Sullivan, John J. *Breaking Ground: The Story of William T. Mulvany*. Cork: Mercier, 2004.
Partsch-Bergsohn, Isa. *Modern Dance in Germany and the United States: Crosscurrents and Influences*. Abingdon: Routledge, 2011.
Seymour, Bruce. *Lola Montez: A Life*. New Haven, CT: Yale University Press, 1996.
Stach, Reiner. *Kafka: Die frühen Jahre*. Frankfurt am Main: S. Fischer, 2016.
Swift, Carolyn. *Stage by Stage*. Dublin: Poolbeg, 1985.
Trueman, Carl R. "John Owen and Modernity: Reflections on Historiography, Modernity and the Self." In *John Owen between Orthodoxy and Modernity*, edited by Willem van Vlastuin and Kelly M. Kapic, 35–54. Leiden/Boston: Brill, 2019.
Walther, Suzanne K. *The Dance of Death—Kurt Jooss and the Weimar Years*. Chur: Harwood Academic Publishers, 1994.
Wills, Clair. *That Neutral Country—A Cultural History of Ireland during the Second World War*. London: Faber and Faber, 2007.
Woodward, Guy. *Culture, Northern Ireland, and the Second World War*. Oxford: Oxford University Press, 2015.

Chapter Two

Erina Brady

Mary Wigman's Irish Disciple?

Deirdre Mulrooney

Was Erina Brady Mary Wigman's Irish disciple? This chapter seeks out documentary and contextual evidence to substantiate 1940s Irish-German Modern Dance pioneer Erina Brady's (1891–1961) alleged training and personal contact with Mary Wigman (1886–1973), the inventor of *Ausdruckstanz*, otherwise known as New German Dance or Expressionist Dance. Born in Germany in 1891 to an Irish father and a German mother, it is widely accepted that Erina Brady sought to spread this form of dance and its philosophy in 1940s Ireland, then an inchoate country full of possibilities. The anti-ballet term *Ausdruckstanz*:

> became common usage after World War II to designate a widespread dance practice in the early and middle decades of the 20th century that flourished in German-speaking Europe. *Ausdruckstanz* emerged from the life reform movement of the early 20th century that promoted diverse practices of physical culture as a way of contesting the industrialisation and urbanisation of modern life. Émile Jaques-Dalcroze's expansion of eurhythmics at Hellerau in the few years immediately preceding World War I, and Rudolf Laban's and Mary Wigman's explorations of movement on Monte Verità during the years of the war, anticipated the dramatic growth of *Ausdruckstanz* in the 1920s and early 1930s.[1]

Considering Brady's work in 1940s Dublin and her assertions in her *Irish School of Dance Art* brochure[2] within this wider international context (see Figures 2 and 3), I first set out in this research to find traces of, and references to, Brady in Mary Wigman's writing, but found these mostly restricted to Wigman's post-war correspondence with Brady's most renowned *Irish School of Dance Art* pupil, Jacqueline Robinson.

Second, this chapter situates Erina Brady and her Irish project among the global pantheon of Wigman's disciples, as evoked by Susan Manning in the following passage:

> The most talented graduates then embarked on their own careers as educators and choreographers of solo, group, and mass dance. Leading dancers criss-crossed Central Europe on tour, and some ventured as far as the Americas and East Asia. The rise of National Socialism after 1933 decisively affected *Ausdruckstanz*: while many dancers remained in Germany and Austria and collaborated with the National Socialists, others went into exile due to their leftist political commitments and/or their Jewish heritage. In the Americas, in Australasia, and in Palestine, émigrés, working together with other dancers, developed and disseminated *Ausdruckstanz*, integrating its practices and principles with a range of other dance forms, including ballet and modern dance.[3]

In this light, I consider Erina Brady's development and dissemination of *Ausdruckstanz* in Ireland in comparison with that of Hanya Holm (1893–1992) who successfully transplanted Wigman's *Ausdruckstanz* to the United States. One might even argue that Brady's work in Ireland constituted a heroic attempt to spread Wigman's enlightened bodily theories to an inchoate country afflicted by an overriding societal repression of the body and its associated arts, in favor of the written word. Additionally, this chapter highlights how, due to Brady's controversial Irish family background she encountered more complex obstacles than most global Wigman pioneers on her mission to spread holistic modern dance to the country of her forefathers.

Erina Brady's ambitious modern dance enterprise flourished in "Emergency"[4] Dublin for approximately a decade, with public performances in the Abbey Theatre, the Mansion House, the Gaiety Theatre, in her *Irish School of Dance Art* Harcourt Street Studio, as well as barefoot outdoor performances in John Betjeman's residence at Collinstown House, Clondalkin.[5] Brady's considerable achievements which had largely vanished from twentieth-century Irish cultural history, which prioritized the written word, resurfaced in the next millennium, thanks initially to Jacqueline Robinson's 1999 Memoir "Modern Dance in 1940s Dublin? Yes, There Was!".[6]

I suggest that the following disjointed traces of Erina Brady's enigmatic existence, lost achievements, and ghostly contribution to the development of dance as an art form in Ireland, offer an eloquent manifestation of the story of the repressed body in Ireland from which to construct a new twentieth-century cultural narrative of dance and the body in Ireland.[7]

ERINA BRADY IN LETTERS AND DIARY ENTRIES BY MARY WIGMAN AND JACQUELINE ROBINSON

Despite the lack of pre-World War II school records, and existing correspondence between Mary Wigman and Erina Brady in the style of Hanya Holm's copious correspondence with Wigman,[8] can it be reasonable nonetheless to consider Brady to be a disciple of Wigman's *Ausdruckstanz* to Ireland in the same vein as Hanya Holm was to the United States?

Though it is widely accepted that Erina Brady, Irish-German Modern Dance pioneer to 1940s Ireland, was a devotee of Mary Wigman and espoused Wigman's theories of *Ausdruckstanz* in her *Irish School of Dance Art* at 39 Harcourt Street (ca. 1939–1951), there is, alas, only one reference to "Erin O'Brady" by Mary Wigman in Wigman's unpublished archives at Berlin's *Akademie der Kunst*, and none in Cologne's *Tanzarchiv Köln*. Brady does not show up in any of Wigman's available cast lists, which is, however, not surprising, given that there is very little documentation available on the students who attended Wigman's classes in her important Dresden school (1920–1944), where Erina Brady claims to have studied and performed with Wigman for three years.[9] However, there are references to be found to Brady in Wigman's 1950s correspondence[10] to Jacqueline Robinson (1922–2000), who after training with Brady in 1940s Dublin, subsequently projected herself into Wigman's orbit in Switzerland, a Mecca for the development of modern dance since the turn of the century. In their subsequent correspondence, Wigman intermittently related "Erin O'Brady" sightings in Switzerland to her ambitious young pupil, who was setting up *l'Atelier de la Danse*, her own school of modern dance in Paris. Forced to reluctantly give up on her Irish School of Dance Art, Brady had left Dublin and returned to her family home, *Casa Erina*, in a picturesque village in Brione in the Swiss canton of Ticino in the early 1950s. As opposed to being dance-related, Wigman's written updates on Brady to Robinson mostly chart Brady's failing health up to 1960, one year before her untimely death from cancer at the age of seventy.

These scant surviving references begin after the 1949 reopening of Wigman's school in Berlin, in connection with Wigman's post-war International Summer School in Zurich, organized by the Swiss Association of Professional Dancers and Gymnasts.[11] Jacqueline Robinson and June Fryer (1926–2011), Brady's two most promising young *protegées*, attended in 1953, inspired by their professional training (1943–1946) in modern dance at Erina Brady's *Irish School of Dance Art* in the style of Mary Wigman.[12]

A single reference in Wigman's personal August 1954 diary,[13] written after her 1954 Zurich summer course when Wigman reflects that seeing "Erin O'Brady" would contribute to bringing her life full circle, hints that

Brady may have played a significant part in her early life. Interestingly, in this correspondence, "O'Brady" is mentioned by Wigman alongside her most intimate and well-known collaborators, Bertha Trumpy and her longtime assistant "Hesschen":

> Ich bin sehr glücklich hier, mag und will an nichts denken, und kann es zu meiner eigenen Überraschung auch. Sobald ich freilich meinen Dschungel verlasse, tritt die Vergangenheit auf mich zu. Marion kam 1½ Tage zu Besuch. Marie, Marthas Älteste, erschien. Nebenan im Teatro die Werres, die Trümpi im Val Resa. Erin O'Brady in Brione, Erika Brünauer in Ascona, und nun noch mein alter Freund Tommy in Ronco. Hesschen meint: 'der Zirkel Ihres Lebens schliesst sich.' Who knows?
>
> (I am very happy here, have no desire to be thinking about anything in particular, and much to my own surprise, am succeeding at this. No sooner have I left my own inner "jungle," than up pops my past to meet me. Marion comes to visit for a day and a half. Marie, Martha's eldest appears. Beside the Theatre, Trümpi shows up in Resa Valley. Erin O'Brady in Brione, Erika Brünauer in Ascona, and now also my old friend Tommy in Ronco. Hesschen says "your life is coming full circle." Who knows?)[14]

This somewhat cryptic mention clearly places "Erin O'Brady," aka Erina Brady, in the pantheon of significant people from Wigman's early life as an artist and as a private person before the war.

Subsequent correspondence from October 1954 to April 1960 from Mary Wigman to Jacqueline Robinson[15] also anchors Brady in Wigman's personal and professional orbit. This lengthy correspondence first began after Robinson met Wigman when she was an observer at her 1952 summer dance course in Montreux, Switzerland:

> I had written to her to inform her of my visit, introducing myself as a pupil of Erina Brady, so I went to greet her but she was so close to the floor, and I was standing, it was no way comfortable. I simply knelt down in front of her, and that is how our first conversation took place, so warm, as though a foretaste of what would later be. And so, for several years, I saw her every summer and on diverse occasions. We never ceased writing to each other, a rich, intimate, wonderful exchange. Mary was a remarkably gifted letter writer. In 1956, when I stayed in Berlin for several months to work at her school, I enjoyed precious moments, both *tête-à-tête* with her at her house and at those delightful parties, where white Rhine wine flowed generously, and Mary would appear alternately serious and frivolous, teasing, profound, tender, and severe.[16]

Mary Wigman's written correspondence to Robinson begins in May 1953, in anticipation of Robinson's attendance at Wigman's Zurich Summer School a few months later. As if Erina Brady was an enigmatic puzzle they were trying to solve, Robinson shared Wigman's correspondence involving allusions to their Dublin modern dance mentor, with another pupil of Erina Brady in 1940s Dublin: June Kuhn (nee Fryer),[17] Ireland's first homegrown modern dancer. Wigman's first rather neutral mention of "Erin O'Brady" is placed at the end of a long encyclical (letter 5 of 50) to Robinson, after she missed her at her 1954 Zurich Summer School:

> Berlin, October, 1954
> Dearest Jacqueline—
> . . .
> I nearly forgot to tell you that I met Erin O'Brady this summer! Have you got her address? Probably! But in any case, here it is:
> Casa Erina, Brione, Sopra Minusio, Ticino, Suisse
> A hearty kiss from
> Mary[18]

When Erina Brady had to close her Dublin *Irish School of Dance Art*, and move back to *Casa Erina* in the Swiss village of Brione, around 1951, her Dublin friend and collaborator, stain glass artist Hugh Barden, visited Brady there to convalesce and paint the idyllic view from her *Casa Erina* balcony.[19] It was around this time that Mary Wigman, whose Modern Dance style Erina Brady had been assiduously spreading to Ireland in her *Irish School of Dance Art* during the 1940s, spotted her again, as noted in Wigman's more expansive 23 November 1954 correspondence (letter 6 of 50) to her young and enthusiastic pupil Jacqueline Robinson. Could this be the same encounter, retold once more with additional revealing detail, that Wigman gives such intriguing significance in her aforementioned August 1954 private diary?

> November 23rd, 1954
> Dear Jacqueline!
> . . .
> Darling, are you getting along with your own work. How do you manage it all? Wife, mother, Hausfrau, dancer and teacher?
>
> Well, I did see Erin O'Brady this summer. And the first moment I got a shock of some kind. Because she has dyed her hair to an orange like color, appearing much younger than I remembered her. She is the same self-managing person she used to be. Leading a very isolated life up in that mountain village. I don't know how she manages it, but evidently, she does.
>
> I can understand very well, what you told me about her influence on you, and that you had to free yourself from her. Thank God you did!

That does not mean that I don't like her—no. I have a sort of admiration for her, understanding at the same time how dangerous such an influence on a young person could be, because she could not do otherwise but take possession of him or her.

How is your group work with Jerome getting on? And the duet with Karin?

So often do I think of you all, wishing you so much to be near and take part in your struggles as well as in your achievements.
My loving thoughts are with you—my wishes,
my greetings. And always
I am
yours
Mary [20]

Here, Wigman seems to be referring to some kind of unpleasant dynamic between Erina Brady and Jacqueline Robinson to which we are not privy. Maybe Brady adopted the role of surrogate mother to the young and impressionable Jacqueline Robinson during her transition from pianist to dancer in Emergency Dublin? Brady was certainly disappointed when her two star pupils, June Fryer and Jacqueline Robinson, left her for pastures new, dashing her dreams of establishing her own dance company after the end of World War II, when borders opened up allowing free travel again throughout continental Europe. This unarticulated frisson reverberates through Erina Brady's letters to Robinson just days after their 1–3 April 1948 performances of her masterpiece "The Voyage of Maeldune" at London's Rudolph Steiner Hall, for which it appears that Jacqueline hadn't bothered to come to Dublin to rehearse:

39 Harcourt Street,
April 8th, 1948
. . . Financially my London venture may have been disastrous for me. As an experience which I could not have had otherwise it has been invaluable.[21]

And a few days later, on April 12th, Brady's next letter to Jacqueline Robinson seems to mark a falling-out between them:

My dearest child,

Mother birds are so wise aren't they? They do everything for their young as long as they are unable to fend for themselves, but when the right moment has come they deliberately turn their young out of the nest, so that they may learn to use their wings. For us poor humans it always is a wrench when we have to do likewise, but when we can become detached whilst still loving as warmly, if

> not more warmly than before, the separation is a sacrifice which will bear fruit for both the teacher and the taught . . .
>
> I shall be writing to your father about the business end of our London venture, and am sorry he too should have been put to expense. As to yourself, I wonder could you let me have the price of the panties. . . . Then, I would like you to send me the two 1000fr notes which you were unable to change, as the Legation here are willing to refund something on them.
>
> And now I have masses of bills to pay and things to see to. So good bye for today.
>
> Ever with very fond love and best wishes,
>
> Erina.[22]

It is a sad letter that apparently marks the end of their association, an association that changed Jacqueline Robinson's life forever by introducing her to *Ausdruckstanz,* and would ultimately lead to her being awarded a *Chevalier des Arts et des Lettres* from the French Government in 1999 for her services to dance.

Wigman and Robinson's subsequent encounters and correspondence continue apace for four years around the topic of Modern Dance, choreography, and teaching, as Jacqueline Robinson establishes her own modern dance School, *l'Atelier de la Danse* in Paris in 1955, without another mention of "Erin O'Brady" until Wigman's nineteenth letter to Robinson on 20 May 1958:

> Berlin, 20/5/58
>
> Dear Jacqueline, this is just to tell you that I am back from the States since a week [sic] and to thank you for your charming letter. . . .
>
> . . .
>
> Berlin again—but I love it as much as I did when I left it. School fine and very vital—
>
> Coming home I found a post-card from Erin O'Brady's friend in Montreux, that Erin, after having come back, got worse and worse—and that she had to go back to the hospital in Berne once more and that the professor there, was not sure if he should operate once more, as he doubted that Erin could stand another strenuous operation.
>
> Her home address:
>
> Chalet Muyarina,
>
> Chernex sur Montreux Suiss [sic]
>
> . . .[23]

Two years later, on 6 April 1960, "Erin O'Brady" gets a final, sad, mention in the ongoing correspondence (letter 24 of 50) between the ambitious Jacqueline Robinson and her mentor Mary Wigman, to whose work Erina

Brady had introduced her in her Dublin *Irish School of Dance Art* in Emergency Dublin:

> 6/4/60
> My dearest, . . .
> I got a letter from Erin O'Brady these days. What a tragedy! She still can't move, has to lie flat on her back, and the utmost she can afford is to crawl on all fours. And nothing but pains, day in day out. If you write her a little note I am sure she will be very happy. I know she loves you very much. Her address: Chalet Muyrarina, Chernex, s. Montreux, Suisse.[24]

Unfortunately, apart from this intermittent chronicling of Erina Brady's sad demise toward the end of her life due to cancer, no other written evidence of the professional modern dance connection between Wigman and Brady has yet emerged. However, given the chaos of World War II and all it entailed with regard to destruction of records, it is reasonable to surmise a professional connection by linking Erina Brady's own version of her training as asserted in her stylish *Irish School of Dance Art* prospectus to available contextual facts.

This absence of clear dance records chimes in with the fact that so far Erina Brady has proven to be the sort of transgressive artist that exists mostly outside of standard archives, with traces of her only to be found dispersed in unlikely places, for example in her secret detective file at the G2 Military Archive at Dublin's Department of Defence in Cathal Brugha Barracks; in Liam Ó Laoghaire's only recently deciphered 1943 film "Dance School" at the Irish Film Archive; in Jacqueline Robinson's last-minute 1999 Memoir "Modern Dance in 1940s Dublin—yes there was!," part-published by this author in *Irish Moves, an Illustrated History of Dance and Physical Theatre in Ireland*, in 2006;[25] in the memories of Brady's pupils[26] who still light up and are so inspired by her, seventy years on; and, in articles like the below 1941 *Irish Independent* "Leader Page Parade" found in the Brady family biscuit tin in their ancestral home in Cavan town in 1996.

PARALLELS BETWEEN ERINA BRADY AND HER AMERICAN COUNTERPART HANYA HOLM

Maybe if Erina Brady had lived, like her American counterpart Hanya Holm, to the age of ninety-nine, instead of dying in 1961 at the age of seventy after a long and debilitating illness, she would have had the opportunity to complete her own memoir, and we would not need to search for these clues and references to substantiate her training with Mary Wigman. Robinson wrote: "On reading over various letters Erina wrote to me that summer, I see that she was

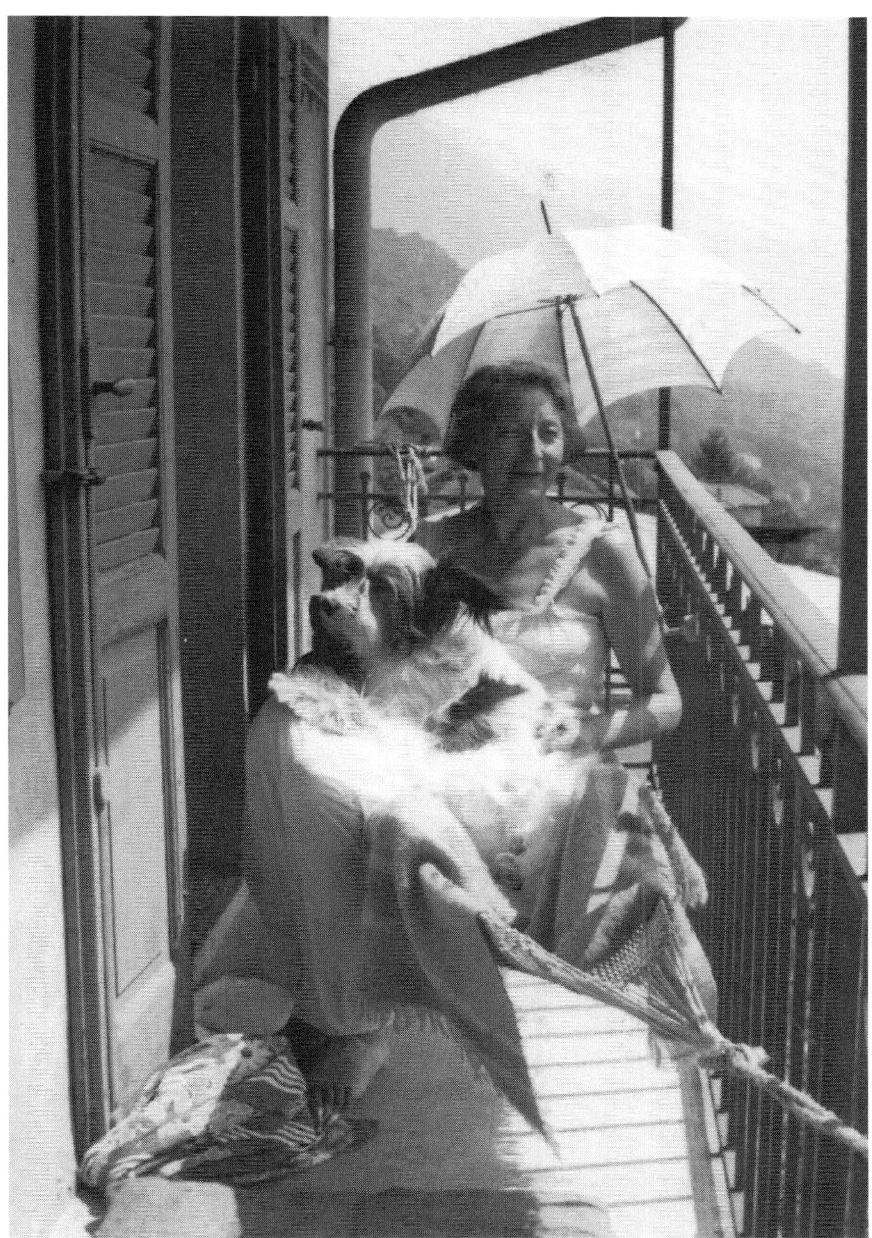

Figure 2.1. Erina Brady and her dog, Scamp, on her balcony in Brione, Ticino, Switzerland, circa 1953. Photograph by Walter Kuhn. Private Collection. Used courtesy of Walter Kuhn.

going through a rather tense period. She had started writing a book. I do not remember whether she told me what it was to be about. Apparently, it never saw the light of day."[27]

However, despite the lack of a paper trail, I would argue we can reasonably ascertain that Erina Brady was in many ways to Ireland what her counterpart, Hanya Holm (who was born in Frankfurt just two years after Erina Brady), was to the United States. Just because correspondence between Wigman and Brady has not been found to date does not mean they did not correspond. I would therefore like to explore the possible parallel existence of Hanya Holm and Erina Brady as disciples of Wigman's *Ausdruckstanz*, in an attempt to understand Brady in the wider context of dancers who studied with Wigman in Germany during the Weimar years, and who then sought to spread Wigman's theories internationally—with varying degrees of success.

Brady came to Ireland in an attempt to transplant the seed of Wigman's *Ausdruckstanz*, or "Dance of Expression," and holistic movement, for about twelve years from approximately 1939 to 1951. This is substantiated, and outlined elsewhere in documentaries by the author, "Dance Emergency"/"*Damhsa na hEigeandála*" (TG4, 2015), and "1943—A Dance Odyssey" (RTE One television, April 2013), featuring Brady's former pupils as eye witnesses and participants looking back on their younger dancing selves, and reminiscing about their childhood dance teacher as filmed by Liam Ó Laoghaire, one of the key founders of the Irish film industry. Erina Brady's former Dublin pupils are now inspiring and enlightened women in their seventies—subtle influencers in Irish society in a variety of areas—to the extent that one, Barbara Sweetman Fitzgerald, even has a CBE in Peace and Reconciliation in Northern Ireland.[28] The rediscovery of Brady's impact on Irish dance and theatre culture began with Jacqueline Robinson's important 1999 Memoir, *Modern Dance in 1940s Dublin? Yes, there was!* (part-published in *Irish Moves*). Trying to piece Brady's legacy together in retrospect, an interesting and crucial triangle between Erina Brady, her pupil Jacqueline Robinson, and their mutual guru Mary Wigman has emerged—the complex dynamics of which come to the fore in letter 6, above, from Wigman to Robinson. Robinson's own belated attempt as respected dance historian to substantiate the elusive early background of her 1940s Dublin teacher, highlights this odd triangular relationship. In letter 6, Wigman implies that the younger Robinson had to "flee" Brady, yet, much later, in her seventies, Robinson expends much energy trying to substantiate Brady's achievements as key disseminator of Wigman's modern dance theories to 1940s Ireland. Poignantly, as if a plea for appreciating Brady's significant, but overlooked cultural contribution, Robinson's 1940s Dublin Memoir is the last thing she writes and seeks to get published, despite a debilitating illness, shortly before her death at the age of seventy-eight in 2000.

ERINA BRADY'S PRE-DUBLIN LIFE AS A DANCE ARTIST

Despite Robinson's efforts, and my own, there are still few substantiated facts about Erina Brady's pre-Dublin life and training, from her birth, on 29 May 1891, in Bad Homburg Vor der Höhe, a posh suburb of Frankfurt, until her arrival to Dublin at the age of forty-eight, after her Cavan father Terence Brady's death in Switzerland in 1937. So, we must rely on Brady's own version of events.

Setting up her *Irish School of Dance Art* on Dublin's Harcourt Street in circa 1941, Ireland's first school of modern dance, Brady made the following assertions about her training in her impressive school prospectus, which is meticulously preserved at the Military Archive, in Dublin's Department of Defence at Cathal Brugha Barracks, Ireland.

> Erina Brady studied Dramatic Art and Production under Claude Benedict, Director of the French Theatre, Canada, and Ballet under Madame de Consoli, of the Scala, Milano. After gaining some knowledge of Eurhythmics at the Jaques-Dalcroze School at Lausanne, she went to Germany to acquaint herself with the Central European methods, and received her first training in Contemporary Dance Art at the Rudolf von Laban School at Frankfurt. Later she studied under Mary Wigman and graduated from her school at Dresden. She gained stage experience in Paris, Rome, Brussels, etc., and teaching experience in England, in Switzerland, and in Germany at the Mary Wigman School, Dresden.[29]

A generation later, in Cavan, in 1996, Erina Brady's second cousin James (Jim) Brady discovered a curious article in a biscuit tin while clearing out his ancestral home in Cavan after his mother's death.[30] This 1941 *Irish Independent*[31] newspaper cutting announced a performance by a mysterious relative called Erina who James Brady had never heard of. "A forthcoming Mansion House recital will display the best of her art, her symbolic dances, her storytelling in the dance. Maimie [sic] Jellett designed some of the costumes."[32]

Through my ongoing research since 2004, I have come to realize that Erina Brady could be economical with the truth, and equivocated on facts in her reinvention of herself when she arrived to Ireland, especially in relation to her secrets about her father and his family story. The 1941 article in the *Irish Independent*, presumably informed by Erina herself, begins romantically:

> Cavan met Cavan one day at Mentone. He, a Brady, was born in Cavan, and was a lecturer in Greek and Latin in the United States. She, an O'Reilly, was born in

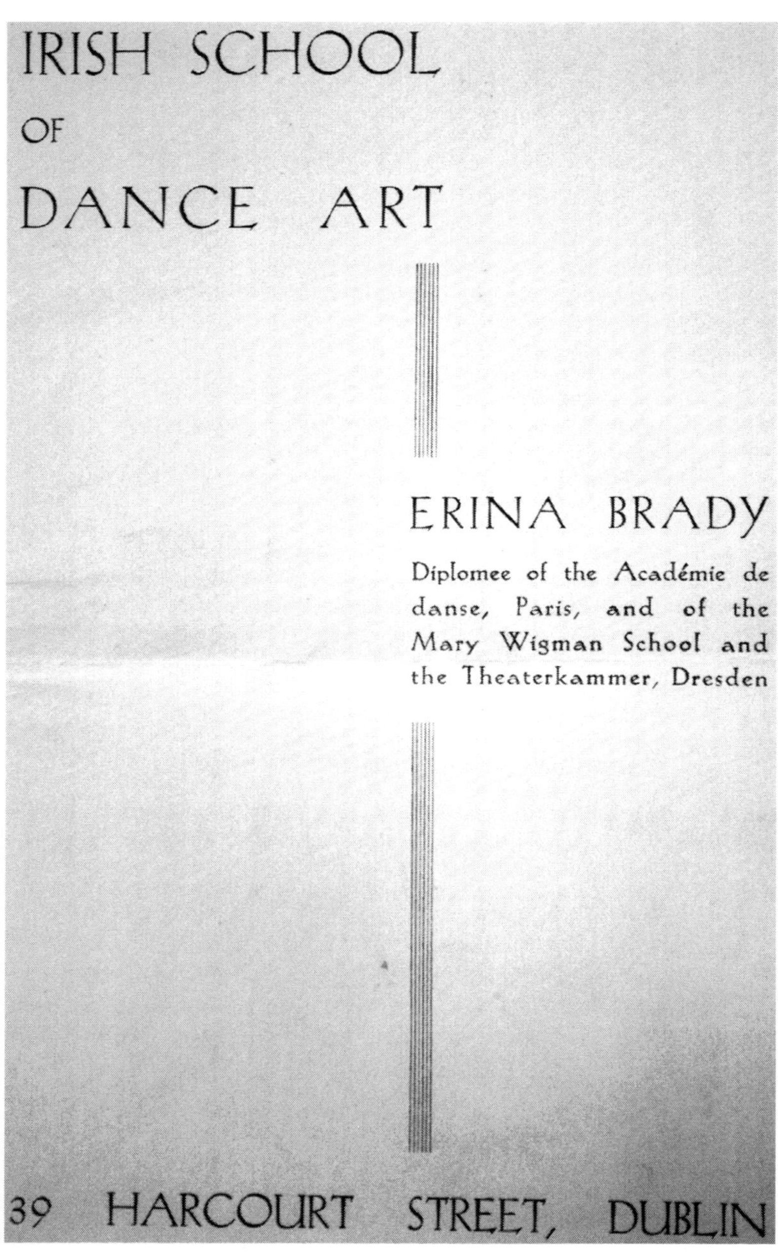

Figure 2.2. Erina Brady's *Irish School of Dance Art Prospectus* (cover). File 'IE/MA/G2/3506—Erina Brady.' The Military Archive at Cathal Brugha Barracks, Dublin, Ireland. Used courtesy of the Military Archive at Cathal Brugha Barracks, Dublin, Ireland.

THE IRISH SCHOOL OF DANCE ART

is the first training centre of Contemporary Dance Movement in Ireland. Its object being to promote the study, practice and appreciation of Dance as an Art Form, there will be a professional and a non-professional department, both of which are under the personal direction of Erina Brady.

ERINA BRADY

studied Dramatic Art and Production under Claude Bénédict, Director of the French Theatre, Canada, and Ballet under Madame de Consoli, of the Scala, Milano. After gaining some knowledge of Eurhythmics at the Jacques Dalcroze School at Lausanne, she went to Germany to acquaint herself with the Central European methods, and received her first training in Contemporary Dance Art at the Rudolf von Laban School at Frankfurt. Later she studied under Mary Wigman and graduated from her school at Dresden. She gained stage experience in Paris, Rome, Brussels, etc., and teaching experience in England, in Switzerland, and in Germany at the Mary Wigman School, Dresden.

PROFESSIONAL DEPARTMENT

AIM. The school aims at giving, besides sound technical training, a general artistic education, with special emphasis on the foundations and principles of dance form, as only on such a basis can a student's talent and personality be developed and the creative instinct stimulated.

TRAINING. To qualify as choreographer, solo dancer, group dancer or teacher of dance, students are required to take a three years' course, on completion of which they pass a final examination entitling successful candidates to the School's Diplomas. Holders of the Diploma for Dance will either be recommended for stage work, or become members of Erina Brady's Dance Group. Holders of the School's Certificate for Teaching may have an opportunity of staying as assistants, or will be recommended for work at schools. After no less than two years of teaching experience they may work independently founding schools for amateur adults and children.

3

Figure 2.3. Erina Brady's *Irish School of Dance Art Prospectus* (page 2). File 'IE/MA/G2/3506—Erina Brady.' The Military Archive at Cathal Brugha Barracks, Dublin, Ireland. Used courtesy of the Military Archive at Cathal Brugha Barracks, Dublin, Ireland.

Germany, her grandfather being Cavan-born. They married and settled down in Switzerland, and their daughter, Erina Brady came to Dublin in January 1939, and established the Irish School of Dance Art here.

Of course, she had been here before. Her articles on the Irish cause in the Swiss papers in the twenties had attracted the encouraging interest of Mr. Sean T. O'Kelly. Her family at that time lived in Lausanne.[33]

However, this article hid another dimension to Erina's complex identity that had little to do with being a modern dance pioneer. More recently it has come to light through my own contact with Erina Brady's family, prompted by several 2011/2012 articles and letters to newspapers,[34] that Erina's father, Terence Brady (b. Cavan 1848–d. Brione, Switzerland, ca. 1937), had been erased from the Brady family tree due to a controversy that was shocking in its time. An ordained Catholic priest who was Dean and Bursar of St. Patrick's School, Cavan, Terence Brady left his Ministry in 1888, to marry Elizabeth Wendland, whom he had met on a November 1887 school fundraising trip to the United States. Unsurprisingly, Father Terence Brady was disowned by his Cavan family when he eloped with the young German woman to St. Martin of the Fields, London on 12 September 1888.[35] This context, which his modern dance pioneer daughter successfully kept secret from her 1940s Dublin milieu must be taken into account when interpreting her actions, assertions, and most importantly, her dissimulations in Dublin. It is curious indeed that neither the formidable Jacqueline Robinson who tried valiantly to find out about Erina Brady's origins in her 1999 memoir, and in her *Dance Chronicle* article "Mary Wigman, a Magician," nor the G2 detectives who applied all the might of their professional skills to figure out Erina Brady's true motivation for landing in 1940s Dublin, discovered this well-hidden family secret which Erina Brady managed to keep to herself. In this politically charged "Emergency" era of great self-inventors like Brendan Bracken and William Joyce,[36] and before the internet and all its digital cross-referencing possibilities, it is not surprising that Ireland's G2 Special Branch were suspicious of the legitimacy of Erina Brady's artistic enterprise, and began to monitor her. The detectives' misgivings were unfounded, however. Erina Brady was, indeed, a modern dancer, inspired by Mary Wigman, and motivated to spread her radically enlightened bodily theories of holistic movement and freedom of expression to Ireland, as I set out to demonstrate here.

Placing the assertions of dance training as outlined in her above *Irish School of Dance Art* Prospectus (meticulously preserved in her G2 detective file at the Military Archive), in a historical framework, Erina Brady, who was born in May 1891 was only five years younger than Mary Wigman, whom she referred to as her teacher and mentor. So, Brady was a contemporary of a pioneer of *Ausdruckstanz*, just a step behind on a parallel path, unlike Jacqueline Robinson, who, at thirty-six years younger, was of a different generation entirely. Brady's own alleged early evolution in dance has a lot in common with that of Hanya Holm, a student of Mary Wigman who is considered one of the "Big Four" founders of modern dance in the United States.

To summarize, Brady's own assertions about her modern dance training in her *Irish School of Dance Art* Prospectus were firstly, that she gained knowledge of Eurhythmics at the Jaques-Dalcroze School in Lausanne; secondly, that she received her first training in Contemporary Dance Art at the Rudolf von Laban School in Frankfurt; and, thirdly, that she later studied under Mary Wigman, graduated from her school in Dresden, and also taught there herself. Influential Swiss composer and teacher Émile Jaques-Dalcroze[37] encouraged his music and dance students to develop a sense of rhythm by translating sounds into movement in a system known as "Eurhythmics." In 1910 Dalcroze's school took up residence five miles outside Dresden at Hellerau, the famous garden city, center of artistic innovation and *Gesamtkunstwerk*. One year later, in 1911, Wigman began her training there with Dalcroze at the age of twenty-seven.

Erina was twenty-four in 1915, when a Jaques-Dalcroze School opened in Geneva, not Lausanne as she mentions in the above quoted *Irish School of Dance Art* Prospectus. So Erina's Dalcroze training necessarily happened at least five years, if not more, after Wigman's. At this point Wigman had already created her iconoclastic, ground-breaking, signature solo *Hexentanz* (1914). Erina's next alleged training, in Frankfurt with Rudolf von Laban[38] (who advocated dance independent of music) as she asserts in her 1940s *Irish School of Dance Art* Prospectus, could not have happened until 1929, when Erina was thirty-eight years old. The fact that Erina's training with von Laban happened considerably later than Wigman's, indicates that Erina was deliberately emulating Wigman, and following in her footsteps.

Interestingly, after qualifying with Dalcroze in Dresden, Mary Wigman turned her back on what she saw as his slavish and subordinate relationship to music. In 1913, when Wigman's friend, the expressionist painter Emil Nolde, saw her solo choreography "Lento" performed in silence, to the rhythm generated by the moving body itself, he recommended that Wigman go to Rudolf von Laban's *Schule der Bewegungskunst* in Monte Verità, another utopian alternative community and place of *Lebensreform* near Ascona, in the Italian part of Switzerland, not far from the Bradys' *Casa Erina.* Nolde, who was using Wigman's iconoclastic dance moves as the model for his paintings in Berlin, felt that Laban's innovations were on the same wavelength as what he was seeing in Wigman's dance.

Wigman wrote of Nolde, and his endeavor to capture live movement on his canvas:

> My acquaintanceship—I had better say my friendship—with the painter Emil Nolde dated far back. . . . Nolde, whenever possible, came to my dance concerts. The managers knew about him and were aware of what was expected from them. They reserved three seats: one for him, one for his tubes and pots of paints, and one for his wife who stood guard lest he should be disturbed.[39]

Opposed to the practice of drawing static models, these painters were more interested in attempting to capture a sense of wild abandoned movement—a hallmark of Expressionist painting and dance. Trying to find Erina here, we can see the parallels with Erina's connection to *The White Stag* artists in Emergency Dublin—Basil Rakoczi, Kenneth Hall, and Patrick Scott, as well as Mainie Jellett and Evie Hone, to name but a few. Though the Irish painters were not known for capturing wild abandoned movement, there was a similar creative synergy between them—reminiscent also of *Gesamtkunstwerk* ("Total Work of Art"), the prevalent ethos during Germany's Weimar era.

At the turn of the century, Switzerland's Monte Verità ("Mountain of Truth"), located on a hill on the west side of Ascona in southern Switzerland was a Mecca of counterculture and the avant-garde, with its anarchists, communists, alienists, vegetarians, theosophists, and anthroposophists influenced by Rudolf Steiner.[40] Interestingly, Steiner schools are closely aligned with the ethos later espoused by Brady in her *Irish School of Dance Art*, and Brady would bring her final, 1946 masterpiece *The Voyage of Maeldune,* starring Robinson and June Fryer to the Rudolf Steiner Hall in London in 1948. I would suggest that there are interesting parallels to be found between the Monte Verità community and the more esoteric practices of W. B. Yeats and his theosophical circle in the Golden Dawn. Herman Hesse, James Joyce, Carl Jung, Isadora Duncan, Rainer Maria Rilke, and D. H. Laurence also crossed paths here. Monte Verità was home to hordes of nature-loving young nudists, feminists, and "vegetablists" who set up communes around the hill. Might Erina have been among them? We can only make an educated guess.

In 1913, Wigman went from Hellerau, Dresden, to Monte Verità—which was where she decided to devote, or even, in her case, to "consecrate" her life to dance. Erina's later teacher, Rudolf von Laban was at the heart of this alternative "*Lebensreform* Colony" during the war years, from 1912 to 1917, as well as of the Zurich arts scene. His Frankfurt movement choirs—as possibly alluded to by Erina in her *Irish School of Dance Art* prospectus—took place a decade later, in the summers of 1924, 1929, and 1930.

So the question is, how do we find Irish-German modern dance pioneer Erina Brady in all of this? This continues to remain a question to be further investigated. However, with Brady's Swiss Family residence,[41] the eponymous *Casa Erina*, located only thirty kilometers from Monte Verità it is hard to imagine that Erina remained oblivious to artistic innovations afoot there, that she did not, in some form, participate. It would be fascinating to think that Brady, liberated daughter of a shunned priest from Cavan, was somehow part of this enterprise, representing Ireland in its midst, joining in the free body expression and barefoot leaping.

TRANSFORMATION FROM HAUSFRAU TO "ÜBERFRAU"

Once at Monte Verità, Wigman never looked back, turning down an invitation to become a teacher at the Dalcroze school in order to pursue her own individualistic vision here. She became Laban's assistant, and he gave Wigman her first performance opportunities, most notably for her radical and iconic *Hexentanz* which she premiered in 1914. Transforming from potential bourgeois *Hausfrau* into the artist and the woman as an *Überfrau*,[42] Hexentanz celebrated the concept of the "New Woman" emerging in Weimar Germany,[43] free from constrictive bourgeois expectations of patriarchy, while giving it a somewhat frightening aura. Erina Brady's "late start" in modern dance is in keeping with Wigman's late arrival to dancing. After two broken engagements, at the age of twenty-seven, Wigman had run away from home, and its ruling concept of becoming a conventional *Hausfrau* to start her dance training with Dalcroze in Hellerau. We have yet to discover Erina's personal story in this context, where the personal is so clearly political.

The problem addressing Brady's third assertion in her *Irish School of Dance Art* Prospectus that she trained, qualified, and taught at Mary Wigman's Dresden school (which existed from 1920 to 1942), is that, unfortunately, there are no records of pupils' names here. Erina was twenty-nine years old in 1920, the year Wigman opened her Dresden School. Robinson's 1999 memoir *Modern Dance in 1940s Dublin—Yes, There Was!*, is our main evidence with regard to Brady's pedigree. Robinson, who began her dance training with Brady in her *Irish School of Dance Art*, is recognized as one of the most important figures in twentieth-century contemporary dance in France. The respected author of *The History of Dance in Modern France 1920–1970,*[44] as well as having been a regular correspondent of Mary Wigman from 1953 to 1970, and the French translator of Wigman's 1973 treatise *The Language of Dance*, Robinson is the reliable witness who rescued Erina Brady from oblivion. The prolific Robinson was also a poet, and, in 1955, founder of *l'Atelier de la Danse*, one of the first modern dance schools in Paris, and author of several more books on dance including *Mon Enfant et la Danse.*[45]

Acknowledging that it was Erina Brady who first introduced her to Mary Wigman, in 1940s Dublin, Robinson states:

> Erina Brady had studied with Wigman in Dresden, been a member of her company, and taught at her school. After leaving Germany, Erina opened her own school, modelled on those Wigman schools that existed in Germany before the war. Mary was in a way our household goddess, our source of inspiration, our model. And Erina would tell us many stories about her. I had never heard of Wigman, or of *Ausdruckstanz,* or modern dance. I was only aware of what I have already mentioned and the common image of the ballet dancer, and I had never questioned or been drawn to question the why, how, and wherefore of dance; simply, I had enjoyed dancing tremendously.[46]

In this volume of the journal "Dance Chronicle," Robinson's 1997 essay, "Mary Wigman, A Magician," which emphasizes the vocational transformation she underwent thanks to Erina Brady, is poignantly juxtaposed with Wigman's 1930–1971 correspondence to Hanya Holm.[47] In her essay, Robinson also gives details of Wigman's 1953 Zurich summer course, which she attended with her fellow dancer June Fryer, and her husband-to-be, the Kurt Jooss dancer Walter Kuhn. It was in 1955, a year after attending these summer courses, and beginning her correspondence with Wigman herself, that Robinson founded her Paris school—a logical sequel to her initial training in Brady's *Irish School of Dance Art*. Robinson gives a detailed account of her 1943–1946 training with Erina Brady in her *Irish School of Dance Art* in her 1999 memoir:

> We were aware of the richness of her past experiences, although she told us little about it in detail. However, those great people, Rudolf Laban and Mary Wigman, with whom she had worked, were present in her studio. There were photos on the walls and very frequent reference to their art and teaching. The family settled in Switzerland. It seems that Erina as a child saw Isadora Duncan dance, and decided she would be a dancer. It is likely that she studied classical ballet in Paris, with Madame de Consoli, and equally likely that she was not satisfied with this type of dance. She returned to Geneva and studied with Emile Jaques-Dalcroze. It seems she was at the time very concerned about the "troubles" in Ireland, and wrote articles in the Swiss press. Thence did she go perhaps to Frankfurt around 1929 to work with Rudolf von Laban. She may have performed with his group. It has proven to be quite a difficult task to ascertain different facts in her pre-Dublin life. Maybe she was known under another name?[48]

Robinson went to great lengths to ascertain facts about Erina's pre-Dublin life, including contacting international renowned Wigman expert Hedwig Müller.[49] Despite her exhaustive research, Robinson never found out that Brady's father had controversially left the priesthood in order to marry her young German mother, a fact that Brady successfully kept hidden from all of her professional acquaintances while promoting holistic Dance of Expression in Ireland. In her memoir, Robinson continues:

> Erina's teaching was very much influenced by the theories and practice of Laban—of Dalcroze also—as far as dance and music relationship are concerned, but principally by that of Mary Wigman. It is presumably in the early 30s that Erina went to Dresden to study with Wigman. Did she perform within her company? Although the name we know is not to be found among the list of "official" teachers at Wigman's school, there is, in a beautiful 1933 prospectus, a reference to classes being given by professional students chosen by Wigman. Maybe Erina was among these? Years later, Wigman did speak to me personally of the fact that Erina taught at her Dresden school.[50]

Indeed, there are obvious aesthetic and choreographic similarities between Wigman's 1930 choreography *Totenmal* [Monument to the Dead] which sought to wed dance and Albert Talfoff's verse in spoken word, in the spirit of *Gesamtkunstwerk*, and Brady's 1946 final Dublin (Abbey Theatre), and London (Rudolf Steiner Hall) artistic triumph *The Voyage of Maeldune*. The fact that Brady's 1946 masterpiece featured Wigmanesque tableaux, and a dramatized recital of Alfred Tennyson's eponymous poem seem to substantiate the above mentioned time frame, and point to the possibility that sixteen years previously in 1930, the thirty-nine-year old Erina Brady, might have been involved in Wigman's *Totenmal*.

Prompted by an encounter with Irish choreographer John Scott at one of his *Irish Modern Dance Theatre*'s performances in Paris, which alerted her to the fact that the dance world in Dublin was unaware of Erina Brady, Robinson knew that it was down to her to set the record straight, despite her own failing health. Robinson states:

> Most certainly these were very important years for Erina. She referred so often to Mary, to other dancers who were with her at the time, to Hanns Hasting and Aladia Montijn, Wigman's musician partners (who both wrote music for Erina). There were fascinating photos on the walls of the studio, and we would gaze and dream over all these fragments of a rich, moving, eloquent world—a world of quest into the possibility of speaking through movement, of reaching towards greater dimensions of being and doing, which we wished to attain.
>
> When did Erina leave Dresden? And why? More unknown elements in this biographical sketch. It seems she worked as a dancer and maybe as a choreographer for the Theatre Mogador in Paris.[51] This theatre staged mostly musical comedies, and toured through Europe. It is there that Erina took part in Rose-marie, in which she was to play again in 1942, in Dublin! [52]

Robinson is referring here to the 1920s Hammerstein operetta-style musical *Rosemarie, A Love Song of the Canadian Rockies,* the smash hit which then became the popular 1936 movie starring Jeanette McDonald and Nelson Eddy. For esteemed pupils of Wigman to take part in musicals was not unusual. This also applied to Hanya Holm. In 1931, Brady's contemporary Holm, became Wigman's appointed disciple to the United States, where she set up a "Mary Wigman School," which later became the "Hanya Holm School." Holm also choreographed Broadway musicals *Kiss Me Kate* (1948), *Out of This World* (1950), *My Fair Lady* (1954), and *Camelot* (1960). Like Erina, Holm also studied at the Dalcroze school before taking up training with Wigman at the age of twenty-eight. She subsequently joined Wigman's Dresden school where she became teaching assistant, in the early 1920s. Wigman herself first performed in the United States in 1930. Wigman's students and disciples Harald Kreutzberg and Yvonne Georgi, led the way for her by performing in the United States in 1929, building up a reputation for "new German dance"—thus providing crucial support and back-up for Holm that the formidable Brady did not have in Dublin.

Maybe cognizant of Holm's success transplanting Wigman's theories to the United States, in contrast to her own Sisyphean battle in Ireland, Erina did advise Robinson to start in America:

> Referring to my future, she advised me to: "go across the ocean [she meant to the United States] before tackling old-old Europe, and tackle Switzerland and France before confronting London. Prejudice once enshrined dies by a slow death, for those who have given hysterical applause at Sadler's Wells don't easily admit that they might have been mistaken. The ballet nevertheless is giving its last kicks and you will live to enjoy the triumphs of our work even there where it suffers persecution today.[53]

It is not surprising to learn that the United States provided more fertile ground than repressive Ireland for Mary Wigman's holistic theories of the body, as we can see from Hanya Holm's success in the United States, in contrast to the difficulties Brady faced in Ireland. Another parallel with Brady is that Holm also attended a Catholic school in Frankfurt for fifteen years. Erina was partly home-schooled by her father, but her upbringing was also Catholic. Unlike Brady, who died in 1961 at the age of seventy, Holm lived until 1992, to the ripe old age of ninety-nine. Holm took on American citizenship before the war in 1939, and unlike Erina Brady, who died in oblivion in Switzerland, she achieved great acclaim and recognition for her contribution to dance as an art form.

Trawling through the archives, there is no lack of good coverage and recognition in the 1940s Irish press for Erina's modern dance activities in 1940s

Dublin. For example, after dissimulating her parental background ("Such is the background of Erina Brady"), the aforementioned *Irish Independent* article of 29 November 1941 continues: "In her spacious, modern Harcourt Street studio-cum-built-in-den hangs a signed photograph of *Die Wigman*, with whom she studied and worked for three years in Dresden. Later, she nearly always spent her holidays there, a respite from producing the ballet for the Paris Mogador Theatre, touring with them all over Western Europe and Italy."[54]

Going according to the reputable Liam Ó Laoghaire's review of Brady's 1941 Mansion House performance in the Irish cultural magazine *The Leader*, we can deduce that Brady's art spoke for itself:

> There is only good and bad dance art. I am not intensely interested in the partisan violences of balletomane or modern but when we come to that simplification, which is so often the accompaniment of greatness, we are aware of a supreme test being applied. Consequently when Erina Brady appeared at the Mansion House lately in her first public recital, one felt she was treading on very dangerous ground. Her first dance revealed a sureness of purpose with a finished technique that led one to believe that she is possibly the finest dancer that has appeared here for years. Her sense of the stage is remarkable, her feeling for music is sensitive, one's impression—that of a flawless artistry.[55]

Ó Laoghaire's shrewd accolade, coupled with the many other eye-witness reports of her work as modern dance pioneer to 1940s Dublin, is a clear indication that Erina Brady should indeed be officially acknowledged as Mary Wigman's disciple to Ireland, even if it requires further research to fit in missing pieces in her story, and she did not have as much enduring success as Hanya Holm on her similar more copiously documented and celebrated mission to the United States.

Twentieth-century dance history in Ireland, a history of apparent non-sequiturs and "failures," is full of gaps and lacunae—for example that of overlooked modern dancer Lucia Joyce, whose own account of events, like Erina Brady's, has not survived either. In the context of this suppressed history of the body, it is extremely important to set the record straight, as Robinson set out to do in her 1999 memoir, and to acknowledge and celebrate Erina Brady's Herculean achievements in her 1940s *Irish School of Dance Art*. When looked at on a wider canvas, quite the opposite of a non-sequitur, Brady's holistic cultural enterprise was a vital step leading toward today's thriving contemporary dance scene in twenty-first-century Ireland, where the body and its associated art form are finally being assigned their rightful pride of place in the Irish cultural landscape.

Without support of any kind, Erina Brady undertook an uphill struggle to transplant *Ausdruckstanz* from Germany to a conservative Ireland that was not yet ready for it. She persevered valiantly in her self-appointed task without recognition in her lifetime and died in oblivion in Switzerland. Today we can be grateful to Erina Brady and acknowledge her hard-won legacy which, luckily for us, we are all heirs to in a more enlightened Ireland that she must have been desperately hoping for. A prophet for Ireland of the coming times, Erina Brady was indeed Mary Wigman's disciple to Ireland, aligning us with all the other countries around the globe to which Mary Wigman's enlightened bodily theories spread from Germany, propelled by a kind of bodily utopianism, and with varying degrees of success.

NOTES

1. Susan Manning, "*Ausdruckstanz* (1910–1950)," *The Routledge Encyclopedia of Modernism* (London: Routledge, 2016), accessed 12 May 2019, https://www.rem.routledge.com/articles/ausdruckstanz-1910-1950. doi:10.4324/0123456789-REM1773-1.
2. *Irish School of Dance Art* Prospectus, ca. 1941. Unpublished File "IE/MA/G2/3506-Erina Brady." Military Archive, Department of Defence, Cathal Brugha Barracks, Dublin.
3. Manning, "*Ausdruckstanz* (1910–1950)."
4. Ireland was neutral during WW2, and the government declared a state of "Emergency," hence the period is referred to in Ireland as "The Emergency."
5. An outdoor performance of Erina Brady's *Irish School of Dance Art* at John Betjeman's residence, Collinstown House, Clondalkin, was filmed in Kodachrome color by Liam O Laoghaire, for "Dance School." His eleven-minute promotional film for Erina Brady's *Irish School of Dance Art* from 1943 has been preserved by the Irish Film Archive, Irish Film Institute, Eustace Street, Dublin 2, Ireland.
6. For further information see Deirdre Mulrooney, *Irish Moves, an Illustrated History of Dance and Physical Theatre in Ireland* (Dublin: The Liffey Press, 2006), 83–113.; Deirdre Mulrooney, "Erina Brady: Irish-German Harbinger of Modern Dance to 1940s Ireland," in *Selected Irish Biographies*, ed. by Sabine Egger (Trier: WVT, 2015), 12–29.
7. For further information, see Deirdre Mulrooney, "'Erina Brady.' Adaptation of 'Dance Emergency.' TG4 documentary Script," English/German, translated by Marc Staudacher . *TANZ Magazine* (April 2015): 52–57. An abbreviated version (in German and English) of this article has been published on the Goethe Institute Ireland website, accessed 19 May 2015, https://www.goethe.de/ins/ie/en/kul/mag/20726284.html. Furthermore, see documentary films on the topic by Deirdre Mulrooney: *Dance Emergency* (TG4, 2014); *1943—A Dance Odyssey* (RTE One, 2013).
8. Published in Claudia Gitelman's essay, with translations by Marianne Forster: "Dance, Business, and Politics: Letters from Mary Wigman to Hanya Holm, 1930–1971," *Dance Chronicle* 20, no. 1 (1997): 1–21.
9. Rouson [sic, no full name given]. Spectator "Leader Page Parade." *Irish Independent*, 29 November 1941, 2.

10. Unpublished correspondence from Mary Wigman to Jacqueline Robinson, comprising fifty letters, from 6 May 1953 to 20 August 1961. Private collection, given to the author by Walter Kuhn after the death of his wife June Kuhn (nee Fryer) in 2011.

11. "For eight successive summers, for two weeks, over 150 dancers of all nationalities have met to work together with the greatest masters. This year the faculty comprised Mary Wigman, whose teaching base is in Berlin, Rosalia Chladek in Vienna, Gertrud Engelhardt in Stockholm, Harald Kreutzberg in the Tyrol, Sigurd Leeder in London, and Victor Gsovsky in Paris—each one representing a specific approach to dance." Jacqueline Robinson in *Art et Danse*, August 1953, cited in Jacqueline Robinson, "Mary Wigman, a Magician," *Dance Chronicle* 20, no. 1 (1997): 26.

12. June Fryer's future husband, Kurt Jooss dancer Walter Kuhn, also attended the Summer School with them.

13. Mary Wigman, from her unpublished 1954 private diary, preserved at Berlin's *Akademie der Künste (AdK)*.

14. Cited from Mary Wigman's unpublished 1954 private diary, *AdK*, Berlin, *Mary-Wigman-Archiv*, No. 467, 23–24. [Trans. by the author]. I am grateful to Dr. Hedwig Müller who kindly shared this quote by email, 23 March 2018; and to Stephan Dörschel, Head of the Archive of Performing Arts, ADK, for sharing the bibliographical reference by email on 29 May 2019.

15. See endnote 4.

16. Robinson, "Mary Wigman, A Magician," 25.

17. June remained Jacqueline Robinson's lifelong close friend from the time they met in Emergency Dublin of the early 1940s, when they were fellow star pupils and performers at Erina Brady's *Irish School of Dance Art*.

18. Wigman, in unpublished correspondence from Wigman to Robinson, letter 5 of 50.

19. Related to the author in person by Hugh Barden's niece, Dora Forster, on 21 May and 21 June 2012.

20. Wigman, in unpublished correspondence from Wigman to Robinson, 6/50.

21. Erina Brady in an unpublished letter to Jacqueline Robinson, 8 April 1948. Private collection, given to the author by Walter Kuhn after the death of his wife, June Fryer, in 2011.

22. Erina Brady in an unpublished letter to Jacqueline Robinson, 12 April 1948. Private collection, given to the author by Walter Kuhn after the death of his wife, June Fryer, in 2011.

23. Wigman, in unpublished correspondence from Wigman to Robinson, 19/50.

24. Wigman, in unpublished correspondence from Wigman to Robinson, 24/50.

25. See Chapter 3 of Mulrooney, *Irish Moves,* 83–114.

26. These are part of TV documentaries and other publications by the author. See following paragraph for details.

27. Jacqueline Robinson, cited in *Irish Moves*, 100.

28. CBE Awarded in 2002, see Ruth Dudley Edwards, "The Subversive CBE" in *The Irish Independent*, 17 February 2002, accessed 12 May 2019, https://www.independent.ie/irish-news/the-subversive-cbe-26239350.html.

29. *Irish School of Dance Art* Prospectus, ca. 1941. Unpublished File "IE/MA/G2/3506--Erina Brady." Military Archive, Department of Defence, Cathal Brugha Barracks, Dublin.

30. James Brady, "A Biscuit Tin," *Genealogical Society of Ireland Journal* 15 (2014): 55–57.

31. *Irish Independent*, 29 November, 1941, 2.

32. Ibid.

33. Ibid.

34. Deidre Mulrooney, "Following Erina Brady's Footsteps," Letter to the *Irish Times*, 6 July 2011; "State's First 'Modern Dance' Performer." June Fryer Obituary, *Irish Times*, 1 October 2011; "Modern Dance Pioneer Had Cavan Roots." Letter to *Anglo-Celt Newspaper*, Cavan, 16 November 2011; "Spot the Artist" Irishwoman's Diary, *Irish Times*, 27 July 2012.

35. Marriage Certificate, "England, Marriages, 1538–1973," Index, accessed 27 Sept 2012, www.familysearch.org/pal:/MM9.1.1/NVJV-TKP, Terence Brady and Elizabeth Wendland, 22 Sept 1888; citing reference: FHL microfilm 1468962.

36. Both are renowned men of mystery from this era: Irish-born Brendan Bracken was Winston Churchill's right-hand man and from 1941 to 1945 Minister of Information, while Anglo-Irish William Joyce was better known as "Lord Haw Haw," wartime broadcaster of Nazi propaganda, for which he was convicted of treason and sentenced to death in 1945.

37. Born in Vienna, 1865, and died in Geneva, 1950.

38. Son of the Military Governor of Bosnia and Herzegovina, born in Bratislava, Austro-Hungarian Empire, in 1879, died in 1958.

39. Mary Wigman in *The Mary Wigman Book: Her Writings,* ed and trans. Walter Sorrell (Middletown, Conn.: Wesleyan University Press, 1973), 55.

40. Mary Anne Santos Newhall, *Mary Wigman* (Oxford: Routledge, 2018), originally published in 2009, 20–21.

41. According to Erina's cousin Constance Brady, Erina's family moved to Switzerland from Frankfurt in the 1930s in response to the rise of Nazism in Germany (Unpublished skype interview with the author, 16 December 2012).

42. Newhall, *Mary Wigman*, 12.

43. Carol Schmid, "The 'New Woman.' Gender Roles and Urban Modernization in Interwar Berlin and Shanghai," *Journal of International Women's Studies* 15, no. 1 (2014).

44. Amsterdam: Harwood Academic Press, 1997.

45. Robinson, *Mon Enfant et la Danse*, (Paris: Editions Universitaires, 1975).

46. Robinson, "Mary Wigman, a Magician," 24.

47. Gitelman, "Dance, Business, and Politics."

48. Jacqueline Robinson, cited in *Irish Moves*, 89–90.

49. Author of the definitive 1986 biography *Mary Wigman: Leben und Werk der grossen Tänzerin* and founder of the Mary Wigman Foundation.

50. Robinson, in *Irish Moves*, 90.

51. Isadora Duncan also performed at the *Théâtre Mogador,* Paris.

52. Robinson, in *Irish Moves*, 90–91.

53. Ibid., 101.
54. *Irish Independent*, 29 November 1941, 2.
55. Ó Laoghaire, Liam, "Dance Recital by Erina Brady," in *The Leader: A Review of Current Affairs, Politics, Literature, Art and Industry*, ed. by Nuala Moran, vol. LXXX, no. 21, 20 December 1941, 517.

BIBLIOGRAPHY

Abbey Theatre Archive: Entry on Erina Brady. Accessed 19 May 2019. http://www.abbeytheatre.ie/archives/person_detail/10305.

Breifne Historical Society. *Journal of Cumann Seanchais Bhreifne* IV, no 16 (1973–75): 525–526.

Brady, James. "A Biscuit Tin." *Genealogical Society of Ireland Journal* 15 (2014): 55–57.

Cunningham, Terence P. and Daniel Gallogly. *St Patrick's College, a Centenary History*. Cavan: St. Patrick's College, 1974.

Dunne, Raymond, and Francis J. Mac Kiernan. *The College Boys, Students of the Kilmore Academy and St. Patrick's College, Cavan 1839–2000*. Cavan: Cumann Seanchais Bhreifne, 2008.

Ferriter, Diarmaid. *Occasions of Sin, Sex & Society in Modern Ireland*. London: Profile Books, 2009.

Gitelman, Claudia, with translations by Marianne Forster. "Dance, Business, and Politics: Letters from Mary Wigman to Hanya Holm, 1930–1971." *Dance Chronicle* 20, no. 1 (1997): 1–22.

———, ed. *Liebe Hanya: Mary Wigman's Letters to Hanya Holm*. Madison: University of Wisconsin Press, 2003.

Green, Martin. *Mountain of Truth: The Counterculture Begins, Ascona 1900–1920*. Hanover and London: University Press of New England, 1986.

Holfter, Gisela and Hermann Rasche. *John Hennig—Exile in Ireland*. Syracuse University Press, 2007.

Karina, Lilian and Marion Kant. *Hitler's Dancers: German Modern Dance and the Third Reich*. New York and Oxford: Berghahn Books, 2004.

Kennedy, SB. *The White Stag Group*. Dublin: The Irish Museum of Modern Art, 2005.

MacKiernan, Francis J. *Diocese of Kilmore, Bishops and Priests, 1136–1988*. Cavan: Breifne Historical Society, 1989.

Manning, Susan. *Ecstasy and the Demon: Feminism and Nationalism in the Dances of Mary Wigman*. Berkeley: University of California Press, 1993.

Manning, Susan, and Ruprecht, Lucia (eds). *New German Dance Studies*. Urbana-Champaign: University of Illinois Press, 2012.

McGrath, Aoife. *Dance Theatre in Ireland: Revolutionary Moves*. Houndmills: Palgrave, 2013.

Müller, Hedwig. *Mary Wigman: Leben und Werk der großen Tänzerin*. Berlin: Quadragia Verlag, 1986.

Mulrooney, Deidre. "Erina Brady: A Forgotten Pioneer of Modern Dance in 1940s Ireland." Goethe Institute Ireland website, April 2015. Accessed 19 May 2019. https://www.goethe.de/ins/ie/en/kul/mag/20726284.html.

———. "'Erina Brady.' Adaptation of 'Dance Emergency.' TG4 documentary Script," English/German, translated by Marc Staudacher . *TANZ Magazine* (April 2015): 52–57.

———. "Erina Brady: Irish-German Harbinger of Modern Dance to 1940s Ireland." In *Cultural Translators—Selected Irish German Biographies II,* edited by Sabine Egger. Trier: WVT, 2015, 12–29.

———. "Following Erina Brady's Footsteps," Letter to *Irish Times*, 6 July 2011.

———. *Irish Moves, an Illustrated History of Dance and Physical Theatre in Ireland*. Dublin: The Liffey Press, 2006.

———. "Modern Dance Pioneer had Cavan Roots." 16 November 2011. Letter to *Anglo-Celt Newspaper*, Cavan.

———. "Spot the Artist." *Irishwoman's Diary*, 27 July 2012.

———, "State's First Modern Dance Performer." June Fryer Obituary, *Irish Times,* 1 October 2011.

Newhall, Mary Ann Santos. *Mary Wigman. Routledge Performance Practitioners*. New York: Routledge, 2009.

Ó Laoghaire, Liam. "Dance Recital by Erina Brady." *The Leader: A Review of Current Affairs, Politics, Literature, Art and Industry* LXXX, no. 21, 20 December 1941, 517.

———. *Invitation to the Film*. Tralee: The Kerryman Ltd., 1945.

Robinson, Jacqueline, *The History of Modern Dance in France, an Adventure 1920–1970*. Amsterdam: Harwood Academic Publishers, 1997.

Robinson, Jacqueline. "Mary Wigman, A Magician." *Dance Chronicle* 20, no. 1 (1997), 23–47.

———. *L'Enfant et la Danse*. Paris: Antoine Vogels, 1988.

———. *Mon Enfant et la Danse*. Paris: Editions Universitaires, 1975.

———. ed. 50 unpublished letters from Mary Wigman to Jacqueline Robinson 1952–1971. Private collection given to the Author by Walter Kuhn, 2011.

Rouson, [sic, no name given]. Spectator "Leader Page Parade." *Irish Independent*, 29 November, 1941, 2.

Schmid, Carol. "The 'New Woman.' Gender Roles and Urban Modernization in Interwar Berlin and Shanghai." *Journal of International Women's Studies* 15, no. 1 (2014): 2. Accessed 19 May 2019. https://ohio.box.com/s/4kfdh4f82wn2xgc0wy2ymsnyd5ko1xtf.

Sorrell, Walter. *Hanya Holm: The Biography of an Artist*. Middletown, Conn.: Wesleyan University Press, 1969.

Wigman, Mary. *The Mary Wigman Book: Her Writings.* Edited and translated by W. Sorrell. Middletown, Conn.: Wesleyan University Press, 1973.

Wills, Clair, "Neutrality and Popular Culture." UCD Scholarcast 5. Series 1 (Spring 2008). Accessed 19 May 2019. http://www.ucd.ie/scholarcast/transcripts/Neutrality_Popular_Culture.pdf

———. *That Neutral Island.* London: Faber and Faber, 2007.

Chapter Three

Duality of Cultural Influences as a Source of Insight and Inspiration

The Collaboration between Aloys Fleischmann and Joan Moriarty 1947–1992

Ruth Fleischmann

Research undertaken by German philologists on the Irish language and ancient literature around the beginning of the twentieth century[1] constituted a source of inspiration to Anglo-Irish writers, painters, historians, and scholars. The Anglo-Irish artists' works, uniquely Irish in theme and form, stimulated many native Irish writers and painters, now liberated from the colonial perception of the land as a country without culture, to follow suit. The great ensuing cultural movement laid the foundations for the political organizations and activities which were ultimately to lead to independence in 1922. The role of the Anglo-Irish intellectuals was crucial. They had roots in two worlds but were half outsiders in both; this uneasy situation brought a small group of the exceptionally gifted among them to explore the indigenous culture and to be inspired by the extraordinary richness of what they discovered. The literary critic Andrew Carpenter has identified what he calls the "doubleness of vision" as one of the salient features of Irish literature.[2]

The work of two later artists with such dual identities is to be sketched here. One is the composer, professor, and scholar of Irish traditional music, Aloys Fleischmann (1910–1992), whose father was a Bavarian musician, his mother born in Cork to German parents. The other is Joan Moriarty, the choreographer and founder of professional ballet in Ireland, who was brought up in England and there became an outstanding Irish traditional dancer and musician. It will be shown how she sought to do for dance what Anglo-Irish artists had done for drama, poetry, and painting, how she collaborated with Fleischmann for nearly half a century, he being engaged in a similar quest, namely seeking to develop an Irish classical art music in touch with contemporary European music while drawing its inspiration from the Gaelic cultural heritage, and how they both devoted their lives to try and bring their respective arts into the lives of ordinary people.

FLEISCHMANN'S GERMAN FAMILY AND IRISH UPBRINGING

Fleischmann's father, Aloys Fleischmann senior, was born in Dachau in 1880, a small Bavarian town close to Munich which was famous for its painters. He was a church musician and composer; in 1905 he married Tilly Swertz, a graduate of Munich's Royal Academy of Music, whose parents had emigrated from Dachau to Cork in 1879. The following year she brought him back to her hometown where he succeeded his father-in-law as cathedral organist. His exile in the rather culturally barren city was somewhat traumatic, but he and his wife found solace in working to develop classical music there, and took pleasure in the company of musicians and music lovers involved in Irish language and drama groups such as Daniel Corkery, Terence MacSwiney, Germaine Stockley, the MacDonnells of Bandon, and a few members of the Ascendancy with similar interests. These people had a considerable impact on Fleischmann in his youth.

Aloys Fleischmann's diaries of 1926 and 1927, begun when he was fifteen, cast an interesting light on the development of his sense of identity. He had begun his schooling at the MacSwiney sisters' Scoil Ita; he became proficient in the Irish language after frequent stays in the Gaeltacht; he was a regular visitor to Corkery's home where he loved the classical gramophone music played for the guests, and the literary discussions, but was unswayed by the political arguments produced by the host and many visitors making the case for Irish republicanism.[3] In an entry of 13 August 1926, he describes an evening walk in Monatrea with his parents' friend, the pianist Sinéad Ní Bhriain: "Miss O'Brien and I talked Irish all the way back. It was dusk, and I thought how in keeping with the lovely Irish landscape is the Irish tongue. We heard a flute-player at some Irish jigs far off, and I thought how I would love my country if I were an Irishman, but being Bavarian, I am split between the two."[4]

That split was to be resolved when he lived among foreigners for the first time as a post-graduate student in Munich from 1932 to 1934. There, under the pseudonym "Muiris Ó Rónáin," he wrote his *Sreath do Phiano* (Suite for Piano), the first work exemplifying his vision of an Irish art-music inspired by the contemporary yet rooted in the spirit of the Gaelic heritage. Two of his Munich professors encouraged him in this enterprise: his composition teacher, Joseph Haas[5] and the music historian Otto Ursprung, an expert on medieval music.[6] Fleischmann's first research on Irish folk music was undertaken in 1936 in response to inquiries from Professor Ursprung.[7] At the end of his life Fleischmann told his friend and colleague Tomás Ó Canainn of his feelings on his return to Ireland in 1934, Wagner's music indicating the path to be taken: "It was on the boat coming back that I began to feel I was riding on the crest of a wave, as we approached Cobh, early in the morning. Ringing in my ears was that marvelous passage from *Tristan*—'Die Irische Königin' (Irish Queen)—Iseult being a Dublin princess. I suddenly began to feel that I had a job to do here."[8]

The "job" to be done was a daunting one. In 1934 Ireland had no professional orchestra, music education was not part of the school curriculum, there was no requirement for music teachers to have recognized qualifications, the career prospects for properly qualified musicians were dismal and most emigrated, there were few opportunities in Irish cities outside Dublin to hear classical music, and fewer still to perform it. Fleischmann resolved to do his utmost to change this and to try to make classical music part of people's lives. His appointment to the chair of music in University College Cork straight after his return from Munich in 1934 put him in a position to set out on this task, which he pursued systematically throughout his life.

He drew his inspiration from his German parents' efforts and successes in promoting classical music in Cork, their adopted city, and from the philosophy of the Cork writer, painter, and musician Daniel Corkery. Corkery was one of the initiators of the Munster Society of Arts, founded at the end of 1923 by twelve writers, painters, musicians, and academics appalled by the devastation caused to the cultural life of the country by war and civil war.[9] Corkery summed up the situation thus: "In no part of the world are the creative arts so dead as amongst us, and nowhere are people less concerned about it. To revive the arts, we must hew in our own quarries."[10] This artistic regionalism was to give expression to the life of the southern province, to explore its Gaelic heritage in literature, the visual arts, and music. It was to be complemented by the study of the arts outside those quarries, and the Society was to provide access to the arts of the European continent. Fleischmann's father was on the music committee of the Munster Society of Arts; its manifesto was adopted by Fleischmann junior. Moriarty was to add a new dimension to the program: dance.

IRISH AND SCOTTISH CULTURAL INFLUENCES ON MORIARTY'S LIFE IN LIVERPOOL

Little is known about Joan Moriarty's youth. The Moriartys had left Mallow in County Cork by 1907, living for a time in Dublin and then moving to England, where Joan was brought up.[11] No documentation of the family's life there up to 1931 has survived. That year Joan began a personal scrapbook of press cuttings which document that the Moriartys were residents of Liverpool and show that the emigrant family took a strong interest in Irish culture. They were members of the Gaelic League, one of the Moriarty brothers played for the Gaelic Athletic Association, and the family had a subscription for the Republican paper, *An Phoblacht*. Joan attended Irish dancing classes organized by the Gaelic League;[12] she became champion Irish step-dancer of Britain in 1931, having been advised to enter for the competition by George Leonard, then champion step-dancer of Ireland.[13] She was also a prize-winning traditional musician with an unusual instrument for a woman: the war pipes. When staying with landed relatives in Scotland, she was first taught by their family piper in Glenapp Castle and subsequently became a pupil in Liverpool of pipe-major Samuel Daly of the Gordon Highlanders, who had trained in the school of piping founded in the Scottish Highlands by the Irish MacCrimmon brothers.[14] She was the first woman to take part in the solo war pipes competition at the GAA Tailteann Games in Dublin, and at the Games of July 1932 was awarded a silver medal. She came first at the Killarney Open Championship in 1933. Her connection with the Scottish Mackay Inchcape family entitled her to membership of the Liverpool Scots Society and therefore to participate (as the first woman piper ever) in the Morecambe and Heysham Scottish Gathering of July 1933.[15]

Moriarty's ballet training is not documented. She studied for a while at Marie Rambert's school[16] until, at the age of fourteen, she became too tall to contemplate becoming a professional ballerina. A relative, Muriel Moriarty-Elliot, a member of the Royal Academy of Dancing, had a school of ballet in Liverpool, which she may have attended. Her immersion in her youth in two dance cultures—one continental, deriving from France and Russia, the other originally from the Irish countryside and cherished by the emigrant communities in Britain—was to have a decisive influence on her subsequent work for dance in Ireland after the family returned to Mallow in the summer of 1933. Her chance to set about implementing a grand plan for ballet in Ireland came in 1945 when—as a traditional musician—she first collaborated with Fleischmann, who early in 1947 agreed to put his Cork Symphony Orchestra at the service of the performing ballet group she was training.

Her ideas on what was needed to make ballet part of Irish culture were as wide-ranging and systematic as were Fleischmann's for music, but the obstacles to be faced and surmounted were greater. First of all, Moriarty had no institutional backing such as Fleischmann had in University College Cork where, though his salary in the early years was small (£75 per annum), it was a fixture. Moriarty, as a private teacher of dance, had a hard struggle to make even a modest livelihood during the depressed war years of the 1940s. Secondly, the public perception of ballet was generally ambivalent. Though classical music was infrequently heard by the majority of Irish people in the first half of the twentieth century, ballet was even more remote from the experience of the average Irish person. It differed from classical music in that it was highly suspect to many in the hierarchy of that most influential institution, the Irish Catholic church. The main obstacle to be overcome by promoters of classical music was generally lack of interest on the part of the public. Promoters of ballet, however, could encounter the sort of hostility that writers constantly and innovative theatrical productions occasionally met with in the puritanical Catholic Ireland of the time.[17] But perhaps more difficult to overcome than the occasional blast from the pulpit was the widespread public perception of ballet as something rather ridiculous, utterly unmanly, and slightly indecent.[18] Thirdly, there was the discouraging fate of the three Dublin performing ballet groups which preceded Moriarty's, and which had vanished one after the other due to the inclement cultural environment. When Eamon de Valera reduced the grant of Ireland's national theatre, the Abbey Theatre, soon after he came to office as Taoiseach in 1932, the directors had to close Ninette de Valois' Abbey Theatre School of Ballet; it had been in operation for six years.[19] The company set up in Dublin in 1936 by Sara Payne (one of the teachers employed by de Valois) had closed in 1945. The Irish Ballet Club, founded in 1939 by an Irish pupil of de Valois, Cepta Cullen, had ceased performances in 1943 after five years, though teaching continued for perhaps another decade.[20]

So, the quest begun by Moriarty with the first public performance of her ballet group on 1 June 1947 in Cork was even more daunting than that on which Fleischmann had embarked in 1934.

THE FLEISCHMANN/MORIARTY CORK BALLET COMPANY COLLABORATION

The forty-six-year collaboration was based on their shared conviction that access to the arts is a basic right capable of bringing great benefit to the individual and to the community. Their experience of Germany and England had generated in both an acute awareness of the significance of the Irish heritage and generated a resolve to delve into it as a source of inspiration. This was to encompass finding themes for ballet in Irish legend, mythology, folklore, and literature, the creation of dance forms fusing elements of traditional Irish dance with ballet, and the composing of new music for the ballets. The partnership brought Moriarty an orchestra for the annual ballet week performances and specially composed ballet music for her choreography; for Fleischmann it brought a new forum for his creative talent and a greater audience both for classical music as well as for new Irish works.

THE CORK SYMPHONY ORCHESTRA

The live orchestral music provided dancers and audience with a dimension of sound which was hardly ever at the disposal of amateur groups, who in the days before tape recorders and audio amplification systems generally danced to piano accompaniment. (Even the Ballet Rambert had to make do with two pianos when it performed in Dublin in 1936, as did Kurt Jooss' Contemporary Dance Theatre in 1946.) The impressive combination of orchestra and ballet company in the annual Cork productions was no doubt one of the factors leading to the successful building of audiences. It meant intensive work for the conductor and players with two months of rehearsals, but there was never any problem in recruiting musicians, and many participated for decades. The rich palette of music added to the orchestra's repertoire, ranging from the great classics of ballet music to compositions by living composers such as Friel, Maconchy, Ó Gallchobhair, Potter, as well as their conductor's works. Fleischmann's tasks were manifold. In a letter of 1982, for instance, Moriarty describes an unexpected problem arising during the preparation for *Giselle* when discrepancies were discovered between the tape recording of Adam's music used at rehearsals in her studio and the hired orchestral score and parts. She wrote to Michel de Lutry, then professor of choreography at the Munich University of Music and Performing Arts, who was to direct the production: "Aloys has had a big job on the music, as he found that a lot of what we are using is not in his score or parts and has had to take it down from the tape and then write out all the parts. But he has at last got it all together and we can begin rehearsals."[21]

From the beginning, Moriarty brought the show to towns outside Cork, though mostly without the orchestra. However, in 1952 the full ensemble performed in Limerick, at the invitation of Dr. James Cowper, parish priest of St. Patrick's parish in the Limerick diocese. The program included the *Nutcracker*, *Sheherazade*, Schumann's *Papillons* orchestrated by Seán Ó Riada,[22] and *The Singer* based on Pádraig Pearse's play with music by Éamon Ó Gallchobhair. It was the first time ballet had ever been performed in the city, and it was enthusiastically received with eight curtain-calls.[23] This is one instance of clerical support for the art of ballet—there were some others. Further centers visited in Ireland were Callan, Clonmel, Fermoy, Killarney, Mallow, Skibbereen, Sligo, Tralee, and Waterford.

FLEISCHMANN'S BALLET MUSIC

Corkery's policy of "hewing in our own quarries" had been adopted for the dance from that first single performance of 1947 for which Moriarty choreographed all five ballets. In 1948 the musical quarry came into operation with Fleischmann's score for Moriarty's new ballet *The Golden Bell of Ko*; it was the first of seven works he was to write for dance and the only one non-Irish in inspiration. The ballet is based on a story Moriarty got from a writer living for a time in Cork who had heard it from a temple monk in the ancient Chinese city of Nankin in the early 1920s—how a bell maker is saved from a tyrannical mandarin by the sacrifice of his three daughters.

In 1951 Fleischmann composed the music for a three-act ballet based on a libretto by the actor and writer Micheál MacLiammóir—the great Englishman who became far more Irish than most of the Irish themselves, and who did Cork the honor of pretending to have been born there. It was *An Cóitín Dearg* [The Red Petticoat], with scenery and costumes designed by MacLiammóir.[24] The libretto had been written for Cepta Cullen, but no record of a ballet choreographed by her has come to light. The story begins and ends in Connemara, with an interlude in New York; it is a tale of emigration and of a happy return home containing elements of the fairy tale as well as of pantomime. Fleischmann described his music as being "astringently contemporary, to some extent neo-romantic, and of course impregnated with the idiom of Irish folk song."[25] It also included some jazz and ragtime elements for the New York episode—somewhat to the surprise of sections of the audience.

In 1956 and 1957 Fleischmann used his research on traditional folk music for the composition of three dance suites for performance at the Cork International Choral and Folk Dance Festival—the choral dance suites *Na Trí Captaení Loinge* and *Bata na bPlanndála*—and the *Cake Dance Suite* for chamber ensemble. Two were first performed by Moriarty's Folk Dance Group, founded in 1957 with members recruited from the Cork Ballet Company; they danced regularly at the Choral Festival, travelled in the 1960s to festivals in France and Germany, and in 1966/67 gave thirteen television performances on RTÉ in its *An Damhsa* [The Dance] series.Two of the Moriarty / Fleischmann ballets were inspired by Irish legend. *Macha Ruadh* of 1955 is based on Myles Dillon's version of the legend of the warrior Queen Macha, founder of Emain Macha, seat of the kings of Ulster. The program note shows the programmatic aims: "in this production of *Macha Ruadh*, music and movement, costuming and décor have been conceived and wedded together to tell a story that is taken from the traditional history of our country, and . . . those responsible for the creation and execution of this ballet and its music are all men and women of Ireland."[26]

That Ballet Week (the premiere of which was attended by President Seán T. O'Kelly) heralded in a new era. The Cork Ballet Company had now reached a sufficiently high standard to be able to perform the classical works; from 1956 guest dancers and producers from leading ballet companies were invited to Cork.

The final Fleischmann/Moriarty ballet came twenty-six years later in 1981 with *The Táin*. It constituted the fulfilment of all they had sought to achieve for ballet in Ireland. The three-act ballet based on the ancient legend of Queen Mebh and Cúchulainn (using Thomas Kinsella's 1969 translation), choreographed by Moriarty, was performed by the National Ballet Company of Ireland; the specially composed music—a 600-page score—was played by one of the state orchestras, the RTÉ Concert Orchestra, at the internationally renowned Dublin Theatre Festival. It seemed that ballet had indeed now become part of the cultural life of the nation.

Two quotations catch perhaps the essence of these people's commitment to the arts. A cutting was recently found in the Moriarty Collection which she had circled in green ink: a few lines from a play by the Spanish poet Jacinto Benavente: "If we want to achieve anything in life, we must subdue reality. We must thrust aside its phantoms which confuse our path and follow only . . . the path of our dreams that leads to the ideal."[27]

Moriarty had subdued the reality of obstacles and hindrances, and for a while her dreams had become reality, though the phantoms returned toward the end of her life. Now, twenty-five years after her death, her dreams of a full-time professional touring ballet company, of an academy to train the nation's most talented to professional level, of dance securely placed within the education system, are back on the Arts Council's agenda, a quarter of a century after their rejection by that body and the disbanding of the national ballet company.[28]

In Fleischmann's *Music in Ireland* of 1952 there is mention of an ancient poem describing Adam and Eve a year after their expulsion from the garden of paradise, deprived of the basis of life: namely of food, clothing, shelter, fire, light, and music. It was an Irish religious poem of the tenth century, the Adam and Eve story in *Saltair na Rann*.[29] That understanding of music as a fundamental element of the human experience was one of the driving forces behind Fleischmann's life in the service of his art, the source of his determination to bring the joy and solace of music and of music-making to those hitherto excluded. Moriarty's work for ballet was fired by a similar conviction—that was the foundation on which their productive and unique collaboration was built. Only one of Fleischmann's many activities was based essentially on teamwork: his involvement in the ballet. Without the help of supporters in his other fields of work, he could not have achieved what he did;

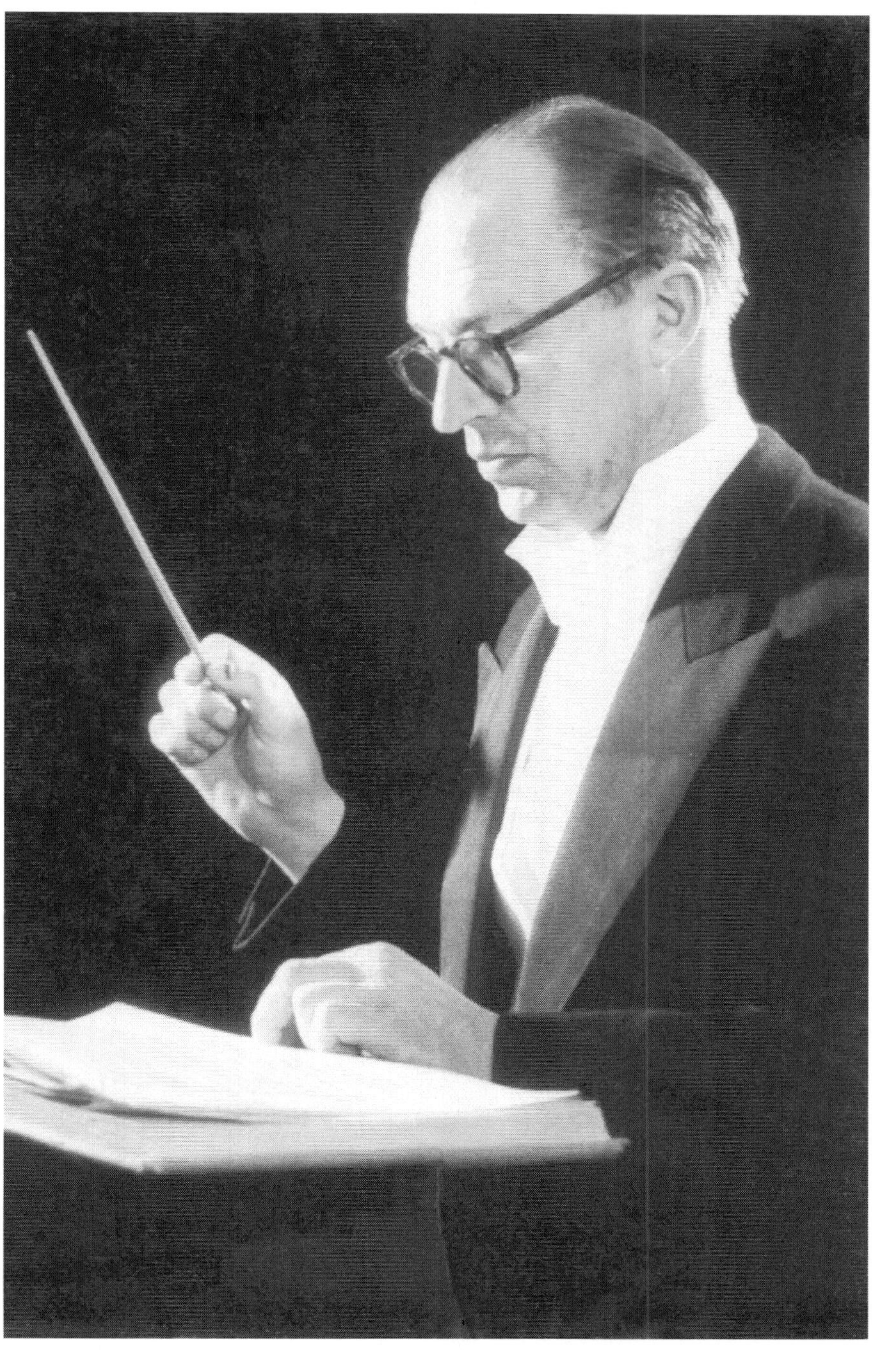

Figure 3.1. Aloys Fleischmann (1958). Photographer, Col. Rory Frewen. Used courtesy of the Frewen family.

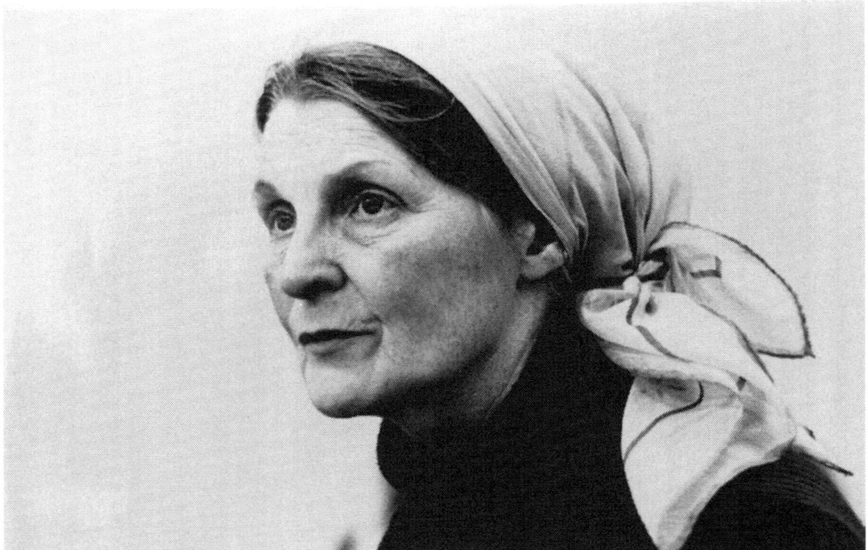

Figure 3.2. Joan Denise Moriarty (1972). Photographer unknown. Used courtesy of Cork City Library, Cork, Ireland (The Moriarty Collection).

but no single individual was indispensable for his work with the Cork Symphony Orchestra for instance, or with the Cork Orchestral Society or Choral Festival, all of which were his area of expertise and initiated by him. Without Moriarty, however, there would have been no ballet and thus no cooperation between the two arts. On the other hand, without his orchestra, without his original compositions, without his general support, the Cork Ballet Company could not have become what it did and, consequently, would probably never have given rise to professional ballet. Theirs was a unique partnership based on equality, on a fusing of different talents, on common aims, and on a shared understanding of the cultural tradition of the previous generation, which they continued and extended.

EPILOGUE

After Moriarty's death, those phantoms evoked by Benavente in his play and which she had for a time overcome, returned with a vengeance in the form of a massive attack on her integrity and her reputation. It has been emphasized above that the collaboration between Fleischmann and Moriarty was one between equals. This might seem patently obvious. However, the denial of that equality is the central libel of a travesty of a biography published in 1995, which presents Moriarty as a nonentity and as a fraud, and Fleischmann as the creator of that impostor who, together with her, is said to have deceived the Irish nation for half a century, funding their private affair through the public purse. The Fleischmann family discovered to their consternation that they had no legal redress, that under Irish law the dead can be libeled with impunity.[30]

The defamatory book, *The Secret Life of Joan Denise Moriarty*,[31] appears to have had an impact on dance research in the academic field. In a doctoral thesis submitted to the University of Limerick by Victoria O'Brien and published in 2011 under the title *A History of Irish Ballet from 1927 to 1963*, Moriarty is written out of the history of Irish ballet. The book is not entitled "A History of Ballet in Dublin," but purports to present the development of ballet nationwide during the period in question. Yet there is no chapter on Moriarty, no study of her work, although she began teaching in 1934, established in 1947 the (to date) most durable Irish ballet performing group and founded Ireland's first professional ballet company in 1959. This extraordinary omission would seem to reflect the viewpoint of *The Secret Life* that Moriarty does not merit research. Furthermore, where she is mentioned in O'Brien's book, her professional integrity is called into question. O'Brien seeks to demonstrate that the Dublin groups she studied exercised a decisive influence on the later development of ballet in Ireland; in this context she turns to Moriarty, coming close to charging her with having plagiarized ballets by Sara Payne and Cepta Cullen.[32] The charges are brought without the accuser having undertaken even the most cursory study of Moriarty's life and work. A mere glance at the Cork Ballet Company programs with their notes on the relevant ballets would have shown that there was no foundation to the imputation of unacknowledged borrowing. Here is the conclusion to a letter written to Moriarty by Cepta Cullen about *Puck Fair* (one of the ballets allegedly replicated by Moriarty without acknowledgement), in which Cullen suggested that Moriarty do new choreography for the ballet planned for the Cork Ballet Week of 1948:

> I shall be in Fermoy for the 20th March and would be happy to give you any help that you may wish. I would also, if I may, like to call and see how the ballet's working out. We here in the Club shall most certainly look forward to and come to the performance. Our very best wishes for your extremely courageous effort on the behalf of "Ballet in Ireland" and anything we can do to help will make us very happy. [33]

It is heartening to catch a glimpse of the solidarity that clearly existed within the Irish dance world at that time.

The presentation of Moriarty in *The Secret Life* as a person of tainted character may have unconsciously influenced the writer of the *History of Irish*

Ballet and led her to jump to unwarranted conclusions in breach of the normal standards of academic ethics requiring sound investigation before damaging accusations are levelled. That negative image may also have given rise to the bizarre idea that Moriarty was largely responsible for the oblivion into which the five short-lived Dublin dance groups had fallen.[34] Had O'Brien set her story of Dublin ballet within the general historical and social context of the period, it would hardly have occurred to her to blame one individual for what was the sad fate of so many valiant pioneers in all fields of Irish life during the first half century of Irish independence.[35]

But the phantoms did not prevail, no more than they had during Moriarty's lifetime. Her collaboration with Fleischmann was commemorated during their respective centenary celebrations in 2010 and 2012, as well as in 2014 on the occasion of the fortieth anniversary of the first performance of Irish National Ballet at an Irish National Ballet reunion in Firkin Crane, Cork. A development of which they could not have even dreamt in 1992 is that their legacies are being made available to the world through their respective websites hosted by Cork City Libraries, on which their digitized papers are being placed. The programs of Moriarty's three companies are now on her website, and Fleischmann's compositions on his. Moriarty's work is documented in her extensive papers, of which Cork City Central Library is now custodian. The Moriarty Collection is by far the largest of its kind in Ireland, and a unique resource for the study of twentieth-century Irish ballet. Many thousands of items have been digitized and will be placed on the website, where they will be freely available. There too will come the digitized ballet section of the Fleischmann Papers, which are stored in the Archives of University College Cork. Both the immense advance in technology, and the significant support of institutions such as Cork City Council, Cork City Libraries, Cork City Ballet, Firkin Crane, CIT Cork School of Music, and University College Cork have ensured the preservation of the Fleischmann and Moriarty legacies, documenting their unique collaborative work for music and dance with an ever increasing amount of the evidence electronically available for all to study and assess.

NOTES

1. Some of the most influential German philologists were Johann Kaspar Zeuss (1806–1856), Ernst Windisch (1844–1918), Heinrich Zimmer (1851–1910) and perhaps above all Kuno Meyer (1858–1919), who produced many translations into English of old Irish lyric poetry, romances and sagas, and who founded the School of Irish Learning in Dublin in 1903 and its journal *Ériu*. See Seán Ó Lúing, *Kuno Meyer 1858–1919: A Biography* (Dublin: Geography Publications, 1991). Meyer was

awarded the freedom of the cities of Dublin and Cork by Irish Parliamentary Party councillors in 1912; the awards were revoked by the city councils in 1915, after he had made his sympathies for the German cause public at a Clan na nGael function in Long Island. Sinn Féin councillors revoked the revocation in both cities in 1920.

2. Andrew Carpenter, "Double Vision in Anglo-Irish Literature," in *Place, Personality and the Irish Writer*, ed. Andrew Carpenter (Gerrards Cross: Colin Smyth, 1977), 173–189.

3. Daniel Corkery wrote short stories, poetry, plays, and a novel, as well as seminal works on the Gaelic heritage. He was an accomplished landscape painter, having taken lessons from Harry Scully at the Crawford School of Art in Cork; he played the cello in George Brady's orchestra at the Blackpool branch of the Cork Gaelic League. See Patrick Maume, *"Life That Is Exile:" Daniel Corkery and the Search for Irish Ireland* (Belfast: Institute of Irish Studies, 1993), 16.

4. Fleischmann Diary 1926. See https://fleischmanndiaries.ucc.ie Both diaries with my introduction and annotations are also accessible on the Fleischmann website hosted by Cork City Libraries, section "Writings." Accessed 20 August 2019. https://www.corkcitylibraries.ie/en/online/read-online/library-publications/

5. See Seámas de Barra, *Aloys Fleischmann.* (Dublin: Field Day Publications, 2006), 24.

6. Ursprung helped Fleischmann publish an article based on his MA thesis in a renowned German music journal: "Die Iren in der Neumen-und Choralforschung," *Zeitschrift für Musikwissenschaft*, 16, vol. 7–8 (1934), 353–355.

7. Letter from Ursprung to Fleischmann, 22 Aug 1935, Fleischmann Papers, Archives of University College Cork, and Ursprung Papers, Bavarian State Library, Ana 343 / Briefe. It is possible that Fleischmann attended lectures on folk music given by Kurt Huber at the University of Munich, but as Fleischmann's letters home of 1934 have not survived, this is not documented. Huber later became a member of the resistance group Die Weiße Rose and was executed by the Nazis in 1943. His unpublished manuscripts were edited by Otto Ursprung after the war.

8. "Aloys Fleischmann in Conversation with Tomás Ó Canainn." *Cork Review* (1992): 13–18.

9. Munster Society of Arts, Members, Objects of the Society, n.d., Fleischmann Papers, Archives of University College Cork.

10. Daniel Corkery, Letter to the Editor, "Munster Society of Arts," *The Cork Examiner*, 26 January 1924, 9.

11. Michael Augustus Moriarty is listed in *Guy's Cork Directory* of 1903 as a solicitor in Mallow; he is not in Guy's 1907 *Directory*, and not in *Thom's Dublin Directory* of 1910—information kindly given to me by Richard Henchion of Cork.

12. See "Maitiu Feis," *The Cork Examiner,* 28 April 1934, 14.

13. *Cork Evening Echo*, 5 April 1931; *An Phoblacht*, 25 April 1931; "Maitiu Feis" in *The Cork Examiner,* 28 April 1934, 14.

14. Joseph Gilmore, "The Cork Ballet Company," *The Threshold* 1, no. 1 (Autumn 1957): 59.

15. *Telegraph*, 16 July 1933; *Sunday Dispatch*, 16 July 1933—Moriarty personal scrapbook, Moriarty Collection, Cork City Central Library, Grand Parade, Cork.

16. The Rambert Dance Company archivist, Jane Pritchard, informed me in a letter of 1 May 1996 that there are no records of Rambert School pupils, only of the dancers who performed with the Ballet Rambert. Ninette de Valois in a letter to *The Irish Times* of 10 October 1985 stated that Moriarty had been a pupil of the Rambert School of Ballet; the dancer and choreographer Domy Reiter-Soffer was told in the early 1960s by Rambert herself that Moriarty had been her pupil.

17. See Michael Adams, *Censorship: The Irish Experience* (University of Alabama Press, 1968); Carolyn Swift, *Stage by Stage* (Dublin: Poolbeg, 1985) and Gerard Whelan with Carolyn Swift, *Spiked: Church-State Intrigue and The Rose Tattoo* (Dublin: New Island, 2002).

18. Because of the widespread prejudice that ballet was effeminate, Moriarty found it difficult to recruit sufficient numbers of male dancers during the early years of the Cork Ballet Company. See Aloys Fleischmann, "The Ballet in Cork," in *Joan Denise Moriarty, Founder of Irish National Ballet*, ed. by Ruth Fleischmann (Cork: Mercier Press, 1998), 16, 20, 62. Even in Sadler's Wells it was deemed necessary to set up a scholarship to encourage boys to study ballet—see Ninette de Valois, *Come Dance With Me: A Memoir 1898–1956* (London: Hamish Hamilton, 1959). In Cork there were occasional clerical denunciations of ballet from 1931 up to 1962: Aloys Fleischmann described two of them in "The Ballet in Cork," 16, 20. There was one further such attack in Cork after a show by Ireland's first professional ballet company, Irish Theatre Ballet—during a sermon on 23 September 1962 in the church of St. Francis, "the nudity of ballet" was denounced as being "only comparable with a house of prostitutes." This is quoted in Aloys Fleischmann's letter of 8 Oct 1962 to the preacher in which he announced his intention of taking legal action against the priest unless an apology for the libel was forthcoming during the next sermon (Fleischmann Papers). An anonymous letter to the Editor of the *Evening Herald*, 10 April 1962, 6, captioned "Ballet picture protest" and signed "Shocked," found a published photograph of five Irish Theatre Ballet dancers clad in black tights "scandalous in the extreme" and a "Threat to the chastity of others."

19. See Christopher Morash, *A History of Irish Theatre 1601–2000* (Cambridge: Cambridge University Press, 2002), 188.

20. See Victoria O'Brien, *A History of Irish Ballet from 1927 to 1963* (Oxford: Peter Lang, 2011), 166–168.

21. Letter of 4 October 1982 from Moriarty to Michel de Lutry in Munich. Moriarty Collection, Cork City Central Library, Grand Parade, Cork.

22. Ó Riada was at that time in his final year at University College Cork, studying for his B.Mus. under Fleischmann. He had attended a recital given by his piano teacher, Tilly Fleischmann, which included Schumann's *Papillons*. Moriarty took up her suggestion that it could make an interesting ballet, choreographed it on the basis of the pianist's libretto; Ó Riada (then known as John Reidy) agreed to orchestrate the work, which was later accepted as one of the assignments for his final examination.

23. Letter from Dr. James Cowper to Moriarty, 7 July 1952, Moriarty Collection. See also: "Ballet Treat for Limerick," *Limerick Leader*, 30 June 1952, 1.

24. In "Design for a Ballet," *The Bell*, Sep 1942, MacLiammóir published the libretto for two of the three acts of *An Cóitín Dearg*. Michael Bowles was to compose

the music, but does not seem to have done so. It is possible that a performance to music by Tyrell Pyne took place in Dublin, but no record of it has been found. See Séamas de Barra, *Aloys Fleischmann.* (Dublin: Field Day Publications, 2006), 101. In 1946 Fleischmann sought permission from MacLiammóir to write music for his libretto, which was readily granted. For further information on MacLiammóir see his autobiographical works: *All for Hecuba: A Theatrical Autobiography* (London: Methuen, 1946; Dublin revised edition 1961 and *Enter a Goldfish: Memoirs of an Irish Actor, Young and Old* (London: Thames and Hudson, 1977). See also Christopher Fith-Simon, *A Biography of Micheál MacLiammóir and Hilton Edwards: The Boys* (Dublin: Gill, 1994).

25. Letter from Fleischmann to Anton Dolin 16 Feb 1959, Fleischmann Papers.

26. See Preface to the Cork Ballet Company program for the gala performance attended by the President of Ireland, 11 May 1955, 3.

27. Jacinto Benavente (1866–1954), *La noche del sábado* [Saturday Night] of 1903. The *Radio Times* of 30 May 1952 quotes the passage in its introduction to a radio adaptation of the play. The speaker is Imperia, a ballerina.

28. See *Arts Council Ballet Policy Review*, 2014.

29. The poem is described by P. W. Joyce in *The Story of Ancient Irish Civilisation.* (London: Longmans, Green & Co., 1907), 83. Reference to this in Fleischmann, ed. *Music in Ireland: A Symposium.* (Cork: Cork University Press, 1952), 40. I am grateful to Liam MacCóil for the information that the quotation comes from *The Irish Story of Adam and Eve from Saltair na Rann*; see the edition with text and translation by David Greene and Fergus Kelly (Dublin: Institute for Advanced Studies, 1976, Vol. 1, Canto XI, 1889–1892), 85.

30. Under German law it is a criminal offense to libel the dead, which ensures that writers and their publishers exercise the same duty of care toward the dead as they do toward the living.

31. My refutation of Sandra MacLiammoir's *The Secret Life of Joan Denise Moriarty* was submitted in Sep 1998 to the Irish Law Reform Commission as a case study demonstrating the need for legislation to protect the dead from defamation; it was placed on the Moriarty website in 2012 (joandenisemoriarty.ie), see the section: Literature on Moriarty.

32. Victoria O'Brien, *A History of Irish Ballet from 1927 to 1963*, 148. See also 70 and 112–113.

33. Letter from Cepta Cullen to Moriarty on 9 March 1948. The Moriarty Collection.

34. Ibid., 147, 149. These charges are presented as facts at the beginning of the *Irish Times* review of O'Brien's book: Michael Seavers, "Correcting a Blind Spot in Irish Ballet." In *The Irish Times,* 27 August 2011, 44.

35. I have placed a critical review of O'Brien's book on the Cork City Libraries website, section: "Literature on Moriarty" at www.joandenisemoriarty.ie; shorter reviews were published in the *Cork Historical and Archaeological Society Journal* (July 2012), *History Ireland* (July/August 2012), *Dancing Times* (August 2012), and *Books Ireland* (September 2012). I am currently working on a Moriarty biography based on the papers in the Moriarty Collection.

BIBLIOGRAPHY

Adams, Michael. *Censorship: The Irish Experience.* University of Alabama Press, 1968.

"Aloys Fleischmann in conversation with Tomás Ó Canainn." *Cork Review* (1992): 13–18.

Arts Council Ballet Policy Review. Dublin: Arts Council, 2014.

Benavente, Jacinto. *La Noche del Sábado* [Saturday Night]. Madrid: B. Velasco, Imp., 1903.

Carpenter, Andrew. "Double Vision in Anglo-Irish Literature." In *Place, Personality and the Irish Writer.* Edited by Andrew Carpenter, 173–189. Gerrards Cross: Colin Smyth, 1977,

Corkery, Daniel. Letter to the Editor, "Munster Society of Arts." *The Cork Examiner*, 26 January 1924, 9.

Cunningham, Joseph P., Fleischmann, Ruth, de Barra, Séamas. *Aloys Fleischmann (1880–1964) Immigrant Musician in Ireland.* Cork: Cork University Press, 2010.

de Barra, Séamas. "Aloys Fleischmann's Ballet Music." In *Joan Denise Moriarty: Founder of Irish National Ballet*, edited by Ruth Fleischmann, 104–113. Cork: Mercier Press, 1998.

———. *Aloys Fleischmann.* Field Day Music 1. Series Editors: Séamas de Barra and Patrick Zuk. Dublin: Field Day Publications, 2006.

de Valois, Ninette. *Come Dance With Me: A Memoir 1898–1956.* London: Hamish Hamilton, 1959.

Fleischmann, Aloys. *Diaries 1926, 1927.* Presented by Róisín O'Brien, introduced and annotated by Ruth Fleischmann, 2013. Accessed 5 June 2019. https://fleischmanndiaries.ucc.ie/.

———. "Die Iren in der Neumen—und Choralforschung," *Zeitschrift für Musikwissenschaft*, 16, vol. 7–8 (1934): 353–355.

———. *Music in Ireland.* Edited by Aloys Fleischmann. Cork: Cork University Press, 1952.

———. *Sources of Irish Traditional Music c. 1600–1855: An Annotated Catalogue of Prints and Manuscripts 1583–1855*. 2 vols., New York: Garland, 1998 [posthumous].

———. "The Ballet in Cork," in *Joan Denise Moriarty, Founder of Irish National Ballet*, edited by Ruth Fleischmann (Cork: Mercier Press, 1998) [posthumous]..

Fleischmann, Ruth, ed. *Joan Denise Moriarty: Founder of Irish National Ballet.* Cork: Mercier Press, 1998.

———. ed. *Aloys Fleischmann (1910–1992): A Life for Music in Ireland Remembered by Contemporaries*. Cork: Mercier Press, 2000.

———. *Refutation of Sandra MacLiammoir's Secret Life of Joan Denise Moriarty.* Cork: Cork City Libraries, 1997 / 2012. Accessed 5 June 2019. https://www.corkcitylibraries.ie/en/online/read-online/library-publications/.

———. ed. *Joan Denise Moriarty: Ireland's First Lady of Dance*. Cork: Cork City Libraries, 2012. Accessed 5 June 2019. https://www.corkcitylibraries.ie/en/online/read-online/library-publications/.

———. Review of Victoria O'Brien's *A History of Irish Ballet from 1927 to 1963*, 2012. Cork City Libraries. Accessed 5 June 2019. https://www.historyireland.com/20th-century-contemporary-history/a-history-of-irish-ballet-from-1927-to-1963/.

———. "Review of Victoria O'Brien's *A History of Irish Ballet from 1927 to 1963*." *History Ireland* (July/August 2012), 13.

Gilmore, Joseph. "The Cork Ballet Company." *The Threshold* 1, no. 1 (Autumn 1957).

Greene, David and Kelly, Fergus, eds. *The Irish Story of Adam and Eve from Saltair na Rann.* Vol. 1. Dublin: Dublin Institute for Advanced Studies, 1976.

Joyce, P. W. *The Story of Ancient Irish Civilisation.* London: Longmans, Green & Co., 1907.

MacLiammóir, Micheál. "Design for a Ballet." *The Bell* 4, no. 6 (September 1942): 394–403.

Maume, Patrick. *'Life That Is Exile': Daniel Corkery and the Search for Irish Ireland.* The Institute of Irish Studies. Belfast: The Queen's University of Belfast, 1993.

Morash, Christopher. *A History of Irish Theatre 1601–2000.* Cambridge: Cambridge University Press, 2002.

O'Brien, Victoria. *A History of Irish Ballet from 1927 to 1963*. Oxford: Peter Lang, 2011.

Swift, Carolyn. *Stage by Stage*. Dublin: Poolbeg, 1985.

———. Whelan, Gerard. *Spiked: Church-State Intrigue and The Rose Tattoo.* Dublin: New Island, 2002.

Zuk, Patrick. "A. J. Potter (1918–1980): The Career and Achievement of an Irish Composer in Social and Cultural Context." Unpublished PhD Dissertation. Durham: University of Durham, 2007.

———, Ruth Fleischmann, and Séamas de Barra. *The Fleischmanns: A Remarkable Cork Family—A Companion to the Fleischmann Centenary Celebration*. Cork: Cork City Libraries, 2010. Accessed 5 June 2019. https://www.corkcitylibraries.ie/en/online/read-online/library-publications/.

Chapter Four

Irish Dance Documentation for the Archive

A Personal Reflection on Irish-German Connections and Intellectual Inheritances

Catherine E. Foley

In 2003, UNESCO (the United Nations Educational, Scientific and Cultural Organization) established its Convention for the Safeguarding of Intangible Cultural Heritage.[1] Prior to this, however, different communities and institutions in specific regions and countries in Europe and other parts of the world had made efforts to document and preserve aspects of their intangible cultural heritage for sociocultural or political reasons. Notions of preservation were, for example, integral to the collections of traditional music, song, and dance undertaken by numerous nation states, or would-be nation states, from the eighteenth century for purposes of constructing and promoting cultural and national identities. Ireland was one of these aspiring nation states and traditional dance played a significant role in this cultural and political representation.[2]

In this chapter, I examine my work as a collector of Irish traditional dance—part of a wider collection of Irish traditional music, song, and dance, for Muckross House, Killarney, County Kerry from 1983–1986. I discuss this process within a wider framework of Irish-German connections and intellectual inheritances which shaped my work and my research.

COLLECTING AND PRESERVING CULTURAL HERITAGE

The act of collection is a transition from primary to secondary oralities/video-oralities. These secondary oralities/video-oralities refer to literary (writing and print) and technological (radio, television, film, and other electronic devices) developments in transmission. In contrast, primary oralities focus on oral (see

Ong 2002), aural, visual, imitative, and kinesthetic transmission.[3] Irish step dancing as intangible cultural heritage has, historically speaking, a relatively short documentation record. Since the eighteenth century—when collections of indigenous performing arts were compiled in Europe as part of eighteenth and nineteenth-century romanticism—Ireland also had its collections.[4] As early as the eighteenth century, the work and philosophy of German philosopher, theologian, poet, and literary critic, Johann Gottfried Herder (1744–1803) influenced thinking in Ireland around German cultural nationalism and by extension other cultural nationalisms including Irish cultural nationalism. Herder, who was acknowledged as the first to coin the term *volkslied* (folk-song), applied it, according to Bohlman (2002) "not only to the music he heard in the local world close at hand, but also to a diverse range of repertoires that were encountered throughout the world of Enlightenment Europe."[5] Herder published two volumes of songs "Voices of the People in Song" (1778) and "Folk Songs" (1779), and also collected folk customs and folk dances. He is acknowledged to have initiated German nationalism but, according to Royal Schmidt, Herder promoted: "Freedom for the expression of national character because of the greater variety of national voices which would ultimately benefit humanity."[6] This notion of a national character influenced intellectuals in other European countries, including Ireland where political reformers were seeking to establish Ireland as a nation state within a context of English colonialism. Thus, during the eighteenth and nineteenth centuries, different cultural societies were established to assist in this endeavor. For example, Irish antiquarian societies were established, including the Dublin Society, which was an enlightened body founded in 1731, to improve the country by promoting agriculture, arts, literature and science. Established in 1893, the cultural nationalist movement, the Gaelic League, advocated a separate Irish cultural nation from that of its colonizer, England. Though the revival of the Irish language was the primary aim of the Gaelic League, it also succeeded in revitalizing the indigenous performing arts through the establishment of a hierarchical system of staged competitions in these arts, including step dancing and named Irish dancing by the Gaelic League. By 1930, an organization of Irish dancing, named An Coimisiún le Rincí Gaelacha was established, under the auspices of the Gaelic League, to promote, popularize and centralize competitions in Irish dancing; from the 1940s this included the registration of teachers and adjudicators. My own training in Irish dancing was within the structures of An Coimisiún and later another organization, An Comhdháil, [7] an organization that split from An Coimisiún due to ideological differences. I qualified as an Irish dance teacher with An Comhdháil in 1977.

Archives, first established during the Age of Enlightenment, contributed to understandings of cultural nationalism and identity politics. For example, in 1900 Carl Stumpf made his first phonograph recordings which laid the foundation for one of the oldest music archives in existence—*The Berlin Phonogramm-Archive*. The institutionalized collections of audio recordings in *The Berlin Phonogramm-Archive* assisted in defining and promoting cultural and national boundaries and their diversity; indeed, the field of comparative musicology emerged within this "Berlin School," and of interest is that an Irish collection was included in the Berlin Archive. This collection was by Fr. Hennebry or Richard de Hindeberg (1863–1916) and consisted of fourteen Wax Cylinder Recordings, five letters, and notes. This collection was based on his 1905 collection of songs in the Ring Gaeltacht and its surroundings in County Waterford. Hennebry published his *A Handbook of Irish Music* in 1928.

Other archives followed, including the establishment of archives in Ireland and, today among others, there is the Archive of the Irish Folklore Commission, National Archives of Ireland, the Muckross House Library Archive, the Irish Traditional Music Archive, and the National Dance Archive of Ireland. These archives are important resources and have assisted in preserving both tangible and intangible cultural heritage as knowledge; knowledge which has been produced and experienced by the people of Ireland. In this chapter, I will focus on one of these archives—The Muckross House Archive, as it houses my work as a collector of Irish traditional music, song, and dance, and in particular, the step-dance collection, the focus of this chapter.

THE MUCKROSS HOUSE ARCHIVE

In 1980, I was selected to work as a collector of Irish traditional music, song, and dance for Muckross House Folk Museum, Killarney, Co. Kerry. The collection project was an initiative of the Trustees of Muckross House in collaboration with Siamsa Tire, the National Folk Theatre of Ireland, and the Kerry County Board of Comhaltas Ceoltóirí Éireann.[8] These organizations were provided with support from the Music Department, University College Cork, and the Irish Folklore Department, University College Dublin.[9] The collection, according to Myers, was to be "a comprehensive and professional collection of the traditional Songs, Music and Dance of Kerry."[10] This regional collection was an attempt to document for posterity the indigenous performing arts of the region—as intangible cultural heritage, for archival purposes.[11] My Irish-German intellectual inheritances, together with my competencies as a practicing musician, singer, and dancer, assisted in preparing me for this work.

IRISH-GERMAN INTELLECTUAL INHERITANCES: A PERSONAL REFLECTION

My notion of "intellectual" follows the work of Antonio Gramsci who states that:

> There is no human activity from which every form of intellectual participation can be excluded: *homo faber* cannot be separated from *homo sapiens*. Each man finally, outside his professional activity, carries on some form of intellectual activity, that is, be he a "philosopher," an "artist," a man of taste, he participates in a particular conception of the world, has a conscious line of moral conduct, and therefore contributes to sustain a conception of the world or to modify it, that is, to bring into being new modes of thought.[12]

Thus, following Gramsci, where *homo faber* cannot be separated from *homo sapiens,* I interpret my intellectual inheritances as being both cognitive, conceptual, and embodied corporeal knowledge.

My Irish-German intellectual inheritances shaped my early research and work as a collector, ethnochoreologist, and ethnomusicologist. This stage of my research was shaped by many influences:

(1) Informal training within a home context: From a young age I played traditional Irish music with my father.[13] Within this home context, I was exposed to intimate social gatherings where traditional music, song, and dance coexisted and an orality of transmission was the norm; traditional music and songs were picked up "by ear" and dances were learned and transmitted informally through observation and participation.

(2) Formal training in Irish step dancing with Peggy McTeggart, Cork. Within this context I was taught by corporeal imitation with musical, verbal, and rhythmic cues; students kept notebooks for their own files where step dances were documented using a written mnemonic system as an *aide memoire*. With this training in Irish dancing—including performance experiences and a teacher's qualification in Irish dance (1977)—I had acquired an embodied and cognitive knowledge of the structures and aesthetic systems of Irish dancing.

(3) Formal training in classical music on piano with the Spanish pianist and composer, Angel Climent [14] and Geraldine Neeson, Cork. Neeson had been taught by Tilly Fleischmann—born in Cork but of German extraction.[15]

(4) The completion of an undergraduate degree in classical music in 1977 with the Anglo-German scholar and composer Aloys Fleischmann,[16] University College Cork. Fleischmann ("Junior") was the son of Aloys Fleischmann (Senior), a teacher, organist, and composer who had been born in Dachau,

Germany in 1880. His mother, Tilly Fleischmann (above)—although born in Cork in 1882, was of German extraction, and was a classical pianist and pedagogue. Fleischmann ("Junior") became Professor of Music at University College Cork, a post he held for forty-six years (1934–1980).[17] As a pedagogue, Fleischmann placed importance on counterpoint and music analysis, among other things, and this rigorous training, together with my Irish dance training and my knowledge of the indigenous performing arts, assisted in my collecting and my later structural analysis of the step dances (see below).

(5) The completion of my doctoral degree (1984–1988) at LABAN in London. During this time, I studied Labanotation and Advanced Laban Studies, among other fields; one of my co-supervisors was Valerie Preston-Dunlop, a former student of Rudolf Laban.[18]

These Irish-German influences and intellectual inheritances combined, impacted on my early research as an ethnomusicologist and ethnochoreologist, while working as a seasonal collector of Irish traditional music, song, and dance for Muckross House, Killarney, County Kerry (1980–1985), and while undertaking my doctoral research at LABAN London, based on the traditional step-dance collection of North Kerry (1984–1988).

COLLECTING AND DOCUMENTING INDIGENOUS PERFORMING ARTS FOR THE MUCKROSS HOUSE ARCHIVE

During the summers of 1980–1982, I identified individual performers of traditional music and song in South Kerry[19] and collected their repertoires of music and songs by audio-recording and transcribing their materials using Western staff music notation, in line with other collectors of music across Europe and in Ireland since the eighteenth century.[20] These materials were deposited in Muckross House for archival and preservation purposes. In 1983, I was asked by the Manager of Muckross House, Edmond Myers, to change from music to dance and to collect for posterity the step dances from a group of elderly step dancers in North Kerry. It was understood by the Trustees of Muckross House, and by Fr Pat Ahern,[21] Artistic Director of Siamsa Tíre, that the repertoires and styles of practice of these dancers, representative of a particular regional, traditional, step-dance practice were, at this point in time, on the decline due to processes of modernity.[22] The Trustees of Muckross House were concerned that this particular practice of step dancing was not being transmitted as before; also I was informed that at the time, younger dancers of the region were more interested in competitive step dancing as taught by local schools of step dancing, registered with the Irish step dancing organization, An Coimisiún (see above).[23] The elderly dancers of North Kerry had been taught by Jeremiah Molyneaux (1883–1965), the last of the itinerant dancing masters in the region, and to the best of my knowledge in Ireland. Molyneaux was part of a lineage of itinerant dancing masters in the region going back to the end of the eighteenth century. These dancing masters had been influenced by a wider system of professional dancing masters in Britain and on continental Europe going back to the fifteenth century.[24] My work with these elderly dancers was, therefore, seen as urgent by Muckross House.

During the summers of 1983–1986, I conducted fieldwork on step dance in the region of North Kerry. I also conducted numerous ethnographic interviews to historicize and contextualize the dance and to understand the worldview of the dancers and those who participated in local dance events.[25] In this chapter, however, I focus solely on the recording and documentation of the dances.

With no video camera provided initially, I used performance—my own dance competence as an ethnochoreological research tool—and learned dances from the remaining students of Jeremiah Molyneaux in their homes.[26] I also used a mnemonic system for writing the dances down as an *aide memoire*; this occurred when learning a step dance at each session with each dancer. This system was an extension of the mnemonic step-dance system taught by Peggy McTeggart to her dance students (see above). At the end of each summer, video recordings of each dancer were also made. Embodying the step dances, however, provided me with a unique opportunity to not only learn the dances but also to gain an embodied sense of the aesthetic values inherent in the dance practice and, indeed, what the dances felt like in my body. As the anthropologist Sally Ann Ness states, "for one to fully understand what performing a choreographed movement means, one must have some appreciation of how getting oneself physically through a choreographed movement can affect a human being, and how it can affect one's own cultural understanding."[27] Embodying the dances was therefore an important methodological research tool. The dances were stored in my body to be remembered and recalled for documentation, analysis, and performance purposes.

THE APPLICATION OF LABANOTATION TO IRISH TRADITIONAL STEP DANCING

Texts of knowledge, as in music and dance documentation, comprise and represent narratives of historical and technological progress and inquiry. The Molyneaux dancers were video-recorded but I was aware that the video recordings would only provide one version of a performance and, in North Kerry, there were numerous versions of each step dance due to the cultural value placed on individual creativity or what the dancers referred to as "putting style into it."[28] Also, I was aware that the mnemonic system I used to document the dances, would not suffice, as it was not accurate enough to reconstruct the dances; it was simply an *aide memoire* for my own personal use. However, other step dancers who had also learned the mnemonic system from Peggy McTeggart, may well have been able to decode the dances, but interpretation and timing might still have been be an issue for reconstruction purposes. I therefore sought an equivalent movement documentation system to Western staff music notation, which I had used for transcribing the songs and music. It was the work of choreographer, dancer, and movement theoretician—Rudolf Laban, particularly his movement notation system—Labanotation, that offered the best solution to me at that time.

Laban (1879–1958), one of the founders of European Modern Dance, also had interests in art, architecture, and theatre. It was in Paris, however, where he was studying painting at École de Beaux Arts (1905–1907) that he endeavored to develop a dance script.[29] Later in Germany, he established a movement choir for amateurs and twenty-five Laban schools for the education of children. He wrote articles and books, performed, choreographed, managed a dance theatre company, a chamber dance theatre company, and opened the Choreographische Institut in Berlin in 1927. In 1928, he published Labanotation or Kinetography Laban, a system for movement documentation. To Laban, the development of a movement notation system was of the utmost importance to make dance equal among the arts. He stated, the "entire history of the art of movement is also the history of striving for a dance notation in which the dancer sees more than a useful tool for his professional education. If this art would have been practiced in previous centuries, we would have today an insight into earlier movement forms and endeavors in our field."[30] Laban had also developed Choreutics, the analysis of human movement in spatial terms, and Eukinetics, the analysis of movement quality. This work was later developed further by his students, including Valerie Preston-Dunlop, my doctoral co-supervisor.

In 1930, Laban was appointed director of the Allied State Theatres in Berlin, a position which provided him with some power and recognition. At the end of this service in 1934, Hitler attended the farewell matinee given in Laban's honor but his contract was not renewed as Laban did not have German citizenship.[31] In 1934, after the National Socialists had taken over power, Laban was appointed director of the Deutsche Tanzbühne, and in 1936, as Germany prepared to host the Olympic Games in Berlin, Laban was commissioned to direct the triumphal celebration of German Dance at the Dietrich Eckart Freilichtbühne (Outdoor Theatre) and to organize a Great International Dance competition in July 1936. While attempting to stage a huge spectacle—*Von Tauwind und der Neuen Freude* (Spring, Wind and the new Joy), involving about 1,000 performers, and while at the height of his career, he was forced to cancel the performance. According to Topaz, "The various parts had been notated and sent to sixty choirs in different cities so that they could be pre-rehearsed. Goebbels attended the final dress rehearsal and was displeased with what he saw. It is widely quoted what his reaction was: 'In Germany there is room for only one movement, the Nazi Movement.'[32] In Goebbels'[33] personal diary, he wrote the following: "Rehearsal of dance work: freely based on Nietzsche, a bad, contrived and affected piece. I disliked it intensely. It is also intellectual. I do not like it. This is because it is dressed up in our clothes, and has nothing whatsoever to do with us."[34] In Isa Partsch-Bergsohn's words, "Goebbels saw through Laban's intentions to use the Nazis for his own goals."[35] Laban had hoped that he could revitalize dance in the theatre but he was to discover that "the Nazis intended to use Laban's movement choir concept as a tool to strengthen body awareness and simultaneously to develop the feeling of racial superiority."[36] For Laban, the Olympics marked his demise in Germany. This meant that his schools were closed and, thus, commenced his exile from Germany, along with many of his followers including Imgard Bartenieff, a student of Rudolf Laban. He eventually took refuge in Britain where he continued his work, particularly on the psychological effects of movement and industry with F. C. Lawrence.[37]

Labanotation or Kinetography Laban, the system of recording human movement, which he devised in 1928, continued to be used by documenters of human movement, including dancers and dance scholars, across diverse disciplines in many parts of the world. In 1960, Gertrude Kurath noted that it was taught in the United Kingdom, United States, Germany, France, Brazil, Argentina, and elsewhere.[38] And, although other forms of dance notation also existed, such as Benesh and Eshkol Wachmann, Labanotation proved to be a popular system for documenting and reconstructing dances from written notation. For example, the ethnochoreologist Elsie Ivancich performed the lead role of the Eldress in a reconstructed Laban score of *The Shakers*, a 1931 work by modern dance choreographer Doris Humphrey, as a university student in the United States in 1956. The theatrical performance with a full cast took place at the University of California in Los Angeles.[39] The use of Labanotation over other human movement documentation systems was also advocated by the German musicologist Felix Hoerburger who, in 1959, stated: "I believe that amongst the existing dance notations the Kinetography (Labanotation) developed by Rudolf von Laban offers a solution. This system is not restricted to one particular national or historical style of dancing, but makes possible the writing down of any corporeal movement.[40]

Labanotation subsequently became a popular movement documentation system for ethnochoreologists, dance anthropologists, and other scholars interested in documenting and analyzing human movement and also examining cross-cultural comparisons. As mentioned above, I also became interested in Labanotation and thus, from 1984 to 1988, I attended Laban in London where, among other things, I was trained in Labanotation, and Advanced Laban Analysis. For my ethnochoreological doctoral research, I not only provided a historical and ethnographic context to the traditional step-dancing community of North Kerry (within the broader Irish dance context), but I also documented and structurally analyzed the step dances in order to provide an understanding of the movement system and the cultural and aesthetic values that comprised the practice. For documenting and structurally analyzing the dances, I used Labanotation, which was the first time that Labanotation had been applied to Irish traditional step dancing.

IRISH TRADITIONAL STEP DANCING IN NORTH KERRY: A MOVEMENT SYSTEM

In this endeavor, I documented and analyzed the step dances, and constructed a hierarchical system of inventories of Irish step-dance movements using Labanotation, to present for the first time, a system of movements accessed and developed by the step dancers as holders of the tradition. This was similar to a kinetic dictionary and a system of hierarchical movements within the three main step-dance categories—Reels, Jigs, and Hornpipes, and I illustrated how the dancers constructed and performed meaningful dances within the tradition by cross indexing their movements with the system.[41] The Labanotated hierarchical inventoried system was thus made up of the following in each of the step-dance categories: elements, cells, motifs, minor phrases, major phrases, and steps or step dances. I argued that "elements" existed on the lowest level of the movement system and were the smallest non-divisible movements; cells—the next level, consisted of two or three elements; motifs were combinations of elements and cells and were fixed in the awareness of the dancer; minor phrases consisted of elements, cells, and possibly motifs; minor phrases were linked to form major phrases; while steps were generally 8-bar choreographic units in any step dance type in Reels, Jigs, or Hornpipes. In total, I documented in Labanotation seventy-three elements in seven categories:

a: positions of feet
b: stepping movements
c: leaping movements
d: hopping movements
e: jumping movements
f: kicking and striking movements
g: gestural movements (tips, touches et al.)

I documented the following number of cells:

102 Hornpipe cells
99 Jig cells
75 Treble Reel cells

And, I documented the following number of motifs:

20 Hornpipe motifs
18 Jig motifs
17 Treble Reel motifs.

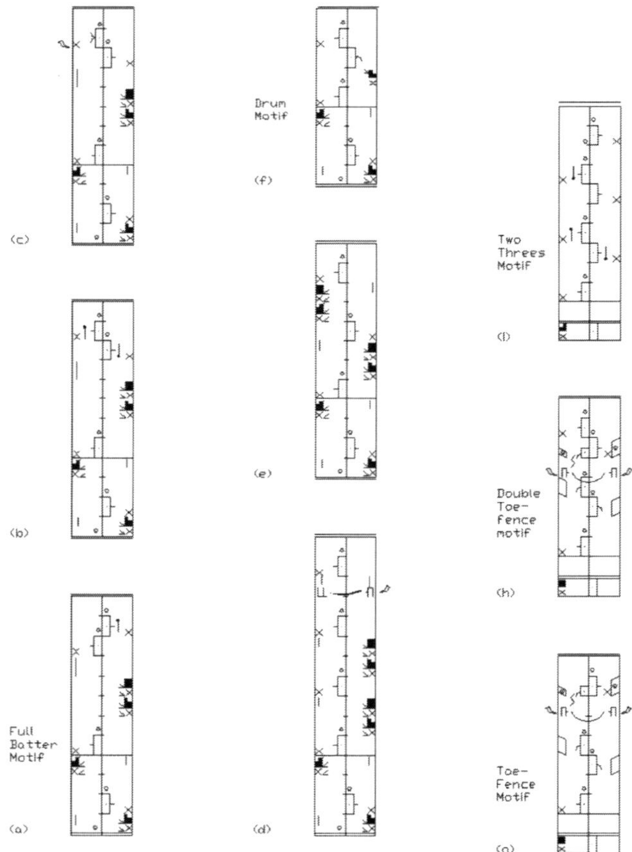

Figure 4.1. Examples of Hornpipe Motifs (a-i) in Labanotation. Labanotation transcriptions by Catherine E. Foley in *Irish Traditional Step Dancing in North Kerry: A Contextual and Structural Analysis* (Listowel, County Kerry: North Kerry Literary Trust, 2012 [1988]), 140. Used courtesy of Catherine E. Foley.

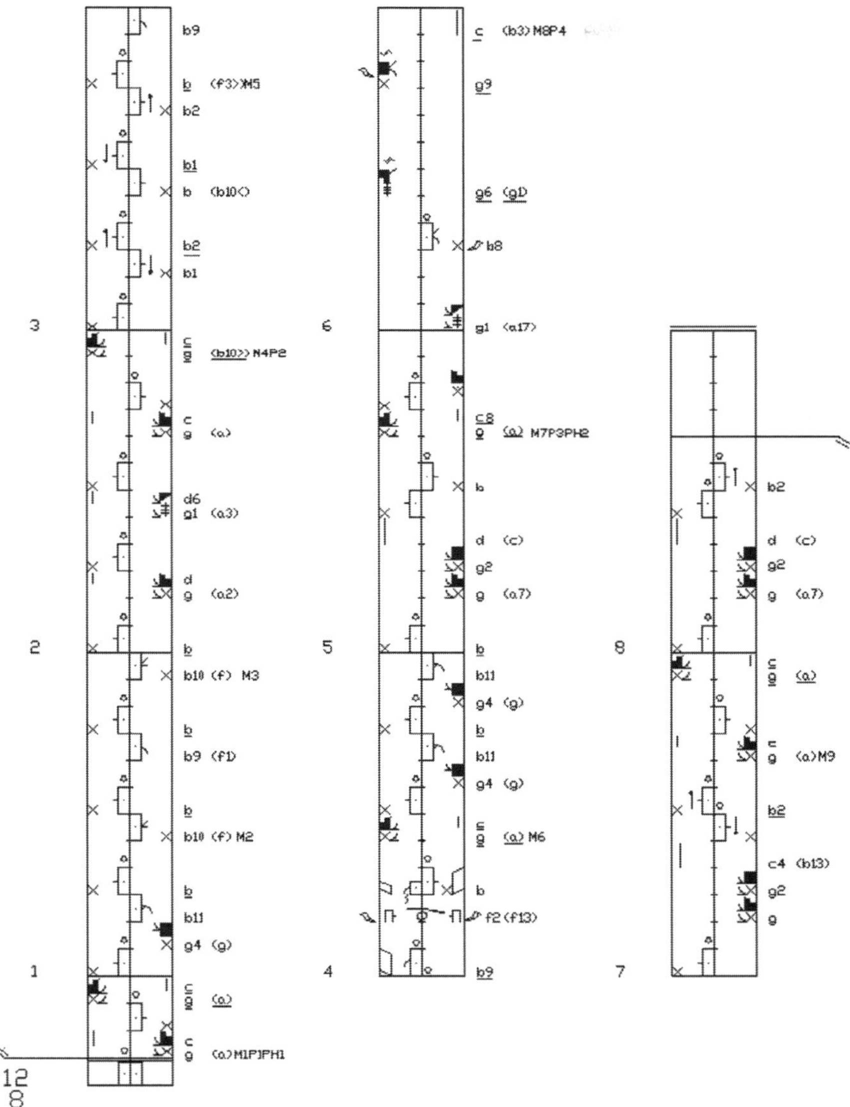

Figure 4.2. Labanotation Transcription "Single Drum Hornpipe Step," including a structural analysis and a cross referencing with the movement inventories. Step Dancer, Michael Carroll. Labanotation transcription by Catherine E. Foley in *Irish Traditional Step Dancing in North Kerry: A Contextual and Structural Analysis* (Listowel, County Kerry: North Kerry Literary Trust, 2012 [1988]), 194. Used courtesy of Catherine E. Foley.

These Labanotated hierarchical inventories were based on my observations, embodiment of the dances, fieldnotes, and video recordings of the dancers. Other teaching sessions and other performances might have provided further variations of these. This work became the foundation for my doctoral thesis (1988) and was subsequently published in 2012.[42]

In 1987, my hand-written Labanotated analytical system and the transcriptions of the step dances were used by Andy Adamson at Birmingham University to refine CALABAN.[43] On completion, the notation of my Labanotated work benefitted from the quality of its readability (see Figure 4.1). When visiting Andy Adamson to see and collect the work, Andy took one of my hornpipe step-dance transcriptions and started to dance it. On seeing Andy dancing, I was convinced that others who could read Labanotation and who were somewhat familiar with the Irish step-dance practice, might also be able to endeavor to reconstruct one of my transcribed step dances.

Through the use of Labanotation, I was therefore able to document, analyze, and illustrate how dancers personally and interpersonally varied step dances as a cultural practice. This showed an important aspect of their practice, that of creativity, which was highly valued in the region of North Kerry. I was also able to document step dances using a universal movement documentation tool, which would ultimately allow for potential reconstruction and for cross-cultural movement comparison and analysis. The documentation of these dances thus assisted in recording them for archival, analytical, and research purposes. However, it was the video recordings of the dances, performed by the holders of the practice, which were the primary records.[44] The Labanotated transcriptions and the hierarchical system of inventories provided other documentation and analytical tools for further analysis, research, and understanding.

CURRENT PRACTICE

Now, for over twenty years, Labanotation has been taught at the University of Limerick to students on the MA Ethnochoreology, the MA Irish Traditional Dance Performance, and the MA Irish Dance Studies programs. Some of these students, and doctoral students, at the university have used Labanotation in their research on Irish dance and other dance practices. In the field in North Kerry, the traditional style of step dancing continues to be danced by a few dancers and it has also been revived within the context of Siamsa Tire, the national folk theatre of Ireland where it exists as a kinesthetic identity marker for the theatre.[45] Also, some of Molyneaux traditional solo set dances and step dances have been taught by me and other step dancers of North

Kerry to students at the University of Limerick and to others. Indeed, some of Molyneaux's traditional set dances are workshopped to be performed by dancers in An Coimisiún dance competitions today.[46] While step dancers may not be literate in Labanotation, some are aware that the step dances can be written down in Labanotation; some dancers also use the concepts of elements and motifs, which I used in my doctoral work, to speak about their practice. Therefore, as musicians learn music notation, I would envisage that in the future dancers may learn Labanotation to aid the documentation and reconstruction of dance as an important human movement activity and as an important part of cultural heritage; in this instance Irish cultural heritage.

CONCLUSION

This chapter examined the emergence of collections and archives with roots in eighteenth-century European romanticism. In particular, it explored my work as a collector of Irish traditional music, song, and dance for the Muckross House Archive, together with the Irish-German connections and intellectual inheritances that were made manifest in my education, early training, and early professional self as a collector, ethnochoreologist, and ethnomusicologist. Focusing on the step-dance component of the collection, I recounted how I used Labanotation to document and analyze Irish traditional step dance for archival and research purposes. This work may allow for the future reconstruction or analysis of this rich aspect of Irish cultural heritage.

NOTES

1. See UNESCO, "The Convention for the Safeguarding of Intangible Cultural Heritage." Accessed 23 May 2019. https://ich.unesco.org/doc/src/01852-EN.pdf

2. Catherine E. Foley, "Nationalism and the Invention of Irish Dancing." Chapter 5 in *Step Dancing in Ireland: Culture and History* (Farnham, Surrey: Ashgate Publishing Ltd., 2013), 131–158; see also Catherine E. Foley, *Irish Traditional Step Dancing in North Kerry: A Contextual and Structural Analysis* (Listowel: North Kerry Literary Trust 2012a [1988]); and Catherine E. Foley, "Perceptions of Irish Dance: National, Global, and Local," *Dance Research Journal* vol. 33, no.1 (New York: Congress on Research in Dance, 2001), 34–45.

3. Catherine E. Foley, "Negotiating the 'native self' and the 'professional self': Ethnochoreological and Ethnomusicological Challenges in the Field" in Anne Margrete Fiskvik and Marit Stranden (eds.) *(Re)Searching the Field: Festschrift in Honor of Egil Bakka (*Bergen: Fagbokforlaget, 2014), 228. See also Walter J. Ong, *Orality and Literacy: The Technologizing of the Word* (London: Routledge, 2002).

4. Printed collections of indigenous music and dance emerged in Ireland during the eighteenth and nineteenth centuries. For example, John and William Neal, *A Collection of the Most Celebrated Irish Tunes Proper for Violin, German Flute or Hautboy* (Dublin: John Neal and William Neal, 1724). Other collections followed, for example, Edward Bunting, *A General Collection of the Ancient Irish Music* (London: Preston & Son 1796); J. J. Sheehan, *Guide to Irish Dancing* (London, Dublin and New York: John Denvir, 1902); J. G. O'Keeffe and A. P. O'Brien, *A Handbook of Irish Dances* (Dublin and London: M. H. Gill and MacMillan, 1902).

5. Philip Bohlman, *A World History of Music* (Oxford: Oxford University Press, 2002), 39.

6. Royal J. Schmidt, "Cultural Nationalism in Herder" in *Journal of the History of Ideas*. Vol. 17, No. 3 (Philadelphia, PA: University of Pennsylvania Press, June, 1956), 407.

7. This change of organization in my training occurred due to my teacher, Peggy McTeggart's shift to An Comhdháil in 1969. She was founding member of this organization.

8. Comhaltas Ceoltóirí Éireann is a cultural nationalist movement established in 1951 for the promotion and preservation of the indigenous performing arts. See Edward O. Henry, "Institutions for the Promotion of Indigenous Music: The Case of Ireland's Comhaltas Ceoltóirí Éireann" in *Ethnomusicology*, Vol, 33/1 (University of Illinois Press: Society for Ethnomusicology, 1989), 67–95.

9. See Catherine E. Foley, *Irish Traditional Step Dancing in North Kerry*.

10. Edmond Myers, Manager of the Trustees of Muckross House, letter to author (27 May 1980: personal archive).

11. Catherine E. Foley, "The Notion and Process of Collecting, Recording, and Representing Irish Traditional Music, Song and Dance: The Muckross House Collection" in *Ancestral Imprints: Histories of Irish Traditional Music and Dance*, ed. Therese Smith (Cork: Cork University Press, 2012b), 107–117; and Catherine E. Foley, "Negotiating the 'Native Self' and the 'Professional Self', 227–242.

12. Antonio Gramsci in Antonio Gramsci, Quintin Hoare, and Geoffrey Nowell-Smith, *Selections from the Prison Notebooks of Antonio Gramsci* (London: Lawrence and Wishart, 1971), 9.

13. My father, Pats Foley, played the melodeon and was also a traditional dancer and singer. He was influenced by his mother, Abbey Lane, who was also a traditional Irish musician (played concertina and fiddle), singer, and dancer, and by neighboring musicians and dancers in the rural surroundings of his home in Glenville, County Cork. I played tin whistle, concertina, and piano, as well as being a singer and dancer.

14. Angel Climent was also church organist at St. Mary's Cathedral (the North Cathedral), Cork, during the 1960s, where notable predecessors were Aloys Fleischmann (Senior) who established a male-voice choir there; my brother, Joe, was one of his choristers; and Hans Conrad Swertz, father of Tilly Fleischmann who married Aloys Fleischmann (Junior) in 1905. See Patrick Zuk, Ruth Fleischmann, and Séamas de Barra, *The Fleischmanns: A Remarkable Cork Family—A Companion to the Fleischmann Centenary Celebration* (Cork: Cork City Libraries, 2010).

15. Patrick Zuk, "Tilly Fleischmann" in Patrick Zuk, Ruth Fleischmann, and Séamas de Barra. *The Fleischmanns: A Remarkable Cork Family*, 9–15.

16. Aloys Fleischmann was the son of Tilly Fleischmann and Aloys Fleischmann (Senior). See Patrick Zuk, Ruth Fleischmann, and Séamas de Barra. *The Fleischmanns: A Remarkable Cork Family* (2010). Also, see Ruth Fleischmann's chapter in this volume.

17. Patrick Zuk, Ruth Fleischmann, and Séamas de Barra (op. cit. 2010). See also Ruth Fleischmann's chapter in this volume.

18. My other doctoral co-supervisor was the sociologist, Paul Filmer at University of London's Goldsmiths College, London, England.

19. I collected specifically within the regions of Kilgarvan, Kenmare, and Sneem in County Kerry between 1980 and 1983.

20. These collectors included Edward Bunting, George Petrie, Breandán Breathnach among others. See Edward Bunting, *A General Collection of the Ancient Irish Music* (London: Preston & Son, 1796); George Petrie, *The Petrie Collection of the Ancient Music of Ireland* (Dublin: M. H. Gill, 1855); and Breandán Breathnach, *Ceol Rince na hÉireann.* vol. 1 (Dublin: An Gúm, 1963).

21. Pat Ahern also completed a BMus degree under Aloys Fleischmann (Junior) and studied piano with Tilly Fleischmann in Cork.

22. Catherine E. Foley, "Step Dancing, Modernity and Change in North Kerry." Chapter 5 in Foley op. cit. (2013), 159–198.

23. See Catherine E. Foley, op. cit., 2001; Catherine E. Foley op. cit., 2012a [1988]; Catherine E. Foley, op. cit., 2013.

24. See Catherine E. Foley, 2013, op. cit. for a more in-depth examination of the itinerant dancing masters in North Kerry and the professional dancing masters on continental Europe. In particular Chapter 2, "The Professional European Dancing Masters," 27–58.

25. See Catherine E. Foley, 2012a [1988]; 2012b; 2013.

26. Foley, 2012a [1988]; 2012b; 2014.

27. Sally Ann Ness, *Body, Movement, and Culture: Kinesthetic and Visual Symbolism in a Philippine Community* (Philadelphia, PA: University of Pennsylvania Press, 1992), 2.

28. Foley, 2012a [1988]; Foley, 2007.

29. Muriel Topaz, 1996.

30. Rudolf Laban in Isa Partsch-Bergsohn, *Modern Dance in Germany and the United States* (Switzerland: Harwood Academic Publishers, 1994). 28.

31. Isa Partsch-Bergsohn, *Modern Dance in Germany.*

32. Muriel Topaz, 1996, 193.

33. Joseph Goebbels was a German Nazi politician and Reich Minister of Propaganda of Nazi Germany from 1933 to 1945.

34. Goebbels in Isa Partsch-Bergsohn, *Modern Dance in Germany and the United States* (Switzerland: Harwood Academic Publishers, 1994), 92.

35. Isa Partsch-Bergsohn, *Modern Dance in Germany*, 93

36. Isa Partsch-Bergsohn, *Modern Dance in Germany*, 91.

37. Laban and Lawrence would co-author the book *Effort* in 1947.

38. Gertrude Kurath, "Panorama of Dance Ethnology." *Current Anthropology:* vol.1, no.3 (The University of Chicago Press on behalf of Wenner-Gren Foundation for Anthropological Research, 1960), 233–254.

39. See also Elsie Ivancich Dunin and Catherine E. Foley, "Seventy Years of the International Council for Traditional Music's Study Group on Ethnochoreology" in *Celebrating the International Council for Traditional Music: Reflections on the First Seven Decades*. Eds. Niala Ceribasic, Don Niles, Svanibor Pettan (Vienna: The International Council for Traditional Music). In press.

40. Felix Hoerburger, "The Study of Folk Dance and the Need for a Uniform Method of Notation." *Journal of the International Folk Music Council 11* (London, England: International Folk Music Council, 1959), 73.

41. See also Adrienne Kaeppler, "Method and Theory in Analyzing Dance Structure with an Analysis of Tongan Dance. "*Ethnomusicology,* vol. 16, no. 2. (Champaign, IL: University of Illinois Press, 1972), 173–217; and Adrienne Kaeppler, "Cultural Analysis, Linguistic Analogies and the Study of Dance in Anthropological Perspective." In Charlotte Frisbie (ed.), Detroit *Monographs in Musicology 9* (Detroit, MI: Information Coordinators, 1981), 25–33.

42. Foley, 2012a [1988].

43. CALABAN, based on AutoCAD (a professional computer graphics program), was developed by Andy Adamson at Birmingham University (UK), and supports the production of high quality Labanotation.

44. See some excerpts from the video recordings of Catherine Foley's Dance Collection of traditional Irish step dance, at the Muckross House Research Library (accessed 23 May 2019). http://www.muckrosshouseresearchlibrary.ie/Dance-Collection.php.

45. Catherine E. Foley, "Globalization and Siamsa Tíre, the National Folk Theatre of Ireland." Chapter 7 in *Step Dancing in Ireland*, 199–226.

46. Catherine E. Foley, "Steps, Style and Sensing the Difference: an Examination of Molyneaux's Traditional Set Dances within Competition Culture," in *Dance, Senses, Urban Contexts: the 29th Symposium of the International Council of Traditional Music's Study Group on Ethnochoreology*, ed. Kendra Stepputat (Institute of Ethnomusicology, University of Music and Performing Arts Graz, Austria), 113–120.

BIBLIOGRAPHY

Bohlman, Philip. *A World History of Music*. Oxford: Oxford University Press, 2002.

Breathnach, Breandán. *Ceol Rince na hÉireann.* vol. 1. Dublin: An Gúm, 1963.

Bunting, Edward. *A General Collection of the Ancient Irish Music*. London: Preston & Son, 1796.

Ceribasic, Niala, Don Niles, and Svanibor Pettan. *Celebrating the International Council for Traditional Music: Reflections on the First Seven Decades*. Vienna: The International Council for Traditional Music. In press.

Dunin, Elsie Ivancich and Catherine E. Foley. *Celebrating the International Council for Traditional Music: Reflections on the First Seven Decades.* Eds. Niala Ceribasic, Don Niles, and Svanibor Pettan. Vienna: The International Council for Traditional Music. In press.

Foley, Catherine E. "Perceptions of Irish Step Dance: National. Local, and Global." *Dance Research Journal*, vol. 33, no.1. New York: Congress on Research in Dance (2001): 34–45.

———. "The Creative Process within Irish Traditional Step Dance." In *Dance Structures: Perspectives on the Analysis of Human Movement,* edited by Adrienne Kaeppler and Elsie Ivancich Dunin, 277–302. Budapest: Akademiai Kiada, 2007.

———. *Irish Traditional Step Dancing in North Kerry: A Contextual and Structural Analysis.* Listowel, County Kerry: North Kerry Literary Trust, 2012a [1988].

———. "Irish Traditional Step Dance Collection. Muckross House Research Library," accessed 23 May 2019. http://www.muckrosshouseresearchlibrary.ie/Dance-Collection.php

———. "The Notion and Process of Collecting, Recording, and Representing Irish Traditional Music, Song and Dance: The Muckross House Collection." In *Ancestral Imprints*: *Histories of Irish Traditional Music and Dance,* edited by Therese Smith, 107–117. Cork: Cork University Press, 2012b.

———. *Step Dancing in Ireland: Culture and History.* Farnham, Surrey: Ashgate Publishing Ltd., 2013.

———. "Negotiating the 'Native Self' and the 'Professional Self': Ethnochoreological and Ethnomusicological Challenges in the Field." In *(Re)Searching the Field: Festschrift in Honor of Egil Bakka,* edited by Anne Margrete Fiskvik and Marit Stranden, 227–242. Bergen: Fagbokforlaget, 2014.

———. "Steps, Style and Sensing the Difference: An Examination of Molyneaux's Traditional Set Dances within Competition Culture." In *Dance, Senses, Urban Contexts: The 29th Symposium of the International Council of Traditional Music's Study Group on Ethnochoreology*, edited by Kendra Stepputat, 113–120. Institute of Ethnomusicology, University of Music and Performing Arts Graz, Austria, 2015.

Gramsci, Antonio, Quintin Hoare, and Geoffrey Nowell-Smith. *Selections from the Prison Notebooks of Antonio Gramsci.* London: Lawrence and Wishart, 1971.

Henebry, Richard. *A Handbook of Irish Music*. Cork: Cork University Press, 1928.

Henry, Edward O. "Institutions for the Promotion of Indigenous Music: The Case of Ireland's Comhaltas Ceoltóirí Éireann." *Ethnomusicology,* vol. 33, no.1. University of Illinois Press, IL: Society for Ethnomusicology, (1989): 67–95.

Hoerburger, Felix. "The Study of Folk Dance and the Need for a Uniform Method of Notation." *Journal of the International Folk Music Council 11.* London: International Folk Music Council, (1959): 71–73.

Kaeppler, Adrienne. "Method and Theory in Analyzing Dance Structure with an Analysis of Tongan Dance." *Ethnomusicology,* vol. 16. no. 2. Champaign, IL: University of Illinois Press, (1972): 173–217.

Kaeppler, Adrienne. "Cultural Analysis, Linguistic Analogies and the Study of Dance in Anthropological Perspective." In *Detroit Monographs in Musicology 9*, edited by Charlotte Frisbie, 25–33. Detroit, Michigan: Information Coordinators, 1981.

Kurath, Gertrude. "Panorama of Dance Ethnology." *Current Anthropology:* vol.1, no. 3. The University of Chicago Press on behalf of Wenner-Gren Foundation for Anthropological Research, (1960): 233–254.

Laban, Rudolf, and F C. Lawrence. *Effort.* London: MacDonald & Evans, 1969 [1947].

Neal, J. and W. Neal. *A Collection of the Most Celebrated Irish Tunes Proper for Violin, German Flute or Hautboy.* Dublin: John Neal and William Neal, 1724.

Ness, Sally Ann. *Body, Movement, and Culture: Kinesthetic and Visual Symbolism in a Philippine Community*. Philadelphia, PA: University of Pennsylvania Press, 1992.

O'Keeffe, J.G. and A. P. O'Brien. *A Handbook of Irish Dances.* Dublin and London: M. H. Gill and MacMillan, 1902.

Ong, Walter J. *Orality and Literacy: The Technologizing of the Word*. London: Routledge, 2002.

Partsch-Bergsohn, Isa. *Modern Dance in Germany and the United States.* Switzerland: Harwood Academic Publishers, 1994.

Petrie, George. *The Petrie Collection of the Ancient Music of Ireland,* Dublin: M. H. Gill, 1855.

Reynolds, William C. "Foundations for the Analysis of the Structure and Form of Folk Dance: A Syllabus." *Yearbook of the International Folk Music Council*, vol. 6. The International Folk Music Council, (1974): 115–135.

Schmidt, Royal J. "Cultural Nationalism in Herder." *Journal of the History of Ideas,* vol. 17, no. 3. Philadelphia, PA: University of Pennsylvania Press, (1956): 407–417.

Sheehan, J.J. *A Guide to Irish Dancing.* London, Dublin and New York: John Denvir, 1902.

Topaz, Muriel. *Elementary Labanotation: A Study Guide.* New York: Dance Notation Bureau, 1996.

UNESCO, "The Convention for the Safeguarding of Intangible Cultural Heritage," accessed 23 May 2019. https://ich.unesco.org/doc/src/01852-EN.pdf

Zuk, Patrick, Ruth Fleischmann, and Séamas de Barra. *The Fleischmanns: A Remarkable Cork Family—A Companion to the Fleischmann Centenary Celebration.* Cork: Cork City Libraries, 2010.

Chapter Five

"Somewhere Between Remembering and Forgetting"

An Examination of the Choreographic Process Inspired by the Poem "The Man Made of Rain" by Brendan Kennelly

Marguerite Donlon

In this chapter, I will first provide a short overview of the different stages of my development as an Irish, female choreographer. I will then present a choreographic process of a dance piece that I created called "Somewhere Between Remembering and Forgetting" inspired by a poem by the Irish poet Brendan Kennelly called "The Man Made of Rain."[1] This piece was commissioned and created for the Stuttgart Ballet, Germany in 2002.

THE BEGINNING: MY DANCE TRAINING IN IRELAND AND ABROAD

Today, I regard myself as an Irish-born contemporary choreographer based between Berlin and Hagen, Germany. Influences from my Irish culture are never too far away, whether it be humor, dance, poetry, music or philosophy. I began my affair with Irish dancing with the idea of breaking rules to make something new. The Irish dancing school I attended as a young child in Longford encouraged us to improvise before we were allowed to learn a reel or a jig. Thanks to this format, I was introduced to improvisational skills at a very young age and I quickly became aware of space and time through movement. This awareness is something that is very important in the world of choreography.

Irish dance was the only form of dance available to me as a young girl growing up in the midlands of Ireland and, as much as I loved it, I began quickly to question why we were not allowed to use our arms. So, I started to study everything I could find about dance in books including encyclopedias. From my studies, I decided that ballet had everything I could have dreamed of, and more. It not only used the feet in all sorts of wonderful ways, but it had elaborate jumps and turns and used the arms in intricate maneuvers. I was fascinated by the complex yet effortless lifts, the formation, the composition, the various types of music and the costumes which were full of fantasy, surrounded by incredible scenery. Ballet, I found, could be abstract or tell stories, it could speak without words and it could touch you like no other art form.

It was then that I started slowly to experiment with combining the arm movements I had seen in ballet with the footwork of Irish dance. Naturally, this was very rudimentary. However, at the age of thirteen, I put all my knowledge together and created my first dance piece called the "Children of Lir." It won second place at an Irish arts competition called *Slógadh*.[2]

A South African artist, Anica Dawson, moved to County Longford in 1978 and opened the dance haven, Shawbrook. I was fortunate to be one of her first students. From my first lesson with Anica, it was an express train for my dance career. Time was not on my side. I was fourteen years old and I believed this to be too old to even dream that a dance career might be possible. At the age of sixteen, I went to England to study dance intensely with a Royal Academy of Dance examiner and teacher called Dorothy Stevens. Her school was a semi-professional dance school in Halifax, Yorkshire and I was her first full-time student. I learned everything I could possibly learn about ballet, modern, jazz, tap and also completed some secondary school examinations. I lived, breathed and ate dance for three years.

Just before my twentieth birthday, I was allowed to take a class with the English National Ballet, which was on tour in nearby Bradford, England. Kevin Hagan was the ballet master at the time and invited me to come to class the next day and he started to work with me during the company break. By the end of the week Peter Schaufuss, the artistic director of English National Ballet, and Kevin Hagan invited me to London to train with the company.

In London, I was offered a type of apprenticeship position. After some weeks of not knowing where this was all going, they asked me to perform all the things I had learned. With huge smiles on their faces, they offered me my first contract and told me I should go to the studio and start learning the new piece that they had just started. I walked in to the studio and, to my surprise, Rudolf Nureyev was leading his rehearsal of "Romeo and Juliet." I was so fortunate to be surrounded by the so-called legends of the ballet world. Very soon I realized there was another form of dance which broke the rules of the slightly more confined classical ballet; this was modern / contemporary dance. This awakened a whole new world for me and I was intrigued.

I was cast in a piece called "Land" by the house choreographer, Christopher Bruce. This was the first time I really understood that there was somebody called a "choreographer" who actually created the dance, sometimes with stories, sometimes without, with classical, rock or pop music, with voice or silence. I learned there was no end to what you could do and I knew this was my world.

I spent my dance career in London with the English National Ballet until I was offered a soloist contract with the Deutsche Oper Berlin in 1990. I had the great honor to perform on one of the biggest stages in Germany, but also other stages including the Metropolitan Opera House in New York, the Kirov in St. Petersburg and the Coliseum in London.

What really excited me most were the choreographers and composers with whom I worked. Each of them left me with a rich gift that inevitably influenced my creative work in some way. Some of those great dance masters were Jirí Kylián, William Forsyth, Maurice Béjart, Kenneth MacMillan, Meg Stuart, Bill T. Jones and Michael Clark.

While I danced professionally until 2000 in Berlin, I started to choreograph my own small pieces in the early 1990s. Eventually, after about fifteen years as a professional dancer, I decided to dedicate all my time to the creative part of my career. In 2001, I was invited to take over as the Ballet Director of the Saarländisches Staatstheater in Germany. I remained there until 2013, creating more than thirty ballets.

THE INVITATION: A NEW BALLET FOR STUTTGART BALLET, GERMANY, 2002

Stuttgart Ballet is a leading German ballet company situated in the south of Germany. It was founded as the court ballet to the Duke of Württemberg dating back to 1609. The modern company was founded by the South African born dancer and choreographer John Cranko in 1961, when he was appointed ballet director. Under his directorship, Stuttgart Ballet became one of Europe's finest dance companies known for its visually arresting style.[3] Cranko's unique fluency as a storyteller can be seen not only in his choreographic works but also in those of the choreographers he influenced, who included Kenneth MacMillan, John Neumeier, William Forsythe and Jiří Kylián. Cranko's work and the work of his students inspired me greatly as a young choreographer.

In the late 1990s, I became connected with the Stuttgart Ballet when I was cast to dance the role of Olga in John Cranko's highly acclaimed production of "Onegin" at the Deutsche Oper Berlin. "Onegin" was taught to us by the then director of Stuttgart Ballet, Reid Anderson. Anderson was the sole owner to the rights of this ballet and was responsible for teaching the piece and other ballets by John Cranko to ballet companies around the world.

Reid Anderson appreciated me as a dancer and artist, and when he heard I had choreographed a successful piece called "Taboo or Not" for the Vienna State Ballet in 2000, he asked to see it and immediately invited me to create a new piece for the Stuttgart Ballet. This was at the beginning of my choreographic career and it was naturally a great privilege as not too many female choreographers were invited to choreograph with the company then, and even today. The ballet I choreographed for the Stuttgart Ballet premiered on 10 May 2002 at the Stuttgart State Theatre. It was one of three ballets presented that evening. It was called "Tanzsichten" ("Dance Views"), a triple bill. The other two pieces, entitled "Cindy's Gift" and "Schere Stein Papier" ("Scissors Stone Paper"), were created by Douglas Lee and Daniela Kurz; my piece was "Somewhere Between Remembering and Forgetting."

The Inspiration for "Somewhere Between Remembering and Forgetting"

"The Man Made of Rain" by Brendan Kennelly

Between living and dying
is the calmest place I've ever been.
He stood opposite me and smiled.
I smiled too, I think, because this was the first time
I'd seen a man made of rain
though once or twice
my heart was chilled by men of ice.
The rain poured through him,
through his eyes, face, neck, shoulders, chest, all his body
But no rain reached the ground,
It ended at his skin.[4]

One summer in the early 2000s, when I was visiting family in Ireland, I heard the Irish poet, Brendan Kennelly, talk on the radio. He read from his poem "The Man Made of Rain," a long poem written in 1998 after his quadruple bypass surgery. The poem documents the shadow lands between life and death. I was instantly inspired. I immediately bought the book and I read it several times. Each time the images became more vivid and I, of course, saw a dance piece.

It was soon after that, that I received the commission mentioned above from the Stuttgart Ballet. I immediately thought about "The Man Made of Rain." I had the great pleasure of meeting Brendan Kennelly in person on a visit to Dublin. He recalled how the poem was inspired by the frightening prospect of heart surgery and how he found himself in a room somewhere between living and dying. He told me of his encounter with the man made of rain who had taken him on a journey past, present and future. His own description, told to me in his soft, lilting, Kerry accent convinced me to use it for my new piece. He was very encouraging and urged me to go ahead.

When I returned to Germany I sat down with my husband, the late Claas Willeke, who had equally fallen in love with "The Man Made of Rain." We decided on which parts we would use and which soundscape would support it. We found two wonderful actors, Katja Riemann and Michael Wenninger who read the selected sections of the poem. Then, Claas fused their voices with an atmospheric, rich carpet of electronic sound called "Ice," "Out of Blue" and "White Strings." We added two pieces from Philip Glass entitled "Strung Out" and "Music in Contrary Motion," as a counterbalance to the electronic score. In her review of the piece for *Stuttgarter Nachrichten*, Andrea Kachelrieß stated:

> Die sanften Stimmen von Katja Riemann und Michael Wenninger zitieren Brendan Kennellys Gedicht "The Man Made of Rain," der Schauer, in dem Yseult Lendvai wie eine Vision zu sein scheintaus einer anderen Welt, dem sich verengenden Korridor, dessen Wände als Grenze, aber auchals Projektionsfläche fungieren. Das Zucken, in das der Frauentanz fließt: all das hat sie fügt einem Ballett hinzu, das so mysteriös ist wie der Ort, den Kennellys Gedicht umkreist—das Nirgendwo zwischen Leben und Tod.[5]

> (The soft voices of Katja Riemann and Michael Wenninger citing Brendan Kennelly's poem "The Man Made of Rain," the shiver, in which Yseult Lendvai seems to be like a vision from another world, the narrowing corridor, its walls acting as a border but also as a surface to project onto; the twitching into which the women's dance flows: all this she adds to a ballet that is as mysterious as the place which Kennelly's poem orbits—the nowhere between life and death.)[6]

"SOMEWHERE BETWEEN REMEMBERING AND FORGETTING": THE CHOREOGRAPHIC PROCESS

Generally, when creating a new dance work, I tend to take several months to prepare and research the theme. By the time I came to choreographing "Somewhere Between Remembering and Forgetting," I was able to recite several passages by heart. It was the atmosphere and images it created that spoke to me; that mood stayed with me as I entered the studio.

As I improvised to create movement and steps, I had a constant stream of random words from the poem: Words such as "Mindbleeding," "Feathers protesting," "Loneliest cry," "Slithery as a snake," "Radiant nothingness," "Drugged pain," "The tongue of rain," "Pigignorant," "Massy Ferguson," "Ballybunion," "Bones and Stories," "Blue Shannon light," "Deeper than Ireland," "Callous bastard," "Oily scrags of sand on Sandymount Strand." Some lines from the poem also stood out, such as:

> I'm walking in the hills that tap their feet
> for dancing streets that I will walk again. . . .

Influenced by Kennelly's use of language, I explored different combinations of the most unimaginable movements: I looped and reversed phrases of movement; I took an upright step to a horizontal level. I was happy to be out of my comfort zone. This was possible because I was inspired by the unfamiliar world Brendan Kennelly had created.

I started the choreographic process by creating steps and movement phrases quickly, allowing my mind and body to recall only what felt relevant from the research. I continued to allow myself to be inspired by the images, words and rhythm of the poem. The movement became more and more disfigured and quirky.

The words helped me get away from my movement habits and enter into a world more unfamiliar to me. It also brought me back to my Irish dancing and I began to explore the intricate footwork from different perspectives. This footwork is especially interesting when it is danced by highly classically trained ballet dancers. The dancers I chose for this piece were exceptional and helped me fuse the Irish footwork with other movement textures. This was also noted by the critic Andrea Kachelrieß on seeing the performance. She stated:

> Marguerite Donlon, seit dieser Spielzeit Ballettdirektorin in Saarbrücken, ist bekannt für die Energie ihrer Choreografien. Wie sie die intensive Beinarbeit des irischen Volkstanzes und die sanften Bewegungen des modernen Tanzes zu einem poetischen Netz verdichtet, ist den Stuttgarter Tänzern neu. Doch Yseult Lendvai, Katja Wünsche, Eric Gauthier, Thomas Lempertz, Jorge Nozal und Javier Amo Gonzales folgen so leicht den sphärischen Klängen von Philip Glass und der speziell in Auftrag gegebenen Partitur von Claas Willeke, das "Somewhere Between Remembering and Forgetting" immer weit von der strenge Form des klassischen Balletts ist. [7]
>
> (Marguerite Donlon, ballet director in Saarbrücken since this season, is known for the edgy energy of her choreographies. How she condenses the intensive footwork of Irish folk dance and the soft movements of modern dance into a poetic net is new to the Stuttgart dancers. But Yseult Lendvai, Katja Wünsche, Eric Gauthier, Thomas Lempertz, Jorge Nozal and Javier Amo Gonzales follow

so easily the spherical sounds of Philip Glass and the especially commissioned score from Claas Willeke, that "Somewhere Between Remembering and Forgetting" is always far from the strict form of classical ballet.)

In the initial choreographic phase, I opened myself up to be inspired by the dancers and their interpretation of my movement. The process became a ping-pong effect that resulted in new interpretations constantly being created. Metaphorically speaking, it was like establishing strong roots and, from there, growing a solid tree trunk and then seeing branches sprouting in different directions. It may have appeared like chaos at first, but with time and distance, it began to form its own unique structure.

During this part of the choreographic process, I mostly worked in silence, but nearly always hummed the intended music and kept the ambient sound in my body. Brendan Kennelly's text and his voice and his words were constantly in my head and that helped to keep me in a specific mood. I had also listened to many interviews he had given and very often I was listening more to the texture, the quality and the sincerity of his voice.

In the beginning of a choreographic process, I tend not to share too much detailed information with the dancers for fear of limiting them. My wish is to give them an open playground, with just enough information to awaken their imagination, yet prevent limiting the process. However, in "Somewhere Between Remembering and Forgetting," I did give the dancers a copy of the texts we would use from "The Man Made of Rain." A copy of the poem was always on my desk in the studio for the dancers and team to read.

I call this first phase of the choreographic process "speed sketching." I believe it is only when a large library of movement material has been created (and this can take several days / weeks), that the real creation starts. When we had a large body of material, I started to compose and carve out "meaning," which for me appeared organically. Nothing was forced. The concept of "flow," generally of importance to me in the choreographic process, went where the energy felt vibrant. The only constant elements were the words from Brendan Kennelly's poem and his voice.

When choreographing, I generally have the bigger picture in sight, whether it be the concept, the story, the mood or the music. The bigger picture is made up of many small parts and it is the details that emerge in these small parts that make the bigger picture unique. My task as a choreographer is to stay open and to allow myself to receive new inputs from my surroundings and to be willing to deviate if it benefits the choreographic process. In this case these inputs not only include the dancers, but the designers and the composers and any other team member involved.

Personally, I would argue that the creative process is about smart editing. It is a unity of instinct, intellect and trusting the skilled knowledge of the professional dancer; the challenge is to find the right balance at the right time. According to the critic, Stefan Dettlinger: "Etwa die Irin Marguerite Donlon. In ihrem Stuttgarter Debut präsentiertr sie mit 'Somewhere Between Remembering and Forgetting' eine zwae ästhetische, in ihren Formen und Figuren aber auch scurrile Arbeit um das Thema Freiheit und Intuition, die alldies neuen Elemente in eine homogene Mischung zu fassen scheint."[8] (In Marguerite Donlon's Stuttgart debut she presented 'Somewhere Between Remembering and Forgetting,' a rather aesthetic piece in its formations and movements, but it is also her unusual work on the subject of freedom and intuition, which seems to combine all these new elements in a homogeneous mix.) (Translation by the author.)

My choreographic process is both virtuosic and dynamic, yet descriptive and realistic. It is very much about people and the personalities of the dancers, about the body and its limitations. It often deals with reflecting what is going on in our world at that moment, whether it be political, environmental or simply a perspective on human behavior. As a choreographer, I embrace challenges and view obstacles as a chance to build on or rethink the choreographic direction, which in turn can often bring new dynamics and ideas to the process.

My creative space has no boundaries, no gravity, no clear past or present. It has no feeling of time at all and no constant rules. It is a space where flow takes control and I happily go with it. It is a space where instinct is given the right of way and intellect has just the right amount of say. It is also a space where I feel no hunger, and tiredness does not exist. Pain, joy and frustration go hand in hand.

After every premiere, if asked how the piece evolved, I have to admit that in that moment I do not know. I am aware of a starting point, which I would always describe as the inspiration, and I am aware of the endpoint, the piece itself. In between is a blur. However, I write and sketch all my ideas and so together with these notes and the rehearsal videos from my assistant, it is possible for me to revisit and patch together the process.

Thus, for "Somewhere Between Remembering and Forgetting," after speed sketching and workshopping with some prepared movement material with the dancers for about a week, I invited them to use the material as if they were building blocks. With that material we began to create our own unique structures. In this second phase of the choreographic process the dancers were encouraged to explore the Kennelly text even further in depth. We then began to combine it to the newly created sound composition from Claas Willeke. With this new dynamic I started creating with them as individuals, forming solos which merged into duets and trios. With each step of the way, more and more comprehension appeared and my task was to gently carve it out,

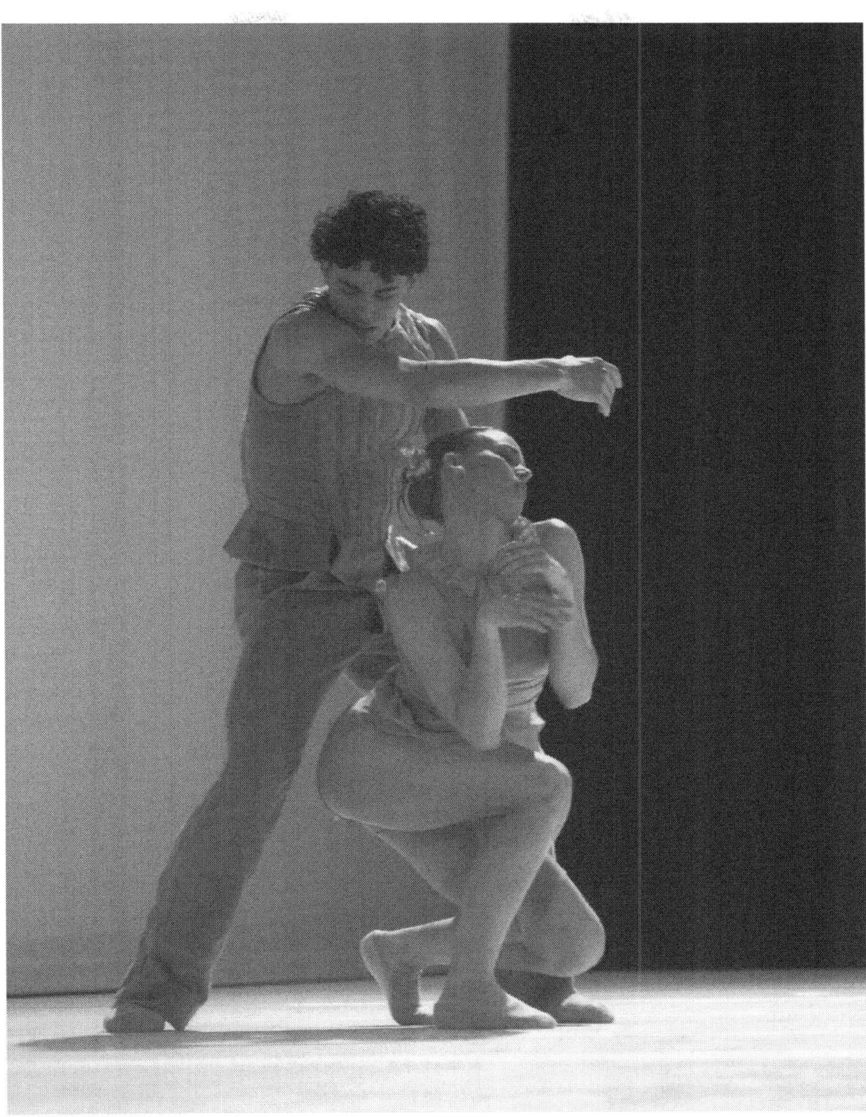

Figure 5.1. Katja Wünsche and Jorge Nozal in "Somewhere Between Remembering and Forgetting," Choreography, Marguerite Donlon. 10 May 2002. Stuttgart Ballet, Germany. Used courtesy of Stuttgart Ballet. Photographer: Bernd Weißbrod.

deciding at every moment what was relevant and what was not relevant to the choreographic work. Throughout this stage of the process of choreographing "Somewhere Between Remembering and Forgetting," I kept seeing a single person wandering through various encounters, which were at times absurd, beautiful and strange. Sometimes this single person was male and other times it was female.

As a choreographer, I am always excited by unexpected misunderstandings or misinterpretations. In my experience these situations often offer wonderful opportunities. I recall my biggest challenge with "Somewhere Between Remembering and Forgetting" was time, or the lack of it. Some days we would have as little as half an hour to rehearse. My production with Stuttgart Ballet was just one of many. Stuttgart Ballet is a world-renowned institution and I was just a small part of the bigger picture. This meant that I did not have the luxury of exploring and trying out different things so I had to come to the studio with a clear plan. Retrospectively, I would say most of the work was done outside the studio. The biggest gift to this whole experience was the brilliance of the dancers and their enthusiasm to create something special with me. I was also very fortunate that the dancers offered to rehearse in their free time. Creative processes vary enormously, and having little time in the studio is the least desirable scenario. However, it did encourage me to put more effort and thought into preplanning.

The ballet, "Somewhere Between Remembering and Forgetting" was danced by Katja Wünsche, Yseult Lendvai, Eric Gauthier, Javier Amo Gonzales, Jorge Nozal, Thomas Lempertz, all professional solo dancers with Stuttgart Ballet. [9]

STAGE, LIGHTING AND COSTUMES

For a choreographer, it is very important to choose the appropriate creative team. For "Somewhere Between Remembering and Forgetting" it was crucial to have a team that would read Kennelly's poem and bring new inspirations to the stage work. I chose the British award-winning light designer Lucy Carter and German costume designer Markus Mass.

Having read the poem, my starting point for "Somewhere Between Remembering and Forgetting" was very visual. I began with the space in which the dance would happen. The stage became an almost temple-like space, white and endless, like a long tunnel which expanded almost forty-nine feet back. It ended with a massive metal door. There were hidden slits on the side walls, which meant the dancers could enter and exit almost without being noticed. At the very end of the piece, the metal door opened slowly to reveal rain pouring down. A single dancer danced effortlessly into the rain, blissfully immersed and moving further away from us, the audience. This image disappeared ever so slowly as the curtain came down.

The all-white space gave Lucy Carter, the lighting designer, the opportunity to play with color and shade. She changed what seemed like an open borderless white space into many different magical universes. In Kennelly's poem he speaks of a room Somewhere Between Remembering and Forgetting. He talks of flowers which don't grow anymore and being allowed to remember and forget. For Brendan Kennelly, the room was both bare and welcoming. Our intention was to create a new space inspired by these words: a space which in turn gave us an enthusing space to blend our creative voices.

The costumes designed by Markus Mass were mostly abstract. Markus Mass used sheer materials for the ladies and raw silk and velvet for the men. These materials helped to create an almost ethereal effect. In shades of pastel green, the dancers' bodies floated against the vast whiteness of the stage.

My aim for "Somewhere Between Remembering and Forgetting" was not to retell or interpret Brendan's story, but simply to allow his poem to inspire me to produce images, emotions and atmospheres that came to my mind each and every time I read the poem.

SOUND AND MUSIC

Claas Wiellke's intellectual approach and his expertise in the music world, especially with improvisation, brought a huge richness to the work. Born in Bielefeld, Germany in 1966, he studied jazz at the University of Fine Arts, Berlin. After some years of playing saxophone with several well-known jazz bands, he began to compose and became more involved with the world of electronics. In 2007, Claas became a professor of jazz theory, composition/improvisation and electronic music at the University of Music, Saarland. His research in teaching and learning improvisation is recognized as visionary and of great value for students and teachers. Artistically, he was one of the founders of and heads of DIE REDNER, a German artist group working with important speeches and exclusive interviews from history-changing personalities such as John F. Kennedy, Charles de Gaulle and Stéphane Hessel.

Claas not only composed for many of my ballet pieces, but also worked together with me on the concepts of these ballets. He was the critical, analytical eye that I was not. Claas died tragically on 13 October 2013.[10]

In relation to the music of "Somewhere Between Remembering and Forgetting," critic Andrea Kachekriess remarks that "Die Tänzer folgen Sie so leicht den sphärischen Klängen von Philip Glass und der speziell von Claas Willeke in Auftrag gegebenen Partitur, dass 'Somewhere Between Remembering and Forgetting' immer weit von der strengen Form des klassischen Balletts entfernt ist. Donlon weiß, wie man Effekte benutzt, ohne sie zu überbelichten."[11] ("The dancers follow the spherical sounds of Philip Glass and the especially commissioned score from Claas Willeke so easily, that 'Somewhere Between Remembering and Forgetting' is far from the strict form of classical ballet. Donlon knows how to use effects without overexposing them.")

It was exciting to see and hear how Claas created an electronic carpet of sound as a base for "Somewhere Between Remembering and Forgetting." He worked on layers upon layers of delicate sounds, which helped to bring us into the mysterious world Kennelly created. I recalled the sound of footsteps echoing down what I imagined was a long corridor. There was of course the sound of rain in various forms. Over this carpet of sound Claas weaved the voices of the actors speaking the text. He managed to find the perfect sound to match the atmosphere that the poem had produced in our minds. It gave space for the imagination to form images, yet it clearly put us somewhere we did not recognize. It was a tonal /musical/ room between here and there which was not familiar. He added two music compositions by Philip Glass entitled "Strung Out" and "Music in Contrary Motion," as a counter balance to his electronic score. The critic Stefan Dettlinger stated: "Zur teilweise mystischen Ambientmusik von Claas Willeke sucht Donlon die ungewöhnliche Bewegung, einen fast verkrampften Spannungszustand am Rande der Normalität. Fast epileptische Szenen Kommen genauso vor wie sich in Endlosschleifen verwickelnde Bewungsabläufe."[12] (To the mysterious, ambient music by Claas Willeke, Donlon seeks unfamiliar movement, an almost cramped state of tension on the edge of normality. Scenes with almost epileptic movement sequences occur entangled in endless loops.)

THE AUDIENCE AND FINDING THE MOOD

As a contemporary choreographer, my aim is for the audience to understand what we are saying. However, I do not create a work to please an audience or to give them what they might think they want. This would be counterproductive. As a contemporary choreographer, I feel I am not only there to create beauty, but to challenge and pose questions, for them and for ourselves.

For each and every creation, there are many layers, and I force myself to look at the same thing from different perspectives. I try to see it from not only my eyes, but the eyes of people from various backgrounds, ages, political stances, cultures, etc. I constantly question, however, when it comes to making a decision to follow my instinct and at that moment nothing else matters. As an Irish contemporary choreographer coming from a classical background, I am known for my unique use of humor. However, "Somewhere Between Remembering and Forgetting" was a more thoughtful and reflective piece. The critic Horst Kroger commented in *Tanz* at the time:

> In Marguerite Donlons Ballett ist es die wunderbar geschmeidige Katja Wünsche. die das Niemandsland zwischen Erinnerung und Vergessen tänzerisch vorgibt—und auch weiterhin beherrscht, wenn später Yseult Lendvai als Alternativfigur sich aus dem Regen schämt. Donlon, aus der Schule des englischen Balletts hervorgegangen, ist die komplexeste unter den drei, stets ist bei ihr der ganze Körper beteiligt, wobei die einzelnen Gliedmaßen oft konträre Bewegungen ausführen. Sie choreographiert gewissermaßen polyphon und knüpft so ein ungemein dicht gewobenes Netz der Beziehungen. Wie sie die miteinander verknüpft und hin—und herfließen lässt zwischen ihren sechs Tänzern, wobei den vier Männern Eric Gauthier. Thomas Lempertz, Jorge Nozal und Javier Amo Gonzales reichlich Gelegenheit geboten wird, such individuell zu profilieren (und Gauthier und Lempertz noch ein bisschen mehr als ihren beiden Kollegen), ist durchaus spannungsvoll zu sehen: ein Tanzrätsel. minutiös durchkonstruiert und so fein strukturiert wie eine Zeichnung von Paul Klee. Da Donlon wohl auch über eine gehörige Portion irischen Humors verfügt, würden wir sie gern bald einmal wiedersehen, vorzugsweise mit einem weniger in irischen Nebel getauchten Ballett—sozusagen in Irisch Dur.[13]

> (In Marguerite Donlon's ballet, it is the wonderfully supple Katja Wünsche which sets the no-man's-land between remembrance and forgetting—and continues to dominate, whilst later Yseult Lendvai is an alternative character who shies away from the rain. Donlon, born out of the English Ballet Schooling, is the most complex of the three pieces, always involving in the whole body, with individual limbs often performing contrary movements. She choreographs in a polyphonic manner, thus forming an extremely dense web of relationships. How she ties them together and flows back and forth between her six dancers, with the four men Eric Gauthier, Thomas Lempertz, Jorge Nozal and Javier Amo Gonzales is given ample opportunity to make an individual profile (and Gauthier and Lempertz a little more than their two colleagues), is quite exciting to see: a dance puzzle. meticulously constructed and as finely structured as a drawing by Paul Klee. Since Donlon also has a good portion of Irish humor, we would like to see her soon, preferably with a ballet less immersed in Irish mist.)

It was and is still the case that I do not shy away from a sense of humor influencing my choreographies, at least in part. In German, in contemporary dance, this is not so common. In my case, it is often referred to as "Irish humor." This observation is usually made by critics outside of Ireland, and has often brought me to the question: What is Irish humor? When I consider that I have lived outside of Ireland for more years than I have lived inside, then might I not be affected by the humor of various other cultures also at this point? The type of humor I am actually interested in involves body language and the interaction between people. I would argue, however, that this does not depend only on culture. I believe many factors are involved such as age, political preference, sexual differences, class distinction and so on. So, can one say that my work includes a sense of "Irish" humor, or is it simply "humor" that can translate across cultures?

EMBRACING CREATIVE CHALLENGES

There is no better or worse, easier or harder way to create a new dance piece. All methods offer exciting opportunities and also some interesting obstacles. An obstacle can be anything from lack of time, miscasting a dancer, a personality clash, a sudden lack of inspiration, an injury to a principal dancer or a traumatic personal loss.

When working on "Somewhere Between Remembering and Forgetting," I was presented with a number of challenges. Due to a lack of time, I was forced to prepare blocks of choreography before my rehearsals. The advantage of this, however, was that the movement was coming directly from my body which was immersed in the poem in every way. The poem offered feelings and images that did not exist in my imagination and brought me to work with movement, space and time in very different ways. I deconstructed my movement, not wanting to recognize a typical dance move I might usually make. I played with dividing the dance into the vast space in a more disfigured way. This, for me, resonated with Kennelly's words:

> Have you been here before, I wondered, will you
> be here again?
> He read my silent wondering.
> "I haven't much time for tenses," he replied.[14]

The other obstacle confronting me was fear. I had just been appointed the new Ballet Director of the State Theatre of Saarland, Germany.[15] It was to be my first Directorship and I felt the pressure of all eyes of the dance world on me. Stuttgart Ballet was world famous and I felt like the intruder who was not qualified. In my first meeting with Brendan Kennelly he spoke about his fear and he told me that the day he faced his fear, eye to eye, was the day he was freed.

> I'm crying because I'm not afraid,
> I said, and I thought I would be.

Fear came to me last night
And slept beside me.
Please let me stay, it said,
Please let me lie with you
And live in you . . . [16]

Facing my "fear" in this choreographic process helped me to grow and go for my own choreographic direction, resisting any pressure to create in a certain way to please the critics or audience. It was important to stay true to myself. It was just as important that my dancers also remained true to themselves as individuals. According to critic Stefan Dettlinger: "In einem hellen, sich nach hinten in regnerische Dunkelheit verjüngenden Raum, organisiert Donlon zwei Tänzerinnen und vier Tänzer in grünem Pastell (Kostüme: Markus Maas), die immer wieder, in Gruppe order einzeln, verschwinden, auftauchen, sich finden, letzlich aber Individuum bleiben." [17] (In a bright regenerating room, moving back toward rainy darkness, Donlon organizes two female dancers and four male dancers in green pastels (costumes: Markus Mass), who disappear again and again, in groups or individually, they appear, they find themselves, but ultimately, they remain their individual selves. Translation by the author).

As a creative artist I embrace the idea of starting with a blank page, because a blank page is never really blank, even if it appears to have no color, no shape and no limitations. It is, however, as daunting as it is inviting. This space can be framed by an inspiration, a concept, an emotion or simply the desire to work with a group of dancers and the curiosity to discover new facets in the artists with whom one is working. I would argue, however, that what comes into the space first, determines a great deal. Generally, it can be emotions and feelings evoked from an inspiration, a clear idea, a story, a piece of music, a person, and in this case a poem and a poet.

CONCLUSION

"Somewhere Between Remembering and Forgetting" emerged in 2002, early in my career as a choreographer and new Ballet Director. However, it made its mark and helped solidify my work as an Irish choreographic artist in Germany. Brendan Kennelly's poem provided me with a unique opportunity to explore modern Irish literature. More than that, "The Man Made of Rain" inspired a visually fluid and yet powerful choreographic piece that created a union between words on the page and steps on the stage.

Working with a deeply descriptive narrative like Kennelly's poem provided me with a secure framework or structure. Nevertheless, it also produced a feeling of confinement which I see positively as "friction." In my world of choreography, friction creates energy, and energy creates power, and power creates a new momentum to move forward to create expressive movement. This expressiveness in "Somewhere Between Remembering and Forgetting" is alluded to by the critic Kachelrieß. She states, "Das Zucken, in das der Tanz der Frau fließt: all dies fügt sie einem Ballett hinzu, das so mysteriös ist wie der Ort, den Kennellys Gedicht umkreist—das Nirgendwo zwischen Leben und Tod."[18] (The twitching into which the women's dance flows: all this she [Donlon] adds to a ballet that is as mysterious as the place which Kennelly's poem orbits—the nowhere between life and death.)

Reflecting upon the choreographic process of "Somewhere Between Remembering and Forgetting" has highlighted the continued importance for me of collaboration: collaboration with artists such as composers, poets, writers, visual artists and more. This provides a space for the emergence of diverse art worlds to create unfamiliar impulses and allow us to enter into new unimaginative territory. It adds challenge and enrichment. Collaborating on "Somewhere Between Remembering and Forgetting" with the poet, Brendan Kennelly, also helped me to see how "fear" is something to befriend. Over a cup of tea one afternoon in Dublin, Brendan Kennelly told me how fear had become his best friend and, from that moment on, he felt freed. This new perspective of fear was a valuable parting gift.

NOTES

1. "Trinity Writers; Nano Facts—What Is Nano: Nanoscience, Physics and Chemistry of Advanced Materials: Trinity College Dublin, the University of Dublin, Ireland: Brendan Kennelly," accessed 30 January 2019. https://www.tcd.ie/trinitywriters/writers/brendan-kennelly/.

2. Gael Linn, "Slógadh," accessed 30 January 2019. https://www.gael-linn.ie/en/about-us/history.

3. Stuttgart Ballet: About, accessed 30 January 2019. https://www.stuttgart-ballet.de/.

4. Brendan Kennelly, "The Man Made of Rain." *Familiar Strangers: New & Selected Poems 1960–2004.* Bloodaxe Books, 2004. www.bloodaxebooks.com.

5. Andrea Kachelrieß, *Stuttgarter Nachrichten*, 13 May 2002 [Translated by Marguerite Donlon].

6. If no other reference is given, all translations in this chapter are by Marguerite Donlon.

7. Andrea Kachelrieß, *Stuttgarter Nachrichten*, 13 May 2002.

8. Stefan M. Dettlinger, *Südkurier*, 13 May 2002.

9. To view "Somewhere Between Remembering and Forgetting," please contact the choreographer via www.donlon.de. Alternatively, a recording of the piece

may be viewed at the National Dance Archive of Ireland, University of Limerick: "The Marguerite Donlon Collection." See the National Dance Archive of Ireland weblink, accessed 19 August 2019, at https://www.ul.ie/library/explore-collections/national-dance-archive-ireland

10. "Claas Willeke," accessed 31 January 2019, http://claaswilleke.wgaller.de/.

11. Andrea Kachelrieß, *Stuttgarter Nachrichten,* 13 May 2002.

12. Stefan M. Dettlinger, *Südkurier*, 13 May 2002.

13. Horst Koeger, *Tanz*. May 2002.

14. Kennelly, "The Man Made of Rain."

15. Staatstheater, Saarländisches. "Saarländisches Staatstheater," accessed 18 February 2019. www.staatstheater.saarland/.

16. Kennelly, "The Man Made of Rain."

17. Stefan M. Dettlinger, *Südkurier*, 13 May 2002.

18. Andrea Kachelrieß, *Stuttgarter Nachrichten,* 13 May 2002.

BIBLIOGRAPHY

Ballett, Stuttgarter. "Stuttgart Ballet: About." Accessed 30 January 2019. https://www.stuttgart-ballet.de/.

Dettlinger, Stefan, M. *Südkurier*, 13 May 2002 [Translation by Marguerite Donlon].

Donlon, Marguerite. "Somewhere Between Remembering and Forgetting." Stuttgart Ballet, Germany, 10 May 2002. For a viewing of the recording of the work contact www.donlon.de or The National Dance Archive of Ireland, University of Limerick, Limerick, Ireland: "The Marguerite Donlon Collection."

Gael Linn, "Slógadh." Accessed 10 June 2019. https://www.gael-linn.ie/en/about-us/history.

German Dance Film Institute Bremen. TYPO3 Version 8LTS. 29 May 2018. Accessed 26 April 2019. http://www.tanzarchive.de/en/members/german-dance-film-institute-bremen/

Kachelrieß, Andrea. *Stuttgarter Nachrichten*, 13 May 2002 [Translation by Marguerite Donlon].

Kennelly, Brendan. "The Man Made of Rain." *Familiar Strangers: New & Selected Poems 1960–2004*. Hexham, Northumberland: Bloodaxe Books, 2004. www.bloodaxebooks.com.

Koeger, Horst. *Tanz*. May 2002. [Translation by Marguerite Donlon].

National Dance Archive of Ireland, accessed 19 August 2019. https://www.ul.ie/library/explore-collections/national-dance-archive-ireland

Royal Opera House, "Lucy Carter," accessed 19 February 2019. http://www.roh.org.uk/people/lucy-carter.

Staatstheater, Saarländisches, "Saarländisches Staatstheater." Accessed 18 February 2019. www.staatstheater.saarland/.

Trinity Writers, and Trinity College. Trinity Writers; Nano Facts—What Is Nano: Nanoscience, Physics and Chemistry of Advanced Materials: Trinity College

Dublin, the University of Dublin, Ireland, "Brendan Kennelly." Accessed 30 January 2019. https://www.tcd.ie/trinitywriters/writers/brendan-kennelly/.
Willeke, Claas. Accessed 30 January 2019. http://claaswilleke.wgaller.de/.

Chapter Six

Creating Tanztheater

Finding Ireland with Pina?

Finola Cronin

In 2016, seven years after the death of Pina Bausch, a major exhibition dedicated to the choreographer's work was mounted in Bonn and Berlin.[1] The exhibits included a replica (almost to scale) of her rehearsal studio, the *Lichtburg,* and extensive archival material of photographs, rehearsal books, and video footage from a selection of her *oeuvre* of over 40 productions. I was invited to participate in an event scheduled as part of the exhibition in Bonn in May of that year and following an hour-long excerpt of Bausch's *Viktor. Ein Stück von Pina Bausch* (1986), joined former colleagues from Tanztheater Wuppertal, Urs Kaufmann and Jan Minarik, in the *Lichtburg* for a public interview. Revisiting *Viktor* we conveyed what we remembered of the creative process that had taken place in Wuppertal and Rome for the work that marked Pina's first international coproduction. We recalled our impulses to create responses to Bausch's questions or *Aufgaben* (tasks) and discussed the construction of sequences and the novelty of rehearsing in Rome. It struck me afterwards that our recollections marked a formal airing of conversations that took place regularly when Bausch's dancers gathered at work or in social settings, and the event in Bonn seemed to prove that the allure of Bausch's work, even for former dancers of Tanztheater, would never wane. The subject of this chapter is the creative process of Pina Bausch—a process that has been identified as groundbreaking within European dance practices of the period. As our conversation that evening illustrated, Bausch's rehearsal methods were pioneering because she facilitated her dancers to become integral to her creation of new works. I focus specifically on the feature of *Aufgaben* that marked the first phase of rehearsals. This phase, lasting approximately ten weeks in my experience, was when dancers presented their ideas in the form of movement, text, small scene, song, and/or image—ideas which contributed, in part, to material for a new work.

Scholarly discussion of Bausch's creative process often includes reference to the *Aufgaben* as "improvisations."[2] Bausch however, was very often at pains to explain that *Aufgaben* should not comprise unstructured impulses.[3] My experience, and the basis of my discussion in this chapter, was that tasks carried out by dancers materialized *composed* answers to Bausch's very open questions.[4] Of those *Aufgaben*, many demanded that dancers recall life experiences and memories, often childhood memories, and in numerous instances the setting of those experiences and recollections might have included a specificity of place, of situation, of language, custom, and practice. Inevitably answering *Aufgaben* demanded research in the form of (re)discovery of one's culture, one's self, and of one's identity. This is not to suggest that Bausch was in search of essentialized characteristics of different cultures. On the contrary, Bausch was asking for individual and collective research to identify what was different and unique amongst our memories and everyday experiences to serve as a catalyst and support her answering of her own questions during the making of new work.

Ciane Fernandes in discussion of Bausch's rehearsal process rightly asserts Bausch's signature and her position as final arbiter: "The dancers' experiences and memories are transformed in the rehearsal process and shaped into aesthetic form."[5] In tracing a genealogy of my responses to *Aufgaben*, I'm interested in ideas put forward by Gabriele Klein who describes Bausch's process, with reference in particular to the international coproductions between the years 1986 and 2009, as a "practice of translation," and she notes that these productions pose "a permanent and complex process of translation between language and movement, movement and writing, between different languages and cultures, and between different media and materials."[6] As the *Aufgaben* arguably contributed material to productions from the late 1970s onwards, both those rehearsed in Wuppertal *and* those realized in coproduction settings, it establishes the *Aufgaben* phase as a fundamental and fixed element of Bausch's creative practice that sits also within Klein's definition of translation as she notes: "cultural translation is a basic principle of collaborative working methods involving people from different cultures [and] Pina's method underscored and reaffirmed processes already at work with the specific mix of nationalities in her company."[7] As importantly in my view, the principle of the *Aufgaben* as composed responses rather than spontaneous improvisations points to that phase of rehearsal as embodied research arising from the conscious summoning by dancers of their culture and experiences.

To consider how I "found Ireland" while working with Wuppertal Tanztheater, I place myself as subject, and trace the *Ursprung* or genesis of select ideas that I researched and subsequently embodied through *Aufgaben*. I detail a small number of the *Aufgaben* I was asked by Bausch in *Viktor. Ein*

Stück von Pina Bausch (1986), *Ahnen. Ein Stück von Pina Bausch* (1987), and *Tanzabend 11. Ein Stück von Pina Bausch* (1991), with reference to my original rehearsal notes, and to my MA Thesis written shortly after I left the company and while still a guest member of Tanztheater Wuppertal. Firstly however, I draw on select sources from the extensive scholarship and writing on Bausch's work, and from interviews that record Bausch's reflection on her process, to consider her aesthetic and why the *Aufgaben* became a fundamental instrument of her creative method.

INFLUENCES: GERMAN AND AMERICAN AESTHETIC AND PRACTICE

Bausch was appointed choreographer of Wuppertaler Bühnen in 1973. Reception to her work was initially quite mixed; in fact, some works were denounced for their perceived portrayal of women as passive victims of male violence. Nevertheless, a loyal following emerged gradually.[8] In 1979 for example, the novelty of her work was captured by Norbert Servos: "[T]he dancers appear not as technical personnel performing the roles; they appear as unprotected with their entire personalities. Their fears and joys possess the force of authentic experience."[9] While we might dispute the idea (following Derrida) that theatre performance can in any way be authentic or unmediated, Servos' account suggests the affective qualities of Bausch's work derived from her aesthetic of theatricality and the arresting scenographic designs by Rolf Borzik and Peter Pabst.

Among the choreographic features of Bausch's style was the inclusion of everyday or pedestrian movement, a feature that Hedwig Müller contends, situates the *Tanztheater* aesthetic as a legacy of the *Ausdruckstanz* movement of the early twentieth century as initiated by, among others, Rudolf Laban, "which had smoothed the way with its rejection of the classical academic style of dance."[10] Müller continues: "If today 'everyday' themes and 'everyday' experiences are acceptable subjects for a theatre of dance orientated towards reality, then this is so only because dance in the Twenties took the first steps in this direction by including 'everyday' movement in its choreography."[11] The everyday choreographic vocabulary, according to Müller, was achieved by "observation of everyday social life for the purpose of dancing," hence *Ausdruckstanz* she claims, gave license "to express personal experience—or what was taken for personal experience."[12]

The course of history would see some works of *Ausdruckstanz* choreographers appropriated by National Socialism ideology, and thus post-war choreographers resisted the use of the term to describe their work. Müller proposes however, that a link endured between pre and post-war developments in modern dance in Germany through Laban's pupil, Kurt Jooss. Jooss fled Germany when the Nazis came to power and just after he gained international acclaim for his ballet *The Green Table* (1932), which depicted the futility and horror of war. On his return to Germany Jooss established Folkwang Tanztheater in 1949 and continued his exploration of social themes in an aesthetic that aimed to present dance as "a technique of dramatic choreography" that was "concerned with libretto, music and above all with the interpretative artists."[13] Jooss was also cofounder and director of the dance faculty at the Folkwangschule based in Essen Werden, where Bausch, in 1955, would begin her dance training and instruction in Jooss' principles of choreographic practice.

A further perspective on Bausch's aesthetic is identified by Susanne Schlicher who writes that her *Tanztheater* was "rooted in the context of the 1968 upheavals [. . .] and the drastic aesthetic changes in post-war German drama theatre," changes she contends, that were led by influential theatre directors Peter Zadek and Peter Stein, among others, who rejected previously "declamatory theatre practices," to present instead a theatre that was "highly visual, physical and often anarchic /chaotic."[14] Schlicher notes also that both German drama and German dance theatre began experimenting in that period with an "aesthetic of images" that eschewed narrative, and she notes that Bausch's use of montage as a dramaturgical structure was derived from film techniques.[15]

Enquiries into dance and its practice were also underway in the post-war era in the United States, and it was there that Bausch journeyed in 1958 as a recipient of a *Deutscher Akademischer Austauschdienst* scholarship (DAAD). Bausch has acknowledged her sojourn in New York, and the influence of choreographers Paul Taylor, Anthony Tudor, Paul Sanasardo and Donna Feuer, with whom she worked while in New York, as pivotal to the emergence of her creative signature.[16] Mark Franko notes that Sanasardo and Feuer's work challenged trends in avant-garde dance in New York at that time. Franko argues that the "task" of modern dance of the 1960s was to "cease presenting movement as a fulfillment of need, as what the dancer needed to do in some psychological or symptomatic way," an aim he claims, that was in marked contrast to the work of Sanasardo and Feuer, which "reinscribed emotion within a social frame."[17] Franko notes also that it is perhaps significant that Pina Bausch worked with Sanasardo and Feuer on the original version of *Laughter After All* (1960), the work that Franko addresses in his chapter.[18] Studying the photographs that accompany Franko's chapter, I am most taken with a sense of the dancers' power and presence in poses that seem to emphasize their embodiment of everyday situations. I am reminded of Bausch's oft quoted comment on her selection of dancers, and her interest not so much in "how they move but in what moves them."[19] For Bausch, it would become important that her performers *be* on stage as *just* a body, and one not so very unlike any other body sitting in the audience.

Norbert Servos claims Bausch's work offers a synthesis of American and European dance aesthetic, an opinion echoed by Ramsay Burt in his seminal work on the Judson Church Dance Theatre.[20] In his monograph, Burt considers the aims of select modern and post-modern dance practitioners on both sides of the Atlantic in the latter decades of the twentieth century to conclude: "[T]hrough their refusal to conform to normative aesthetic expectations, these (sic) unruly bodies of European and American dancers were creating a context in which embodied experience could become a site of resistance against normative ideologies rather than an affirmation of them."[21] Yvonne Rainer, a leading American choreographer and filmmaker was among the most radical of choreographers who espoused new ways of thinking about dance. Her claim in the early 1960s that: "[D]ance is hard to see. It must either be made less fancy or the fact of that intrinsic difficulty must be emphasized to the point where is almost impossible to be seen" resonated throughout the New York dance scene.[22] Rainer's sentiment, in my view, has parallels to Bausch's concerns of 1978: "[W]hy are we dancing at all? How it is developing now is quite dangerous. Everything is routine, and no one knows anymore why we're doing the movements. It is a strange sort of vanity, which is growing more and more away from people. And I believe that we once again need to come closer."[23] Arguably while Rainer and Bausch would find quite different solutions to engage audiences, their concerns, in my view, illustrate a shared mission.[24]

Returning to Germany in the early 1960s, Bausch worked closely with Kurt Jooss, and performed and choreographed for Folkwang Tanzstudio, and was awarded the Choreography Prize in Cologne in 1969. From 1973 at Wuppertaler Bühnen, she set about gathering an ensemble of solo dancers to transform the Wuppertal Ballet into Tanztheater Wuppertal. In the years that followed, Bausch engaged dancers from numerous countries with diverse dance techniques and demonstrated her intent that the uniqueness of each dancer be available to be seen onstage. Approximately five years after her arrival in Wuppertal, Bausch began the process of setting *Aufgaben* during the creative process asking questions of dancers; seeking their observations and perspectives of everyday life.[25] On stage, dancers' culturally inscribed bodies emerged in performances that foregrounded difference of culture within and across the ensemble to become a feature of Bausch's work. While it is not unusual that dance companies engage dancers from a range of nationalities, a distinction of Bausch's choreography was how she used the working process to formally present ideas of cultural diversity, a feature of her work, which, in my view, became one of the strongest markers of her political position of inclusivity, and one of her most significant legacies.

Bausch's motivation to "bring dance closer" served as a catalyst for works that explored gender relations and wider social issues, and arguably the means to do so necessitated her finding a process to create work "from the inside out," and from material that surfaced out of the social moment in which she lived: "I know only the times we're in. I can only speak about what I feel."[26] A focus of bodies as "sites of resistance" to challenge normative social and political hegemonies would become integral to Bausch as the leading exponent of German Tanztheater. The dancer's body moreover as corporeal material, as a human body that is also "personal, social, emotional, animal, mineral, vegetable, sexual, biological and psychological, and as an agent of motion," would become the central mediator for her interrogation of her art as a medium of expression.[27] I auditioned for Pina in 1984 and in early 1985 arrived in Wuppertal to learn works from the repertoire. In January 1986, rehearsals began in Wuppertal at the *Lichtburg* for a new work, and in February of that year the company travelled to Rome for three weeks to embark on Pina's coproduction with Teatro Argentina in Rome.

EMBODYING RESEARCH: TRACING *AUFGABEN*

Viktor. Ein Stück von Pina Bausch (*Viktor. A Piece from Pina Bausch*) (1986)

> *Etwas wie eine Maus erzählen/ Totschießen spielen/ Wozu man ein Messer nicht benutzt/ Etwas versteigern/ Kinderballett/ Sehr schöne Sachen sagen—ganz einfach*
>
> (Narrating something like a mouse/ Playing shooting dead/ Mermaid/ What one doesn't use a knife for/ Auction something/ Children's ballet class/ Say something very beautifully—very simply)[28]

The atmosphere at the start of the rehearsal process had an element of the ludic; this arose from the provision of diverse items of costume, accessories, and sundry objects hidden from view behind three large mirrors that formed a sort of backstage area available to the ensemble for preparation of their *Aufgaben*. Here was where embryonic ideas were tested, movements rehearsed, collaborative ideas discussed and arranged. My practice, and my observation of the practices of my colleagues, was to note ideas before I presented them to Pina and amend as necessary post-presentation.

The *Aufgabe Kinderballett* (Children's Ballet Class) on 31 January evoked my early training in classical ballet in Dublin. For the annual ballet exams and reviews of syllabi, the region's ballet teachers and young dance students assembled. The group of ballet teachers left an impression—appearing to me at the time as glamorous women carefully made-up with red or purple lipstick, hair high in elaborate piles, often wearing fur coats, and patent stiletto heels displaying beautifully turned-out feet. We were fortunate to have live music accompaniment and I remembered one pianist in particular, an elderly woman, who played the piano wearing a big wool coat. My *Aufgabe* for *Kinderballett* merged the idea of a cold elderly pianist body with a glitzy shod, fur-coated ballet teacher. To this figure I added a much later experience I had of a dance teacher who arrived to class each morning and after shakily descending the three steps to the ballet studio, sat slumped in his chair while gesturing in the general direction of the pianist to begin playing for the class.

For presentation to Pina, I composed a figure of an incoherent, bored, and possibly hung-over ballet mistress. I selected from costume rails a pair of red patent shoes and a heavy full-length sealskin coat. The patent leather shoes had spilt open on the side and were a little too big so that I could not lift my feet and this of course, helped create my shuffle walk. My colleagues Antonio Carrallo and Benedict Billet had also an idea in response to "*Kinderballett*" and thought to set a scene where Antonio would act as a new pupil who copied Benedict in order to follow the exercises. Combining our ideas, the scene unfolded thus: Benedict and Antonio placed themselves in a corner of the *Lichtburg*. Dragging a chair, I entered and pulled my coat tightly around me to sit opposite the pair. I called out "*Plies*" and began counting the exercise in a monotonous barely audible voice. I was totally self-absorbed and only occasionally reminded Antonio to "pay attention." I remained oblivious to Benedict's diligent efforts and Antonio's growing disinterest. According to my notes, after we finished our scene Pina asked me to repeat my entrance walk with the chair. I recorded in addition, that my "back was slightly curved" and that "I was falling out of my shoes."[29]

On 7 March, in Rome, Pina set the *Aufgabe, Spüren von Etwas* (Traces of Something). I remembered a story about a flock of migratory birds that dive to their death mid-Atlantic, to a place that scientists assume existed before the land mass broke apart during last Ice Age.[30] My response to this task was verbal—no other theatrical form was needed. For the production, in part two of *Viktor*, Pina structured the scene *Kinderballett* followed by *Spüren von Etwas*, which had been renamed, *die Vögel* (The Birds), and as directed by Pina, I related the story in a voice devoid of emotion. Occasionally I repeated sentences or lost my place in the story as my attention was drawn to Antonio as he busied himself tying Benedict (who languished in *Arabesque* position) to the wall with strips of white linen.

Etwas Versteigern (Auction Something), an *Aufgabe* asked on 30 January was atypical in that it was not an open question but rather concerned an experience Pina had at an auction room in Rome, and she asked a number of us to recreate the tension and suspense of the event. I attempted a clipped, sharp, and very fast stream of text, and my effort was selected for the performance. The auction was eventually repeated in a number of different contexts of *Viktor*. Its first outing came after the opening scene when large pieces of furniture and smaller household items are carried briskly downstage and exhibited to the audience. In the second act, lap dogs in the form of three or four diverse breeds such as Pekinese, Shih-Tzu, and/or Chihuahua were sourced to be presented on the auctioneer's table upstage, and then walked or carried downstage to the audience. The auction was also staged in the production's final scene when the entire cast assembled onstage to sit on the floor and with legs outstretched and heads bowed, advance slowly downstage.

What I was trying to replicate in my enactment of an auction, an event that I had never attended, was the familiar sound of cattle auctions that were aired routinely on radio in the 1960s and 1970s by the national Irish radio, Raidió Éireann, I had always found the broadcaster's rapid-fire delivery captivating but incomprehensible. It seemed to have a secret dynamic code, but its repetitive rhythms and musical cadence, was alluring and mesmeric.

Ahnen. Ein Stück von Pina Bausch (*Ancestors. A Piece from Pina Bausch*) (1987)

In answer to the question from Pina "*A Dance from your Country*" in January 1987, I had an idea to do an Irish dance step, but as I had only very limited experience of traditional Irish dance from classes in school (among sixty other nine-year olds), I could only execute the most basic steps of a Reel. In the *Lichtburg* I unearthed a heavy black wool dress with a tight taffeta skirt that I thought would work well to inhibit my movements. I arranged a tartan scarf across one shoulder tied under my arm and attached a bunch of house keys to a safety pin and fastened it to my chest. The unorthodox image was completed by the addition of a hair net secured with clips. In the performance, I entered downstage with the Irish dance steps, the "side sevens" and "skips," and traversed the stage and then travelled over and back, repeating the sequence until two colleagues entered to lay me out on a stretcher and carry me offstage.

Tanzabend 11. Ein Stuck von Pina Bausch (*Dance Evening 11. A Piece from Pina Bausch*) (1991)

Kopf in den Sand stecken/ Stolz/ Ablenken/ Überlebenskünstler/ Seltsame Heilung/Zerbrechlich (Head in the sand/ Pride/ Distract/ Survival Artist/ Strange healing/ Fragile)

Tanzabend 11 marked Bausch's second international coproduction and was a partnership with *Festival de Otono de Madrid*. This was to be my final creation with Bausch and by that time the pattern of conscious creation of material was familiar, as were the challenges of the *Aufgaben* to delve deep and research sources. As my former colleague Barbara Kaufmann (nee Hampel) conceded: "[T]he word improvisation is not correct. We discover something, busy ourselves—we are searching. Sometimes it comes quickly, sometimes one works for a long time behind the mirror. Some themes are overwhelming."[31] From my own notes I recorded: "Every attempt has to be made to find form, either through dance or theatre. However, the notion of form, is not to be understood as a complicated or complex requirement, simplicity or refinement, were often more closely connected to the 'truth' of the endeavor." [32]

In response to *Überlebenskünstler* (Survival Artist), I re-created a ballet class scenario based on my experiences as a student of Molly Lake. Lake had studied with the Russian ballet master Serafina Astafieva, and with the Italian master Enrico Cecchetti, and had danced in the companies of Anna Pavlova and Markova-Dolin in England. She formed Ballet Continental with her husband Travis Kemp and toward the end of her career was ballet teacher at the London School of Contemporary Dance where Kemp was principal. Curiously, Lake taught class accompanied by Kemp. Lake directed the class, calling out the order of exercises and pacing the room to adjust a student's arm or give a correction, but she relied on Kemp to ensure that students heeded her comments. I asked Dominique Mercy to enact Kemp, and together we strolled around the rehearsal stage in Madrid in February of 1991 instructing our imaginary students. I re-created Lake with help of a blouse and a tight skirt to restrict my movement and wore high heels. Sometimes Mercy supported my elbow to indicate my fragility, while at other times he walked a little behind me to convey his subordinate role. He carried out my directives to the students sometimes demonstrating *port des bras* or pointing his feet to indicate that increased turnout was required. This scene was renamed "*Molly*" and in March and April in the *Lichtburg* was selected in various sequences with diverse other *Aufgaben* until it found its place in the second act of the production.

CONCLUSION

The details on *Aufgaben* I presented to Bausch give a brief account of a process of embodied research and they amount to a very small sample of the *Aufgaben* I presented to Bausch in answer to the hundreds of questions that she asked. The writing of the responses in advance of showing them to Pina underpins the emphasis on accuracy and the attention to detail of costume, gesture, position in space, the tempo of delivery of text and so on, in other words, the comprehensive record required so that material could be re-presented precisely when requested later in the rehearsal process. The arc of an *Aufgabe* response was thus a monitoring of an idea from its impulse and the work to convey that impulse into form. Integral to that (re)search is, I believe, that while the dancer's *Aufgabe* was to find the particular in one's culture, its presentation always demanded form to make sense to Bausch. The *Aufgaben* phase can thus be considered as an intrinsic part of an artistic process that illustrates what Gabriele Klein notes is the "paradox of translation." She writes that translation "is always also confronted with the paradoxical relationship between identity and difference. The paradox is that translation actually removes the difference, in other words, the translation should correspond with the original, and yet, at the same time, identity can only emerge from difference."[33]

Throughout my period of working with Pina the business of spending time with memory, and specifically tasked to do so during the *Aufgaben* phase, elicited a sustained period of formal reflection on the culture I came from and on my changing connection to that culture while living abroad. In answer to the question did I find Ireland while working with Pina, retrospectively I understand how I was, to quote Ninette de Valois, "a hoarder of matters Irish" as I actively researched Irish poetry and literature, history and current affairs excavating memory and revisiting experiences shaped to greater and lesser degrees by my upbringing.[34] Whether Ireland is to be found in Bausch's work is altogether another question. Perhaps the strongest flavor of Ireland in her work is a scene in the production *Auf dem Gebirge hat man ein Geschrei gehört. Ein Stück von Pina Bausch* (*On the Mountain a Cry was Heard. A Piece from Pina Bausch*) (1984) where Jean Francois Durore enters downstage left clutching a small shoebox to his chest. He sits on the earth-covered stage with his legs outstretched and removes something from his box. He lies down and places the item at his head. He then stands up and repeats the sequence marking the length and breadth of the stage. After a short period, Dominique Mercy joins Durore onstage. Mercy is shrouded in a black shawl and wearing a long skirt and carries a chair and a spade. With unsteady and hesitant steps Mercy arrives upstage and attempts to bury the chair. While Durore carefully measures the span of his body leaving traces on the dark earth, Mercy fails to conceal his chair. The scene is accompanied by a rendition of the traditional Irish lament *An Cailín Deas Crúite na mBó* (*The Young Girl Milking the Cow*) played by Irish piper Finbar Furey. Bausch, had never visited Ireland and to my knowledge, knew little of Ireland or her history, but for me, she captured a sense of Ireland in that scene of torturous sorrow, resignation, and resilience.

Leading protagonist of Wuppertal Tanztheater, Meryl Tankard noted of Bausch's rehearsal process that "[I]t was the first time a director had encouraged me [sic] to project my own personality on the stage and it opened up a whole new world."[35] I would concur that the evocation of one's autobiography was a singular experience—by turn stimulating, challenging, and uncomfortable. Not all *Aufgaben* were answered by all dancers, and Bausch is on record as acknowledging the courage required to stand up and show work.[36] Yet Bausch's *Aufgaben* can also be viewed as invitations to the dancer to invest in her creative process, which in my view led ultimately to the great sense of agency one experienced as contributor to that process, an agency also palpable in performances where one acted as "the locus of subjective presence" in the (re)creation of one's life experience.[37]

NOTES

1. *Pina Bausch und das Tanztheater* [*Pina Bausch and Tanztheater*], Kunst-und-Ausstellunghalle, Bonn, 4 March and 26 July 2016; Martin-Gropius-Bau, Berlin, 16 September 2016–9 January 2017.

2. Ciane Fernandes, *Pina Bausch and Tanztheater Wuppertal: The Aesthetics of Repetition and Transformation* (New York and London: Peter Lang, 2002). See Chapter 2, "The Creative Process," 25–34.

3. Interviewed by Jochen Schmidt in 1978, Bausch recalls that her training in Folkwangschule included scheduled improvisation hours. She clarifies: "But they weren't improvisations—instead one composed a little, made some dance and little studies. In any event I was one of those who was a little more active in this direction," in "Nicht wie sich Menschen bewegen, sondern was sie bewegt" ["Not how people move, but what moves them"] in *Pina Bausch Wuppertaler Tanztheater*: *Von Frühlingsopfer bis Kontakthof* [*Pina Bausch Wuppertaler Tanztheater: from Rite of Spring to Kontakthof*], eds., Hedwig Müller, Norbert Servos, Gert Weigelt (Köln: Ballett Bühnen-Verlag, 1979) 5–8. Reproduced in *O-Ton: Pina Bausch: Interviews und Reden* [*O-Ton: Pina Bausch: Interviews and Talks*], Stefan Koldehoff; Pina Bausch Foundation, Madelene Zuther eds. (Bonn: Pina Bausch Foundation, 2016), 38. (Translated Finola Cronin). Further interview citations may reference the interviews and talks by Pina Bausch collected in this publication.

4. Bausch's resistance to disclosing theme at the outset of her creative process is on record: "[W]hen I talk too much about it then I have already tainted it. I always have the feeling that I must protect it. I must also be silent about it, so that it is left untouched. I want the people to use their fantasy." Jochen Schmidt Interview 1978, in *O-Ton,* Koldehoff, Pina Bausch Foundation, Zuther, eds., 41. (Translated by Finola Cronin).

5. Fernandes, *Pina Bausch*, 26.

6. Gabriele Klein, "Practices of Translation in the Work of Pina Bausch and the Tanztheater Wuppertal," *Inheriting Dance: An Invitation from Pina*, Marc Wagenbach, Pina Bausch Foundation, eds. (Wuppertal: Pina Bausch Foundation, 2014), 26.

7. Klein, in Wagenbach, *Inheriting Dance* (Ibid.)

8. For further reading on reception to Bausch's work see *Pina Bausch Dance Theatre or The Art of Training a Goldfish:* by Norbert Servos (Cologne: Ballett-Bühnen-Verlag), 1984. For American reception to German Tanztheater and Pina Bausch's work see *The Drama Review* (TDR) vol 30, no. 2, 1986, 33–106.

9. Norbert Servos, "Pina Bausch: Dance and Emancipation," in *The Routledge Dance Studies Reader,* ed. Alexandra Carter (London: Routledge 1998), 42.

10. Hedwig Müller, "Ausdruckstanz" and the New German Dance Theatre in Germany," in *The Pina Bausch Sourcebook: The Making of Tanztheater*, ed. Royd Climenhaga (London & New York: Routledge, 2013). 19. Also note, Müller includes in her reference to *Tanztheater* aesthetic not only the work of Bausch but also works of her contemporaries Hans Kresnik, Susanne Linke, and Gerhardt Bohner.

11. Ibid. Quotation marks Müller.

12. Ibid.

13. Kurt Jooss, quoted by Müller, in Climenhaga, *Pina Bausch Sourcebook*, 15.

14. Susanne Schlicher, "Preface" in Fernandes, *Pina Bausch*, xvii.

15. Schlicher (Ibid.) Schlicher's description of Bausch's dramaturgy reveals the strong influence of Brecht on Bausch and indeed Servos signals this influence in his description of her works' non-linear and fragmentary scenes, juxtaposing of image, and ideas of estrangement where the familiar every day is isolated to appear strange. Servos, in Carter, *Dance Studies*, 36–45.

16. Pina Bausch Interview Edmund Gleede *". . . ich empfinde Menschen sehr stark,"* [*". . . I find people to be very strong"*] 1975. in *O-Ton,* Koldehoff, Pina Bausch Foundation, Zuther, eds., 24.

17. Mark Franko, "Five Theses on Laughter After All," in *Moving Words: Re-writing Dance*, ed. Gay Morris (London and New York: Routledge, 1996), 50.

18. Ibid. 52.

19. Pina Bausch, Interview Jochen Schmidt (1978) in *O-Ton*, Koldehoff, Pina Bausch Foundation, Zuther, eds., 37.

20. Pina Bausch, Interview Norbert Servos in *Pina Bausch Dance Theatre* by Norbert Servos (Munich: K. Kieser Verlag, 2008), 20.

21. Ramsay Burt, *Judson Dance Theater: Performative Traces* (London and New York: Palgrave Macmillan, 2006), 20–21.

22. Yvonne Rainer, "A Quasi Survey of some 'Minimalist' Tendencies in the Quantitatively Minimalist Dance Activity Midst the Plethora, or an Analysis of Trio A," in *Minimal Art: A Critical Anthology*, ed. Gregory Battcock (New York: E.P. Dutton and Co. Inc., 1968), 271.

23. Pina Bausch, Interview Jochen Schmidt (1978), in *O-Ton,* Koldehoff, Pina Bausch Foundation, Zuther, eds., 38.

24. Rainer used everyday movement and gesture but aimed to erase any aspect of emotional expression and most notably, repetition (see her seminal work *TRIO A*).

Bausch used everyday movement also but her work was expressive and presented micro-narratives in episodic structures. Bausch's choreography employed the use of repetition described as "serial repetition" in Burt, *Judson Dance Theatre*, 141.

25. Bausch acknowledges that the impulse for asking questions of her performers began with her production *Blaubart. Beim Anhören einer Tonbandaufnahme von Béla Bartóks Oper "Herzog Blaubarts Burg." Ein Stück von Pina Bausch* [*Bluebeard. While Listening to a Tape Recording of Béla Bartók's Opera "Duke Bluebeard's Castle." A Piece from Pina Bausch*] (1977), and was further explored in *Er nimmt sie an der Hand and fürht sie in das Schloß, die andern folgen* [*He takes her by the hand and leads her into the castle, the others follow*] (1978), a coproduction with Schauspielhaus Bochum. See *O-Ton*, "*Vorwort,*" in Koldehoff, Pina Bausch Foundation, Zuther, eds., 9. See also Pina Bausch Interview in Norbert Servos, *Pina Bausch* (2008), 239.

26. Pina Bausch, Interview Ruth Berghaus (1987), in *O-Ton*, Koldehoff, Pina Bausch Foundation, Zuther, eds., 92. See also Royd Climenhaga, *Pina Bausch: Routledge Performance Practitioners* (London: Routledge 2009), 11.

27. Valerie Preston-Dunlop & Ana Sanchez-Colberg, *Dance and the Performative: A Choreological Perspective: Laban and Beyond* (London: Verve Publishing, 2002), 9.

28. *Viktor*, *Fragen, Themen, Stichworte aus den Proben* [*Viktor, Questions, Themes, Cues from the Rehearsals*] by Raimund Hoghe, *Viktor. Ein Stück von Pina Bausch* Programme (Wuppertal: Wuppertaler Bühnen), 1986.

29. Rehearsal Notes *Viktor*, Finola Cronin Wuppertal, January–March, 1986.

30. The text accompanied a work of Rebecca Horn, *Der Spiegelbad* [*The Mirror Bath*] (1982). Exhibition: Rebecca Horn, Kunsthaus, Zürich, 11 June–24 July, 1983.

31. Barbara Kaufmann (nee Hampel), Interview Finola Cronin, Copenhagen, 10 August 1996, in Finola Cronin, *Dance in Time: A Perspective on the Rehearsal Process of Pina Bausch and Tanztheater Wuppertal* (Unpublished MA diss. University College Dublin, NUI, 1996), 51.

32. Finola Cronin, *Dance in Time* (Ibid.).

33. Klein, in Wagenbach, *Inheriting Dance*, 27.

34. Ninette de Valois, *Come Dance with Me* (London: Hamish Hamilton, 1959), 24.

35. Meryl Tankard quoted in Royd Climenhaga, *Pina Bausch: Routledge Performance*, 2009, 13.

36. Pina Bausch, Interview Eva-Elisabeth Fischer (1992), in *O-Ton*, Koldehoff, Pina Bausch Foundation, Zuther, eds., 160.

37. Climenhaga, *Sourcebook*, 2013, 113.

BIBLIOGRAPHY

Battcock, Gregory, ed., *Minimal Art: A Critical Anthology*. New York: E.P. Dutton and Co. Inc., 1968.

Bausch, Pina. *Viktor.* Wuppertal: Wuppertaler Bühnen Productions, 1986.

———. *Ahnen.* Wuppertal: Wuppertaler Bühnen Productions, 1987.

———. *Tanzabend 11.* Wuppertal: Wuppertaler Bühnen Productions, 1991.

Burt, Ramsay. *Judson Dance Theater: Performative Traces*. London and New York: Palgrave Macmillan, 2006.

Carter, Alexandra, ed., *The Routledge Dance Studies Reader.* London: Routledge, 1998.

Climenhaga, Royd. *Pina Bausch: Routledge Performance Practitioners.* London: Routledge, 2009.

Climenhaga, Royd, ed., *The Pina Bausch Sourcebook: The Making of Tanztheater*. London & New York: Routledge, 2013.

Cronin, Finola. *Dance in Time: A Perspective on the Rehearsal Process of Pina Bausch and Tanztheater Wuppertal.* Unpublished MA dissertation. Dublin: University College Dublin, National University of Ireland, 1996.

———. Rehearsal Notes, *Viktor,* 1986. (unpublished)

Fernandes, Ciane. *Pina Bausch and Tanztheater Wuppertal: The Aesthetics of Repetition and Transformation.* New York and London: Peter Lang, 2002.

Hoghe, Raimund. *Viktor Program*, Wuppertal: Wuppertal Bühnen, 1986.

Koldehoff, Stefan, Pina Bausch Foundation, and Marlene Zuther, eds., *O-Ton: Pina Bausch: Interviews und Reden*, Bonn: Pina Bausch Foundation, 2016.

Morris, Gay, ed., *Moving Words: Re-writing Dance.* London and New York: Routledge, 1996.

Müller, Hedwig, Norbert Servos, and Gert Weigelt. *Pina Bausch Wuppertaler Tanztheater*: *Von Frühlingsopfer bis Kontakthof.* Koln: Ballett Bühnen-Verlag, 1979.

Preston-Dunlop, Valerie, and Ana Sanchez-Colberg. *Dance and the Performative: A Choreological Perspective Laban and Beyond.* London: Verve Publishing, 2002.

Servos, Norbert. *Pina Bausch Dance Theatre.* Munich: K. Kieser Verlag, 2008.

Valois, de, Ninette. *Come Dance with Me.* London: Hamish Hamilton, 1959.

Wagenbach, Marc, Pina Bausch Foundation, eds., *Inheriting Dance: An Invitation from Pina*. Wuppertal: Pina Bausch Foundation, 2014.

PART II

Chapter Seven

Samuel Beckett, Kleist, and Oskar Schlemmer

Choreographing in Prose, Drama, and Television

Susan Jones

Throughout his career, Samuel Beckett's interest in human motion underscored the activities of the subjects of his prose and the protagonists of his plays. Always alert to the philosophies of human mobility and the traditions of physical theatre, Beckett incorporated into his work responses to a variety of philosophical ideas focusing on the relationship between the mechanical and the human as well as aspects of theatre related to puppetry, mime, and *commedia dell'arte*. The knock-about comedy of *Godot*, the painful progressions of *Molloy*, and the "funambulistic staggering" of *Watt* attest to this preoccupation with the possibilities, as well as the trials and limitations, of activity and physical disability behind the impulse to "go on." However, in the late work a more intensive focus on the design and patterning of movement reveals in Beckett a distinctive choreographic sensibility. In this essay I shall first explore one of the ways in which Beckett develops this choreographic texture in the late TV play, *Quadrat I and II* (1981). During the later works, Beckett sometimes illustrates a striking commonality with formalist choreographic innovations of the early twentieth century emerging from German *Ausdruckstanz* (expressionist dance), and in one particular instance, his dance play *Quadrat I and II* demonstrates an extraordinary affinity with the work of Bauhaus director Oskar Schlemmer. In this work Beckett uncannily shares with Schlemmer the philosophical underpinning and choreographic patterning of one of the *Bauhaus Dances*, *Raumtanz* (Space Dance, 1926). The common ground for Schlemmer and Beckett's later drama lies in a source of inspiration provided by Heinrich von Kleist's 1810 essay, "Über das Marionettentheater." Yet this was not the only source for Beckett's turn to the choreographic in his later years. In the second half of the chapter I shall show how his dance play was not an isolated exception but a development emerging from the prose of the 1960s and 1970s in which Beckett had explored the possibilities of limited physical movement defined by the configurations of geometricized spatial forms. In this respect Beckett reflects the geometrical design of early *danse d'école*, where the human body, placed at the center of an imaginary sphere, positions her/himself and moves always in relation to its circumscribed form.

KLEIST'S MARIONETTE

Beckett first read Kleist's 1810 essay when he began directing his own plays in the 1970s. "Über das Marionettentheater" constitutes a dialogic discourse on the relationship of self-consciousness and grace[1]. From the perspective of literary studies, Kleist's importance as a figure of German literature related principally to his contribution to drama and to the Romantic movement. Nevertheless, Kleist frequently subverted clichéd assumptions about Romanticism, introducing skeptical and paradoxical strategies to his exploration of human subjectivity, focusing on moments of individual doubt and crisis. In exploring a variety of generic forms, including poetry, novels, short stories, and essays that discussed matters of aesthetics, psychology, and metaphysics, Kleist showed the range of his reading of contemporary philosophers such as Kant, Fichte, and Schelling. In the Marionette essay Kleist illustrated his theme through the use of a Platonic dialogue in which an unnamed, dramatized narrator gives the example of the puppet as the perfect exponent of grace in dance. The essay consists of a conversation between the narrator and Herr C, a professional dancer, who discuss the implications of three anecdotes that illustrate the way in which self-consciousness impedes the expression of natural grace. Kleist's structural economy masks a highly complex presentation of a theme that had been treated by Schiller in his discussion of "Gracefulness and Dignity" (1793) as a moral issue, one that may in turn be analyzed as a Romantic response to Kant's aesthetics, in which Schiller attempted to shift the subjectivist turn in Kant to "regain an objective notion of the beautiful."[2] Kleist's rhetorical strategy, however, generates an ironic distancing between narrator and authorial position. While Herr C privileges the mechanized grace of the puppet, he leaves open the status of the puppet master who ultimately controls the technology.[3]

Kleist became especially important to Beckett during the later stages of his career, when he turned to directing his own plays. He had received Kleist's essay from the actress Nancy Illig in 1969 and it struck a chord with Beckett's envisioning of how his plays should be performed.[4] James Knowlson remarks on the choreographic style for the late plays, which coincided with Beckett's role as director: "When [Beckett] came to direct his own plays in the 1960s and 1970s, he brought to his task the intense concentration and meticulous precision of the choreographer."[5] Beckett's response to Kleist's essay influenced considerably the tenor of his instructions to actors, and he frequently recommended that they read it.

Beckett would, however, have encountered the essay's themes of self-consciousness and grace through his reading of Kleist's philosophical predecessors, such as Kant and Schiller, and his interest in movement also stems from his knowledge of French traditions and Cartesian philosophy. Of particular interest was his reading of Arnold Geulincx's philosophy, whose focus on the body as machine may have influenced the composition of the early novel *Murphy* (1938).[6] Kleist's Marionette essay later supplemented the ideas drawn from these earlier philosophical discussions. Kleist's perspective on the philosophical problem of the relationship between human movement and self-consciousness gave rise to many literary and choreographic responses to the movement of the puppet. One could surmise that Beckett had in part absorbed Kleist's ideas unknowingly through his spectatorship of revivals of the Ballets Russes' 1911 production of *Petrouchka* in 1934 and 1935 in London, during the time in which he was completing *Murphy* (the narrator observes that Murphy's heart was "all that a heart should be. Buttoned up and left to perform, it was like Petrouchka in his box.")[7] Petrouchka, of course, suffers a tragic demise having been granted the "gift" of self-consciousness by the Showman. But the full impact of Kleist's essay entered Beckett's later career when he used it as a rehearsal guide for actors. When directing the actress Katherine Schultz for the part of Winnie (*Happy Days*) in Berlin in 1971, Beckett concentrated on "the rhythm and timing of her movements," even "quoting Kleist's essay on the marionette theatre to reinforce his argument . . . that precision and economy would produce the maximum grace."[8]

Beckett's shift to choreographic design as the focus of the dramatic event appeared in his TV play *Ghost Trio* (1975), and he turned to the Kleist essay when rehearsing with Ronald Pickup in this work. According to Knowlson, on this occasion Beckett quoted the passage from the essay in which Herr C gives the example of the bear fencing more effectively with his paw than the human with his rapier. The creature without self-awareness responds unselfconsciously to the fencer's movements and is not deceived by false passes. The bear's movements are in addition achieved with the strictest economy and maximum grace. Knowlson, who was present at this exchange, writes that Beckett applied Kleist's example to the figure F in *Ghost Trio* "as he moves to the window or the door, or looks up from the pallet to the mirror":

> From the two different kinds of movement in the play, one sustained, economical, and flowing, the other abrupt and jerky as "F" "thinks he hears her," it is as if Beckett's figure is poised midway between two worlds. For his "man in a room" is still, in spite of everything a creature bound to a world of matter, not quite the still-life figure that at moments he appears to be. Nor is he totally free of self-consciousness, as his look in the mirror indicates, or wholly indifferent to the world of the nonself, as his responses to stimuli from outside or from within his own mind suggest.[9]

The dual quality of the figure's movement looks back to Beckett's reference in *Murphy*, to the two gestural extremes of the Petrouchkan figure—the languid and the hysterical—the enclosed figure torn between the unselfconsciousness of the puppet and the self-awareness of his human incarnation. Unlike Petrouchka, the figure of *Ghost Trio* manifests these extremes of physical being within the context of a far sparer modernist aesthetic. In fact, the choreography seems most acutely to illustrate the figure's hovering between seemingly distinct realms, between hyper-awareness and unselfconsciousness. Beckett represents the distinction most effectively without the use of language, instead using qualitative shifts in the human body's movement in relation to the distinctive rhythmic divisions it creates within time and space. Before he sees himself in the mirror, the protagonist of *Ghost Trio* thus shows the lack of self-consciousness advocated by Kleist in the puppet's movement.

In his advice to actors, Beckett drew from Kleist's essay the expression of some of his most profound aesthetic principles. As C. J. Ackerley and S. E. Gontarski have observed, by comparing the human dancer with the marionette, Kleist suggests the superiority of the latter because it is "lacking in self-awareness and affectation, which destroy natural grace and charm." Thus the essay offers a "thesis on self-consciousness and motion whereby the presence of the one destroys the dynamics of the other."[10] But the ambiguity of Kleist's authorial position, achieved through the ironic positioning of the two voices of his dialogue, leaves open a further possibility, that of "going through" consciousness in order to reach once more a pre-lapsarian state. In performance dance terms, one might think here of the studied naturalness of Isadora Duncan and many other exponents of modern dance whose movement styles suggest pure spontaneity but reveal highly crafted choreographic effects. In Kleist's essay, the image of the puppet as perfect example of grace suggests a somewhat counterintuitive theory, yet it demonstrates a paradox of subjectivity encountered by the trained dancer. In Kleist's picture the human dancer would have to be disciplined in such a way as to eliminate conscious thought. To some extent this is what a number of specialized dance techniques aim for: the physical body is trained through repetitive action so that the mind's response to muscular activity becomes intuitively focused on a gravitational center in the way that Kleist described the puppet. The practitioner is not in an unselfconscious state but achieves something much closer to what Herr C envisions as the skillful puppet master's alignment of his own body with that of the puppet's center of gravity. Beckett requires something similar of his actors. In a demonstration of the Kleistian paradox, the actor conveys the nature of the curse of self-consciousness.

Yet the Beckettian actor draws on a physical discipline that is in itself paradoxical, requiring a highly self-conscious effort to "think oneself into the habitual" so that to some degree she/he stylizes habitual movement in order to show unselfconscious action. Beckett's later interpretation of Kleist helps to explain a shift from his interest in the pathos and threatening gestures of puppet-like movement in *Godot* and *Endgame* toward the bare abstraction contained in the rhythm, pace, and geometry of mechanical movement in his later work.

OSKAR SCHLEMMER (1888–1943)

Of all the choreographies associated with Kleist's essay, the work of the Bauhaus architect, designer, painter, and choreographer Oskar Schlemmer most strikingly anticipates the mathematical precision of Beckett's treatment of the moving figure in his late work. Oskar Schlemmer provided one of the most original responses to *Ausdruckstanz*. Schlemmer was principally associated

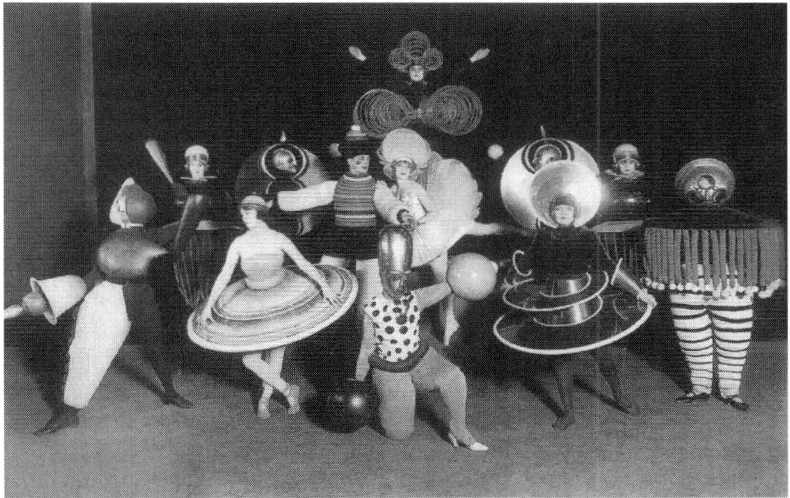

Figure 7.1. Costumes by Oskar Schlemmer (Bauhaus) for *Triadisches Ballett*, at Metropol-Theater in Berlin. Photograph by Ernst Schneider, 1926 © Getty Images.

with the Bauhaus but had initially been born in Stuttgart, where he trained as a painter, moving into sculpture, design, and architecture for a time before adding dramaturgy and choreography to his interests. Schlemmer joined the Bauhaus in Weimar in 1920. This avant-garde arts institution, established by Walter Gropius in 1919, embraced a whole range of visual arts, although theatre had not been part of its original manifesto. But a theatre workshop was established in 1921 and a theatre quickly became central to Paul Klee's design for the building, which was eventually created when the institution moved to Dessau. "Bau und Buhne" (building and stage) was the title of his original drawing for the architectural plans. Thus, from its inception the Bauhaus theatre productions incorporated a strong element of design and costuming, reflecting the talents of the visual artists who ran it. Schlemmer's interests in the theatre lay in the exploration of human form in space and time, which explains his turn to choreography.

Schlemmer became a director of the Bauhaus theatre, a position he held from 1923 to 1929, but in 1922 he had already created *Das Triadische Ballett* (Triadic Ballet), an extraordinarily innovative dance work illustrating his philosophical theories about human form and art.[11] Schlemmer incorporated ballet into this work perhaps because the puppet-like movement of his figures could most easily be expressed though its symmetrical forms. The dancers were clad in highly constructed, technologically daring costumes and masks made out of materials such as wire and plastics, reflecting his interests in abstract design and puppet-like forms as well as his responses to modernity and the industrial age. Schlemmer's figures created a drama of conflict between the subject's apparent absence (hidden behind the elaborate costume) and his or her humanity (revealed through gestures and movements). Above all, he emphasized the mathematical disposition of the bodies in space and the rhythms with which they moved. In this ballet Schlemmer showed the human figure as art object but revealing his or her humanity and grace in spite of a puppet-like concealment.[12]

Schlemmer's chief literary influences included Kleist's "Über das Marionettentheater" (1810), and the British dramaturge Edward Gordon Craig's important essay on the "Über-Marionette" (1908), which had also been inspired by Kleist. As we have seen, Kleist's essay debates the question of whether the ballerina, subject to self-consciousness, can attain grace in her movements. Schlemmer was inspired by the skeptical strategies employed by Kleist but also informed by Gordon Craig, who, drawing on Kleist, claimed that "If you could make your body into a machine . . . and *if* it could obey you in every movement for the entire space of time it was before the audience . . . you would be able to make a work of art out of that which is in you."[13] Ernst Scheyer observes that Schlemmer had built on a dance "vision" first initiated in 1912, with the addition of two major elements: "One is the mechanical-technological, a fusion of the ideas of Kleist's puppet theatre and the devices of constructivism. The other is a metaphysical humor, not very different from that of Paul Klee."[14] Schlemmer's dance forms were often identified with *Ausdruckstanz* because they showed the ways in which the human spirit and expression prevails in spite of being encased in the restrictive materials of modern technology in experimental costumes and masks, and in spite of being limited by strict, puppet-like or mechanical movements, often based on ballet technique.

By situating Schlemmer's work as part of the complex theoretical and historical moments in which *Ausdruckstanz* developed, we find that expressionism incorporated several Romantic philosophical perspectives on the idea of grace that we traditionally associate, as we saw above, with the discipline of ballet. Elements of Schiller's discussion of grace endured in modern dance at the same time as the moral idea of grace emerged in modern depictions of the practice of ancient Greek dance, where harmony of the body and mind is an aid to achieving a state of physical and spiritual "grace." But the graceful expression of the human body in this period lies in tension with the recovery of its Nietzschean, atavistic side—its overt propulsion of rhythms, ungainly leaping, and gestures reaching beyond a rational geometric enclosure of movement based on a center point of human equilibrium. Kleist's perspective, giving rise to skeptical literary and choreographic responses throughout the nineteenth and twentieth centuries, posed the question of whether a state of grace is humanly possible, whether self-consciousness prevents the achievement of grace, and whether this situation may be seen as a curse, a playful conundrum, or as a center of the puppet-master's control over the mechanized object. *Ausdruckstanz*, with its inclusive shift in focus from dance to many forms of movement, thus facilitated new ways of representing important issues of modernity in dance and literature.

SCHLEMMER'S RAUMTANZ AND BECKETT'S QUAD

Beckett saw Schlemmer's art work when he was in Dresden in the 1930s and was introduced to Dresden intellectuals by the dancer Gret Palucca. Palucca had known Schlemmer as Bauhaus director and was familiar with his choreographic work, but Schlemmer's dance experiments had ceased to be performed by the 1930s and Beckett would not have seen a performance of his choreography at that time. Yet Beckett's late work, especially the television dance play *Quadrat I and II* (1981, originally entitled *Quad*)—where four hooded figures enter and exit a suspended square, moving in predetermined patterns and never engaging in dialogue—shows a distinct affinity with Schlemmer's choreography, a conceptual link that occurs through their common assimilation of Kleist. In his *Bauhaus Dances* (1926), Schlemmer drew principally on the theories of Kleist's marionette essay. Beckett's role as director of his own work shows the way in which Kleist's theories influenced his ideas about the movement of actors onstage. The economy and movement patterns of Schlemmer's *Bauhaus Dances* demonstrates an uncanny correspondence with Beckett's dance play, prompting the speculation that Schlemmer provided an actual source for Beckett's play.

A revival of interest in Schlemmer's dance work occurred between the 1960s and 1980s in Europe and the United States. A reconstruction of the *Triadic Ballet* (1922) and *Bauhaus Dances* (1926) by the British scholar Margaret Hastings was performed in Germany and a filmed version appeared on German TV in 1968 (in German and English versions), not long after Beckett had returned to Berlin to rehearse a German production of *Endgame*. Of further interest may be the fact that Beckett produced *Quadrat I and II* in Stuttgart, where Schlemmer initially trained and where the Schlemmer archives are in part housed. Then, in 1982, the same year as the transmission of *Quadrat I and II*, Debra McCall's reconstruction of *Bauhaus Dances* were first performed in New York. The conceptual affinities between Schlemmer's dances and Beckett's late work are suggested by the geometric precision of the choreography's design, in the figures' physical placement in the stage space, and in the similarity of their philosophical impulses and generic forms. It seems that when Beckett was commissioned to produce a work for the Süddeutschen Rundfunk in Stuttgart he drew on an aesthetic that had marked the city's association with twentieth-century traditions of contemporary dance and theatre.[15]

Bauhaus Dances (1926) still looks startlingly "contemporary" today, and one dance in particular, *Space Dance* (Raumtanz), seems uncannily to anticipate Beckett's *Quadrat I and II*. In *Space Dance*, three figures move around a grid that has been outlined on the stage, dividing the space into quadrants and triangles, with lines intersecting at the center. The figures are encased in padded all-over suits, color-coded red, blue, and yellow, with blank, circular masks to cover the face, the only decoration suggested by two circular eye-holes. The figures traverse the lines of the grid in mathematically precise divisions of movement—one striding, one walking, one running, always following the triangular patterns of the grid. They never meet at the center, always narrowly missing each other. Schlemmer explores the notion of human encounters and the relationship between the human body and the stage space in terms of mathematical design, and the mechanical and rhythmical workings of the physical body. He interrogates the way in which generic distinctions are created physically in drama as comedy, pathos, and anger and examines how they are produced, not only through the quality of movement on the grid and the appearance of the figures—which are sometimes disturbing, at other times endearing—but also through the mathematical precision of the figures' movement, which creates either the tragic isolation or the comic near-collision of the figures in space. As Schlemmer himself observed, "human consciousness lies behind the mechanical figure"[16]: behind the abstraction of the presentation lies the unavoidable humanity of the protagonist.

In Beckett's *Quadrat I and II*, the marked-out grid only appears as a diagram in manuscript notes; on the TV screen the lines are not drawn on the stage as in *Space Dance*. But within the frame of the TV screen the unblemished "quad" appears suspended in space, and the protagonists move along imaginary straight lines intersecting at the center. Each figure completes a prescribed trajectory, always appearing and disappearing at the limits or corners of the quad. But rather than following the triadic geometry of Schlemmer's *Space Dance*, in which three figures appear and move around the triangles drawn on the floor, Beckett explores in *Quadrat* the figural relationships associated with placing the triangular paths of four figures within the spatial patterning of the "quad." Four slightly hunched figures dressed in robes with cowls covering their head suggest the hypocrites in canto 23 of Dante's *Inferno* (in *Quadrat I* each figure's cloak is a different color—red, blue, yellow, white). They shuffle around the grid, each step following a precise mathematical and rhythmic division of pace. The figures move, like Schlemmer's, in triangular paths that traverse the square, each appearing successively until four occupy the space, then one by one moving off the quad at one of the corners into darkness. Each figure turns left at the center (like the occupants of the *Inferno* as they spiral downwards) and, as in *Space Dance*, near collisions ensue as the numbers of moving figures on the grid increase and then diminish.

For the original *Quad* Beckett intended the sequence to occur once only, the piece to be filmed in color and performed to a score for percussion. But then Beckett decided to repeat the sequence in black and white, the movements performed to a metronome beat rather than to the percussive sounds of the first sequence. Thus in the final version, *Quadrat I and II*, Beckett had the sequence shot twice, once in color and once in black and white, where the figures in their hooded cloaks most closely resemble Gustave Doré's 1861 illustrations for the hypocrites of the *Inferno* (widely popularized in the early twentieth century). The colors are reduced from four to two, the score reduced to its absolute basic rhythmical component, so that the sound which had filled the space in *I* is replaced by the double "to and fro" beat of the metronome in *II*. Thus the numerical paring down of four to its square root suggests, in visual and auditory terms, the logical economy of form to which Beckett strove.

Beckett's manuscript drawings and textual instructions for the figures' movement in *Quadrat I and II* resemble Schlemmer's designs for his *Bauhaus Dances* with their figures placed in the center of a complex geometrical pattern on a grid.[17] But Schlemmer's work may have provided a late allusion in a series of sources for Beckett's play. According to Anna McMullan, Beckett's 1981 dance play did not appear *ex nihilo* (and in the next section we will discuss Beckett's interest in geometry in the "Residua"). McMullan makes a striking case for Beckett's never completed "J. M. Mime" (1963) as precursor of his televisual experimentation in *Quadrat I and II.* She claims that although the earlier mime is based on the idea of the quincunx taken from Sir Thomas Browne and others, the first geometric diagrams for this piece "anticipate the plotted movements and playing area of *Quad.*"[18] Her idea is of some interest here because it suggests the longer gestation for this TV piece in an idea which might have been rekindled in the wake of a resurgence of scholarly interest in Schlemmer's work in the late 1960s and before Beckett turned to the medium of television with *Ghost Trio* (1975). Gontarski, Knowlson, and others have associated the scenario of "J. M. Mime" with the two published mimes, *Act Without Words I* and *II*, both of which place human bodies in a severely restricted environment. However, McMullan observes that

> in "J. M. Mime," there are no specified gestures in the first pages of the manuscript—it is the movement patterns and the possible routes which are sketched out. Beckett therefore resorts to text, first dialogue and then monologue, and the interplay between text and *mise en scene*, to present a sense of the subjectivity of the players and their confinement within the rules of the structure they inhabit (completely transformed into physical and visual text in the mimes).[19]

McMullan suggests that through the medium of television, Beckett found a way to overcome this "disjunction between the abstract formality of the geometric moves . . . and the textual dialogue/monologue that led to the abandonment of 'J. M. Mime.'" McMullan also shows how *Quad* retrieves from the earlier piece "the concepts of the square playing area and the movement along the sides and towards the center, the major difference is that the midpoint 'O' which creates the quincunx in 'J. M. Mime,' is (a)voided as a 'danger zone.'"[20] In fact, one could argue that Beckett did not ultimately abandon the disjunction between geometric patterning and the corporeality of the speaking figures but instead refined it in *Quadrat I and II*, creating a far greater intensity of dramatic "affect" as the figures' willed propulsion to follow the geometric pattern at every moment promises to end in (but always avoids) violent confrontation at the center. In this respect one might argue that Schlemmer's *Space Dance* provides the interim choreographic development between "J. M. Mime" and *Quadrat I and II.*

Beckett's exploration of genre in this piece also resembles aspects of Schlemmer's enquiry, where the movement of the figures creates a shift between the extremes of comedy and tragedy. Yet Beckett's figures suggest a far bleaker and more menacing trajectory. Beckett had described the center of the quad as "a danger zone," so that while at first the shuffling figures tend to generate laughter in the viewer, the tension increasingly builds toward terror as the moving figures relentlessly repeat their endless shuffling, their dogged avoidance of the central point building an atmosphere of near hysteria until, one by one the figures leave the space and all that remains is the emptiness of the suspended square.

BECKETT'S SHORT PROSE: "RESIDUA"

The late TV play *Quadrat I and II* appears in some ways to be the terminus of Beckett's debt to Kleist, and in this work the connection to Oskar Schlemmer as a source for this play arises from the two artists' shared interest in Kleist. However, in order to extend our understanding of Beckett's late play it is useful to establish neglected aspects of Beckett's earlier presentation of geometricized forms containing a precisely choreographed body in the prose experiments of the 1960s, and the way in which these offered interim sketches for the highly pared-down dramatization of "going on" and its relationship to the imagining of last things in his one dance play. I shall focus here on the "Residua," a group of texts written and often abandoned and rewritten in new forms across the 1960s and 1970s, in which I believe Beckett turns to the choreographic to negotiate a "dead end" in prose-writing.[21] In a curious way, Beckett's focus on the geometric positioning and pacing of figures of these texts recalls the geometrical order and patterning of *danse d'école* of the sixteenth and seventeenth centuries (the antecedent of "traditional" ballet), when the textual evidence of dance notation shows the classical patterning of early modern and baroque dance. Given Beckett's interest in the discussions of human movement and mechanical "grace" in the seventeenth-century Cartesian philosophy of Geulincx, the analogy is not quite as far-fetched as it might seem.

Mark Nixon identifies this discrete period of experimentation in Beckett's prose writing. He observes how Beckett initiated a series of short texts in 1964 "that concentrates on the workings of the imagination in order to construct geometrically defined 'closed spaces,' in which human figures are placed or rather arranged." These came to represent what Beckett often referred to as "residual" pieces, and all focus on an imagining of the human figure trapped within the limitations of a geometrically constructed space. Nixon observes, "The opening of the English extract [of *Faux Départs*] is a version of material found in *All Strange Away*, while the three French extracts anticipate *Imagination morte imaginez* and 'Imagination Dead Imagine' in its English translation (1965)."[22] Nixon concludes that the brief passages of *Faux Départs* suggest the initiation of what would become stages in a new kind of experimentation, giving rise also to texts such as *The Lost Ones*, *Ping*, and *Lessness*. For most critics, the focus of these texts lies in what David Watson calls their constant reopening "their site of representation, disrupting its totality" and that to "talk of the texts as merely representing something is to ignore the ritualistic processes of textual repetition, the process of performativity, the linguistic performance of the body in relation to desire and language, its dialectical relationship to the subject positions it adopts and refuses."[23]

In order to explore this kind of "play of the text" with ritualistic and performative processes, it is useful to identify how Beckett drew on specific aesthetic tools for this group of prose pieces. One area of inspiration stemmed from his enduring interest in mathematics (and in this respect Beckett resembles the Cartesian philosophers' predilection for the abstraction of geometry). Yet the evidence of Beckett's letters as well as manuscript diagrams of works such as *Film*, *Ghost Trio*, or *Quad* confirms that the mathematical aspect of his experimentation with form worked in tandem with a concern for the choreographic and the choreographed body. On the reverse side of a letter of 22 September 1964 to Barbara Bray, Beckett drew a series of diagrams which the editors of the 1957–1965 volume consider to be "a schematic of body positions, presented with permutations."[24] These drawings seem to be related to the text of *Le Dépeupleur*, which was not published until 1970. But the drawings confirm Beckett's earlier preoccupation with spatial geometry and with the potential limitations of body position and movement when the figure is placed at the center of an imaginary circle or square (three inches by three inches). In fact, such problems of the body's positioning in space has occupied choreographers since classical times (and pre-historical times too), and what is striking about Beckett's enquiry is the proximity of the nature of his exploration to a long history of the relations of geometry and dance theory.

Beckett's focus on mathematics throughout his work has been explored thoroughly by Chris Ackerley in "Samuel Beckett and Mathematics." Ackerley shows the depth and variety of Beckett's uses of geometry, algebra, and arithmetic throughout his work, and in all genres. In relation to the short texts under discussion here, Ackerley shows how "the mathematical metaphor which dominates the later works is that of the mind turning to measurement as the memory fades."[25] However, I would argue that Beckett's particular form of experimentation in this period, closely related to his use of precise mathematical calibration, expresses mathematics as a contemplation of the movement of the body, thus marking a significant turn to the choreographic. This kind of choreography is not so much associated with the music-hall comedy turns of *Godot* (although mathematical dispositions of space can be found there too), but a far more abstract, stylized form. The imagining of the designed movement of figures, not just the positioning of them, within the confines of a geometrically constructed space, and an imagining of such movement as a mathematically calibrated form of action, executed with absolute precision of pace and rhythm, constitutes an important aspect of Beckett's representation of the subject in all these works.

Two examples suffice to show the turn to choreographic specificity as the body is placed in limited or restricted spaces. Part 4 of *Faux Départs* (in English) anticipates the title of a later piece in its first line, "Imagination Dead Imagine," also containing material to be found in *All Strange Away* (published 1976), but here it specifically announces the first of a number of preoccupations of this period of prose-writing. It describes a place in which the narrative voice (described in *All Strange Away* as "a last person") positions a dying figure between alternating moments of darkness and light: "A closed space five foot square by six high" (70). The voice later imagines him (the dying man) not simply positioned in stillness in this cuboid, but also in action: "Try as well as sitting standing, walking, kneeling, crawling, lying, creeping, in the dark and the light" (70). The infinity of this place of limbo is imagined as an excruciating, unending juxtaposition of movement and stasis: "Say a lifetime of walking crouched and drawing himself up when brought to a stand" (70).

All Strange Away echoes the opening of Part 4 of *Faux Départs*, which in turn grew out of "Fancy Dying." This "elliptical text," as Nixon puts it, responds to the fourth *Faux Départ* and was abandoned early in 1965 but finished in 1973 for a limited edition published in 1976. Nixon encapsulates concisely its place in the Beckett prose texts of this period, claiming it "represents the first in a series in which objects and figures are arranged and rearranged in confined spaces with mathematical precision. It deliberates on the conditions inside the entombed place, paying detailed attention to temperature, lighting and dimensions, as well as to the relationship between silence and sounds, and between degrees of whiteness. The language is minimal, estranged, sparse, yet suggestive."[26]

What is also striking about this piece is how it shifts between the dimensions of distinctive geometrically constructed spaces (moving between cuboid, cube, and rotunda), and how the minimal actions of male/female imagined figures are precisely choreographed to reflect the repetition of movement within a restricted environment. These movements are not simply indicated in a general sense by a series of present participles as in the fourth *Faux Départ*: "sitting, standing, walking, kneeling, crawling, lying, creeping" (73); or by describing the psychological effect and quality of action and situation: "Falling on his knees in the dark to murmur, no sound, Fancy is his only hope" (74). Beckett further articulates in longhand the equivalent of a passage of dance notation that exactly represents the nuance of a piece of choreography with directional, spatial, and temporal indicators and a sense of body weight and transfer of weight between limbs. First he situates the main figure: "The back of the head touches the ceiling, say a lifetime of standing bowed" (74). But, noting the directional value of the description (Beckett's use of the word *deasil*, meaning clockwise, from the Gaelic, indicates positive qualities, adding an ironic flavor to the account), the geometrical detailing of first the cuboid of diminishing dimensions, then of a rotunda, enables precise location and positioning of characters: "Call floor angles deasil, a, b, c and d and ceiling likewise e, f, g and h, say Jolly at b and Draeger at d, lean him for rest with head at a and head at g, in dark and light" (74). Likewise a suggestion of movement from position to position is mathematically constructed in this tightly limited space: "For nine and nine eighteen that is four feet and more across in which to kneel, arse on heels, hands on thighs, trunk best bowed and crown on ground. And even sit, knees drawn up, trunk best bowed, head between knees, arms round knees to hold all together" (75). Here we sense how the weight is distributed through the seated figure and how the energy driving the clasping of arms keeps the body in this position. Next, the excruciating positioning of two figures lying down head to toe with knees drawn up and constantly shifting with discomfort through four possible configurations captures the kinesthetic actuality of the situation: "And even lie, arse to knees say diagonal arc, feet say at d, head on left cheek at b. . . . So on other four possibilities when begin again" (75).

A female figure, named in the text as Emma, is both present and not present, here in the story and imagined in the mind of the narrator, the erotic memories/imaginings of a lover interpolated into the tortured restriction of the figure's environment. Later in the piece the focus turns to narrative flashes revealing this female figure repeating a stylized movement in an increasingly shrinking space, which has become a rotunda. The narratorial un-anchoring of the voice from its text, the prose's un-anchoring of itself from conventional grammatical phrase, its punctuation within and outside conventional sense, creates a constantly dizzying dialectical effect, simultaneously combining hard-edged mathematical precision and poetic lyricism in an image of physical discomfiture and choreographed expressiveness. Thus when the cube first shrinks in size we have the practical account, "Call floor angles deasil a, b, c, and d and in here Emma lying on her left side, arse to knees along diagonal db with arse toward d and knees towards b though neither at either because too short and waste space here too some reason yet to be imagined" (77). But then the description of the pose is shortly followed by moments of poetic intensity interpolated into a lighting plot: "Slow fade of ivory flesh when ebb ten seconds and gone. Long black hair when light strewn over face and adjacent floor. Uncover right eye and cheekbone vivid white for long black lashes when light." Her restricted movement is choreographed: "Left hand clinging to right shoulder ball, right more faint loose fist on ground till fingers tighten as though to squeeze, imagine later, then loose again and still any length, so on. Murmuring, no sound, though say lips move with faint stir of hair" (77).

The situation is repeated, this time imagined within the even greater restriction of a rotunda. With repeated pose, at first the woman's concertina-d shape is described as lying on the floor "arse wedged against wall at c and knees wedged against wall ab a few inches from face and feet wedged against wall bc a few inches from arse" (82), but now the choreographic description is enhanced so precisely we can envision the stylized simplicity of her self-embrace, "left hand most clear and womanly lightly clasping right shoulder ball so lightly that slip from time to time down slope of right upper arm then back up to clasp, right no less on upper outer right knee lightly clasping" (82). The articulation of the embodied figure, whose minimalist gestures are restricted by the space, is conveyed in the language of mathematical precision and the driest of tones, but whispers of lyricism leak out of the description, a hint of expressiveness in the "lightly slip from time to time down the slope," "the lightly clasping" hand—the language of poetry breaking through in the hand movements' suggestion of a sigh, just as, in a later piece the pure poeticism of *Lessness* (1969), in "the blue celeste of poesy" (132), seeps through the tortuous situation and apparent fixity of certain moments in a movement toward the end.

In the TV play *Quadrat I and II* (1981) Beckett to some extent pushes the ideas of these prose pieces to their furthest development, this time *dramatizing* through precise and repetitive pacing a hellish scenario of perpetual movement at the end of time in a "ballet" of mathematical configurations. Again Ackerley explains that *Quad* integrates both geometry and arithmetic: "the quad is set out geometrically, but the movements of the players defined arithmetically, with absolute precision."[27] But, as we have seen, other choreographic sources lie behind this work. *Quad*'s proximity to Schlemmer's choreographic experimentation also suggests one of the most convincing inspirations for Beckett's formal structuring of the movement of this play.

Yet our discussion of Beckett's prose pieces reveals how mathematics and geometry stimulated the writer's choreographic interest before he embarked on *Quad*, whose relationship to Bauhaus dance reminds us that *Ausdruckstanz* traditions had themselves spawned several choreographers and dance practitioners interested in movement as constituted by geometric form. The theories supporting such ideas of containment of the human body within the framework of geometric planes and solids belong to the field of kinesthetics during the period of early twentieth-century dance, and among innovators in this field, Rudolf Laban (also emerging from *Ausdruckstanz*) provides an intriguing theoretical expression of movement in space that curiously anticipates this area of Beckett's work, and brings into play the importance of the short prose for Beckett's experimental testing of choreographic form for the late drama. While the underpinning of what Laban identified as "Choreutics," an innovative system of the analysis of human movement, stems from a far more optimistic view of the function of human movement than Beckett's skeptical gestures toward a Dantean Hell, Laban nevertheless created exercises for dancers in three-dimensional spaces in a way that provides an insight into Beckett's kinesthetic practice. Laban's exercises were executed within architecturally constructed frameworks based on the Platonic solids (regular complex polyhedrons such as the cube, dodecahedron, or icosahedron). They showed the extension/limitations of the body within the geometric form, while Beckett explored the minutiae of movement caused by the restriction of the body within the architectural confinements imagined in the "Residua."

Beckett's abstract "choreographic" aesthetic here relates to the very history of choreographic form, including those techniques that can be traced all the way back to the early development of *danse d'école* in the sixteenth and seventeenth centuries as a positioning of the body at the center of an imaginary circle or sphere (we can of course also think of Vitruvian man and Leonardo's drawings). More specifically related to the Beckettian uses of closed spaces and geometrical patterns in the "Residua," the history of choreographic uses of geometrical figuration shows the ways in which Beckett (perhaps inadvertently) borrows from a tradition originating in classical sources including Aristotle's *Poetics* and Plato's *Timaeus* that have been read through early modern interpretations (even though Beckett is frequently skeptical of or refutes such a tradition). Most importantly, this is a tradition which shows how choreographic patterning emerges in the act of creating text. Furthermore, as Mark Franko has convincingly shown, there is not simply a close relationship of dance and writing in the early modern period in Europe, but the practice of the choreographic in this period produces dance *as* text.[28]

Franko's argument might be employed to facilitate a reading of Beckett's residual prose texts *as* choreography, where imagined embodiment/movement, recorded as geometric pattern on the page, enables the text's theorization of the rupture of linguistic meaning and the impossibility of closure.

In a chapter on geometrical dance in fifteenth and sixteenth-century France and Italy, Franko identifies the way in which the arrangement of figures into geometric patterning (recorded on the page) in sixteenth-century court dance manuals on the one hand provides, in its production of meaning, a formal *textual* representation (by the body) of the king's authority. But in the very spatialization of these patterns (imagined, or in actual performance) in the movement *between* poses these geometric dances illustrate the essential aesthetic conundrum of choreographic form, that of the relationship of stillness and movement (Franko shows the opposition as "figura/schema," arising in part from Quintilian's rhetorical terms).[29] In Franko's interpretation of these ballets, the pose is frequently associated with the mimetic, a symbol of authority, whereas the movement between poses bears no specifically symbolic meaning and thus gives rise to dance as possessing the material of destabilization of meaning. This relationship of the mimetic and the non-mimetic in the practice of these dances constitutes dance as theory itself. It opens up a breach between the prescribed dis-individuation of the body brought about by formal pattern (the individual figure subsumed into the social chorus that renders symbolically a "given" meaning in their poses and groupings), and the movement between poses, a gap, a space through which unscripted, individual interpretative expression might flow. Franko does not at this point in his book focus on twentieth-century choreography (although his coda takes the teleology of his argument toward the geometric configurations of Oskar Schlemmer), but this discussion of early modern geometrical dances hints at one way in which we could think about Beckett producing, in the imaginings of the body in these prose pieces, an intriguingly similar theorization. Beckett's implementation of the choreographic as a category in these prose works enables a new kind of textual experimentation, in which the writing produces a particular kind of tension between disciplined form and poetic utterance. The constraints of geometric and mathematical form govern the human obedience to an implied authority (Beckett may initially have been thinking of his reading of Geulincx, whose *Ethics* stipulates the Divine originator of human movement), and yet through the design of movement and stillness within the geometrical solids in which these figures appear the strict mathematical expression of the positioning of the body gives way to moments of unconstrained poetic sublimity. Thus the prose of this period renders, in its bizarre textual representations of the body, the productions of a choreographic imagination.

Beckett was looking for a way to "go on" out of the "dead end" of fiction as completed the decade before in the trilogy—and there are plenty of "faux départs." But in the "Residua" he imagines the subject placed during her/his last moments in a series of geometrically designed solids. These are in a way apocalyptic habitats, humans trapped within severely limited spaces, yet these radical texts express the "passion" of the gestures of *ballet d'action* leaking through into the text through the medium of minutely detailed movement in what is otherwise dense and clinical prose. The limitation of the body suggests a wrenching despair, and yet a curiously lyrical poetry emerges in the expression of mathematically precise, finely tuned choreographed movement. Beckett creates an entirely original form of prose poetry—and indeed he uses these pieces to move toward and experiment with the dramaturgical environments of the late (highly choreographed) TV plays. Thus it was fortuitous that Beckett read Kleist's essay at the point at which his drama focused more intensively on the minutiae of pace and movement. His proximity to Schlemmer's work, which also found inspiration in Kleist, reinforces Beckett's debt to the Kleistian paradox of the marionette's grace. But Beckett's choreographic imagination is complex. He had already experimented with the mathematics of the choreographic. In fact, the aesthetics driving Beckett's "Residua" make us consider how one of the most innovative conditions of Beckett's writing during the 1960s and 1970s is his envisioning an abstract kind of choreography as an important component of the production of prose.

In sum, the intersection with choreographic forms in Beckett's prose and TV experimentation raises questions about the language of movement and gesture as a distinct category of his work, especially in the latter focus on economy of form and on the contemplation of "last things." While his one dance play, *Quadrat I and II*, reveals the terminus of a hellish perspective on bodily entrapment in perpetually predetermined cycles of movement in restricted space, other areas of his work in fact offer momentary access, through the minutiae of intense movement of the hands, the arms, the elbow, the kneeling human form, to the *possibility* (however skeptical the presentation) of attainment of the grace denied to the human by Kleist in his marionette essay. While such gestures occur intermittently throughout Beckett's work, we encounter these choreographies most frequently and with greatest effect and force during the period in which Beckett undertakes the final contemplation of the subject, the focus on last things—not just the last "breath" but the last "word," the last "movement." Such gestural vocabulary generates an intensity of being that can be described as a lyrical, wordless poetry produced by the body's deliberate disturbance of the air, hinting at a visual indication of direction, a movement toward "the nothing" ("grace to breathe that last void" in *Ill Seen Ill Said*), frequently bearing within it the trace of the sacramental. We find such choreography elsewhere during the 1980s in the raising and lowering of the arm and turning of the page in *Ohio Impromptu* and in *Still*, the kneeling of the woman in prayer in *Ill Seen Ill Said* or the gestures of the disembodied hands anointing the head in *Nacht und Träume*.

The choreography in these pieces implies something close to what Giorgio Agamben describes in his *Notes on Gesture*, that gesture is essentially always a gesture of not being able to figure out something in language.[30] Perhaps such observation leaves open the possibility of the ultimate non-closure of Beckett's "What Is The Word" (published posthumously in 1989). Is this both a gesture of last rites ushering the subject into the "void" and a gesture that nevertheless acknowledges the impossibility of closure in language?[31] What is revealing is that we find Beckett using different choreographic possibilities throughout his work from the 1960s onwards: borrowing from the formal experimentation of an aspect of *Ausdruckstanz* of the early twentieth century, but also integrating into his work the subversive force and power of gesture, the minutiae of pace and movement encountered between the poses of much earlier dance forms.

NOTES

1. The essay "Über Das Marionetten Theater" was first published in four instalments in the daily *Berliner Abendblätter* from 12 to 15 December 1810. Kleist was editor of the newspaper. An English translation of this essay appears in Roger Copeland and Marshall Cohen, eds., *What is Dance? Readings in Theory and Criticism* (Oxford: Oxford University Press, 1983).

2. Lucia Ruprecht, *Dances of the Self in Heinrich von Kleist, E. T. A. Hoffman, and Heinrich Heine* (Aldershot, Hampshire: Ashgate Publishing, 2006), 21. For a close reading of Kleist's narratorial ambiguity in this essay in relation to his other "occasional writings" see Hilda Meldrum Brown, *Heinrich von Kleist: The Necessity of Art and the Ambiguity of Form* (Oxford: Oxford University Press, 1998), 60–94.

3. The question of whether the perfect attainment of human grace is possible brings out the paradoxical condition of the subject who dances, who must strive for the perfect alignment of gravity of the puppet, even though self-consciousness gets in the way of achieving this and is bound to fail. The implications for dance arise from the essay's implicit questioning of the subjectivity of the dancer and from its anticipation of later modernists' explorations of the dancer as either creative medium or as aesthetic object, as in the theories of Mallarmé and Valéry. For the choreographer, the issue of individual subjectivity compared to the perfection (or the limitation) of the inanimate object stimulated a host of choreographic interpretations of the puppet figure in the nineteenth and twentieth centuries.

4. Dirk Van Hulle, and Mark Nixon, *Samuel Beckett's Library* (Cambridge: Cambridge University Press, 2013), 77.

5. James Knowlson, *Damned to Fame: The Life of Samuel Beckett* (London: Bloomsbury, 1996), 194.

6. Kleist's essay also complements the theories of Denis Diderot. See Mark Franko, *Dance as Text: Ideologies of the Baroque Body* (Cambridge: Cambridge

University Press, 1993), 145. Franko observes that Diderot imagines in *Paradoxe sur le comédien* (written 1773, but published later than Kleist's essay in 1830) a "performance machine capable of reproducing perfected theatrical acts *ad infinitum*"—an actor as automaton who can repeatedly reproduce an exact expression or feeling. In fact, closer to Beckett's modernist context, Bergson had alluded to the Kleistian puppet in relation to dance in a section on "The Aesthetic Feelings" from Chapter 1 of *Time and Free Will*; see Henri Bergson, *Time and Free Will: An Essay on the Immediate Data of Consciousness*, trans. by F. L. Pogson (1910; London: Allen and Unwin, 1971), 11–13.

7. Samuel Beckett, *Murphy* (1938; New York: Grove Press, 1957), 3.

8. Knowlson, *Damned to Fame*, 584.

9. Knowlson, *Damned to Fame*, 633.

10. C. J. Ackerley and S. E. Gontarski, eds., *The Grove Companion to Samuel Beckett* (New York: Grove Press, 2004), 470.

11. Schlemmer had in part been inspired by Arnold Schoenberg's musical setting (1912) for Albert Giraud's cycle of poems *Pierrot lunaire* (1884). The American choreographer Glen Tetley created a notable ballet of *Pierrot Lunaire* (1962) for his own company, later mounted for Ballet Rambert.

12. Through Edward Gordon Craig's association with Duncan and Stanislavsky in Russia, but also through experimental German and Russian drama, including the work of Meyerhold and Alexander Tairov, such ideas were absorbed by choreographers such as Fokine and Massine.

13. Edward Gordon Craig, "The Actor and the Ueber Marionette," *The Mask* (1908), 8. For background, see also Olga Taxidou, *The Mask: A Periodical Performance by Edward Gordon Craig* (Amsterdam: Harwood Academic Publishers, 1998); and Jonathan Pitches, *Vsevolod Meyerhold* (London: Routledge, 2003).

14. Ernst Scheyer, "Foreword," *Dance Perspectives* 41 (Spring 1970), 32. Scheyer's special issue explores the work of Mary Wigman and Oskar Schlemmer. See also Susanne Lahusen, "Oskar Schlemmer: Mechanical Ballets?" *Dance Research* 4, no. 2 (Autumn 1986), 65–77; and Juliet Koss, "Bauhaus Theater of Human Dolls," *The Art Bulletin* 85, no. 4 (December 2003), 724–745.

15. Films (1986) of *The Bauhaus Dances of Oskar Schlemmer*, reconstructed by Debra McCall, in the New York Public Library for Performing Arts, *MGZIC 9-1566 and *MGZIC 9-1567. Clips of Schlemmer's "Space Dance" can be seen on YouTube at http://www.youtube.com/watch?v=UKfNkrmZtSg and a clip of the German TV performance of Beckett's *Quad* can be seen on Youtube at http://www.youtube.com/watch?v=298--7BTTnI

16. Quoted in Franko, *Dance as Text*, 150. In the Epilogue to this book (133–152), Franko outlines the development of theories of mime and pantomime in the work of Montaigne, Noverre, and Diderot. See also Angelica Gooden, *Actio and Persuasion: Dramatic Performance in 18th-Century France* (Oxford: Oxford University Press, 1986). Beckett's responses to the French traditions and theories of mime are also important in tracing the antecedents of his choreographic method in the plays.

17. *Quad*, in *Collected Shorter Plays of Samuel Beckett* (London: Faber and Faber, 1984), 293.

18. Anna McMullan, "Samuel Beckett's 'J. M. Mime': Generic Mutations of a Dramatic Fragment," *Samuel Beckett Today/Aujourd'hui* 16, no. 1 (June 2006), 338–339.

19. McMullan, "Samuel Beckett's 'J. M. Mime,'" 339.

20. McMullan, "Samuel Beckett's 'J. M. Mime,'" 339.

21. Samuel Beckett, "Residua," in *Texts for Nothing and Other Shorter Prose, 1950–1976*. London: Faber and Faber, 2010. Page numbers cited in the text.

22. Mark Nixon, Introduction to Samuel Beckett, *Texts for Nothing and Other Shorter Prose, 1950–1976* (London: Faber and Faber, 2010), xii–xiii.

23. David Watson, *Paradox and Desire in Samuel Beckett's Fiction* (Basingstoke: Macmillan, 1991), 115.

24. George Craig, Martha Dow Fehsenfeld, Dan Gunn, and Lois More Overbeck, eds., *The Letters of Samuel Beckett, Vol. 3: 1957–1965* (Cambridge: Cambridge University Press, 2014), 629n7.

25. Ackerley, "Samuel Beckett and Mathematics," http://www.uca.edu.ar/uca/common/grupo17/files/mathem.pdf (n.d.), 20.

26. Nixon, Introduction to *Texts for Nothing,* xiii.

27. Ackerley, "Samuel Beckett and Mathematics," 18.

28. Franko, *Dance as Text*, 15–30.

29. Franko, *Dance as Text*, 16.

30. Giorgio Agamben, "Notes on Gesture," in *Infancy and History: The Destruction of Experience*, trans. Liz Heron (London: Verso, 1993), 135–140.

31. For a compelling discussion of neurological conditions in relation to Beckett's late work, see Laura Salisbury, "'What Is the Word': Beckett's Aphasic Modernism," *Journal of Beckett Studies* 17, nos. 1–2 (2009), 78–126.

BIBLIOGRAPHY

Ackerley, C. J. "Samuel Beckett and Mathematics," http://www.uca.edu.ar/uca/common/grupo17/files/mathem.pdf (n.d.)

Ackerley, C. J., and S. E. Gontarski, eds. *The Grove Companion to Samuel Beckett*. New York: Grove Press, 2004.

Agamben, Giorgio. "Notes on Gesture." In *Infancy and History: The Destruction of Experience*, 135–140. Translated by Liz Heron. London: Verso, 1993.

Beckett, Samuel. *Murphy*. 1938; New York: Grove Press, 1957.

———. *Collected Shorter Plays of Samuel Beckett*. London: Faber and Faber, 1984.

———. *Texts for Nothing and Other Shorter Prose, 1950–1976*. London: Faber and Faber, 2010.

———. *The Letters of Samuel Beckett, Vol. 3: 1957–1965*. Ed. George Craig, Martha Dow Fehsenfeld, Dan Gunn, and Lois More Overbeck. Cambridge: Cambridge University Press, 2014.

Bergson, Henri. *Time and Free Will: An Essay on the Immediate Data of Consciousness*. Trans. by F. L. Pogson. 1910; London: Allen and Unwin, 1971.

Brown, Hilda Meldrum. *Heinrich von Kleist: The Necessity of Art and the Ambiguity of Form*. Oxford: Oxford University Press, 1998.

Copeland, Roger, and Marshall Cohen, eds. *What Is Dance? Readings in Theory and Criticism*. Oxford: Oxford University Press, 1983.

Craig, Edward Gordon. "The Actor and the Ueber Marionette." *The Mask* (1908).

Franko, Mark. *Dance as Text: Ideologies of the Baroque Body*. Cambridge: Cambridge University Press, 1993.

Gooden, Angelica. *Actio and Persuasion: Dramatic Performance in 18th-Century France*. Oxford: Oxford University Press, 1986.

Knowlson, James. *Damned to Fame: The Life of Samuel Beckett*. London: Bloomsbury, 1996.

Koss, Juliet. "Bauhaus Theater of Human Dolls," *The Art Bulletin* 85, no.4 (December 2003), 724–745.

Lahusen, Susanne. "Oskar Schlemmer: Mechanical Ballets?" *Dance Research* 4, no. 2 (Autumn 1986), 65–77.

McMullan, Anna. "Samuel Beckett's 'J.M. Mime': Generic Mutations of a Dramatic Fragment," *Samuel Beckett Today/Aujourd'hui* 16, no. 1 (June 2006), 333–345.

Moynihan, D. S., and Leigh George Odom. "Oskar Schlemmer's 'Bauhaus Dances': Debra McCall's Reconstructions," *The Drama Review* 28, no. 3 (Autumn 1984), 46–58.

Nixon, Mark. Introduction. Samuel Beckett, *Texts for Nothing and Other Shorter Prose, 1950–1976*. London: Faber and Faber, 2010.

Pitches, Jonathan. *Vsevolod Meyerhold*. London: Routledge, 2003.

Ruprecht, Lucia. *Dances of the Self in Heinrich von Kleist, E. T. A. Hoffman, and Heinrich Heine*. Aldershot, Hampshire: Ashgate Publishing, 2006.

Salisbury, Laura. "'What Is the Word': Beckett's Aphasic Modernism," *Journal of Beckett Studies* 17, nos. 1–2 (2009), 78–126.

Scheyer, Ernst. "Foreword," *Dance Perspectives* 41 (Spring 1970), 1–32.

Taxidou, Olga. *The Mask: A Periodical Performance by Edward Gordon Craig*. Amsterdam: Harwood Academic Publishers, 1998.

Van Hulle, Dirk and Mark Nixon. *Samuel Beckett's Library*. Cambridge: Cambridge University Press, 2013.

Watson, David. *Paradox and Desire in Samuel Beckett's Fiction*. Basingstoke: Macmillan, 1991.

Chapter Eight

Rhythm and Color

Reading Lucia Joyce and the Legacy of Dance in the Works of James Joyce and Samuel Beckett

Siobhán Purcell

The role and significance of the body in modernism has received much critical attention, but rarely has this attention addressed the body as an aesthetic vehicle in and of itself. Given the importance of discussions of the body in terms of form, the legacy of dance has been overlooked in theorizing modernist aesthetics. Susan Jones has written:

> As literary aesthetics disrupted traditional assumptions about narratology, poetics, and historiography writers sought modes of representation to express more adequately what they perceived to be the disjunctive "modern" subject, whose experience of consciousness, of identity, of the passage of time and memory was above all skeptical.[1]

In Jones's work, we hear echoes of Beckett's characters, characters for whom the experience of the passage of time becomes the text itself. Jones's identification of the modern subject at once identifies the disjunctive in modern dance and modernist literature but also describes an experience of bodily contingency that typifies the modernist experience of embodiment. This experience characterizes modern dance as well as of literary representation. As Alexandra Kolb has put it: "Modern dance in particular was a movement which incited numerous writers to put pen to paper."[2] As Deirdre Mulrooney's work about the overlooked Irish-German dancer Erina Brady has shown, the legacy of dance in Irish and European modernism has a depth needing to be plumbed. Studying exemplary and interesting figures such as Brady outlines a cultural moment, including a breadth of historical figures and a depth of personal considerations. In attempting to retrieve forgotten figures within the modernist movement, all too often women, Mulrooney's descriptions of "bodily modernism" and of this hybrid-identity dangerous female body are of particular importance.

The richness of the influence of dance on modernist literature is such that small examples often yield a wealth of unexplored connections and networks. In this chapter, I would like to take one small local example of concurrence between dance and modernist text and to trace the overlooked connections between them. Exploring this local example will allow this study to move amongst Germany, Paris, and Ireland and to tackle gender politics, questions of heredity and of ability, of text, performance, and the body. In tracing this bodily modernism, this chapter focuses on the overlooked contributions of Lucia Joyce to the works of both James Joyce and Samuel Beckett during the 1930s. Lucia Joyce, daughter to James and, for a time at least, romantically engaged with Samuel Beckett, appears in fictional versions in the pages of these authors' works. As a dancer and as an interlocutor of the body, Lucia Joyce connects the works—and lives—of both authors. What we shall see is a focus that shifts from describing Lucia Joyce's promising career as a dancer in the 1920s, and narratives of strength and grace, to representing Lucia in terms of disability. The physical prowess and artistry that marked her early career is replaced following her institutionalization with a predominant emphasis on her impaired body: rather than an artist of the body, she becomes all body; her disabled identity both takes from her identity as a dancer at the same time as it ignores it. I will further argue that dance is an increasingly important motif in the works of both Joyce and Beckett at this time. Lucia's influence may be traced in the significance of early twentieth-century ideologies of movement in their works. She haunts the works of both Joyce and Beckett. She represents a real-life example of an artist of movement who is represented in their works as a dancer and also as an institutionalized voice; in each author's works she comes to represent the avant-garde aesthete *and* the impaired outsider. Considering the artistic output of Lucia Joyce allows for a better understanding both of how disability is read *in* modernism and how disability extends those features *of* modernism already present within established works.

In the works of Joyce and Beckett, we see a playful undermining of contemporaneous preoccupations with bodies politic and the idealized boy. Both authors subvert nationalist ideas of heroism, as it existed in inter-war Ireland and Germany, and explore the value of non-normative bodies. This valuing of difference comes not only thematically but also formally; both authors play and explore the conventions of classical form in favor of a literary form that is self-reflexive and difficult. Indeed, it may be argued that a culture of dance is already present within the texts, represented by and contributed to by Lucia Joyce. The legacy of her career and her dance and the catastrophe of her treatment provide a valuable context in which to situate the works of both Joyce and Beckett. Recovering the value of Lucia Joyce's work also shines a light on the bodily, dancerly, performative nature of the high modernist works of the inter-war period.

Lucia Joyce spent much of the 1920s as a student of dance. She began her training in eurhythmics with the Jaques-Dalcroze Institute (1925–1929) before attending the Akademia, the newly established school of Raymond Duncan, brother to Isadora Duncan, in Paris. In addition to dance classes, the Akademia was based on the idea of the Platonic Academy and, heavily inflected by Duncan's neoclassical belief in maintaining the proximity of labor and modes of production to life itself, also offered courses in the arts and crafts, including printing, ceramics, and weaving. Duncan's school emphasized ascetic self-reliance and crafted a pseudo-classical curriculum that instructed the entire body. The school is parodied in the opening pages of Beckett's first, unpublished novel, *Dream of Fair to Middling Women.* "And all day it was dancing and singing and music and douches and frictions and bending and stretching and classes—Harmonie, Anatomie, Psychologie, Improvisation with a powerful ictus on the last syllable in each case."[3] The Duncan school prioritized a holistic emphasis on movement, including movement through drawing.

Lucia Joyce then studied with the British dancer and choreographer Margaret Morris, even planning to become a physical therapist in the Morris style, and also met Loïs Hutton and Hélène Vanel. Calling themselves *Rythme et Couleur*, Vanel and Hutton had a well-defined and active sense of aesthetic purpose: their art was inclusive. As spokesperson for the group, Vanel published a number of articles collected in their newsletter entitled *Cahiers rythme et couleur.* The *cahiers* included the artistic output of many of their students, including painting by children as young as four years of age who took dance lessons in their school. Vanel also wrote and illustrated short pieces on the importance of movement not only for dance but indeed for all other art forms: "Le *mouvement,* tout au contraire des formes et des couleurs, demande une appreciation directe, instantanée, decisive, et par conséquent, personelle."[4] With this attention to movement, Hutton and Vanel emphasized the value of the line, whether executed by the body or the pencil. As Vanel explains,

> Dans la peinture, nous cherchons le rythme: rythme dans l'espace, rythme des lignes qui bondissent et se brisent, s'entrelacent, tournoient, fuient, rythme des volumes qui surgissent s'illuminent dans les profendeurs, se retirent, s'affacent, ayant chacun sa place et sa valeur inevitable, et partout et dans tout, l'equilibre.[5]
>
> (In painting, we seek rhythm: rhythm in space, rhythm of lines that leap and break, intertwine, spin, flee, rhythm of volumes that arise and illuminate the

> depths, withdraw, each having its place and its inevitable value, and everywhere and in everything, equilibrium.)

The emphasis on painting speaks to the holistic and wide-ranging nature of the group's avant-garde approach to modern dance; their interrogation of form in the midst of movement demonstrates a concerted effort to marry the media of dance, mime, painting, and text. It is in this vein that Lucia's work for her father may also be read. We see this emphasis on rhythm in Lucia's letterings in her father's work, which bristles with the dynamism of Hutton and Vanel's democratization of art.

The group moved to Paris and changed their name to *Les six de rythme et couleur*, and it was here that Lucia Joyce joined the troupe. They were noticed in Paris, even attracting the attention of the great dance critic André Levinson. In a profile from March 1928 in the *Paris Times* after her performance in *La Princesse Primitive,* one commentator remarked that "When she reaches her full capacity for rhythmic dancing, James Joyce may yet be known as his daughter's father."[6] At this time, she even appeared in a film by Jean Renoir as a toy soldier (1928). The peak of her career as a dancer came in late May 1929 at an international competition at the Bal Bullier. Dancing to Schubert's *Marche Militaire* in a fish costume of her own design, she won the affections of the audience though she did not win the competition. As James Joyce reported to his mentor Harriet Shaw Weaver in a letter dated 28 May 1929, "Lucia's disqualification for the dancing prize was received by a strong protest from a good half of the audience (*not* friends of ours) who called out repeatedly 'Nous reclamons l'irlandaise! Un peu de justice, messieurs!'"[7] Following her success in this competition, she embarked on formal ballet training (for the first time) with Lubov Egrova, at the age of 21, training six hours a day.

Les six de rhythme et couleur were the inspiration for the RAYNBOW girls of Book II of *Finnegans Wake*:

> And they leap so loopl, looply, as they link to light. And they look so loovely, loovelit, noosed in a nuptious night. Withasly glints in. Andecoy glants out. They ramp it a little, a lessle, a lissle. Then rompride round in rout.
>
> Say them all but tell them apart, cadenzando coloratura! R is Rubretta and A is Arancia, Y is for Yilla and N for greeneriN. B is Boyblue with odalisque O while W waters the fleurettes of novembrance.[8]

The influence of dance is clear; reimagined as colors of the rainbow, Joyce's language bends and stretches to accommodate his intended affect. The rhythm of the prose "and they leap so looply, looply, as they link to light" patterns children's games. The rainbow girls dance through time, the young becoming old and the old becoming young. Joyce's language strives to recreate the whirl of the dance: they "rompride round in rout." As Carol Shloss writes:

> Her repertoire group, Les Six de rythme et couleur, seemed to inspire Joyce to invent his own troupe of Rainbow Girls—the young, heavenly dancers who entertained him in imagination and became the vehicle by which he could make explicit an analogy between language and body language, between words and dance. Both of them were wrested from a world of constant flux, whose evanescence became increasingly interesting to him.[9]

Joyce's adaptation of the real-life troupe demonstrates his interest in the materiality of expression and furthers his emphasis on medium. With the Rainbow Girls, the movements of the body become themselves meaning and language is rendered incarnate.

By October 1929, Joyce revealed to Harriet Shaw Weaver that Lucia had turned away from this promising career and had "come to the conclusion that she has not physique for a strenuous dancing career the result of which has been a month of tears as she thinks that she has thrown away three of four years of hard work and is sacrificing a talent."[10] This biographical turning point has been traced and considered in Joyce's own work, such as in the Nuvoletta scene of *Finnegans Wake*, by Joyce's biographers like Richard Ellmann and also by Lucia Joyce's biographer Carol Shloss. Each examination of the event emphasizes a different aspect of Lucia Joyce's decision—the loss of a potential career, resentment that may have begun to develop with the family—but retrospective knowledge of the situation that was to come has perhaps hindered a full understanding of this event.

By the early 1930s, it was clear that Lucia's mental health was in crisis, and she became an inpatient in a number of sanitariums around Europe. Having given up a career in dance, Lucia looked to other media and began designing ornate letters as a way of generating income. She produced an alphabet of letterings, called "lettrines" in the language of *Finnegans Wake,* hand-drawn and meticulously designed to complement pieces of text. The letters took on some of the dynamism of her dancing, now married to the stasis of the written word. The lettering thus took literally the words of Hélène Vanel: "Donc, mentalement, ceui qui dessine, danse. La fermeté et l'audace de la ligne ne viennent-elles pas du rythme imprimé a la main qui conduit le crayon?"[11] (So, mentally, whoever draws, dances. Does the firmness and daring of a line not come from the rhythmic impulse of the hand which guides the pencil?) Lucia's replacement of the ephemeral performativity of dance with the fixity and silence of the written word suggests a formal interrogation of the rhythm of the poems which she illustrated. Lucia Joyce's illustrations appeared in four published works: *Pomes Penyeach*, *A Chaucer ABC*, *Storiella as She is Syung*, and *The Mime of Mick, Nick and the Maggies.* In her illustrations, in particular in *A Chaucer ABC* and *Pomes Penyeach,* the letters of the alphabet express the shapes and movements of the human body. They lend the page with a kinetic rhythm and mimic the lines of figures in motion. The letterings contrast the precise and exacting typeface in which the text is cast, juxtaposing the regularity of the typeface with dynamic and performative embellishments that echo the works themselves. In bringing the forms of poetry and dance together, Lucia's works probe the distinctions between media and performativity. When in 1927 André Levinson described dance as the writing of the body, "the alphabet of the inexpressible," his words evoke Lucia's alphabet, which seems to conform less to typographical form than the contours and sinews of the body.[12]

The letterings echoed the Duncans' emphasis on a fully embodied response to art—from type and text right through to modern dance. As Elizabeth Duncan's student, Yvonne Berge recalled that students were trained in art and design as a means of "making the pupils' bodies well fitted for harmonious movement":

> Every morning we received drawing lessons from one of the best teachers from Csiseck in Vienna. In these classes we were introduced alternately to expressionism (on huge sheets of paper), kinetism, graphic musical and rhythmic expression, composition, lettering, placards and the nude. This graphic work undertaken in conjunction with dance, was extremely enriching and stimulating. Music, painting, dance, theatre and literature all came together to form a perfect whole.[13]

Duncan's emphasis on the very physicality of expression, even on the page, inflects how we may understand the dancerly qualities of Lucia's own lettering. Indeed, the Duncans' insistence that all material would be produced on-site (even designing the typeface which they used to publish pamphlets by hand) emphasizes the personal, individual labor associated with production by hand. Lucia's letterings, never mass-produced on any great scale, recall the performativity of dance by insisting on their uniqueness, their individuality, and the distinctness of the artist's body who rendered them.

The letters first appeared in Joyce's second collection of poetry, *Pomes Penyeach,* with initial letters designed and illuminated by Lucia Joyce, published by Obelisk Press in 1932. This deluxe edition is charming and lavish, designed as something of a vanity piece, and destined for libraries and collectors. When the work was published, critics such as Louis Gillet and Fritz R. Vanderpyl acclaimed the marriage of antique material with art deco design, and many commentators remarked upon Lucia's close proximity, on one hand, to the Irish tradition of illuminated manuscripts such as the Book of Kells, and on the other, to Joyce's formal innovations. At times, Lucia's illuminations also write *back* to her father's text, offering a different perspective, a new emphasis and a broadened form that undoubtedly alter the way that both her own lettrines and Joyce's poems may be read.

Pomes Penyeach was intended as a collection of songs, thus, the decision to embellish or illuminate the work challenges the very textuality of the collection. Indeed the performativity of the poems differentiates the work from many of Joyce's others. Intended for performance, the poems were not typed but handwritten in emerald ink, a simulacrum of the act of writing itself. As Paul Valéry had written,

> *A poem,* for example, is *action,* because a poem exists only at the moment of being spoken; then it is *in actu.* This act, like the dance, has no other purpose than to create a state of mind; it imposes its own laws; it, too, creates a time and a measurement of time which are appropriate and essential to it: we cannot distinguish it from its form of time. To recite poetry is to enter into a verbal dance.[14]

In recording this moment of transmission, the text teeters between the fleetingness of the act and the permanence of the page. Like the dancerly quality of Lucia's letterings, this formal blurring implies a sense of the Joyces' collaboration achieving a unique *frisson.*

The experiences of the body and in particular of sensations come to the fore of the work. Recurring themes of visual impairment are offset by Lucia's illuminations; darkness and grayness pervade the collection, lightened and made all the more visible by the vibrant chiaroscuro of Lucia's works. As the lettrines reflect upon the poems, the poems, in turn, reflect upon the quiet presence of the initials. The gradual diminishing of vision and visual culture form an eroding backdrop in the poems themselves, while the edition is perhaps the most strikingly visual piece in all of Joyce's oeuvre. The materiality of the book itself also extends the collection's emphasis on frailty. The delicate rice paper of the edition, and the illegible slants of Joyce's handwriting, are bolstered and strengthened by the boldness of the lettrines. Though Lucia appears as the subject of a number of the poems themselves, she also appears as co-contributor, sloughing away the paternalistic layers of the poems themselves, modifying and qualifying them with her bold contributions.

The first such instance of these exchanges occurs with the metareferential "A Flower Given To My Daughter." Based on a real event in the Joyces' lives, the poem recalls an occasion when Joyce's former lover, Amalia Popper, presented Lucia, then aged six, with a white rose. The poem reflects upon the relationship of address to addressee: whom does the poet speaker address? It also self-referentially invokes the presence of the person to whom the poem is dedicated on the page.

The flower, which is presented to the "blue-veined child," is repeated in the delicate and ornate filigree of Lucia's introductory F. [15] The white rose, held in the tail of the F, contrasts the frail, pastel colors evoked by the poem itself: "sere and paler / than time's wan wave." [16] Given the presence of the white flower, the poem is positively fertile. We observe here one of the many visual puns that typify Lucia's playful lettrines; with its pale pastel pink coloring, Lucia moves between the French and English and harnesses both the rose flower and the rose color. This fleshy coloration is fitting; as Norbert Lennartz writes, "Joyce's poems anatomize the speaker's progeny and represent them only as bodily fragments . . . diaphanous, 'blueveined' objects of utmost delicacy, as in 'A Flower Given to My Daughter.'"[17] The lettering invigorates the work, lending a simultaneity and performativity to the piece, providing an embodied response to the thematic content of the work. The opening image of frailty is thus elaborated by Lucia's lettrine while also disavowed by her very presence within the volume; in contrast to the many sickly children of the collection, here Lucia, the very daughter upon whom the encounter is based, has become herself the fully fleshed-out artist, present on the page in a strident, self-identified declaration. Her letters carve out a bold space on the page and contrast the timid sloping of her father's distinctive handwriting; they are clear, beautiful and declarative.

In "Bahnhoffstrasse," Lucia's illustration manages, again, something of this simultaneity denied to the written word. The poem is based on a real event in Joyce's life: his first attack of glaucoma, which he experienced in Zurich in August 1917 and which required an immediate operation.[18] "Bahnhofstrasse," as it exists in this collection, diminishes much of the necessary tension of the poem. In this edition, a protective Japanese macre-paper overlays the work and renders the poem, at first glance, gauzy and difficult to read. The ambiguity of "the signs that mock" the speaker also blurs the narrative for the reader; the obfuscation brought about by the eye attack, while not explicitly addressed in the poem saving articulations of the "star of pain," by virtue of the macre-paper overlay doubly complicates the visual in the poem.[19] While the poem may very well be about temporary loss of vision, the very fact of its existence on the page, further lightened by Lucia's illustration, exemplifies a tension at the heart of the poem. The materialism of the special edition resonates with the theme of the poem. Lucia's lettrine for this poem further complicates the very form of the work.

Like an imagist poem, Joyce's poem is intensely visual; it approximates a painting or an image, a scene neatly condensed to its very essence. Lucia's illustrated T, far from presenting a piteous or impassive scene, presents a human-like figure in motion, one fist curled and raised above the head. The spasm of pain described as a "trysting and turning star" is embellished in

Lucia's initial, lending a kinetic energy to the piece.[20] Lucia's illustration serves also to further undermine the "blindness" of the poem; her illuminated letter incorporates the "grey way" and "violet signals" described in the poem. Instead of dulling the event described, Lucia's lettrine energizes the piece, rendering the poem's emotional affect all the more demonstratively. The poem is aural but Lucia's lettering reveals much of the visual emphasis of the poem, embellishing it with an intensely corporeal configuration.

Lucia's involvement in this publication of *Pomes Penyeach*, while elaborating upon her father's work, is ultimately a singular moment of productive creativity in the midst of a deeply troubling decade. Though the lettrines were screen-printed for *Pomes Penyeach*, Lucia's potential success as an illustrator was foreshortened by the disastrous misplacing of the originals by the publishers Burns and Oates. Excerpts of *Finnegans Wake,* then referred to as *Work in Progress,* were published in a series of "fragments" that appeared throughout the late 1920s and 1930s. In these published fragments of *Work in Progress*, Lucia's illustrations occupy a lesser role than they had in *Pomes Penyeach*, in effect book-ending the works.

The illuminations further the formal experimentation of the work, particularly with regards to symbolism of the letter, while also reflecting certain aspects of the content. In fragments from *Finnegans Wake,* Lucia's illustrations occupy a lesser role than they had in *Pomes Penyeach*, though they are explicitly tied to dance: in *The Mime of Mick, Nick and the Maggies,* published separately by Servire Press in 1934, the illustrations appear on the cover and after the final word, reflecting on what is to come and what has been. Lucia's drawings collaborate with the text instead of merely accompanying it. The cover further demonstrates the polyphony of the work: a figure dancing—maybe pirouetting—is clearly visible, but it also takes the shape of a cityscape atop a running river. The front illustration of the work is substantially more involved than a lettrine, taking up most of the cover. Pointedly, the cityscape pirouettes between the words "JAMES JOYCE," engulfing both the title and the author by its sheer size. The towering apartment block nestled along the riverbed gives the drawing not only a sense of movement but also renders the topography of a city. The bold indigo coloring of the title image, contrasted by shades of silver and gray, gives a clue to the riddles posed in the chapter itself. The illustration is one of the only thematic points of fixity within the text itself, and it takes the form of a dancer.

In *A Chaucer ABC,* Lucia Joyce's letterings were used to illustrate a beautiful edition of *The Prayer of Our Lady.* The physical form and shapes of modern dance are further confirmed in this acrostic poem which Lucia's alphabet accompanied in 1936. By this point, Lucia was institutionalized and, against her wishes, would remain so until her death almost fifty years later in 1982. By such time, critics had begun to adopt the paternalistic tone that characterizes much of the discussion of her life: while the legacy of dance is clearly apparent in her lettrines for *A Chaucer ABC,* her artistry as a dancer had already begun to fade into a supportive myth of her father's genius. Louis Gillet writes in the Introduction to the work:

> She used to dance. Those who saw her declare that she was enchanting. I can well believe it; I have seen her walk. Then her fancy changed. She wanted to prove that she has as much wit in the tips of her fingers as in the tips of her toes. She bestirred herself and began to draw.[21]

Gillet's identification of a kind of latent energy which pivots from the body to the page identifies the unique kineticism of the drawings while simultaneously disavowing the kind of considered artistic response which Lucia's drawings surely figure. Indeed, the passivity of this changing "fancy" erodes the meaningfulness of Lucia's engagement with the works of her father, disempowering and stripping the work of its vitality.

The narrative of Lucia Joyce's life became inflected by the 1930s rhetoric of degeneration and eugenics: as the Second World War dawned, Joyce's efforts to find a cure for his daughter became increasingly frantic. It is clear from his letters that he compared Lucia's health to that of Nijinsky: "He was supposed to be an absolutely hopeless case of *dementia praecox* and yet according to sensational reports a week ago in the press he is now miraculously cured as a result of insulin treatment."[22] Indeed, it is at this point that Beckett and Joyce each begin to underscore the importance of disability in their works. Both Beckett and Joyce interrogate contemporaneous pseudoscience; hereditary science is mocked in much of Joyce's work, and in Beckett's case, his early work as a translator of the Surrealists reveals an exceptional sensitivity to the contingencies of medical diagnoses such as hysteria (*This Quarter* 1932) and a thorough contempt for racist discourse (*Negro Anthology*). Uniting this sensitivity was a profound distaste for resurfacing notions of "degeneration." The language of degeneration, popularized by Max Nordau in the 1890s, sought to compare modern artists to physically "degenerate" people and vice versa. In the beginning of the twentieth century then, degenerate, or sometimes "decadent" art became that which was impure, abnormal, outside of the confines of acceptable normative standards. As Barron describes, degenerate art referred to "art that is unclassifiable or so far beyond the confines of what is accepted that it is in essence 'non-art.'"[23] The rich points of reference that shaped modern dance—moving away from classical form, inverting typical understandings of grace—echo the Nordauian rejection of the modern in the 1930s. The dancer's body, far from immune to political baggage, bears the cultural, accumulated weight of racialized, gendered, and nationalistic ideology. In this way, the disabled body and the modern dancer's body are two points along a continuum of degeneracy, and the distinctions between the two are collapsed. As Ramsay Burt has written, "notions of physical hygiene and of the body's capabilities that are mediated through dance are gendered and are socially and historically specific. The subjective experience of embodiment is also conditioned by ideologies of national identity."[24] Thus, the transitions in depictions of Lucia Joyce from a dancerly figure to a disabled figure testify to the complex politics of embodiment in the modernist period. By problematically codifying her as disabled, the legacy of Lucia Joyce's dance career is collapsed.

As Joyce sought to extricate Lucia Joyce from incarceration, Beckett travelled around Germany, witnessing first hand the collision of aesthetic and bodily discourse in the decrees and propaganda that targeted so-called *entartete* or degenerate art. These travels around Germany, recorded in a series of diaries he kept, currently housed at the University of Reading, depict Beckett's experience of the Nazis' denouncing of modernist art: "All the lavatory men say 'Heil Hitler.' The best pictures are in the cellar."[25] The perceived "degeneracy" of modernist art and the attempts to depict modernist painters as disabled or mentally ill coincides with Beckett's trend of depicting increasingly disabled figures in his works. Indeed, some of his early characters are based on Lucia Joyce and markedly depict her as "crippled." In his 1934 collection *More Pricks Than Kicks,* for example, Lucy, one of Belacqua's many girlfriends, is involved in a motorcar accident and becomes disabled as a result.

> Lucy came a sickening cropper backwards down the rampant hind-quarters, the base of her spine, then of her skull, hit the ground a double welt, the jennet fell on top of her, the wheels of the car jolted over what was left of the jennet, who expired there and then in the twilight, *sans jeter un cri.* Lucy however was not so fortunate, being crippled for life and her beauty dreadfully marred.[26]

This maiming and subsequent killing off of Lucy establishes a tradition of representing Lucia between two poles, one that turns upon her physical beauty and grace and the other on a metaphorical and sometimes literal emphasis on physical impairment.

Joyce read the story and, in a letter to his daughter-in-law, Helen Joyce, commented on Beckett's collection, singling out the appearance of Lucy for comment: "Beckett has brought out his book *More Pricks than Kicks*. One of the characters is named Lucia but it is quite different. She is a cripple or something. Haven't time to read it. But looked at it here and there before quitting Paris. He has talent, I think."[27]

The excerpt is interesting for a number of reasons. Firstly, Joyce admits to not having read it, he has only looked at it, but he is already familiar with the character of Lucy, despite her rather brief and somewhat aborted appearance in the collection. Secondly, it would seem to be one of the first, if not the first, occasions of Joyce having acknowledged Beckett's talent as a writer, even in the emotive and uncomfortably familiar recognition of Lucia and Beckett's strained relationship. Thirdly, it is regrettable though somewhat inevitable that Lucia's own views are entirely absent or omitted from the reception. Finally, the fact of Joyce recognizing his daughter as the basis for Lucy's character is all the more remarkable, for in acknowledging that the nature of the "crippling" is "quite different," he indirectly addresses the nature of Lucia's own troubles. It is the nature of this "difference" that seems especially significant for, here, Joyce distinguishes between the states of mental distress that Lucia experiences, and the physical, acquired nature of mobility impairment. For Joyce, it would seem that Lucy's disability thus metaphorizes or perhaps analogizes Lucia's distress, a distress that "cripples" her. The fact of Beckett rendering Lucia's own distress along these lines, in the form of an acquired physical impairment, foreshadows a number of Beckett's most famous characters.

We can trace Lucia Joyce as the inspiration for a number of characters within a number of Beckett's later works as well: "First Love," *Molloy*, and *Waiting for Godot.* Perhaps the most famous may be the character of Lucky in *Waiting for Godot.* Pozzo tells Estragon and Vladimir, "He used to dance the farandole, the fling, the brawl, the jig, the fandango and even the hornpipe. He capered. For joy. Now that's the best he can do."[28] In "joy" we hear echoes of Lucia's surname, and in the enslaved Lucky's dance, we may hear echoes of Lucia's almost victory, danced in her fish costume in 1929: Pozzo tells us that Lucky "thinks he's entangled in a net." As Jones has shown, Beckett's later works are utterly dancerly. And as Josephine Starte suggests, "Beckett's plays are remarkably choreographic in quality."[29] The dance-like qualities of Beckett's works are such that new and rather remarkable productions of his works in the twenty-first century have often played between the ideas of physical constraint and of strict measure. Often physical impairment precipitates such innovation; toward the end of her life, the late Rosemary Pountney adjusted her performances of *Footfalls* to accommodate her physical discomfort in taking the precise steps necessitated by the stage directions. In her place, a spotlight took the necessary steps, reminding the audience of the very physicality and contingencies of the human body, even when absented from the stage. [30] In recent productions of *Not I* by Lisa Dwan and Jess Thom, the constraint of the performer's body required by the script, far from absenting the human body, reveals the very physicality of the spoken word and of the body that speaks it.[31] In this way, the body on stage becomes not a vessel for the actor but a performance of physicality in its own right, a silent and dance-like invocation of pure presence.

As the noted dance disability theorist Petra Kuppers observes, the impact of disabled practitioners occupying the stage focuses much of the performative tensions of the work: when disabled bodies take to the stage, "Ways of telling become important: nuances inflect familiar stories, allow new perspectives on different forms of embodiment to emerge. The performance is the reiteration of the seemingly familiar in a bracketed, framed format; a conscious placement of one's body into the visible, tangible scene of a show."[32] Lucia Joyce's rehearsing of her father's words did this work on the page as once her dancing had on the stage; using her training, she inflected familiar stories with something uncanny, lending something of embodiment to the written word. As Mark Franko has remarked, the "history of dance and politics can often be read and deconstructed in the encounters between performance and the print discourse that marks its passage with a discursive afterlife."[33] This discursive afterlife is clear in the emphasis on physical culture is clear in stagings of Beckett's works and also in adaptations of Joyce's: one need only think of Olwen Fouéré's 2014 *riverrun*.[34] In examining the legacy of Lucia Joyce, I hope to stake a claim on the contested hierarchies and particularities of literary modernism. Moreover, these concerns are not merely biographical; they are formal and ideological: the erasure of Lucia's presence within this oeuvre, as well as the diminished importance of her own work, demonstrates the necessity of reinterrogating the representation of dance in these works and of championing and reclaiming the voices of women, the institutionalized, and the disabled.

NOTES

1. Susan Jones, *Literature, Modernism, and Dance* (Oxford: Oxford University Press, 2013), 3.
2. Alexandra Kolb, *Performing Femininity: Dance and Literature in German Modernism* (Oxford: Peter Lang, 2009), 6.
3. Samuel Beckett, *Dream of Fair to Middling Women* (New York: Arcade Publishing, 1993), 13–14.
4. Helene Vanel, *Cahiers Rythme et Couleur: Prose Poèmes Croquis Annales Photographies* (Semestriel No. III, Mai 1926. https://gallica.bnf.fr/ark:/12148/bpt6k1341972/f1.item), 89.
5. Vanel, *Cahiers Rythme et Couleur*, 69–70.
6. *Paris Times*, "On the Left Bank" (14 March 1928), quoted in Carol Schloss, *Lucia Joyce: To Dance in the Wake* (New York: Picador, 2005), 6.

7. James Joyce, *Selected Letters*, edited by Richard Ellmann (London: Faber and Faber, 1992), 339.

8. James Joyce, *Finnegans Wake* (London: Faber, 1975), 226.

9. Shloss, *Lucia Joyce*, 426.

10. *Letters of James Joyce: I Edition*, ed. Stuart Gilbert (New York: Viking, 1957), 285.

11. Vanel, "Le Mouvement," *Cahiers Rythme et Couleur*, 91.

12. André Levinson, "The Idea of the Dance: From Aristotle to Mallarmé," in *What is Dance? Readings in Theory and Criticism*, ed. Roger Copeland and Marshall Cohen (Oxford: Oxford University Press, 1983), 50.

13. Quoted in Jacqueline Robinson, *Modern Dance in France (1920–1970): An Adventure* (London: Routledge, 2013), 54.

14. Paul Valéry, "Philosophy of the Dance," In *What Is Dance? Readings in Theory and Criticism*, ed. Roger Copeland and Marshall Cohen (Oxford: Oxford University Press, 1983), 63.

15. James Joyce, *Poems and Exiles*, edited with introduction by J. C. C. May (London: Penguin, 1992), 44.

16. James Joyce, *Poems and Exiles*, 44.

17. Norbert Lennartz, "'The Ache of Modernism': James Joyce's Pomes Penyeach and Their Literary Context," *James Joyce Quarterly* 47, no. 2 (2010): 202.

18. Richard Ellmann, *James Joyce, New and Revised Edition* (Oxford and New York: Oxford University Press, 1983), 205.

19. James Joyce, *Poems and Exiles*, 53.

20. James Joyce, *Poems and Exiles*, 53.

21. Louis Gillet, Preface to Geoffrey Chaucer, *A Chaucer A. B. C. being a hymn to the Holy Virgin in an English version, from the French of Guillaume de Deguilleville*, initial letters designed and illuminated by Lucia Joyce (Paris: Obelisk Press, 1936), i.

22. *Letters of James Joyce: III Edition*, ed. Richard Ellmann (New York: Viking, 1966), 406.

23. Stephanie Barron and Peter W. Guenther, *Degenerate Art: The Fate of the Avant-garde in Nazi Germany* (Los Angeles: Los Angeles County Museum of Art, 1991), 11.

24. Ramsay Burt, *Alien Bodies: Representations of Modernity, 'Race' and Nation in Early Modern Dance* (London and New York, Routledge: 1998), 5.

25. *The Letters of Samuel Beckett, Vol 1: 1929–1940,* ed. Martha Dow Fehsenfeld and Lois Overbeck More (Cambridge: Cambridge University Press, 2009), 384.

26. Samuel Beckett, *More Pricks Than Kicks*, vol. 4 of The Grove Centenary Edition (New York: Grove, 2006), 159.

27. Joyce, *Letters III*, 316.

28. Samuel Beckett, *Waiting for Godot*, in *The Complete Dramatic Works* (London: Faber and Faber, 2006), 27.

29. Josephine Starte, "Beckett's Dances," *Journal of Beckett Studies* 23, no. 2 (2014): 181.

30. *Footfalls,* dir. Jonathan Heron, Samuel Beckett Theatre, Dublin, July 2012.

31. *Not I,* dir. Touretteshero, Battersea Arts Centre, London, 28 Feb–17 March 2018, and *Not I, Footfalls and Rockaby,* dir. Walter Asmus, An Taibhdhearc, Galway, July 2014.

32. Petra Kuppers, *Disability and Contemporary Performance* (New York: Routledge, 2004), 2.

33. Mark Franko, "Dance and the Political: States of Exception," *Dance Research Journal* 38, nos. 1–2 (2006): 7.

34. *riverrun,* dir. Olwen Fouéré, Projects Arts Centre, Dublin, 6 October 2013.

BIBLIOGRAPHY

Barron, Stephanie, and Peter W. Guenther. *Degenerate Art: The Fate of the Avant-garde in Nazi Germany*. Los Angeles: Los Angeles County Museum of Art, 1991.

Beckett, Samuel. *The Complete Dramatic Works.* London: Faber and Faber, 2006.

———. *Dream of Fair to Middling Women*. New York: Arcade Publishing, 1993.

———. *Footfalls,* dir. Jonathan Heron. Samuel Beckett Theatre, Dublin, July 2012.

———. "German Diaries" [Six Volumes, late September 1936 to early April 1937], RUL MS (unnumbered), Beckett International Foundation, Reading University Library.

———. *The Letters of Samuel Beckett, Vol 1: 1929–1940*. Ed. Martha Dow Fehsenfeld and Lois More Overbeck. Cambridge: Cambridge University Press, 2009.

———. *More Pricks Than Kicks*. Vol. 4 of The Grove Centenary Edition. New York: Grove, 2006.

———. *Not I*. Dir. Touretteshero. Battersea Arts Centre, London, 28 Feb–17 March 2018.

———. *Not I, Footfalls, and Rockaby*. Dir. Walter Asmus. An Taibhdhearc, Galway, July 2014.

———, *Riverrun*. Dir. Olwen Fouéré. Projects Arts Centre, Dublin, 6 October 2013.

Burt, Ramsay. *Alien Bodies: Representations of Modernity, 'Race' and Nation in Early Modern Dance*. London and New York, Routledge: 1998.

Chaucer, Geoffrey. *A Chaucer A. B. C. being a hymn to the Holy Virgin in an English version, from the French of Guillaume de Deguilleville.* Initial letters designed and illuminated by Lucia Joyce. Preface by Louis Gillet. Paris: Obelisk Press, 1936.

Ellmann, Richard. *James Joyce*: *New and Revised Edition*. Oxford and New York: Oxford University Press, 1983.

Franko, Mark. "Dance and the Political: States of Exception." *Dance Research Journal* 38, nos. 1–2 (2006): 3–18.

Jones, Susan. *Literature, Modernism, and Dance.* Oxford: Oxford University Press, 2013.

Joyce, James. *Finnegans Wake*. London: Faber and Faber, 1975.

———. *Letters of James Joyce: I Edition.* Ed. Stuart Gilbert. New York: Viking, 1957.

———. *Letters of James Joyce: III Edition.* Ed. Richard Ellmann. New York: Viking, 1966.

———. *The Mime of Mick, Nick and the Maggies: a Fragment from Work in Progress.* Illustrations designed by Lucia Joyce. The Hague: Servire Press, 1934.

———, *Poems and Exiles.* Edited with introduction by J. C. C. May. London: Penguin, 1992.

———. *Pomes Penyeach.* Inscribed letters designed and illuminated by Lucia Joyce. Paris: Obelisk Press, 1932.

———. *Selected Letters of James Joyce.* Edited by Richard Ellmann. London: Faber and Faber, 1992.

———, *Storiella as She is Syng: a section of Work in Progress.* Illustrated by Lucia Joyce. London: Cornivus Press, 1937.

Kolb, Alexandra. *Performing Femininity: Dance and Literature in German Modernism.* Oxford: Peter Lang, 2009.

Kuppers, Petra. *Disability and Contemporary Performance.* New York: Routledge, 2004.

Le Bihan, Adrien. James Joyce travesti par trois clercs parisiens (dont Louis Gillet et Michel Crépu de la Revue des Deux-Mondes), Cherche-bruit, 2011.

Lennartz, Norbert. "'The Ache of Modernism': James Joyce's *Pomes Penyeach* and Their Literary Context." *James Joyce Quarterly* 47, no. 2 (2010): 197–211.

Levinson, André. "The Idea of the Dance: From Aristotle to Mallarmé." In *What Is Dance? Readings in Theory and Criticism*, ed. Roger Copeland and Marshall Cohen, 47–55. Oxford: Oxford University Press, 1983.

Mulrooney, Deirdre. "The lost story of James Joyce's daughter as a Parisian dancer." *The Irish Times* 21st June 2018.

Robinson, Jacqueline. *Modern Dance in France (1920–1970): An Adventure.* London and New York: Routledge, 2013.

Shloss, Carol. *Lucia Joyce: To Dance in the Wake.* New York: Picador, 2005.

Starte, Josephine. "Beckett's Dances." *Journal of Beckett Studies* 23, no. 2 (2014): 178–201.

Titus, Edward, ed. *This Quarter* V.1 (1932).

Valéry, Paul. "Philosophy of the Dance." In *What Is Dance? Readings in Theory and Criticism*, ed. Roger Copeland and Marshall Cohen, 55–65. Oxford: Oxford University Press, 1983.

Vanel, Hélène. *Cahiers Rythme et Coeleur: Prose, Poemes, Croquis, Annales, Photographies.* Semestriel No. III, Mai 1926. https://gallica.bnf.fr/ark:/12148/bpt6k1341972/f1.item

Chapter Nine

Yeats's Transgressive Dancers

Margaret Mills Harper

The work of W. B. Yeats traces a long arc. Over the course of his life, which extended through the late Victorian and Edwardian periods, the early years of the twentieth century, the Great War in Europe and revolution in Ireland, the high modernist 1920s, and the urgent 1930s, the style of Yeats's poetry and drama also shift radically, from early, sinuous Celtic-Twilit lyrics to harsh, emotionally uncomfortable work made when Europe slouched towards the Second World War. Some impulses are constant throughout his long and restless career, however. One of these is certainly a commitment to the idea of art, and within that, the notion of performance. For Yeats, to be human was to be in a constant state of longing: "a hunger for the apple on the bough / Most out of reach," as he puts it in the poem "Ego Dominus Tuus."[1] This yearning for fullness cannot be satisfied, or arguably even understood, but it may be expressed in words or action—and to a large degree, in Yeats, words are action. It is hard to overstate the importance of performance and performativity for understanding him.

Yeats was of course a playwright, founder and manager of the Irish national theatre, and a tireless promoter of drama. Theatre and theatricality saturate his *oeuvre*. Rather surprisingly (because he knew little about it, technically speaking), dance in particular plays a large role in his thinking and practice. Not only is dance important to an understanding of Yeats, but he also occupies an interesting place in the history of Irish modern dance. He consistently promoted innovative practices and institutions (most notably the Abbey School of Ballet), and he worked productively with dancers and choreographers, such as Michio Ito and Ninette de Valois. The influence of dance on Yeats's work, especially his dance plays, has received thoughtful attention.[2] Figures of dancers also populate his poetry rather densely, appearing at cruxes of a number of his most well-known works. These dancers embody the artifice and otherness that are hallmarks of Yeats's ideas. They are human forms engaging in highly artificial movements, elaborately suggestive of unfulfilled desire and symbolic action. They also occur at identifiable fault lines in Yeats's works as overdetermined emblems, often pointing to emotional and conceptual issues that were yet to be worked through. Dancers, as I hope to show, point to moments when Yeats reaches beyond what he understands or can encompass. They are signs of unharnessed poetic energy, impossibility made possible.

PERFORMANCE

Yeats's first choice of medium was visual. His father, brother, sisters, and daughter were all visual artists, and he went to art school as a young man. Soon, however, he decided that "Words alone are certain good," or so the speaker pronounces in a repeated line from the poem Yeats kept as the first in many volumes of collected poetry, "The Song of the Happy Shepherd" (*VP* 64–67). Yeats could not show the energy of endless desire in visual media: his "vision" (or "visions") required a temporal element. It also demanded stillness, however. Thus, as suggested in this poem, which is certainly an *ars poetica* for the young poet, the temporality of his chosen work must not occur in dance or music (partly, it must be admitted, though he does not say as much, because of his profound lack of talent in either of those arts). The pronouncement about words occurs at the end of a statement dismissing dance and music specifically. For an art that could capture what is necessary, that is, the "dreaming" truth that occurs "in thine own heart," the Shepherd, a figure out of pastoral tradition, proclaims,

> But O, sick children of the world,
> Of all the many changing things
> In dreary dancing past us whirled,
> To the cracked tune that Chronos sings,
> Words alone are certain good.

Nonetheless, the Shepherd does "sing" (this is, after all, his "Song"). Furthermore, the friend for whom he mourns, in a poem that contains grief as well as joy, was of a dancing lineage:

> And I would please the hapless faun,
> Buried under the sleep ground,
> With mirthful songs before the dawn.
> His shouting days with mirth were crowned;
> And still I dream he treads the lawn,
> Walking ghostly in the dew,
> Pierced by my glad singing through. . . .

Traces of Mallarmé may inhere in this hapless faun, as well as a hint of theatrical treading the boards or even dance in the phrase "treads the lawn"; the scene hints at the uses to which Mallarmé's poem "L'Après-midi d'un faune" was put in the decade after the publication of Yeats's poem in 1885, by Debussy (1894), and then Nijinsky (1912). The central moment of "The Song of the Happy Shepherd" is the Shepherd's advice (to readers who presumably are those "sick children of the world") to take up a shell from the seaside and speak into its hollow opening so it can "reword" one's utterance. After so enjoining his hearers, he announces, "I must be gone"—into his own dream of his ghostly fellow and final imperative: "dream thou!" (67) The poem is deeply invested in the iterated self and the emptiness implicit in such action. In manuscript and first printed versions, the poem explicitly calls for performance: the manuscript is headed "enter a Fawn / Holding a shell."[3] The text in the *Dublin University Review* begins with the information that the poem is "*Spoken by a Satyr, carrying a sea-shell,*" and a mock stage direction ("*He carries a sea-shell*") remains in its first appearance in a book-length collection, *The Wanderings of Oisin and Other Poems* (1889).

When the lure of the actual stage, and with it the idea of a national literary theatre, took hold in practice around the turn of the twentieth century, Yeats was inevitably drawn to a form of total theatre. As Katherine Worth notes, Yeats "grasped . . . that words were not enough" for his purposes. Instead, "a technique of intense physicality was needed. All the resources of the theatre—scene, color, music, dance and movement—had to be brought into play."[4] Yeats's theatrical art, like his poetry, was also consistently symbolic, attending to representations rather than things themselves, suggestions rather than direct presentation. Among the ideas that Yeats brought into his drama (influenced by his deep commitments to the occult, including membership in a magical order, as well as his discovery of Nietzsche) was the conviction that the deepest of human needs requires the distance of art or ritual to be expressed. The self must reach not necessarily into some unspecified interior but beyond itself towards an exteriorized otherness or other. What it finds there must be performed, (re-)enacted in space and time, form joining rhythm and movement, in order to be valid.

UNPURGED DESIRE

In the 1880s and 1890s, the young Yeats's dancers are nearly always associated with fear of the feminine. They are supernatural, *unheimlich*, and powerful, showing the clear influence of the cultural tradition of female love objects or Romantic *femmes fatale*. Their appearance often bodes ill for the men who encounter them. After the turn of the century, this stock image occurs with less frequency. In Yeats's middle period, there are relatively few dancers in the poetry, though he was developing an innovative style of theatre during this period: minimalist, ritualized, exotic, and incorporating dance. In 1916, the first of what he called his dance plays, *At the Hawk's Well*, was performed in Lady Cunard's drawing room in London, characterized by R. F. Foster as a place where "the avant-garde mingled with high society."[5]

A new and significantly more complex energy attends dancers and dancing in the later periods of Yeats's work, that is, in the 1920s and 1930s. The earlier themes are folded into presentations of greater ambiguity. Dancers densely populate Yeats's poetry and drama following 1917, after his introduction to the Japanese Nōh drama through Ezra Pound's study and editorial work on the scholar Ernest Fenollosa, his marriage to George Hyde Lees, and the automatic writing that the Yeatses began during their honeymoon. In this period, too, Yeats was intensely interested in or worked with several self-choreographing modern dancers, including Loie Fuller, Michio Ito, and Ninette de Valois.

The philosophic system whose ideas most profoundly affected the rest of Yeats's life uses dance as a prime metaphor. The structured ideas that came through the automatic script were founded on geometric form and dynamic movement. As it developed in the intense mediumistic collaboration between the Yeatses and the two editions of *A Vision*, the "system" became an impersonal and totalizing structure that purports to encompass intensities of human desire and expression, including acceptance of fate as it operates in and through many reincarnated lives. In the first version of *A Vision*, Yeats invents a narrative featuring two simultaneous expressions of the eternal truths. One emanates from Europe and takes the form of an old book written by a fictional author (in the woodcut made by Yeats's friend Edmund Dulac, this fictional personage, Giraldus, looks a good deal like W. B. Yeats). The other is found in a mysterious tribe who dance symbolic patterns on the orientalized sands of the Arabian desert.

In the work from what are arguably Yeats's most productive decades, the 1920s and 1930s, *A Vision* is always in the background. The late dancers and dance as an idea also partake of Yeats's ongoing work on understanding and living the system. They are much more socially and aesthetically progressive, or transgressive, than is sometimes realized. The late dancers exhibit personal and sexual agency that is complex and ambiguous. They are less similar to the traditions of Keats's "La Belle Dame sans Merci" than they might seem. They are still figures of desire, but the confessional poet often uses them to express specific attachments to actual women. As such, they have more agency as individuals than the earlier dancers. One of these women was Maud Gonne's daughter Iseult, who is one of the models for the dancers in Yeats's volume *Michael Robertes and the Dancer*.[6]

With the system in mind, as well as the marital collaboration between Yeats and his much younger wife George it represents, these later dancers can be seen to embody unresolved energies that drove Yeats's modernity. In the later work as in the earlier, dance and dancers occupy unsettled territory.

The figure of the still and moving dancer, with mask or dead face, which Frank Kermode argues is "the central icon of Yeats and of the whole [Romantic] tradition," is static, unworldly beauty. She (the dancer in this conception is always female) functions as an embodied correlative to a formal theory of poetry.[7] Other dancers populate Yeats's late drama and verse, though, and they point to alterations in theory as well. These dancers are depicted in relationships with men and other women. In the title poem to the volume *Michael Robartes and the Dancer* (1921), the first collection after the major changes in Yeats's work that usually lead critics to identify a new period, the voice identified as *She* and presumably the dancer in the title speaks back to the learned but possibly old-fashioned *He*, presumably Robartes, as he lectures her on how to become just such a Romantic image. "They say such different things at school," she muses (*VP* 397). The poem comments on Yeats's relationship with Iseult Gonne, the daughter of his long-adored Maud. This dancer is given more agency and character than the earlier dancers, and the drama of the dialogue poem lies in the ambivalence of the power dynamic between the two speakers: he does most of the talking, but are his pronouncements to be accepted by readers or are they the useless attempts to seduce a modern woman by a pompous older man?

The light touch of this poem and the next in the volume, "Solomon and the Witch," overlie a new energy, which hints at transference of gendered identities. This is not a troubadour debasing himself before a silent beloved but a man who claims to understand the performance of femininity better than the woman to whom he speaks. He has "principles to prove me right," he says, in asserting that "blest souls are not composite" (*VP* 396–397). Solomon too lectures Sheba for most of their poem, but she has both the last word, which is of sexual desire, rendering all his talk irrelevant.

Later poems build upon the truths of composite souls as well as desire. By and large, they incorporate the suggestion that self-awareness is possible only by realizing that self is other, always alien and strange, and that finding that otherness and strangeness is the only route to self-discovery. A critical aspect of that strangeness is that it works against subjectivity as well as for it. The self is radically unstable, changing from moment to moment. Put differently, the dancer is not only stillness in motion; she (or he) also always moves in surrounding stillness—two incompatible conceptions violently yoked together. The final couplet of the poem "Mohini Chatterjee" nods in this direction with its evocation of live bodies dancing eternity: "Or, as great sages say, / Men dance with deathless feet" (*VP* 496).

In other words, dance still points to the poet reaching beyond himself, in the system-influenced poetry of the later period no less than the poetry raised over the sexual fears and personal romantic crises of Yeats's earlier periods. The poem that follows "Mohini Chatterjee" in the volume *The Winding Stair and Other Poems* (1933) is the mighty "Byzantium" (*VP* 497–498). It links "death-in-life and life-in-death" in a setting where human life is joined on the pavements of the city with ghostly figures that are indefinable, "an image, man or shade, / Shade more than man, more image than a shade." The lifeless, deathless images seem to triumph over the "mire and blood" of the mortal ones, but the final stanza forces all into a set of images that whirl nearly out of control, the "fury" of human life broken by spirit, spirits carried on live dolphins, water dissolved by fire, a dancing floor breaking the living feet that might dance on it, the sea torn by the life in it as well as the art that torments it:

> Those images that yet
> Fresh images beget,
> That dolphin-torn, that gong-tormented sea. (*VP* 498)

These final images of the poem "Byzantium" are uttered by a speaking voice that readers are meant to identify as the speaker of the earlier "Sailing to Byzantium," an old man with a heart "sick with desire / And fastened to a dying animal" (*VP* 408). "Byzantium," like its companion poem, is dramatic. No longer sailing, the speaker is now inexplicably in the purgatorial place where "The unpurged images of day recede." The movement of the poem pushes in succeeding stanzas from a description of the setting (the city at midnight), to unresolved antinomies of living/dead image/human/shade, to the metal bird imagined in the earlier poem now bitter with scorn of the living, to a searing vision of "flames . . . flames begotten of flame" that vanish into moving non-movement, "Dying into a dance / An agony of trance." Words and images repeat themselves in an "unpurged" jumble. The impossible Byzantium cannot be expressed: by the last stanza, the syntax breaks down into a series of exclamatory noun clauses, then a sentence that obsessively repeats itself rhythmically in the trimeter of a last quatrain. Then the quatrain itself dissolves: the final two lines ignore their line break and become a single six-beat line, and the end-rhyme disappears into the short *o* sounds in *dolphin* and *gong* and assonance and alliteration of *torn* and *tormented*. The connection is made in sound and image, not logic. The ending of the poem points to a paradox operating in much of Yeats's late work: broken bodies, including the bodies of formal lines and presumed bodies of speakerly personae, also dance.

BEYOND THE POLES

One of the standard ways of thinking of Yeats's modernist poetry, using a term of which he was fond (which was taken from Dante), begins with the idea of Dantean unity of being, and the poet's injunction to himself to "hammer your thoughts into unity."[8] This kind of interpretation relies on older notions of high modernism as a movement that was anxious about disunity, presenting fragmentation as an indication of something fundamentally wrong.[9] Yeats's modernist dancers twirl to a different tune. Dancers in such poems as "The Double Vision of Michael Robartes" and "Among School Children," animated by the philosophy of *A Vision*, embody the always changing relationship between strictly opposing polarities rather than the poles themselves. In the conceptual commitments that suffuse Yeats's late work, there has been a shift, from stressing artificiality or distance from the real, to focusing on the energy that causes that split. Given that art and life are always related to each other, what kind of repulsion pushes them apart, and what kind of magnetism attracts them to each other? Definition and balance are overcome by transgression, refusal of stability, and the operations of unharnessable power.

Lack of stability has not dominated any number of characterizations of Yeats's mature work. Given his powerfully persuasive (even domineering) voice and his continuing attachment to traditional poetic form, it has been easy to imagine Yeats's aesthetic to be pervaded by a notion of mastery. His work revels in opposing polarities, but, or so goes a well-established narrative, Yeats's work always also yearns for a state that would transcend them. Thus, critics (including this one) have written about antinomies such as chance and choice, life and art, life and death, love and hate, male and female, self and anti-self, egalitarian and hierarchical, and so forth—not to mention the host of polarities in the elaborate geometrically based terminology of *A Vision*: Sun and Moon, east and west, Primary and Antithetical, light and dark. These binaries exist in a system that imagines them in the context of a total figure, however, a larger if unreachable whole of which they are the two sides. The system describes such a unified whole in discussions of the Thirteenth Cone (or Cycle), that is, a spiritual abode beyond the twelve cycles or gyres, or perhaps a totality that exists beyond the always changing whirls of energy between oppositions that drive the universe. (There must be such in a philosophic structure that requires what Hegel might call an antithesis to every thesis.)[10]

This way of thinking may suit the sensibilities of readers interested in and influenced by analyses of literary modernism as a western European and North American movement led by writers such as Pound and Eliot, but it may miss some of the messiness of Yeats. Imagining Yeats as a binary thinker who yearns for synthesis of oppositions misses a quality he often refers to using words like *wildness* or *the wild* or, crucially, expresses by means of dance. The third term in Yeatsian systems is often less a resolution of two opposites than a way of expressing an impossibility: imagining the satisfaction of desire, without even proposing that such a state is imaginable.[11] Even the poem "Ego Dominus Tuus," seemingly the most binary of poems, does not exactly end with the figure of a mysterious anti-self conjured up in the final lines. The poem, written in December 1915, is in the form of a dialogue between two figures with the oppositional designations *Hic* and *Ille*, who illustrate the idea of self and anti-self. The poem concludes with a strange start of fear that birds might carry away the ultimate secret to "blasphemous men," an inexplicable last item in a series of increasingly distant imagined images. The birds make the poem fly away, like the bird at the final lines of "The Tower" or the swans in "The Wild Swans at Coole," or the bird song at the end of Emer's dance in the play *The Death of Cuchulain* or at the conclusion of the related poem "Cuchulain Comforted." Daniel Albright's notes to the poem quote from a conversation with Yeats that took place in 1916, as recorded by a minor member of his circle. The notes show Yeats, a great talker, expounding upon the escape from the binaries of conscious self and subconscious other as something both necessary to art and made possible only through performance:

> Then talked of Freud & Jung and the subconscious self, applying them to art; said the great thing is to reduce the conscious self to humility, as by imitation of some ancient master, leaving the unconscious free to work: said all reading of contemporaries & imitation of them was bad. The self in poetry must be a dramatist, regarded by poet as spectator.[12]

"THE DOUBLE VISION OF MICHAEL ROBARTES" AND "AMONG SCHOOL CHILDREN"

A dancer occupies a central position in "The Double Vision of Michael Robartes," a poem published first in the 1919 printing of *The Wild Swans at Coole.* Positioned between two other figures in the middle section of a three-part poem, this dancer may be a useful first illustration of the complexity represented by dance in Yeats's late work. The poem is based almost directly on an aspect of the system of *A Vision*, in particular, the states of the soul symbolized by the dark and full moon, the first and fifteenth lunar phases. The second part of the poem, set on the fifteenth phase or full moon, describes three figures, the central one of which is a dancer. The other two are a Buddha (representing ultimate emotional wisdom) and a Sphinx (representing "triumph of intellect"). Between them moves a dancer. She also represents something impossible, as are all figures at the full moon, since they consist purely of one principle rather than the mixture of qualities that life requires. She has "outdanced thought" and attained "bodily perfection," meaning that attention entirely on physical sensation alone can create mental stillness, so that the mind "moved yet seemed to stop / As 'twere a spinning-top" (*VP* 383–384).

The dancer, more than her two companions, embodies not perfection but a different kind of impossibility, the simultaneous affirmation and negation of movement within movement, time overthrown in a moment of time, a figure that is dead and yet "flesh and bone." In the third part of the poem, the speaker or dreamer, named Michael Robartes in the title, is brought to what he calls "a pitch of folly" as he is "caught between the pull / Of the dark moon and the full, / The commonness of thought and images / That have the frenzy of our western seas" (*VP* 383–384). This is not nihilism (after all, it occurs in a rhyming, rhythmic, stanzaic form of great vitality, and the poem ends with the making of a "song"). Rather, it suggests another impossibility: the containment within a structure of something antipathetic to form. At the end of the poem, Robartes recounts having "made my moan" then "kissed a stone," two acts beyond language, and afterwards "arranged . . . in a song" his visionary reward in ruin.

This dancer is good preparation for probably the most well-known of Yeatsian dancers, the one at the mighty conclusion of the poem "Among School Children," from *The Tower* (published in 1928). That dancer (in good part because of the tonal and formal resonance of the verse) seems an image of triumphant unity if there ever was one, the union of the real and the imagination, the creative act and the creating actor, form and matter. But that power occurs in a setting that is also fundamentally unresolved. The poem, if you recall, is concerned with the problem of time. The speaker, an old man, cannot reconcile memory and present circumstance, hope with remorse. The poem begins in a school, with the speaker observing the children as a distinguished visitor (Yeats was a member of the Seanad Éireann or Senate in the new Free State and made such a visit to a Montessori School in Waterford as part of his official duties).[13] He looks at the children and is suddenly transported into a memory of his beloved and himself when young. Further musing on her in old age leads to a thought about whether a mother's love for a baby would exist if she knew the child as an old man. This thought is expressed by means of an allusion to Porphyry and Plotinus, and the poem then moves into a discussion of other ancient thinkers.

Philosophically speaking, the issue is ontological, between difference (that which changes over time) and identity (which remains through time). The intellectual direction of the latter half of the poem begins with Platonic form, touches down on the issue of human image-making, calls out to those very "Presences," suggests the possibility of unity of body and soul (labor and "blossoming or dancing"), and then finishes with two images suggested by the last: a chestnut tree and a then dancer. Two questions are raised: in which of its parts—leaf, blossom, or bole—is a tree essentially comprised? Then,

> O body swayed to music, O brightening glance,
> How can we know the dancer from the dance? (*VP* 446)

The famous final quatrain might read as if the answers to the two questions are *none of the above* and *we can't*. Yeats has hammered his thoughts into unity and nothing can withstand their tempered strength. The philosophical problems that have driven the poem, of essence over time, part to whole, and being to doing, are solved. The chestnut tree is itself though changing through seasons and from part to part, and a dancer is indistinguishable from her dancing or from dance as an abstraction. Opposites—part to whole, multiplicity to singleness, identity through time, creating and created—disappear in a magnificent concluding unity, made of the balance of four near-perfect lines.

But what if the energy of the questions left hanging and also suggesting answers, as questions must by their very form, is a stylistic correlative to some unthinkability beyond the binary of the One and the Many? The autobiographical speaker loves Plato and Plotinus, whose thought underpins the poem, but then he bids them go back. The great tree and dancer succeed the old scarecrows of great philosophers and the aged "smiling public man" Yeats has become, in terms of the movement of the poem, but they do not displace them. As Vendler notes, the poem as a whole arrives very late at what she describes as its "sublime moment of address," the three odal apostrophes to those Presences that are "self-born mockers of man's enterprise," tree, and dancer.[14] The performed voice of the poem has turned from awkward stick figure into a tree or dancer himself, alive with "great-rooted" energy, whose "Labor is blossoming or dancing," beautiful with embodied art.

If the poem is read with attention to its play of power and gender, a further possibility emerges. If the ending is interpreted as expressing certainty or transcendence, the final questions are posed by a masculine speaker to an equally knowledgeable "we," with the dancer addressed only as a body and eroticized glance. Doubts and difficulties are overcome by poetic potency, and the speaker has overcome the identity with which the poem begins, of a foolish and embarrassingly undesirable old man, trapped in a public role and exiled from the "passion" known by the female figures that are opposites to his current state. The poem is preoccupied with nuns, children, Yeats's remembered beloved, a "youthful mother," "careless Muses," and perhaps the mysterious "Presences / That passion, piety or affection knows" in the climactic penultimate stanza. These figures collectively pose trouble for the masculine identity of the "I" of the first stanzas and the collective "we" it claims by the famous final line. He imaginatively enters, or is entered by, the images he invokes. The poem may not only gesture towards the traditional poetic form of an ode by means of these apostrophes, but also towards a magical summons or mystical undoing. He is tree and dancer, but also another worshipper of images like nun or mother, also a breaker of hearts as well as one whose heart may be broken, another "self-born mocker" as well as man whose enterprise is mocked. Tim Armstrong argues that the tag "self-born" belongs to a theme of sexual self-renewal in late Yeats, implying "a reintegration of the feminine and the masculine within the self."[15] The poem may well point to the sexual explorations of Yeats's final decade, along with the transgressive eroticism of some of the poetry from these years (including figures like Crazy Jane from the sequence *Words for Music Perhaps* and Ribh the hermit from *Supernatural Songs*).

CONCLUSION

A correlative to the final questions of "Among School Children" may be found in the gyres of the system, which are neither found nor invented, neither totalized nor fragmented. They are over determined, overly rigid in structure, but also never still and infinitely pulsing with movement, so that *A Vision* resorts to such absurdities as stories of Arab tribes dancing diagrams into the sands of the desert, or terms as Thirteenth Cone as a way of describing them. In one passage, the Thirteenth Cone is envisioned as "a sphere because sufficient to itself; but as seen by Man it is a cone. It becomes even conscious of itself as so seen, like some great dancer, the perfect flower of modern culture, dancing some primitive dance and conscious of his or her own life and of the dance."[16]

This sphere or cone is less a noun, an object that can be named, than the turning of attention to the dance that is the need for naming. Desire is one word for this state. Energy is another. An object becomes a subject, "conscious of itself as so seen," and that semi-divine subjectivity is both primitive and modern, organic (flower rather than tree as in "Among School Children" and possessed of life) and artificial (dancer). Its gender is indeterminate, as are a number of its cultural antecedents, notably the Hindu Lord of the Dance and a "mediaeval story" about a Guardian Angel mentioned in the sentence following the passage quoted above.

I do not want to end this chapter with my own transcendent solution to the jagged edges of thought and feeling that Yeats uses in his late poems featuring dancers. Nor do I want to imply that Yeats rested in more than a temporary pleasure in success. Existence outside binaries does not come without a cost, as can be seen in a little lyric that is not one of the great philosophical poems such as "Among School Children." In the very late poem "The Crazed Girl," based on a real episode with a woman that very nearly caused a scandal, the self is divided with disastrous consequences.[17] Neither these consequences nor the self-division are transcended, as many interpretations would have it, but they can be accepted and valued. The text of the irregular sonnet begins:

> That crazed girl improvising her music,
> Her poetry, dancing upon the shore,
> Her soul in division from itself . . .

The poet declares that the girl, "hiding amid the cargo of a steamship" with a broken knee-cap is not pitiful or absurd but "a beautiful lofty thing" or at least something "heroically lost, heroically found." (*VP* 578)

Dance plays a role here, too. The second stanza claims that she "stood in desperate music wound," the last word repeated twice in the next line, suggesting that the poet is also "wound" (or indeed wounded) in desperate music like the dancing figure. Perhaps both she and he make, in the final lines of the poem, "no common intelligible sound." Instead, they both sing the final snatch of song: "O sea-starved, hungry sea." Both crazed girl and old poet are living out the principles of the system, the poem suggests. "Her soul in division from itself" is danced in a winding gyre into something the poet calls a "triumph," though she is mentally ill, her knee injured so that she cannot physically dance, and unintelligible. That triumph hardly represents healing from her "crazed" condition, but the poet declares her "a beautiful lofty thing." That phrase echoes the identical phrase from the previous poem in *Last Poems*, "Beautiful Lofty Things," where it is used for a litany of people Yeats has admired most: the nationalist John O'Leary, his father, Standish O'Grady, Lady Gregory, and Maud Gonne. (The word *crazed* also suggests a connection with Crazy Jane, one of Yeats's most outrageous and disturbing personae.) Once again, dancers can be found in a location where Yeats, despite his own need for closure and mastery, faces, expresses, and accepts crucial insecurities and instabilities.

NOTES

1. W. B. Yeats, "Ego Dominus Tuus," in *The Variorum Edition of the Poems,* ed. Peter Allt and Russell K. Alspach (New York: Macmillan, 1957), 368 (hereafter cited in text as *VP*).

2. See Richard Allen Cave, *Collaborations: Ninette de Valois and William Butler Yeats* (Alton: Dance Books, 2011); Sylvia C. Ellis, *The Plays of W. B. Yeats: Yeats and the Dancer* (London: Macmillan, 1995); Susan Jones, *Literature, Modernism, and Dance* (Oxford: Oxford University Press, 2013), especially chap. 1, "A Poetics of Personality: Mallarmé, Fuller, Yeats, and Graham"; and Deirdre Mulrooney, *Irish Moves: An Illustrated History of Dance and Physical Theatre in Ireland* (Dublin: The Liffey Press, 2006), especially chap. 2, "The Neglected Chapter: Salvaging the Abbey School of Ballet."

3. W. B. Yeats, *The Early Poetry, Volume II:* The Wanderings of Oisin *and Other Early Poems to 1895; Manuscript Materials*, ed. George Bornstein (Ithaca and London: Cornell University Press, 1994), 202–203.

4. Katharine Worth, *The Irish Drama of Europe from Yeats to Beckett* (London: Athlone Press of the University of London, 1978), 3.

5. R. F. Foster, *W. B. Yeats: A Life. II: The Arch-Poet* (Oxford: Oxford University Press, 2003), 40.

6. See Elizabeth Butler Cullingford, "Yeats and Women: *Michael Robartes and the Dancer*, in *Yeats and Women*, ed. Deirdre Toomey, 2nd ed. (London, Macmillan, 1997), 223–251.

7. Frank Kermode, *Romantic Image* (London: Routledge and Kegan Paul, 1957), 89.

8. The first appearances of both of these phrases occur in the automatic script. "Unity of being" is first mentioned on 3 September 1918, in an answer to one of Yeats's questions dictated by the Control Thomas of Dorlowitz through George Yeats. "Hammer your thoughts into unity," also in George Yeats's hand, is advice to W. B. given by the Control Ameritus on 24 November 1919 (*Yeats's* Vision *Papers*, 4 vols., gen. ed. George Mills Harper, assisted by Mary Jane Harper, vol. 2., *The Automatic Script: 25 June 1918–29 March 1920*, ed. Steve L. Adams, Barbara J. Frieling, and Sandra L. Sprayberry (London: Macmillan, 1992), 41, 492. On "unity of being," see *A Vision: The Revised 1937 Edition*, ed. Margaret Mills Harper and Catherine E. Paul (New York: Scribner, 2015), 353–354n37. In "If I Were Four-and-Twenty," also written in 1919, Yeats writes, "One day when I was twenty-three or twenty-four this sentence seemed to form in my head, without my willing it, much as sentences form when we are half-asleep: 'Hammer your thoughts into unity.' For days I could think of nothing else, and for years I tested all I did by that sentence" (in *Later Essays*, ed. William H. O'Donnell [New York: Scribner, 1994], 34).

9. A useful corrective to this readerly hope for overcoming of disunity, even in poems that purport to offer reconciliation, may be found in Evan Radcliffe, "Yeats and the Quest for Unity: 'Among School Children' and Unity of Being," in *Colby Library Quarterly* 21, no. 3 (1985): 109–121. See also Michael Wood, *Yeats and Violence* (Oxford: Oxford University Press, 2010), an extended reading of "Nineteen

Hundred and Nineteen," a poem or poetic sequence that, *inter alia*, features the dance of Loie Fuller.

10. For thoughtful and knowledgeable analysis of this concept (as many others), see Neil Mann, *A Reader's Guide to Yeats's* A Vision (Clemson, SC: Clemson University Press, 2019), chap. 10, "The Divine: One and Many."

11. The sections describing the Thirteenth Cone are confused in the first edition of *A Vision* (1925), as Yeats was when the topic was brought up in the sessions of automatic writing. By 1937, when the second, heavily revised edition of the book was published, Yeats had worked through the ideas (and also read Hegel, among a number of other philosophers), so that the concept is explained with greater clarity. It remains a small aspect of the whole system, arguably more attractive to literary critics than it was to either W. B. or George Yeats.

12. Daniel Albright, ed., *W. B. Yeats: The Poems* (London: J. M. Dent / Everyman, 1992), 585n. The conversation as recalled by Henry Woodd Nevinson is quoted by Ronald Schuchard in his essay, "An Attendant Lord: H. W. Nevinson's Friendship with W. B. Yeats," in *Yeats Annual* No. 7, ed. Warwick Gould (London: Macmillan, 1990), 120.

13. George Yeats accompanied her husband on the visit to St. Otteran's School. Her witty description of the day to her friend Tom MacGreevy does end on a note more somber than W. B.'s poem that also gives a curious counterpart to elements in the poem like the "young mother," the linkage of young mother with nuns as worshippers of images, and the triumphal final line: "They [the nuns] make one feel ashamed, ashamed of life and drinking and smoking and caring for nothing not even husband and children or relations (who really does?) or anything but a line written in a book and a particular person that is but a part of one's own supreme egotism" (cited in Ann Saddlemyer, *Becoming George: The Life of Mrs W. B. Yeats* [Oxford: Oxford University Press, 2002], 320–321.

14. Helen Vendler, "Thinking in Images, Thinking in Assertions," chap. 4 in *Poets Thinking: Pope, Whitman, Dickinson, Yeats* (Cambridge, MA: Harvard University Press, 2004), 102. Vendler also argues for incorporation of incompletion in the exultant final images of the poem by way of a reading of the whole: "The poet means us to understand . . . that life is imperfect as it unfolds and yet perfect as it rounds to completion, lofty in its public, private, and collective yearnings and yet persistently, and enigmatically, disappointing until it can be re-evaluated *in extenso*" (99–100).

15. "Giving Birth to Oneself: Yeats's Late Sexuality," in *Yeats Annual* No. 8, ed. Warwick Gould (London: Macmillan, 1991), 47.

16. W. B. Yeats, *A Vision: The Revised 1937 Edition*, ed. Margaret Mills Harper and Catherine E. Paul (New York: Scribner, 2015), 175.

17. The woman was Margot Ruddock; Foster describes the episode in *The Arch-Poet*, 542–544.

BIBLIOGRAPHY

Armstrong, Tim. "Giving Birth to Oneself: Yeats's Late Sexuality." In *Yeats Annual* No. 8, edited by Warwick Gould, 39–58. London: Macmillan, 1991.

Cave, Richard Allen. *Collaborations: Ninette de Valois and William Butler Yeats.* Alton: Dance Books, 2011.

Cullingford, Elizabeth Butler. "Yeats and Women: *Michael Robartes and the Dancer.* In *Yeats and Women*, edited by Deirdre Toomey, 223–251. 2nd ed. London, Macmillan, 1997.

Ellis, Sylvia C. *The Plays of W. B. Yeats: Yeats and the Dancer.* London: Macmillan, 1995.

Foster, R. F. *W. B. Yeats: A Life. II: The Arch-Poet 1915–1939*. Oxford: Oxford University Press, 2003.

Harper, George Mills, ed., assisted by Mary Jane Harper. *Yeats's* Vision *Papers*. Vol. 2. Edited by Steve L. Adams, Barbara J. Frieling, and Sandra L. Sprayberry. 4 vols. London: Macmillan, 1992–2001.

Jones, Susan. *Literature, Modernism, and Dance.* Oxford: Oxford University Press, 2013.

Kermode, Frank. *Romantic Image.* London: Routledge and Kegan Paul, 1957.

Mann, Neil. *A Reader's Guide to Yeats's* A Vision. Clemson, SC: Clemson University Press, 2019.

Mulrooney, Deirdre. *Irish Moves: An Illustrated History of Dance and Physical Theatre in Ireland.* Dublin: The Liffey Press, 2006.

Radcliffe, Evan. "Yeats and the Quest for Unity: 'Among School Children' and Unity of Being." *Colby Library Quarterly* 21, no. 3 (1985): 109–121.

Saddlemyer, Ann. *Becoming George: The Life of Mrs W. B. Yeats*. Oxford: Oxford University Press, 2002.

Schuchard, Ronald. "An Attendant Lord: H. W. Nevinson's Friendship with W. B. Yeats." In *Yeats Annual* No. 7, edited by Warwick Gould, 90–130. London: Macmillan, 1990.

Vendler, Helen. "Thinking in Images, Thinking in Assertions." Chap. 4 in *Poets Thinking: Pope, Whitman, Dickinson, Yeats*. Cambridge, MA: Harvard University Press, 2004.

Worth, Katharine. *The Irish Drama of Europe from Yeats to Beckett.* London: Athlone Press of the University of London, 1978.

Yeats, W. B. *The Early Poetry, Volume II: "The Wanderings of Oisin" and Other Early Poems to 1895; Manuscript Materials.* Edited by George Bornstein. The Cornell Yeats. Ithaca and London: Cornell University Press, 1994.

———. *Later Essays*. Edited by William H. O'Donnell. New York: Scribner, 1994.

———. *The Poems.* Edited by Daniel Albright. London: J. M. Dent / Everyman, 1992.

———. *The Variorum Edition of the Poems*. Edited by Peter Allt and Russell K. Alspach. New York: Macmillan, 1957.

———. *A Vision: The Original 1925 Edition.* Edited by Catherine E. Paul and Margaret Mills Harper. *The Collected Works of W. B. Yeats.* Vol. 13. George Bornstein, general editor. New York: Scribner, 2008.

———. *A Vision: The Revised 1937 Edition.* Edited by Margaret Mills Harper and Catherine E. Paul. *The Collected Works of W. B. Yeats*. Vol. 14. George Bornstein, general editor. New York: Scribner, 2015.

Chapter Ten

"I as a Text," I as a Dance

On the Relationship of Contemporary Dance and Contemporary Poetry with Reference to Anne Juren, Martina Hefter, Monika Rinck, and Philipp Gehmacher

Lucia Ruprecht

The title of Judith Butler's Adorno Lectures, held at the Institute for Social Research at Johann Wolfgang Goethe University in Frankfurt am Main in 2002, is *Giving an Account of Oneself*[1]. As the literal German translation, "Rechenschaft von sich selbst ablegen," does not capture all the nuances of the English title, emphasizing accounting and explaining rather than telling a narrative about the self, the German title of the lectures is *Kritik der ethischen Gewalt* (A Critique of Ethical Violence).[2] This title points to the intention of Butler's reflections on accountability. Her lectures devise a new form of ethics, which is based on the fact that the subject "can never fully be accounted for:"[3]

> It would be, perhaps, an ethics based on our shared, invariable, and partial blindness about ourselves. The recognition that one is, at every turn, not quite the same as how one presents oneself in the available discourse might imply, in turn, a certain patience with others that would suspend the demand that they be self-same at every moment. Suspending the demand for self-identity or, more particularly, for complete coherence seems to me to counter a certain ethical violence which demands that we manifest and maintain self-identity at all times and require that others do the same. . . . When we claim to know and to present ourselves, we will fail in some ways that are nevertheless essential to who we are. We cannot reasonably expect anything different from others in return. . . . This can constitute a disposition of humility and generosity alike: I will need to be forgiven for what I cannot have fully known, and I will be under a similar obligation to offer forgiveness to others, who are also constituted in partial opacity to themselves.[4]

I cite Butler's reflections on accountability at such length here because I would like to keep the ethical impulse in mind when attempting to approach the choreography of Anne Juren and Philipp Gehmacher, and the texts of Martina Hefter and Monika Rinck, even if the connections between this impulse and practices of contemporary art cannot be covered comprehensively in the following.[5]

In her Munich speech on poetry, Ulrike Draesner speaks of the poetic genre as a "Gattung der Überforderung" (genre of excessive demands).[6] The same might apply to contemporary dance. Both poetry and dance are semantically never quite fathomable. For exactly this reason, one might argue, they need to be commented on. However, the choreographies and writings of the artists discussed here also already comment on themselves. They are dance pieces and texts which convey insights on their own aesthetics. On the back cover of the first edition of her collection of noteworthy terms which she calls *begriffsstudio* (concept studio), Monika Rinck quotes Niklas Luhmann, who points out that scholarship is not lacking in "gelehrter Prosa" (learned prose), but in "gelehrter Poesie" (learned poetry), which, according to Luhmann, is the only mode that is able to give expression to the "eigentümlichen Weltstimmungsgehalt wissenschaftlicher Theorien" (specific mood value of academic theory). Theory, Luhmann suggests, should always be accompanied by "eine[r] Art Parallelpoesie . . . die alles noch einmal anders sagt und damit die Wissenschaftssprache in die Grenzen ihres Funktionssystems zurückweist" (a kind of parallel poetry which says everything that theory says in different words, thereby limiting theoretical language to the confines within which it is functional).[7] The notion of parallel poetry exemplifies the specific achievements of artistic research such as the "researching art" created and presented by contemporary dance and literature.[8] This fences in my own academic language, keeping it within the borders of its functionality and defining the task of this chapter as the attempt to observe and constellate findings that already have been formulated by dance and poetry.

If the term parallel poetry is used for both the chosen literary and dance pieces, this implies an equally poetical and theoretical style in each.[9] As the analyses undertaken in the following will show, contemporary dance and contemporary poetry express ideas that correspond to content generally marked as theoretical thinking—in this case, Butler's reflections on accountability. (Theoretical) Art and theory participate in the same "mood value." Among other things, this mood value deals with the question how "I" can be said at all, if this "I" is a physically and discursively composed subject—I as a dance, "I as a text"—that can never completely access itself, while inevitably addressing a "you."[10] Butler refers to the Italian philosopher Adriana Cavarero here who anchors social experience in the dyadic encounter between the

"I" and the "you," and therefore within a "fundamental dependency on the other," even if the other is not the same as the self.[11]

What is there to say about more specific processes of interaction between contemporary literature and contemporary dance? While this relationship has generally not been given much attention in current scholarship and writing, it used to be very different about a hundred years ago. The time around 1900 saw not only the birth of a new aesthetic of dance, performed on a practical level and commented on in critical reviews, but also of a poetics of dance which was produced in the act of literary writing. This new poetics—as an exploration of possible forms of writing rather than a set of rules—associated dance with an embodied type of scripture. Writers were fascinated by non-verbal expressiveness, and by the fleeting nature of danced signs that assembled and dissolved themselves in perpetual motion.[12] However, literary descriptions of dance at the turn of the century rarely emerged from the writer's own experience of movement. They remained scenes of reception, or, as Gabriele Brandstetter put it, "Lektüren" (readings) of choreographed movement, the dynamics of which would be transferred into writing.[13] If it is present at all, the infatuation with dancers that often triggered or accompanied this reception process is only retrospectively alluded to in contemporary literature, as in the melancholic epigram preceding two dance poems in Martina Hefter's *Nach den Diskotheken* (After the Discotheques): "Nijinski in seiner Kammer schläft, bedeckt mit Gedichten. Lasst ihn."[14] (Nijinsky sleeps in his chamber, covered by poems. Let him.)

What I am trying to show here is that there is a fundamental difference between dance writing around 1900 and 2000, not only with regard to poetological and erotic concerns. There are only few contemporary texts that comment on dance; but those which do seem to emanate from the author's own experience of movement, sometimes more expressly, sometimes less so. Contemporary texts also show a relatively broad understanding of dance, expanding it into everyday movement, which is put in relation with the act of writing. Hefter regards her poems "als Erweiterungen körperlicher Bewegung" (as an extension of physical movement). In her volume *Vom Gehen und Stehen. Ein Handbuch* (Walking and Standing. A Handbook) she states that she is interested in "die subjektiven Eindrücke, die man von ihr (der körperlichen Bewegung) haben kann, entweder als Person, die die Bewegung ausführt, oder als Person, die jemand anderen in der Bewegung betrachtet" (the subjective impression that it (physical movement) generates, either in the person that performs the movement, or in the person that observes someone else's movement).[15] This subjective, biographically informed focus on movement beyond its established choreographic modes provides a striking link to contemporary practices of dance; both poetry and dance seem to be compelled to devote further artistic research to it. Therefore, even if, as stated above, one might find less poetological writing about dance today, there can be no doubt about the presence of *poetological writing*—and *poetological dancing*.[16] The editors of the collection *Poesie und Begriff* (Poetry and Concept), which assembles statements by various contemporary poets, define their understanding of poetics as "Eröffnung eines Erkenntnisraums" (making available of a space of insight) that brings together poetry and concept formation. This goes beyond a definition of poetics as a possible form of writing, and it also exceeds the "Frage nach dem Machen eines Textes" (question about the making of a text).[17] Rather, this kind of poetology is interested in poetic concepts. They are described as follows:

> Wie für den philosophischen ist auch für den poetischen Begriff charakteristisch, dass er eine Welt ohne Vorbild bezeichnet, uns in eine Wirklichkeit versetzt, die es vor ihm für uns nicht gab. Er stellt ungewöhnliche Beziehungen her, legt neue Wege an, macht spürbar, dass etwas geschieht.[18]
>
> (What characterizes not only philosophical but also poetic concepts is that they describe a world without precedent, placing us in a reality that has not existed for us before. Poetic concepts create unusual relations, pave new paths, and make it perceivable that something is happening.)

Such an understanding of the poetic formation of concepts corresponds to an equally poetic formation of movement in dance. By approaching an only gradually accessible knowledge on the peripheries of comprehensibly formed language and movement, contemporary dancing and writing open new spaces of insight. In the process, language comes close to physicality and movement; therefore the description of a poetic work sometimes reads like the description of a dance. Referring to Draesner's poetological speech once more, writing poetry means "sich von der Eigenbewegung der Sprache . . . von ihren Eigen-Möglichkeiten . . . zu Laut gebenden Stimmen führen zu lassen . . . mit Hilfe der eigenen Körperlichkeit" (to let oneself being led by the inherent motion of language . . . and its own possibilities . . . to voices of sound . . . by means of one's own physicality). Draesner also puts this as follows:

> Poesie ist, was geschieht, wenn wir die in den Schatten geräumte Sprachlautlichkeit aus dem Horn fließen lassen. Wenn wir anfangen, den Wortkörper—Körper der Sprache, wie er auf der Seite steht, diesen vereinfachten reduzierten abstrahierten Körper—zu lesen—zu entbinden.[19]
>
> (Poetry is what happens when we let the sonic dimension of language, which tends to be kept in the shadow, flow freely. When we start to read and to release

the body of words, which is the body of language as it is written on the page, in simplified and abstract ways.)

Draesner defines the sonic dimension of language that exists beyond its semantic encoding (even though it contributes to this encoding) in four ways: as language's meter, "Puls" (pulse) or "Denk-Fühlstrom" (stream of thoughts and feelings); as "Wortlaut" (word-sound) or "Klang und Charakter des einzelnen Wortes" (sound and character of the single word); as "Tempo" (tempo) in the sense of a "Bewegung-durch-Zeit" (movement-in-time), which is suggested by "die Sprachstruktur des Textes selbst" (the language structure of the text itself); and, finally, as a "Melodie der Vokale" (melody of vowels)" which is lending the verse "ein bestimmtes Licht" (a certain illumination).[20]

With regard to the choice of words and content, Draesner's definition of the sonic dimension of language may apply in particular to her own understanding of poetry. However, pulse, stream of thoughts and feelings, and movement-in-time also potentially offer ways to approach a poem by Monika Rinck. Rinck's *tour de trance* rightly incited Michael Braun to claim that poetry seems sometimes "wie eine Nachbardisziplin der Kinetik" (like a neighboring discipline of kinetics).[21] The rotary motion of the poem might indeed be called a study of kinetics, here in the shape of a nearly unnoticeable, catastrophic circling of non-human size. The subtitle of *tour de trance* is *"my task, she said, was poisoning time."* This is taken from the English translation of Maurice Blanchot's musings about female poisoners, in which he assumes that, rather than having an interest in killing people, these historical women were fascinated by the poisonous manipulation of temporality. Time becomes an "imperceptible consumption."[22] Rinck's poem makes this process of consumption or emaciation perceptible through the image of a massive, and simultaneously slowed down, implosion of energy. Despite the scale of the dimensions that are invoked, *tour de trance* also reminds us of a subjective experience of decelerated dancing, initiated by a chemical drug, of movement dragging along while rotating, and the dancer hallucinating an otherworldly catastrophe as long as the drug lasts. With reference to Blanchot, death due to poisoning might then be the end of the trance, the return to sobriety. The title *tour de trance*—reminiscent of Rinck's *begriffsstudio*—is a poetic concept, in that it places us in a reality that did not exist for us before. *Tour de trance* contrasts the speed records invoked by its near-homophone *Tour de France* with an eventual loss of sense of time. The latter dissolves within the cyclic movement, and it does so in the shape of a dance poem:

tour de trance
my task, she said, was poisoning time

wie sich alles drehte, wiederholte, dehnte,
und rotierte, die wärme war a space so vast,
so katastrophisch groß, war sie arena
worin die trümmer von objekten trieben,
wilde schläge in der ferne, keiner hörte,
jeder fühlte, die wellen der erschütterung.
wo etwas fehlte, wurde alles größer,
drehte sich, rotierte, kam ins schlingern
und blieb dann in der mitte liegen.
die müdigkeit war eine kur, das gewicht
der atmosphäre, halluzinogene leere
federte, es drehte sich jetzt weniger
als wären die schläge, in dem was sie sind
gegenstand der verdünnung, als würde
die zeit, der reißende raum, präzise und
zärtlich vergiftet, in ihrem gewebe stiege
die chemische schwäche, es schäumte,
erstickte, das weiße lager der krusten,
das sich formierte, wird reicher und toxisch
verrauschten die schläge, es dreht sich,
dreht sich unmerklich, und steht.[23]

tour de trance
my task, she said, was poisoning time

how everything turned, repeated, expanded
and rotated, heat was *a space so vast*,
so disastrously large, was an arena
in which the wreckage of objects drifted,
savage impacts in the distance, no one heard,
everyone felt, the pulsing aftershocks.
where something was missing, it all got bigger,
turned, rotated, lurched about
and then came to rest in the centre.
fatigue was a cure, the weight
of the atmosphere, hallucinogenic heaviness
cushioned, it was turning less now,
as if the impacts, in their very substance,
were subject to dilution, as if
time, torrential space, were being precisely and
tenderly poisoned, the chemical weakness
rising in its fabric, frothing, suffocating,
the accumulated white layer of
crusts becoming richer, the impacts
fading into toxic noise, it turns,
turns imperceptibly, and stops.[24]

"It turns," we read instead of "she turns," or "I turn." If this means that "turn" refers to the repercussions of an oversized, impersonal dynamic, rather than the dancer's own, this also casts light on the understanding of language in the poem. Within such a partly impersonal language, the debris of (conceptual) objects floats in a precisely describable way. In this sense, the poem is about a language of that which comes to "rest in the center," following an aesthetic process that is always also based on contingency. When an interviewer in conversation with Rinck remarked, "You seem to use 'found' language or colloquialisms often too," she replied: "Well, what is NOT found?"[25]

Rinck's mainly internet-based *begriffsstudio* is an archive of such discursive findings, a growing list of potential elements or seeds of poems that still need to be worked on. But the list might also be understood as a poem in progress, as active as the "active archive" of *walk + talk*. *walk + talk*, originally curated in 2008 by Philipp Gehmacher for Tanzquartier Vienna, is an open series of lecture performances by dance artists, which have been shown in varying constellations in Brussels, Stockholm, and other cities since. The series has also been extensively documented on the internet. Strictly speaking, the web version goes beyond a mere documentation as it reproduces, comments on, and continues the series in a different medium. In addition, the documentation makes accessible the statements by the performers on their dancing in form of a written, tag along script to the video recording, thus transforming them into a visualized (rather than merely oral) running commentary. The format of the lecture performances (i.e., movement and comment) is therefore duplicated once more on the internet platform by means of its association of recorded movement and speech, the latter's transcription, and the exact allocation of time slots for these comments. This not only enables one to revisit the event on stage, it also adds to the aspects of *walk + talk* that turn it into a piece of artistic research.

Contemporary dance and contemporary poetry possess their own archival directories and annotations, their structures of transmission and commentary, working with what people understand, but also with what is willingly or unwillingly misunderstood.[26] In the section "Sitzen. Stehen. Gehen. Sätze." (Sitting. Standing. Walking. Sentences.) in Hefter's *Handbuch,* the first person narrator articulates the wish for an archive of movement: "Ich möchte alle Bewegungen meines Lebens konservieren. Ich möchte gern eine Kiste mit Bewegungen an einige Leute vererben." (I would like to conserve all the movements of my life. I would like to hand down a box with movements to a number of people.) Within the section "Stille Post" (Chinese Whispers) she plays with purposeful misunderstandings that are then guided "in Richtung Plausibilität und Verständlichkeit" (in the direction of plausibility and comprehensibility), but this is "angesichts des Verfahrens von vornherein ein Fake" (in view of the process, fake from the outset).[27] Rinck explains that she found the words for her *begriffsstudio,* for example, when misunderstanding radio programs, or when translating, but she did so also in conversations, on the internet, on the street—words and phrases overheard, subjective finds that are then transferred into the seemingly systematic sequence of a list which is in fact unsystematic and contingent. Might we compare purposefully misunderstood words with a kind of purposefully misunderstood body in dance? Interestingly, there is an overlap between Draesner's statement about the mobilization of an otherwise "in den Schatten geräumten Sprachlautlichkeit" (a sonic dimension of language which is confined to an existence in the shadow) with Gehmacher's statement about the kind of body that occupies him and that he wants to exhibit, which is a "fragile, material body, a broken and uncoordinated body: just about everything that makes up the shadow-side of the civil body, the body we care for and symbolize."[28] In the same way as poetic language plays with common semantic values, by avoiding, extending or narrowing them, dance work aims to step behind common ways of moving. It establishes bodily practices that escape the aesthetic codes of dominant body images, devoting themselves instead to often subjective, sometimes minute, kinetic experiences and observations, which are then processed in a productive manner. Similar to the exploration and transformation of found concepts in poetry, dance explores and transforms found movement.

Anne Juren's contribution to *walk + talk* on 16 March 2011 in the Kaaistudios in Brussels shall serve as an example here, and as beautiful complementary piece to Rinck's poem, since both approach the state of entrancement in a clairvoyant, distant, but also evocative way; and both put a clear end to the trance. What follows is an excerpt from the script of Juren's performance. In the beginning, she simply stands on stage and starts to shake her body, trying out different qualities and focal points for her movement, or using different body parts, until she develops it into a dance that is choreographed more fully, but nevertheless still impacted by repetition:

> 00:17:11 00:17:17
> Shaking is a nice feeling.
> 00:17:18 00:17:43
> It's so full of possibility of a continuous movement. I will feel the muscles, organs, and skin shaking by itself.
> 00:17:44 00:17:56
> Marina Abramović was using shaking for the performance she did in 1972, *Freeing the Body.*
> 00:18:02 00:18:44

She was shaking, getting in trance for about six hours, before collapsing by exhaustion. I was kind of intrigued by what she meant by freeing the body. Then I decided to reenact this performance. So I went into the studio, covered my head, got undressed, and started dancing for six hours.
00:18:46 00:19:29
After fifteen minutes, I realized, in order to continue, I have to find a strategy. And then I started to understand that for me, less than thinking freedom as a state, like 'I'm free,' freedom can be seen as a construction of the body.
00:19:31 00:19:59
So I was in transit, I was changing constantly quality, and managed to keep the six hours. And I realized that each change was more and more bringing a certain connection towards the viewer.
00:20:01 00:20:04
This is my response to Marina.
00:23:06 00:23:08
Thank you.[29]

As Gehmacher states, *walk + talk* is among other things concerned with the attempt "Ich zu sagen" (saying "I").[30] Most performers articulate this attempt in indirect ways. Their underlying question might be "what do I perceive?" rather than "who am I?" Juren demonstrates this when she shows how she perceived Abramović's shaking and how she works with it.[31]

In *Risiko und Idiotie*, Rinck writes:

> Welcherart ist das Gelenk zwischen Werk und Biographie? . . . Dass eine Verbindung besteht, ist selbstverständlich, allerdings liegt zwischen dem Dichter und dem Text die Arbeit, die ein Chaosgenerator, ein Prisma, eine Verrichtung; die Lektüre, Diebstahl, Entfremdung, Gnade und Verstockung ist und die die biografische Verbindung auflöst.
>
> (What kind of a link exists between text and biography? . . . It is self-evident that there is a link. However, between the poet and the text there is the process of work, which is a generator of chaos, a prism, a performance; which comprises reading, stealing, estrangement, grace, and obduracy and thereby dissolves the biographical link.)

The processing of biographical material establishes "dann später irgendwann ein ganz neues und auf viel bessere Art fiktives Ich" (at some point in the future a completely new and much better fictitious self).[32] Despite—or perhaps precisely because of—its commitment to cultivating body and language, the work on the self always takes into account that control is limited. Butler associates this with a loss of sovereignty that is in fact required for a coherent theory of humanely conceived subjectivity. Hefter calls it a "Stürzen ins

Kippeln" (a falling into a tilt). In the section "Sitzen. Stehen. Gehen. Sätze" of her *Handbuch*, she writes:

> Ich möchte nicht vom Sitzen sprechen. Ich möchte im Sitzen nicht reden. Ich möchte auch nichts so Großartiges machen, dass es jeden Menschen in seinen Sitz presst. Ich spüre, dass, wenn ich jetzt noch länger darüber nachdenke, das Sitzen kulminiert, ein Stürzen ins Kippeln wird. Ich will hier sitzen, als würde ich lieber gleich gehen. Die Bedeutungen wechseln so schnell die Bewegung, dass es aussieht, als renne das Zimmer.[33]
>
> (I do not want to talk about sitting. I do not want to talk sitting. I also do not want to do something so grand that it pushes everyone back into their seats. I feel that, if I keep thinking about this even longer now, the act of sitting will topple over, becoming a falling into a tilt. I want to sit here as if I would rather just leave. Meanings change their movement so quickly that it looks as if the room was running.)

In his version of *walk + talk*, when performing on 7 December 2013 in Stockholm, Gehmacher says after one minute and twenty-nine seconds that his performance is about the attempt "to somehow expose a certain sense of physicality as such," and after three minutes and fifteen seconds: "It's maybe just the attempt to expose a sense of subjectivity and how these people live with their art form" ("these people" are the other performers of *walk + talk*).[34] Around this point in time he is exploring a torsion—a countermove of head, neck, shoulder, and arm—which is the result of moving his face to the left with his left hand, while the right arm, mostly stretched out—sometimes bent—moves to the right side, backwards, and upwards. This is a kind of experimental stretching which, however, strongly stresses the fact that whether he is talking or not, his face is covered in an unusual, only partially functional way by his hand. The movement has the character of resolutely trying out how to avert his gaze, in more or less complete, more or less partial ways, and doing so explicitly, but not compulsively. This does not give the impression of being associated with shame, but it does to some extent block out the audience's view of the performer, while making his own explorations seem like the palpations of a blind man; a sensing-measuring that does not at all forget about its environment. The stretched-out arm indicates this by marking the outlines of its kinesphere. Furthermore, it is a movement of the arm that will be described by Gehmacher as an essential gesture of making contact, testing the boundary between self and world.[35]

The works of Gehmacher, Hefter, Juren, and Rinck do not present us with an unquestioned sovereign subject, but with one that gives account of movement possibilities, of him- or herself, one that looks for recognition and recognizes others, and that tries out different forms of addressing that go beyond the self, be it in writing or in performance. Juren's sequence of movement, for example, is an answer to Abramović, while her comments at the same time establish a connection with the spectator. With this perspective in mind I am turning once more to Butler, whose Adorno lectures reflect on how a subject that is inaccessible to itself should be thought of as an ethical one.[36] Referring to Cavarero, Butler argues that the "I" encounters "not only this or that attribute of the other," but the other as a being that is "fundamentally exposed, visible, seen, existing in a bodily way and of necessity in a domain of appearance." Turning to the self, she continues:

> *This* exposure that I am constitutes, as it were, my singularity. I cannot will it away, for it is a feature of my very corporeality and, in this sense, of my life. Yet it is not that over which I can have control.[37]

Singularity delimits the extent to which individuals can be replaced or justified, although it is this singularity that we share with others. Our exposure to a public that is sometimes "intimate" and sometimes "anonymous . . . cannot be narrated,"[38] partly because there is always

> a bodily referent here, a condition of me that I can point to, but that I cannot precisely narrate, even though, without a doubt, there are stories about where my body went and what it did and did not do.[39]

Giving account will thus always fail to a certain degree; but one nevertheless attempts to narrate the self, not only to oneself but also to others, whether these others are imaginary or real: "No account takes place outside the structure of address."[40] In Butler, "the ethical valence of the situation is thus not restricted to the question of whether or not my account of myself is adequate, but rather concerns whether, in giving the account, I establish a relationship to the one to whom my account is addressed and whether both parties to the interlocution are sustained and altered by the scene of address."[41]

The dances and poems described in this chapter are such scenes of address. They show an ethical commitment as their "ability to affirm what is contingent and incoherent in oneself may allow one to affirm others who may or may not 'mirror' one's own constitution," as Butler writes.[42] Her disposition of the non-sovereign subject is present in the mood value of the poetic and dancerly attempts at accountability by Gehmacher, Hefter, Juren, and Rinck.

NOTES

1. A version of this chapter was first published in German under the title "'Ich als Text,' Ich als Tanz. Überlegungen zu Anne Juren, Martina Hefter, Monika Rinck und Philipp Gehmacher," in *Sprache im Technischen Zeitalter* 216 (2015), pp. 405–416. It was written on the occasion of "Step-Text," a two-part event hosted by the Zentrum für Bewegungsforschung at Freie Universität Berlin and Literarisches Colloquium Berlin in April and July 2015, organized by Gabriele Brandstetter and Sigrid Gareis, who also edited the special journal issue of *Sprache im Technischen Zeitalter.* The translation in this volume is by Lena Mahnke, Sabine Egger, and Mayuri Goswami, revised by Lucia Ruprecht. This also applies to translations of citations, if given in brackets and not otherwise referenced.

2. Judith Butler, *Kritik der ethischen Gewalt. Adorno-Vorlesungen* 2002, Institut für Sozialforschung an der Johann Wolfgang Goethe-Universität, Frankfurt am Main, trans. Reiner Ansén (Frankfurt am Main: Suhrkamp, 2018).

3. Judith Butler, *Giving an Account of Oneself* (New York: Fordham University Press, 2005), 19.

4. Ibid., 41–42.

5. For further readings that align Butler's *Giving an Account of Oneself* with contemporary dance, see Christina Thurner, "Es war einmal ein Statement. Anne Teresa de Keersmaekers Tanzsolo *Once* als politische Reflexion," *Forum modernes Theater* 1 (2005), 95–107, and Jeroen Peeters, "How to knit oneself a private political body? On deufert & plischke's *Directory* project," in *Through the Back: Situating Vision between Moving Bodies* (Helsinki: Kinesis 5, 2014), 157–186.

6. Ulrike Draesner, *Die fünfte Dimension. Münchner Reden zur Poesie*, ed. by Holger Pils and Frieder von Ammon (Munich: Stiftung Lyrik Kabinett, 2015), 24.

7. Cited after Monika Rinck, *begriffsstudio 1996–2001* (Berlin: edition sutstein, 2001), appendix, commentary on term no. 16.

8. For artistic research, see also Sybille Peters (ed.), *Das Forschen aller: Artistic Research als Wissensproduktion zwischen Kunst, Wissenschaft und Gesellschaft* (Bielefeld: Transcript, 2013).

9. See also Thomas Meinecke, "Ich muss nicht schreiben, um nicht verrückt zu werden," in Daniel Lenz, Eric Pütz, *Lebensbeschreibungen. Zwanzig Gespräche mit Schriftstellern* (Munich: text + kritik, 2000), 149.

10. I am citing the title of Thomas Meinecke's book *Ich als Text* (Frankfurt am Main: Suhrkamp, 2012).

11. Butler, *Giving an Account*, 33. See also Adriana Cavarero, *Relating Narratives: Storytelling and Selfhood* (London: Routledge, 2000).

12. I am thinking of the paradigmatic modernist texts on dance by Hugo von Hofmannsthal, Rainer Maria Rilke, Stéphane Mallarmé, Paul Valery, T. S. Eliot, and others. For discussions of these, see Gabriele Brandstetter, *Poetics of Dance: Body, Image, and Space in the Historical Avant- Gardes* (New York: Oxford University Press, 2015); Gregor Gumpert, *Die Rede vom Tanz: Körperästhetik in der Literatur der Jahrhundertwende* (Munich: Fink, 1994); Susan Jones, *Literature, Modernism, and Dance* (Oxford: Oxford University Press, 2013); Julie Townsend,

The Choreography of Modernism in France: La Danseuse, 1830–1930 (London: Legenda, 2010).

13. See Gabriele Brandstetter, *Tanz-Lektüren. Körperbilder und Raumfiguren der Avantgarde* (Freiburg: Rombach, 2., extended edition 2013) .

14. Martina Hefter, *Nach den Diskotheken* (Berlin: kookbooks, 2010), 7.

15. Martina Hefter, *Vom Gehen und Stehen. Ein Handbuch* (Berlin: kookbooks, 2010), 76.

16. For poetological dances, see also Laurence Louppe, *Poétique de la danse contemporaine, la suite* (Brussels: éditions Contredanse, 2007).

17. Ric Allsop's understanding of a poetry of movement as "a creative practice rather than a critical act" supposes a dichotomy between creativity and theoretical enquiry that I do not wish to subscribe to. See "Some Notes on Poetics and Choreography," *Performance Research: A Journal of the Performing Arts* 20, no. 1 (2015, Special Issue on Poetics & Performance): 4.

18. Armen Avanessian, Anke Hennig, Steffen Popp, "Vorwort der Herausgeber," in *Poesie und Begriff. Positionen zeitgenössischer Lyrik* (Zurich: diaphanes, 2014), 7.

19. Draesner, *Die fünfte Dimension,* 19–22.

20. Ibid., 22–23.

21. Michael Braun, "Drehung im rhythmischen Zeremoniell. Zu den Gedichten von Monika Rinck," *Sprache im Technischen Zeitalter* 42 (2004): 4.

22. Maurice Blanchot, "Two Versions of the Imaginary," in the *Gaze of Orpheus and Other Literary Essays*, ed. by Adams Sitney (Barrytown: Station Hill, 1981), 85. I wish to thank Monika Rinck for the reference.

23. Monika Rinck, *tour de trance*, in *zum fernbleiben der umarmung: Gedichte* (Berlin, kookbooks, 2007), 74. *tour de trance* is a compelling contemporary complement to Rilke's dance poem *Spanische Tänzerin.*

24. Monika Rinck, *tour de trance*, in *to refrain from embracing*, trans. Nicholas Grindell (Providence RI: Burning Deck, 2011), https://www.lyrikline.org/en/poems/tour-de-trance-1832.

25. Monika Rinck,"*maintenant* #4: monika rinck," interview by S. J. Fowler, *3 AM MAGAZINE*, http://www.3ammagazine.com/3am/maintenant-4-monika-rinck/.

26. Swantje Lichtenstein's experiment of a commentary without any reference text tests the limits of such structures, see her *Kommentararten */!* (Berlin: Verlagshaus Berlin, 2015).

27. Hefter, *Vom Gehen und Stehen*, 56, 76.

28. Gehmacher quoted in Jeroen Peeters, "Shadow Bodies: On Philipp Gehmacher's Incubator," in *Through the Back*, 137.

29. Anne Juren, *walk + talk 14-Kaaistudio's Brussels*, 16 March 2011, http://olga0.oralsite.be/oralsite/pages/Anne_Juren_WT_14/index.html.

30. "The attempt of saying 'I' was paramount." Philipp Gehmacher, *Introduction. walk+talk, a few facts*. February 2013, http://oralsite.be/pages/Walk_Talk_Documents.

31. In his poetics lectures entitled "Ich als Text" (I as a Text) Meinecke worked with the question "What do I perceive?" in his own way. He comments on his practice of collecting discourses by others in a collection of discourses about himself,

sequencing answers to the questions (even if not asked directly) "How are my texts perceived?" and "How am I perceived within and through my texts?"

32. Monika Rinck, *Risiko und Idiotie. Streitschriften* (Berlin: kookbooks, 2015), 16.

33. Hefter, *Vom Gehen und Stehen*, 54.

34. Philipp Gehmacher, *walk + talk 23-Kulturhuset Stadsteatern Stockholm*, 7 December 2013, http://olga0.oralsite.be/oralsite/pages/Philipp_Gehmacher_WT_23/index.html.

35. For Gehmacher's choreographies of "utterance," see Constanze Klementz: "Gehmachers Äußerung artikuliert ein physisch-reflexives Vermögen, das . . . in einem Zwischenraum siedelt: dem der Intersubjektivität. Für Gehmacher ist hier der Ort der Problematisierung des Subjekts. . . . Seine ‚utterance' veräußert aber immer auch die Frage nach ihrem Potenzial, nach der Möglichkeit, sich hervorzubringen, zu zeigen und mitzuteilen, in einer ständigen sprunghaften Ver-Stellung des einen durch das andere durch das Dritte. Getragen von der Oszillation zwischen Körper-Sein und Körper-Haben, Sprache-Sein und Sprache-Haben. Wesentlich immer in Relation zu, im Hin-Blick auf: me, the world, you. (Philipp Gehmacher). ("Gehmacher's utterance articulates a reflective physical possibility, which . . . settles in a space in-between: a space of intersubjectivity. For Gehmacher, this is the place where the subject can be engaged with. . . . His 'utterance,' however, always also disposes of the question about its own potential, the potential to produce itself, to show *and* communicate in a constant, erratic disguise of one through the other through the third. This is carried through in the oscillation between being a body and having a body, being language and having language. Essentially always in relation to something: *me, the world, you.* (Philipp Gehmacher), in "Sehen lassen, was nicht geschah, um gesehen zu werden. Zur Be-Gründung alternativer Zeit- und Raumerfahrung in dem choreografischen Format *walk+talk*," www.philippgehmacher.net, June 2010, http://sarma.be/docs/2894.

36. Rinck also refers to Butler and Cavarero, in *Risiko und Idiotie*, 19, footnote 11, where she asks which mood might already be inherent in postures taken during acts of speech.

37. Butler, *Giving an Account*, 33.

38. Ibid., 34–35.

39. Ibid., 38.

40. Ibid., 36.

41. Ibid., 50.

42. Ibid., 41.

BIBLIOGRAPHY

Allsop, Ric. "Some Notes on Poetics and Choreography." *Performance Research: A Journal of the Performing Arts* 20/1 (2015), Special Issue on Poetics & Performance, 4–12.

Avanessian, Armen, Hennig, Anke, and Popp, Steffen, eds. *Poesie und Begriff. Positionen zeitgenössischer Lyrik.* Zurich: diaphanes, 2014.

Blanchot, Maurice. "Two Versions of the Imaginary," in the *Gaze of Orpheus and Other Literary Essays*, ed. by Adams Sitney Barrytown: Station Hill, 1981, 79–90.

Brandstetter, Gabriele. *Poetics of Dance: Body, Image, and Space in the Historical Avant- Gardes* New York: Oxford University Press, 2015.

———. *Tanz-Lektüren. Körperbilder und Raumfiguren der Avantgarde*. Freiburg: Rombach, second, extended edition 2013.

Braun, Michael. "Drehung im rhythmischen Zeremoniell. Zu den Gedichten von Monika Rinck." *Sprache im Technischen Zeitalter* 42 (2004), 4–7.

Butler, Judith. *Giving an Account of Oneself.* New York: Fordham University Press, 2005.

———. *Kritik der ethischen Gewalt. Adorno-Vorlesungen* 2002, Institut für Sozialforschung an der Johann Wolfgang Goethe-Universität, Frankfurt am Main, trans. Reiner Ansén Frankfurt am Main: Suhrkamp, 2018.

Cavarero, Adriana. *Relating Narratives: Storytelling and Selfhood.* London: Routledge, 2000.

Draesner, Ulrike. *Die fünfte Dimension. Münchner Reden zur Poesie*. Edited by Holger Pils and Frieder von Ammon. Munich: Stiftung Lyrik Kabinett, 2015.

Gehmacher, Philipp. *Introduction. walk+talk, a few facts*. February 2013, accessed 15 August 2019. http://oralsite.be/pages/Walk_Talk_Documents

———. *walk + talk 23-Kulturhuset Stadsteatern Stockholm*, 7 December 2013, accessed 15 August 2019. http://olga0.oralsite.be/oralsite/pages/Philipp_Gehmacher_WT_23/index.html.

Gumpert, Gregor. *Die Rede vom Tanz: Körperästhetik in der Literatur der Jahrhundertwende*. Munich: Fink, 1994.

Hefter, Martina. *Nach den Diskotheken*. Berlin: kookbooks, 2010.

———.*Vom Gehen und Stehen. Ein Handbuch*. Berlin: kookbooks, 2010.

Jones, Susan, *Literature, Modernism, and Dance*. Oxford: Oxford University Press, 2013.

Juren, Anne. *walk + talk 14-Kaaistudio's Brussels*, 16 March 2011, accessed 15 August 2019. http://olga0.oralsite.be/oralsite/pages/Anne_Juren_WT_14/index.html.

Klementz, Constanze. "Sehen lassen, was nicht geschah, um gesehen zu werden. Zur Be-Gründung alternativer Zeit- und Raumerfahrung in dem choreografischen Format *walk+talk*," www.philippgehmacher.net, June 2010, http://sarma.be/docs/2894.

Lichtenstein, Swantje. *Kommentararten */!* Berlin: Verlagshaus Berlin, 2015.

Louppe, Laurence. *Poétique de la danse contemporaine, la suite*. Brussels: éditions Contredanse, 2007.

Meinecke, Thomas. "Ich muss nicht schreiben, um nicht verrückt zu werden," in Daniel Lenz, Eric Pütz, *Lebensbeschreibungen. Zwanzig Gespräche mit Schriftstellern*. Munich: text + kritik, 2000, 145–155.

———. *Ich als Text*. Frankfurt am Main: Suhrkamp, 2012.

Peeters, Jeroen. *Through the Back: Situating Vision between Moving Bodies*. Helsinki: Kinesis 5, 2014.

Peters, Sybille, ed. *Das Forschen aller: Artistic Research als Wissensproduktion zwischen Kunst, Wissenschaft und Gesellschaft*. Bielefeld: Transcript, 2013.

Rinck, Monika. *begriffsstudio 1996–2001*. Berlin: edition sutstein, 2001.

———. *zum fernbleiben der umarmung: Gedichte*. Berlin, kookbooks, 2007.

———. *to refrain from embracing*. Translated by Nicholas Grindell, Providence RI: Burning Deck, 2011. https://www.lyrikline.org/en/poems/tour-de-trance-1832.

———. *Risiko und Idiotie. Streitschriften*. Berlin: kookbooks, 2015.

Thurner, Christina. "Es war einmal ein Statement. Anne Teresa de Keersmaekers Tanzsolo *Once* als politische Reflexion," *Forum modernes Theater* 1 (2005): 95–107.

Townsend, Julie. *The Choreography of Modernism in France: La Danseuse, 1830–1930*. London: Legenda, 2010.

Chapter Eleven

Dancing between Transgression and Transformation in German Literature after 1945 and 1989

Johannes Bobrowski and Katja Petrowskaja

Sabine Egger

In the texts by Johannes Bobrowski and Katja Petrowskaja to be discussed in this chapter, dancers transgress and challenge existing boundaries. Both texts constitute examples of poetic memory, an autobiographical writing in the wider sense, in which dance allows for movement between times, places and spaces of memory and of belonging. In their texts, both writers address their personal and collective experience of the Holocaust and the Second World War as part of a European history that has its center in Central and Eastern Europe. While Johannes Bobrowski's short narrative "Der Tänzer Malige" (1965, The Dancer Malige), engages with the topic from a perpetrator's or contemporary witness's perspective, and is written by an author, born in 1917, who participated in the invasion of Poland as a German soldier, Katja Petrowskaja's *Vielleicht Esther* (2014, Maybe Esther) reflects on her Jewish family history from the perspective of a third generation victim. Petrowskaja was born in 1970, studied Slavonic Studies in Estonia and the United States, and gained a PhD in Moscow, before moving to Berlin with her German partner in 1999. Having learned the language only as an adult, writing in German allowed her to approach her own biography and family history through a distinctive poetic language and in the context of different memory discourses.[1] The author explores her Jewishness as something only marginally present in her childhood everyday life as the daughter of two Ukrainian intellectuals, in a household marked by a cosmopolitan and European sense of belonging, in the former Soviet Union. This differs from Bobrowski's traumatic first-hand experience, and a kind of writing that is in part pushed forward by a dynamic of guilt and atonement.

In both texts analyzed, however, boundaries between historical reality and imagination, different grand narratives and subjective memory, as well as those between victim and perpetrator are crossed or even shifted through a poetics of dance. Furthermore, the trope of dance employed can in both cases be interpreted as an autopoietic reference that draws on the meaning of dance in Hasidic thought and literature, and in Central Eastern European Jewish culture. Hasidic dancing produces a spiritual uplift and enhances social relationships; it is both an expression and a stimulator of joy, even in the face of darkness or historical trauma. Dancing for pleasure in the face of social marginalization and living conditions in ghettos was also part of secular Jewish culture in European cities and towns since the Middle Ages. In the texts discussed, this religious practice and ritualized activity is adapted to modern, secular dance forms, constituting a transgressive movement, as described by Michel Foucault.[2] Transgression in this sense is a liminal practice that forces the poetic language of memory to acknowledge that which it cannot acknowledge, which is beyond a boundary. The act of transgression as a dialectical process both challenges an existing boundary, and makes this boundary visible. I aim to show how such boundaries are momentarily subverted or questioned in the texts discussed without necessarily being dissolved beyond this moment. The temporary nature of such a transgression or subversion, as well as the somewhat ironic secularization of Hasidic dance in both texts, also suggests elements of the carnivalesque, as defined by Mikhail Bakhtin.[3]

JOHANNES BOBROWSKI: BALANCING BETWEEN *L'ART POUR L'ART* AND *ART ENGAGE*

Johannes Bobrowski was born to a German-speaking family in the East Prussian town of Tilsit (today Sovetsk) in 1917, and spent his childhood in Königsberg (today Kaliningrad) with summers on his grandparents' farm in the borderlands of the river Memel, where he experienced a multiethnic village life in which Lithuanian, Russian and Jewish traditions intermingled, before participating in the German invasion of Poland and Russia in the Second World War, and the family relocating in East Berlin after 1945.[4] However, Bobrowski did not regard himself as a Socialist GDR author, but rather as a German writer, influenced by the modernism of Baudelaire, Mallarmé and Trakl, and in close contact with contemporaries on both sides of the East-West border.[5] His work gained attention in both Germanies after he was awarded the prestigious prize of the West German Gruppe 47 for his poetry in 1962.[6] In the prose fiction he increasingly turned to in the 1960s, he explores the complexities of individuals, ethnic communities and their relations in historical contexts. His largely modernist aesthetics, however, which also influenced his fiction, deviated from the official Socialist discourse. The latter prescribed both a Marxist interpretation of history and a Socialist Realist style of writing, with workers as its target readership, while rejecting modernist, experimental writing as *l'art pour l'art*. In "Der Tänzer Malige," Bobrowski uses dance to create a dual structure in Bakhtin's sense of the carnivalesque, which overturns dominant perspectives. The text is an example of a *Wirkungsästhetik* (aesthetics of effect) that cannot be grasped in the framework of a simple opposition of *l'art pour l'art* and *art engagé*, and it thus places Bobrowski's fiction in-between the prevalent discourses in East and West German literature of the time.[7]

In an interview with the Deutschlandsender Berlin in 1964, Bobrowski outlined the main theme of his work as the "Verhältnis der Deutschen zu den Nachbarvölkern, und eben die Frage der deutschen Verschuldung. . . . Man kann sich, glaube ich, von der Geschichte nicht dispensieren" (relationship between the Germans and their neighbors, and, in particular, the question of German guilt. I think one cannot exempt oneself from history).[8] Having participated in the Second World War in Central and Eastern Europe as a German soldier, the relationship between individual and collective responsibility for this past are at the heart of Bobrowski's writing. In his texts, he attempts to establish a literary dialogue with the Jewish and other Eastern European victims of National Socialism. Apart from being based on Christian humanism, the ethical framework for this dialogue is influenced by Martin Buber's philosophy of "I and Thou," which, in turn, includes ideas of Central Eastern European Hasidic thought and tradition.[9] Bobrowski's fictional texts draw on the latter as well as on the author's personal experience, portraying German soldiers as figures with positive and negative character traits in stories containing autobiographical references.

The story told in "Der Tänzer Malige" begins in August 1939 in a "kleinen . . . Landstadt" (164) (small . . . country town). By means of the geographical detail given, the town can be identified as Mohrungen, East Prussia (today Morag), the place of birth of J. G. Herder, where Bobrowski's own unit was stationed before the beginning of the war. For readers not familiar with the author's biography, the setting puts it in the larger historical context of the German invasion of Poland. The story is told in the present tense, and in a mode of zero focalization (with an omniscient narrator), but from a post-war perspective. The narrator remains rather detached from the events, until the closing part of the frame narrative points to some kind of participation on his part. Already the detailed description of the unnamed small town at the beginning of the story as a place, dominated by a strikingly empty market square which seems impossible to cross, and various, equally non-convincing attempts by the narrator to explain this contradiction indicate a *verkehrte Welt*, a world turned upside down.

The following passages provide an insight into the everyday life of the soldiers stationed there. Initially the impression of a civil normality still prevails, narrated in a casual tone—the soldiers pass their time playing cards, drinking beer. Military training presents merely a tedious exercise (164–166). However, the soldiers' behavior soon deteriorates. On the one hand, the narrator's unchanged casual tone makes the nailing of a live chicken to the ground and the racist remarks of the commanding officer, Lieutenant Anflug, also seem somehow normal (166). On the other, the tone takes aback readers who share the author's fundamental ethical values. The perversion of normality reaches its abyss in Rozan, a Polish town nearby,[10] when Lieutenant Anflug orders a group of elderly Jews to pull a heavy cable drum up a steep river bank, only to kick it down the slope each time they have nearly reached the top (167–168). For the reader, the allusion to Sisyphus underlines the absurdity of Anflug's order and of the National Socialism he represents. For the watching soldiers, however, from whose point of view the story is told here, this act represents merely part of their daily routine.

What appears strange in connection with the incident in their world is the reaction of Malige, a soldier who worked as a dancer and circus artist in civil life. Malige suddenly dances down the slope, lifts up the cable drum and carries it uphill for the Jews:

> er springt ein paar Schritte vor, hat jetzt die Beine in einen Tanzschritt gebracht, so eine Art Prozessionsschritt, Hüpfer, schnelle Schrittfolgen, plötzliches Stehnbleiben, vor, zwei Schritte zurück. An Anflug vorbei, der es sehen müßte, aber anderes zu tun hat, bis zur Kante des Abhangs vor. Und jetzt—das ist nun schon wahre Kunst—mit der gleichen Schrittfolge den Hang hinab, nicht ein bißchen schneller, Zeitlupe sozusagen. Wohl verrückt geworden, schreit Anflug. Das kann er jetzt nicht mehr übersehen, dieses Affentheater. (168)
>
> (he hops a few steps forward, bringing his legs into a dance movement, a kind of processionary step, a little jump, a few sequences of quick steps, stopping suddenly, forwards, two steps backwards. Passing Anflug, who has to see it now, but is too busy doing other things, he goes right to the edge of the slope. And now—this is real art—with the same sequence of steps down the hill, not one bit faster, in slow motion, so to speak. Have you gone mad, Anflug shouts? He can't overlook it anymore, this madness.)

This act results in the momentary dissolution of those structures giving meaning to the world created by National Socialism, with Malige's dance exposing the inherent madness of this world from the perspective of humanity. A humane gesture manifests itself through a completely absorbing, joyful, and highly artistic form of dance. Anflug, standing at the top of the slope "flounders" as the dancer approaches him; "he puts one foot forward, grabs for his field cap, for his belt, has begun to scream, screams like an animal—orders or something—a meaningless jumble. And he sees Malige, dancing towards him, closer and closer, only a few more meters to go, his head thrown back, mouth open."[11]

In the narrative, this act of rebellion goes beyond a practical act of help and military disobedience, because it changes the perception of those soldiers watching him at this point in time. The description of Malige picking up the cable drum and dancing back up the hill with it is from the perspective of Maschke, one of the other soldiers who are completely fascinated by Malige's performance:

> Maschke . . . rennt an den Abhang, steht, sieht: Malige ist unten angekommen, breitet die Arme, bewegt sie wie Flügel, ein grüner Vogel in einem Dohlenschwarm, fordert offenbar seine Zuschauer, die alten Herrschaften dort unten, zum Platznehmen auf, er, Malige, . . . hat die Kabeltrommel bereits ergriffen, sie aufgehoben—wie ein Zauberkistchen, wo gleich die Tauben herausflattern werden und hinterher ein Sonnenschirm, der sich von selber öffnet, so leicht jedenfalls—und ist noch immer in seinem Tanzschritt, den Kopf zurückgeworfen. Und jetzt, die Trommel vor sich her tragend, als müßte er sie festhalten, sie flöge ihm sonst fort, den Hang aufwärts, nicht ein bißchen langsamer oder schneller. . . . / Von den Wagen herüber, der ganze Zug kommt gerannt—Kretschmann, Zelt, Wiechert, Markschies, Naujoks—steht, blickt dem Tänzer entgegen, tritt zur Seite, als er über den Hang auftaucht, vor der Kante noch einmal den Schritt zurück tut, die vier kurzen Schrittchen folgen läßt und nun, oben angekommen, die Kabeltrommel im Arm, auch noch den Hüpfer. (168–169)

> (Maschke . . . runs over to the slope, stands there, sees: Malige has arrived at the bottom, spreads his arms, moving them like wings, a green bird in a flock of jackdaws, apparently asking his audience, the elderly gentlemen there below, to take their seats, he, Malige . . . has already caught hold of the cable drum, and lifted it—like a little magic box, out of which the pigeons are about to emerge, flapping their wings, followed by a parasol opening all by itself, as effortlessly as this anyway—and has, while still dancing, thrown back his head. And now, carrying the drum in front of him, as if he had to hold it back to keep it from flying away, up the slope, not a bit more slowly or more quickly. . . . / Over from the trucks, the whole platoon come running over—Kretschmann, Zelt, Wiechert, Markschies, Naujoks—stand, look toward the dancer, step aside, as he appears over the slope, takes a step back in front of the edge, followed by four short little steps and now, having reached the top, with the cable drum in his arm, even takes the little jump.)

At this moment, the world of National Socialism is changed into a humane one. That the onlooking soldier Maschke, from whose point of view the narrator watches the event, associates it with a circus performance might emphasize the illusionary character of this world, created by the artist Malige. Nevertheless, for a moment it turns into reality for him and the other soldiers and changes power relations, if only temporarily. In the story, the change does not go much beyond this. Lieutenant Anflug is transferred to another post after the event, due to his "unmögliche[m] Verhalten" (169) (dreadful behavior). But the smoke that will engulf the Polish town in the future, as announced by the narrator at the end, thus metonymically pointing to the burning down of Polish villages and towns in the course of the German invasion and the ovens of the concentration camps to be built in occupied Poland, indicates that Malige's act has not saved its Jewish inhabitants from the Holocaust.[12]

By refusing to adjust his movement to the "normality" of the National Socialist world, the dancer Malige questions not only power relations, but also patterns of perception within this world. His dance deconstructs the racist perspective of Anflug and the other soldiers by transforming their "Haufen Juden" (bunch of Jews) into his dignified audience of "alte Herrschaften" (167–168) (elderly gentlemen). The Lieutenant's transformation into a screaming animal due to his rage at Malige's dance performance acts as a counterpart to it. Maschke's initial difficulty with fitting Malige's dancing steps into his existing categories and terminology becomes evident when he describes a "Hüpfer, schnelle Schrittfolgen; plötzliches Stehnbleiben, vor, zwei Schritte zurück" (little jump, a few sequences of quick steps, a sudden stop, forward, two steps back) as a "Prozessionsschritt" (processionary step). The resulting change of his perspective into an aesthetic one is apparent from his commentary: "das ist nun schon wahre Kunst" (now this is real art), and the poetic language of the following sentence: "Malige ist unten angekommen, breitet die Arme, bewegt sie wie Flügel, ein grüner Vogel in einem Dohlenschwarm" (168) (Malige has arrived at the bottom, spreads his arms, moving them like wings, a green bird in a flock of jackdaws). The latter differs noticeably from the laconic, even colloquial everyday language used for other passages narrated from the soldiers' perspective. Malige's "wahre Kunst" is therefore to turn his humanitarian action into an aesthetically fascinating performance.

Malige does not even seem to be aware of the ethical dimension of his action, but focuses exclusively on the perfection of his movement at this moment in time. He balances between control and sensual commitment to the movement itself, which finally propels the dancer toward the commanding officer, "mit zurückgeworfenem Kopf, offenem Mund" (his head thrown back, mouth open). The focus on the movement itself is the precondition for its success. This includes the overcoming of physical boundaries: it turns the heavy cable drum into a "Zauberkistchen" (little magic box) that moves up the hill as if by itself. Malige is dancing up the slope, "die Trommel vor sich her tragend, als müßte er sie festhalten, sie flöge ihm sonst fort" (168) (carrying the drum in front of him, as if he had to hold it back to keep it from flying away). It is the aesthetic quality of the dance that has an effect on his current audience and opens at least a window of hope for future performances of this kind. That the dancer will be transferred for disciplinary reasons to a frontline cabaret seems "bei seinem Können wahrscheinlich oder immerhin möglich" (169) (likely or, at least, possible in view of his ability).

The character of Malige can be read as a mask behind which the author Bobrowski approached memory of the Holocaust in the literary landscape of the 1960s. In this sense, his dance would be a contribution to the debate on the incompatibility of moral obligation and aesthetic play taking place in both German states. Malige is the embodiment of an autonomous subject who literally dances apart (*zertanzt*) this contradiction through his art. In contrast to the pure playfulness of the Anacreontic artist—which is partly reflected in postmodern writing—the moral obligation to remember, and the awareness that neither a literary "dance" nor any other form of remembrance can be an atonement for past silence, provides the essential framework for the postwar writer Bobrowski.[13] At the same time, this is inextricably linked to the belief that a moral obligation cannot weigh down the aesthetics of a text on a formal level.[14] With regard to dominant memory discourses in East and West Germany of the time, the dance in "Malige" thus goes beyond the carnivalesque, and could be interpreted as an act of transgression in Foucault's sense: a liminal practice that forces its own poetic language to acknowledge that which it cannot acknowledge, which is beyond a boundary.[15] The interpretation that Malige's liberation of the Jews from their Sisyphus-work is an existentialist act,[16] giving a glimpse of hope, is contradicted by the darkness of the final image in the text:

> Ich weiß nur, was ich erzählt habe. / Höchstens noch: daß es Abend wird. . . . Und daß nichts einen hindern würde, über die Brücke zu gehen und durch die Stadt, jetzt in der Dunkelheit, begegnete man sich nicht selber, ausgerechnet hier, in dieser polnischen Stadt, ohne auch nur einen Grund dafür zu finden. (169)

> (All I know of is what I have told you. / At best there remains: that evening is closing in. . . . And that nothing would stop you from going over the bridge and through the town, now in darkness—were it not that you would meet yourself, here of all places, in this Polish town, without even finding a reason for it.)

Individual and collective guilt prevents the subject at the end from "crossing the bridge" in an autonomous aesthetic act. The narrator finds himself stranded and estranged in a dark place, reminiscent of a modernist writer incapable of making sense of history and his individual existence.[17] Despite such modernist elements, the text remains essentially a realistic narrative, with the dance not questioning or transforming relations between sign and meaning, subject and world, past and present on the level of language. Malige's dance remains a symbol to be read within the firm ethical framework of a memory discourse based on guilt and atonement. However, and more problematic, not least in view of this framework, is that while binary relations between Jewish victims and German perpetrators are questioned through Malige's act of solidarity, they are not fundamentally transformed. By making the Jewish characters metaphors of a passive Other, it could even be argued that the text draws on traditional stereotypes of Central Eastern Jewish culture as one of passive victimhood and archaic, strange customs conventionally associated with Hasidic culture from a Western, Christian perspective, and turned into a propaganda tool by the National Socialists.

KATJA PETROWSKAJA—"FLEET-FOOTED, DANCING HER WAY INTO WORLD HISTORY"

In his article on Katja Petrowskaja's work for the German daily, *Die Welt,* Jan Küveler remarks that to overcome the impossibility of a literary approach to the Holocaust from an ethical perspective, as stated by Theodor Adorno in 1949,[18] what is needed is a multi-sensory, experiential literature. Such a literature could, according to Küveler, generate a level of reflection that succeeds in overcoming traumatic gaps or voids in German and Jewish collective memory—or, as he continues, a pair of "Beine" (legs) to virtually travel the distance from the present to a difficult past by means of an embodied kind of writing.[19] By addressing voids in a European history, in which German, Jewish and Post-Soviet discourses tend to collide and merge, by means of the remembering subject's corporeal and imaginary dance movement through this history (or by imagining others doing so), Petrowskaja's *Vielleicht Esther* constitutes an act of transgressive memory on various levels. This also includes the crossing of boundaries between individual experience and historiography, self and Other. At the same time, this act of transgression is exposed as a performative practice in the book, thus putting a question mark over its own ethical value, and, to a certain extent, over any binding ethical framework for a memory discourse.

Petrowskaja, born in the Ukrainian capital Kiev in 1970, grew up in a family where being Jewish, and the specific historical experience linked to it, was hardly talked about. In part, this silence can be attributed to the marginalization of the Holocaust in the official Soviet memory discourse of the Second World War, in line with the exclusion of religious and ethnic belonging. Similar to Bobrowski's writing in the context of GDR memory discourses, Petrowskaja's *Vielleicht Esther* (2014), thus widens dominant (post-)Soviet discourses to include memory of the Holocaust from an explicitly Jewish perspective. At the same time, writing in German about events taking place in the "European East" (formerly communist countries which tended to be regarded as far away from a (West) German perspective during the Cold War, and as a cultural Other in different historical periods) expands the German framework of memory, from a national to a transnational one.[20] Making this transnational perspective part of a confident, "Jewish" approach, including a playful, self-ironic distance, transgresses boundaries of German memory which are still largely in place both in public debate and the literary canon of the twenty-first century. Tracing the history of her ancestors through the twentieth and back into the nineteenth century, the author-narrator's journey leads her across Europe, to cities like Vienna and Moscow, to the Warsaw Ghetto, Babi Yar, or Mauthausen—all of them in some way or other sites of her family history. Biography and family history are thus linked to specific—historical—places or sites. Her movement between places connects these to each other and to different points in time, by this creating an embodied literary space in the sense of Michel de Certeau.[21] On the one hand, the focus of this journey is on family members, like Petrowskaja's grandmother Rosa, who embody the Jewish contribution to European culture as enlightened, modern and cosmopolitan, but still intricately connected to traditional Hasidic culture. On the other, the journey follows traces of those family members who fell victim to the Holocaust and to other instances of historical violence. The Esther mentioned in the book title is one of these. The author-narrator identifies with their marginal status, and with their suffering as a trope of Jewish history and belonging.[22]

On her journey she is again and again confronted by voids in her family history, reflecting the marginalization of traumatic events and experiences in Jewish and post-Soviet discourses. This is exemplified by the absence of the massacre on Jews committed by the National Socialists at the ravine of Babi Yar in Kiev from different memory discourses.[23] It was one of the largest mass executions during the Holocaust, and confronts the author-narrator with an experience of alterity going beyond family or ethnic boundaries, to the level of humanity. Inextricably linked to the author-narrator's place of childhood, it is also a site of genocide, including members of her own family among the victims: "Kiew war einer von vielen Orten, wo es passierte, man sagt, es sei das größte zweitägige Massaker des Holocaust. 33771 Menschen tötete man in zwei Tagen. Eine merkwürdig genaue Zahl." (186) (Kiev was one of many locales where it took place; it is said to be the largest two-day massacre of the Holocaust. Thirty-three thousand, seven-hundred and seventy-one people were killed in two days. An oddly precise number. *ME* 166) While largely blended out of Soviet history, from a Jewish—and a humane— perspective the scale of this atrocity which far exceeded the above number, and is incomprehensible both on a rational and affective level, necessarily seems to render it a void, thus demanding a process of memory in spite of its incomprehensibility and without any closure imaginable. Ambiguity, as a recurrent feature of the stories told in *Vielleicht Esther*, is closely linked to such voids. The "maybe" (vielleicht) in the book title already alerts the reader to ambiguity as a feature of remembrance, and in turn, to the existence of different modes of historical narrative. That "maybe" is further expanded on in the blurb of the German original: "Hieß sie wirklich Esther, die Großmutter des Vaters, die 1941 im besetzten Kiew allein in der Wohnung der geflohenen Familie zurückblieb? . . . Wenn aber schon der Name nicht mehr gewiss ist, was kann man dann überhaupt wissen?" (Was her name really Esther, the father's grandmother who was left alone in the apartment of the family who had escaped? . . . If not even the name is a certainty, what can one know at all? S.E.)

The narrator feels a sense of pride in being part of a family lineage whose members have placed high value in educating themselves and others, thus representing a European tradition of Enlightenment. Die "Meinigen" (my family) (28; *ME* 21) tend to be extraordinary individuals in their respective environments. This exceptionality also applies to Simon Geller, an assimilated Jew who around 1860 founded a school for deaf-mute children in Vienna to teach them to speak, and, in doing so, began a family tradition to be continued through several generations. Deaf children were regarded as mentally handicapped and found themselves excluded in a traditional Jewish culture, where spoken language and music played a central role. Enabling them to speak was therefore a significant step toward their emancipation and potential inclusion. However, the potential idealization of an assimilated Jewish culture is immediately questioned by the way the memory process itself is imagined: The chapter titled "Ein Flug" (55) (A Flight, *ME* 47) puts the narrator in flying pursuit of Schimon Heller who escapes with her into a mythical space reminiscent of one of the Shtetls painted by Chagall, where flying appears as an aerial dance. Together with the reference to his Jewish name "Schimon" (49) (Shimon, *ME* 41), this image recalls a non-assimilated, traditional Jewish world which, despite its shortcomings and strangeness from the narrator's point of view, is also an integral part of her family history and of European history. But this world is accessible only through imagination, sensory perception and movement.[24]

Furthermore, the image of the chase, combining mythical elements of Chagall's modernist perspective on Hasidism with elements reminiscent of contemporary fantasy, points to the difficulties inherent in remembering a complex past from a third-generation point of view:

> ich habe es probiert, sie fliegen Richtung morgen, parallel zu Zeit und Raum, manchmal quer dazu, der eigenen Flugbahn folgend und den weisen und strengen Büchern, die wir nie lesen und verstehen werden, die Wege des Städtchens schimmern dunkelgrün, mein nächtlicher Spaziergang, meine Jagd nach Schimon, . . . (56)
>
> (I've tried to, they fly toward tomorrow, parallel to time and space, sometimes crosswise, following their own trajectory and the wise and stern books that we will never read and understand, the paths in the towns [sic!] shimmer, dark green, my evening stroll, my hunt for Shimon, . . . *ME* 47–48)

Her attempt to remember and narrate what cannot be narrated thus jumps between various modes and media in the course of the book, combining the autobiographical with mythological reference, photographs and archive material. Variable focalization allows the narrator to slip into the roles of different family members. She puts herself physically into their places by visiting historical sites where they led their lives.

> Die Vermeidung des Konjunktivs macht aus einer Vorstellung eine Erkenntnis oder sogar einen Bericht, man nimmt die Stelle eines anderen ein, katapultiert sich dorthin, auf diese Tabelle zum Beispiel, und so erprobe ich jede Rolle an mir selbst, als gäbe es keine Vergangenheit ohne irgendein Als-ob, Wenn oder Falls. (45)
>
> (Avoidance of the subjunctive turns imagination into recognition or even statement, you take another's place, catapult yourself there, into this chart, for example, and thus try out every role for myself as though there was no past without an *if*, *as though*, or *in that case*. *ME* 36)

While remembering, and belonging, thus turns into a performance, giving apparently a free choice of roles to play, this freedom of choice is taken back again in other passages, tying the author-narrator to historical experience, different ethical, cultural and political frameworks. In another passage she compares her journey to a google search limited by algorithms (12; *ME* 6). Moments of empathy and understanding are soon questioned again, or commented on ironically. The stories of family members are told in a humorous or absurd way, while she is constantly acknowledging the impossibility of doing so. The author-narrator fails to find a coherent frame in which to bring together these stories and perspectives, gradually accepting its fragmentary nature as a strength of her narrative.

Her grandmother Rosa, with whom she shares a strong emotional bond and who is present throughout the book, personifies the transgression of boundaries which is central to the narrator's idea of Jewish identity and belonging.[25] In those chapters explicitly dedicated to Rosa, she appears as a beautiful woman who, in her love for dancing, brings together traditional Jewish culture and international modernism. Going blind as an old woman further refines her sharp sense of hearing and the gestural language she uses in everyday conversation with all around her, including those who can hear. This gestural language is something which has become natural to her after her training and life-long work as a teacher for the deaf (66; *ME* 57). Rosa is the last family member to continue this tradition which for Petrowskaja defines their Jewishness, combining enlightened thinking, sensory perception and grace. Her grandmother transforms gesturing into a form of dance:

> Rosas Hände, die in der Gebärdensprache immer lebendig waren, fanden auch im Ruhestand keine Ruhe, ... Sie hatte ihr ganzes Leben mit Gehörlosen verbracht, sie sprach jeden Tag Gebärdensprache, ihre Schüler nannten Rosa Mi-ni-a-tur-na-ja-mi-mi-ka, Miniatur-Mimik, als wäre es ihr Name . . . Sie habe die schönste und scheueste Mimik aller Hörenden gehabt, erzählte mir eine alte Lehrerin aus ihrer Schule. (63)
>
> (Rosa's hands, which were always animated by her use of sign language, didn't rest even in retirement. . . . She had spent her entire life with the deaf, she spoke sign language every day, her students called Rosa Mi-ni-a-tur-na-ya-mi-mi-ka, miniature mimic, as though this was her name . . . An elderly teacher from Rosa's school told me that she had the most beautiful yet bashful signs and gestures of all the hearing members of that community. *ME* 53)

Rosa is essentially a modern woman. Her independence and active engagement, not only for the deaf but also for the blind when older, bears witness to this, as much as does her frantic attempt to write down her memories as she loses her own vision. Dancing Charleston is one art form in which she immerses herself as an act of rebellion. Another is singing opera and operetta pieces, which makes her part of the cosmopolitan, modern Central Eastern Europe of the 1920s. Nicola Rayner writes about the Charleston:

> One of the best known craze dances, its rhythm and steps are an instant shorthand for the Roaring Twenties, for the Jazz Age, for a generation running wild in an era of new freedoms and rebellions. This was a dance where toes turned in, knees knocked, legs kicked high and arms went into big scarecrow poses. It's an extravagant, thrill-seeking dance.[26]

Rosa, who dreamt of becoming an opera singer, sneaks out of the house to dance and go to the opera in order to enjoy herself and escape the selfless teaching and learning environment at home (65–66; *ME* 56). Family photographs show her dancing on the table as her future husband proposes to her with a bunch of roses (68; *ME* 58–59). When she becomes a speech and language therapist and teacher for the deaf, she "tanzte und sang für ihre Schüler, wann immer sie konnte. Noch mit 75 Jahren führte sie mir ihre Lieblingsstücke vor" (66) ([was] dancing and singing for her students whenever she could. At the age of seventy-five, she still entertained me with her favourites, *ME* 56). This is also an act of rebellion through song and dance, against teaching becoming a purely academic, physically restrictive practice. By dancing Charleston and singing opera and operetta pieces for her deaf pupils, Rosa thus transgresses unspoken boundaries which have turned an enlightened family tradition into a somewhat disabling practice.

Through her singing and dancing for entertainment purposes and as an expression of her own enjoyment of physical movement, Rosa transforms both, rational ideals of education and traditional Central Eastern European Hasidic traditions of dance and gesture as an embodied expression of life and joy for religious reasons, while, at the same time interlinking them. This is, in effect, a change of paradigms (i.e., a change of places as described by Jacques Derrida in "Choreographies"): "The most innocent of dances would thwart the assignation á residence, escape those residences under surveillance; the dance changes place and above all changes *places*. In its wake, they can no longer be recognized."[27] This transformation also applies to the absurdity of singing to a deaf audience, an act that reflects Jewish traditions of joyful dance and song in the face of darkness and death,[28] a reference made at different points of *Vielleicht Esther*.[29] Further examples include the narrator expecting the community beginning to dance at the funeral of her granduncle Abram/Arnold (207–206), in view of the absurdity of his survival until then, or her father's joke when he cannot remember the details of his flight from the German soldiers as a child. The latter refers to a tradition of Jewish humor, which, according to Freud, contains dialectical elements of self-depreciation and self-praise. The author-narrator concludes: "Ein Witz ist wichtiger als eine richtige Antwort, das Wort ist mehr wert als das Ergebnis." (166) (A joke is more important than a correct answer, the word more than the outcome. *ME* 146)

Rosa's transgressive and transformative dancing encapsulates the poetics of memory in *Vielleicht Esther*. The following quotation can therefore be understood as an autopoietic reference. The image of Rosa, encompassing the movement of her legs in dance, rather than restricting herself to that of the arms and hand—the latter having become both a highly developed skill and a disability in her family over the centuries[30]—evokes a transgressive memory discourse, bringing together very different experiences in an emphatic, sensory and highly complex narrative. This narrative, despite traumatic events and dead ends encountered, transforms contemporary memory discourses within German, Jewish and European context into a narrative of survival:

> Das Wichtigste waren aber ihre Beine, sagte meine Mutter, . . . Meine Babuschka hatte tatsächlich sehr schöne Beine, sie war leichtfüßig, noch im Krankenhaus, kurz vor ihrem Tod, zeigte sie den Krankenschwestern wie man Charleston tanzt, das war als die Krankenschwestern die Zimmer lüfteten und Rosa aufstehen musste trotz ihrer Schmerzen, sie konnte nur noch liegen und tanzen. . . . und dann, so erzählt meine Mutter, hielt Rosa vor allen Kranken eine Rede, sie sprach über die zwanziger Jahre in Moskau, wie sie Tanzen gelernt hatte, tanzend erzählte sie von der Neuen Ökonomischen Politik und wie sie die Rede von Trotzki . . . hatte miterleben dürfen. . . . leichtfüßig tanzte sie mitten in die Weltgeschichte hinein. (67–68)

> (But the most important thing about Rosa was her legs, my mother said. . . . My babushka's legs were exquisite. She was fleet-footed, even in the hospital shortly before her death, and showed the nurses how to do the Charleston when they came to air out the room and Rosa had to get up despite her pain—she was only able to lie flat or dance; . . . My mother told me that Rosa gave a speech in front of all the patients, talking about the 1920s in Moscow and how she learned to dance, and while dancing she chatted about the New Economic Policy and how she had been present at Trotsky's speech . . . she deftly[31] danced her way into world history. *ME* 58)

It is this nimble approach to an atrocious history of suffering that the author-narrator aims to adapt for her own narrative performance: "La-la-la Human Step hieß die Tanz-Performance, bei der ich wieder einen Hans kennenlernte. Danach gingen wir tanzen." (278) (*La la la Human Step* was the name of the dance performance where I met another Hans. We went dancing afterward. *ME* 248). The narrator and the DJ with the paradigmatic German name "Hans" she meets at a dance performance in Vienna spend the night dancing until the morning. This is after her research in an Austrian concentration camp on the reasons for her grandfather's survival of this camp leaves her without any clear insight regarding his guilt or innocence. The last page of *Vielleicht Esther* recalls, in a somewhat ironic tone, Hans and herself "chatting" about their grandfathers who were both prisoners of war, his as a German in Siberia, hers a Soviet Ukrainian in Austria. "[W]ir raveten, oder we were raving for peace, die ganze Nacht, für den Weltfrieden, für Dionysos und in memoriam Otto von Habsburg,"[32] who was, according to Austrian media covering his funeral in 2011, the last crown prince and quasi "emperor" of an "old," cosmopolitan Europe that was destroyed by nationalism and anti-Semitism.

In "Malige" and *Vielleicht Esther*, secularized versions of Hasidic dance, characterized by the dancer's total immersion in the movement and his or her ability to captivate the audience, create moments of transgression or liminality. In "Malige," the resulting carnivalesque defeat of power on the level of plot, at the same time suggest a literature of commitment transgressing the antagonism of *l'art pour l'art* and *art engagé* determining literary discussions in the 1960s. Facing the memory of his participation in an inhumane system, the act of writing cannot resolve the contradictions inherent in the author's past experience and the process of remembering. Instead, it must remain a continuous effort in bringing these contradictions together in the literary text as a piece of art, indebted to modernism as well as realism, and marked by the experience of the Second World War. However, despite its originality and unsettling poetic potency, this form of transgression does not lead to a questioning of the author's parameters of guilt and atonement as such. It does not challenge the binary system of Jewish victims and German perpetrators, with the victims conforming to the stereotypical image of Jews as an archaic and passive Other. Petrowskaja's text, on the other hand, while drawing on traditional images and tropes of Hasidism as a prominent feature of Eastern European culture before the Holocaust, thus making them an integral part of its poetics and the author's Jewishness, also ironically subverts these—for example with Hasidic dance merging into Charleston in the context of Viennese modernism of the 1920s.The result is a transgressive dance that challenges existing boundaries while acknowledging their presence. This use of dance reflects the memory and identity discourse in the book, which moves between an inside and outside perspective, between past and present, empathy and absurdity, as a dance combining spontaneity and performance. Such a postmodern performance, playing with dominant perceptions of self and Other, perhaps rather imaginable for an author like Petrowskaja, who belongs to a different generation and has a different cultural and experiential background, undermines these structural polarities. (That the texts compared belonging to different genres may be a further factor to be taken into account here.) Nevertheless, the memory discourse in *Vielleicht Esther*, comes closer to Derrida's conception of dance as a type of disordering, dismantling or deconstruction that alters the paradigms through which it moves.[33] In addition to the disordering of binary concepts of identity, dance as a form of narrative in Petrowskaja's book is also about how to address blank spaces in memory and history, and the abandonment of definite answers, including linear historical narratives and binding ethical frameworks.

NOTES

1. *Vielleicht Esther* taps into the "Eastern European turn" in recent German-language literature, which has seen a surge in voices from Eastern Europe in the last two decades (Brigid Haines, "Introduction: The Eastern European Turn in Contemporary German-Language Literature," *German Life and Letters* 68, no. 2 (2015): 145–153). A substantial number of these voices are those of young authors for whom German is not their first language.

2. Michel Foucault, "A Preface to Transgression," in *Language, Counter-Memory, Practice. Selected Essays and Interviews*, ed. with an introduction by Donald F. Bouchard (London and Ithaca, NY: Cornell University Press, 1980), 29–52.

3. Mikhail Bakhtin, *Rabelais and His World* (Bloomington: Indiana University Press, 1984).

4. This section on Bobrowski is partly based on ideas developed in Egger, Sabine, "The Good German between Silence and Artistic Deconstruction of an Inhumane World: Johannes Bobrowski's Narratives *Mäusefest* (1962) and *Der Tänzer Malige* (1965)," in *The Good German in Literature and Culture*, ed. Christiane Schönfeld and Paul O'Doherty (Rochester, NY: Camden House, 2013), 85–97.

5. These included, for example, Günter Grass, Ingeborg Bachmann, Peter Huchel and Uwe Johnson. Bobrowski also corresponded with Paul Celan.

6. The group of post-war writers who called themselves the Gruppe 47 played a central role in public and literary memory discourses of WW2 and the Holocaust, as well as regarding the post-war German literary canon. Its members understood themselves as having an impact on public debate through their literary and non-literary work, but took a moral rather than political stance when confronting the cataclysm or "Zivilisationsbruch" of the Holocaust in their writing (Dan Diner and Seyla Benhabib, eds., *Zivilisationsbruch: Denken nach Auschwitz* (Frankfurt am Main: Fischer, 1988)). East German literature of the time, on the other hand, was dominated by Social Realism. In the course of the 1960s, the literary debate in both fields of German literature focused on the need for a literature of commitment, a discussion based on the antagonism of *l'art pour l'art* and *art engagé*. The Frankfurt Auschwitz trials of 1963–1965 influenced this debate both in East and West Germany.

7. Bobrowski repeatedly distanced himself from a literature reduced to its "didaktisch-polemische[n] Absicht" (didactic-polemic aim), e.g. in his contribution to a panel discussion during the International Writers' Convention in Weimar and Berlin, May 14–20, 1965. At the same time, he argued for a poetics of small steps when writing about National Socialism, including the portrayal of "Nazis als mittlere Leute von ganz üblichem Verhalten" (cited in Holger Gehle, "Verständigung und Selbstverständigung—Zur Prosa Johannes Bobrowskis," in *In der Sprache der Täter: Neue Lektüren deutschsprachiger Nachkriegs- und Gegenwartsliteratur*, ed. Stephan Braese (Opladen/Wiesbaden: Westdeutscher Verlag, 1998), 79).

8. "Vom Hausrecht des Autors. Ein Interview des Deutschlandsenders" (1964), in Johannes Bobrowski, *Gesammelte Werke*, vol. 4, *Die Erzählungen, vermischte Prosa und Selbstzeugnisse*, ed. Eberhard Haufe (Stuttgart: DVA, 1999), 477. At the same time, however, he is critical of the idea that literature could provide "eine Art

Wiedergutmachung" ("Benannte Schuld—Gebannte Schuld" (1962), in Bobrowski, *Gesammelte Werke* 4, 446). Page numbers from "Malige" and other texts given without further reference in the first part of the chapter, discussing Bobrowski's writing, refer to this publication. Translations are by Sabine Egger / S.E.

9. See Sabine Egger,"Martin Buber und Johannes Bobrowski. Ethik und Erinnerung in der sarmatischen Lyrik," *Literaturkritik.de* 19, no. 4 (2017), accessed May 14, 2019, http://literaturkritik.de/public/inhalt.php?ausgabe=201704#toc_nr1923.

10. Bobrowski's own unit participated in the taking of the Polish town Rozan during the war, i.e., this is one of several references, geographical and historical, interlinking the story with the author's biography. However, these references are not made explicit to the reader unfamiliar with the author's life.

11. "Anflug oben schwankt, setzt einen Fuß vor, greift nach seiner Feldmütze, nach dem Koppelzeug, hat zu schreien begonnen, wie ein Tier, Befehle oder so was, ein sinnloses Durcheinander. Und Malige, sieht er, tanzt auf ihn zu, immer näher, ein paar Meter noch, mit zurückgeworfenem Kopf, offenem Mund." (168–169)

12. Smoke is a topical image of the Holocaust in post-war German poetry, including poems by Nelly Sachs or Paul Celan's "Todesfuge" (1948, Death Fugue). Bobrowski would have been familiar with the work of these authors, as well as with that of their contemporaries. See Reinhard Tgahrt and Ute Doster, *Johannes Bobrowski oder Landschaft mit Leuten. Katalog zur Ausstellung des Deutschen Literaturarchivs im Schiller-Nationalmuseum* (Marbach am Neckar: Deutsche Schillergesellschaft, 1993), 445.

13. When posted in Poland, Bobrowski seems to have been on friendly terms with his superior, on which the character of Lieutenant Anflug is based. See Andreas Degen, *Bildgedächtnis: Zur poetischen Funktion der Sinneswahrnehmung im Prosawerk Johannes Bobrowskis* (Berlin: Erich Schmidt Verlag, 2004), 104. According to his sister Ursula, Bobrowski hit the Anflug character in the face after he had ordered a maltreatment of Jewish civilians similar to the one in the story, but continued to correspond with him through letters after the war (Degen, *Bildgedächtnis*, 104).

14. The lightness carrying away the dancer is reminiscent of the poet's playfulness in baroque Anacreonticism. At the end of the eighteenth century, dance was a widely used allegory of life, love and other art forms than dance itself. See also Bobrowski's afterword in the collection of baroque poetry he edited, *"'Wer mich und Ilse sieht im Grase . . .'"* (1964). Bobrowski himself employs the image of a dancing artist for the writer in other texts, such as in the early short narrative "Tribunal" (1950) and in *Levins Mühle* (1964). In *Levins Mühle*, a group of Jews, Gypsies and other outsiders engage in a traditional Polish folk dance as an act of resistance against the anti-Semitic mill owner. Also, the painter and poet Philippi, who can be interpreted on one level as a caricature of the author, dances, rather than walks, as an act of defiance against aesthetic conventions.

15. See Foucault, "A Preface to Transgression."

16. It is likely that this is a conscious reference to Camus's 1943 adaptation of the Sisyphus myth as a philosophical essay, *The Myth of Sisyphus*. In 1957, Bobrowski had written a review of Camus's *Der Fall* for the journal *Das Buch von drüben*, published by the Altberliner Verlag Lucie Groszer. The liberation from a reflecting

consciousness embodied by Heinrich von Kleist's "Gliedermann" might be another intertextual reference to consider in this context.

17. Modernist literature, including Sartre, Camus, Proust, Joyce, Beckett or Kafka, remained largely excluded from the canon of East German literature until the mid-1960s, largely because of the "decadent" bourgeois world view expressed in it. Franz Kafka's work, for example, was not published in the GDR until 1965. See, for example, Stephen Brockmann, "Resurrected from the ruins: the emergence of GDR culture," in *Rereading East Germany. Literature and Film of the GDR*, ed. Karen Leeder (Cambridge: Cambridge University Press, 2015), 35–51.

18. This refers to his much-cited dictum: "To write poetry after Auschwitz is barbaric." Theodor W. Adorno, *Prisms* (Cambridge, MA: MIT Press, 1983), 34.

19. Jan Küveler, "Der Holocaust ist unsere Antike," *Die Welt*, 11 March 2014, accessed 10 June 2019, https://www.welt.de/kultur/literarischewelt/article125670065/Der-Holocaust-ist-unsere-Antike.html.

20. In her article from 2017, Jessica Ortner states that "a considerable number of Eastern European migrant authors of Jewish origin are currently lifting Holocaust memory in a German context to a new level" (Jessica Ortner, "The Reconfiguration of the European Archive in Contemporary German-Jewish Migrant Literature: Katja Petrowskaja's novel *Vielleicht Esther*." *Scandinavian Jewish Studies* 28, no. 1 (2017): 38.

21. Michel de Certeau, *The Practice of Everyday Life* (Berkeley: University of California Press, 1984).

22. Ich hatte keinen Grund zu leiden. Trotzdem litt ich, von früh an, obwohl glücklich und geliebt, umgeben von Freunden, es was mir peinlich zu leiden, ich litt immer wieder an dieser manchmal schneidend scharfen, manchmal wermutherben Einsamkeit, . . . (23) (I had no reason to suffer. Yet I did suffer, from early on, although I was happy and loved and surrounded by friends, embarrassed to be suffering, but suffering still with a loneliness that ranged from razor-sharp to bleakly bitter . . . *ME* 17) Page numbers from this text given without further detail here and in the following refer to the German original: Katja Petrowskaja, *Vielleicht Esther*. Berlin: Suhrkamp, 2014. Translations are taken from Katja Petrowskaja, *Maybe Esther*, trans. Shelley Frisch (London: Fourth Estate, 2018), abbreviated as *ME*).

23. This applies in particular to memory discourses in the former Soviet Union. At the same time, the passage on it in the book goes beyond a criticism of such an absence, and of the marginalization and persecution of Jews in the Ukraine or Russia, also during the 1930s and 1940s. What is proposed here is a multidirectional memory discourse.

24. The blending of assimilation and tradition, and the inherent contradiction, is also expressed in the narrator's interpretation of her aunt's recipe for Kwas: "als ob Europa und die Juden aus einer Wurzel stammten . . . dass alle Juden, auch die die gar keine Juden mehr waren, sich zu den letzten Europäern zählen durften, schließlich haben sie alles gelesen, was Europa ausmacht." (31) (as though Europe and the Jews were descended from one root . . . that all Jews, even those who were no longer Jews at all anymore were among the last Europeans, having, after all, read everything that constitutes Europe, *ME* 23). On the role of Jewish education culture as the "Kitt"

(glue) holding together the now lost multicultural Central European society, see Karl Schlögel, *Die Mitte liegt ostwärts. Europa im* Übergang (Munich: Hanser, 2002), 14.

25. In one passage, Rosa's continuous presence is put in the images of Soviet hairpins the author-narrator keeps finding on her journey (61; *ME* 51–52).

26. Nicola Rayner, "How the Charleston Changed the World," *Dancing Times*, 15 May 2013, accessed May 14, 2019. https://www.dancing-times.co.uk/how-the-charleston-changed-the-world/.

27. Jacques Derrida and Christie V. McDonald, "Choreographies," in *Bodies of the Text*, ed. Ellen W. Goellner and Jacqueline Shea Murphy (New Brunswick: Rutgers University Press, 1995), 145.

28. See Michael Fishbane, *The Exegetical Imagination: On Jewish Thought and Theology* (Cambridge, MA: Harvard University Press, 1998), 173–184, 226–231.

29. See also Rosa's Yiddish singing and dancing on her seat, when listening to a record of Yiddish music the author-narrator has brought back from her visit to Warsaw, a movement infecting the granddaughter, despite her finding this somewhat ridiculous (77; *ME* 66).

30. The author-narrator is told by her mother that "die Beine der Frauen unserer Familie wurden in jeder Generation schlechter, sie verkümmerten buchstäblich . . . das lag daran, dass die Frauen unserer Familie jahrhundertelang an sechs Tagen der Woche vor ihren Schülern standen." (68) (the legs of the women in our family grew worse with every succeeding generation . . . because the women in our family had spent centuries standing in front of their students six days a week . . . *ME* 58).

31. "Light-footed" or "nimbly" might have been a better translation here than "deftly."

32. "We raved, or we were raving for peace, the whole night, for world peace, for Dionysus and in memory of Otto von Habsburg." (*ME* 248)

33. Derrida, "Choreographies," 94.

BIBLIOGRAPHY

Adorno, Theodor W. *Prisms.* Cambridge, MA: MIT Press, 1983.

Bakhtin, Mikhail. *Rabelais and His World.* Bloomington: Indiana University Press, 1984.

Bobrowski, Johannes. *Gesammelte Werke*, vol. 4, *Die Erzählungen, vermischte Prosa und Selbstzeugnisse*, edited by Eberhard Haufe. Stuttgart: DVA, 1999.

Brockmann, Stephen. "Resurrected from the Ruins: The Emergence of GDR Culture," in *Rereading East Germany. Literature and Film of the GDR*, edited by Karen Leeder, 35–51. Cambridge: Cambridge University Press, 2015.

de Certeau, Michel. *The Practice of Everyday Life*. Berkeley: University of California Press, 1984.

Degen, Andreas. *Bildgedächtnis: Zur poetischen Funktion der Sinneswahrnehmung im Prosawerk Johannes Bobrowskis.* Berlin: Erich Schmidt Verlag, 2004.

Derrida, Jacques and McDonald, Christie V. "Choreographies," in *Bodies of the Text*, edited by Ellen W. Goellner and Jacqueline Shea Murphy, 141–156. New Brunswick: Rutgers University Press, 1995.

Diner, Dan and Benhabig, Seyla, eds. *Zivilisationsbruch: Denken nach Auschwitz*. Frankfurt am Main: Fischer, 1988.

Egger, Sabine. "The Good German between Silence and Artistic Deconstruction of an Inhumane World: Johannes Bobrowski's Narratives *Mäusefest* (1962) and *Der Tänzer Malige* (1965)," in *The Good German in Literature and Culture*, edited by Christiane Schönfeld and Paul O'Doherty, 85–97. Rochester, NY: Camden House, 2013.

———. "Martin Buber und Johannes Bobrowski. Ethik und Erinnerung in der sarmatischen Lyrik," *Literaturkritik.de* 19, no. 4 (2017). Accessed May 14, 2019, http://literaturkritik.de/public/inhalt.php?ausgabe=201704#toc_nr1923.

Fishbane, Michael. *The Exegetical Imagination: On Jewish Thought and Theology*. Cambridge, MA: Harvard University Press, 1998.

Foucault, Michel. "A Preface to Transgression," in *Language, Counter-Memory, Practice*. Selected Essays and Interviews, edited with an introduction by Donald F. Bouchard, 29–52. London and Ithaca, NY: Cornell University Press, 1980.

Gehle, Holger. "Verständigung und Selbstverständigung—Zur Prosa Johannes Bobrowskis," in *In der Sprache der Täter: Neue Lektüren deutschsprachiger Nachkriegs- und Gegenwartsliteratur*, edited by Stephan Braese, 79–102. Opladen and Wiesbaden: Westdeutscher Verlag, 1998.

Haines, Brigid. "Introduction: The Eastern European Turn in Contemporary German-Language Literature," *German Life and Letters* 68, no. 2 (2015): 145–153.

Küveler, Jan. "Der Holocaust ist unsere Antike," *Die Welt*, 11 March 2014. Accessed 10 June 2019, https://www.welt.de/kultur/literarischewelt/article125670065/Der-Holocaust-ist-unsere-Antike.html.

Ortner, Jessica. "The Reconfiguration of the European Archive in Contemporary German-Jewish: Migrant-literature Katja Petrowskaja's Novel *Vielleicht Esther*." *Scandinavian Jewish Studies*, 28, no. 1 (2017): 38–54.

Petrowskaja, Katja. *Vielleicht Esther*. Berlin: Suhrkamp, 2014.

———. *Maybe Esther*. Translated by Shelley Frisch. London: Fourth Estate, 2018.

Rayner, Nicola. "How the Charleston Changed the World," *Dancing Times*, 15 May 2013. Accessed 14 May 2019. https://www.dancing-times.co.uk/how-the-charleston-changed-the-world.

Schlögel, Karl. *Die Mitte liegt ostwärts. Europa im Übergang*. Munich: Hanser, 2002.

Tgahrt, Reinhard and Doster, Ute. *Johannes Bobrowski oder Landschaft mit Leuten. Katalog zur Ausstellung des Deutschen Literaturarchivs im Schiller-Nationalmuseum*. Marbach am Neckar: Deutsche Schillergesellschaft, 1993.

Chapter Twelve

Dance and the Postmodern Subject in "Libidoökonomie" and "Der Kranich auf dem Kiesel in der Pfütze" by Feridun Zaimoglu

Joseph Twist

TURKISH DANCES BETWEEN THE TRIVIAL AND THE RADICAL

Dance plays an important role in how Turkey is imagined by others, which is reflected in how the country markets itself abroad. The Turkish entry to the 2003 Eurovision Song Contest, "Every Way that I Can" by Sertab Erener, is a salient case in point, as the song's Turkish musical features and lyrics of female seduction were accompanied by a dance routine and costumes heavily indebted to belly dance.[1] The organizers of the opening ceremony in Istanbul the following year stuck with this winning formula for her reprise, which featured a scantily clad harem of male belly dancers (*zenne*), followed by a group of whirling dervishes during the second song.[2] Perhaps more so than any other Muslim-majority country, Turkey is associated with its famous forms of dance, despite the fact that dance and music remain a contested area within some conservative Islamic sects. Whereas belly dance, often viewed as depraved, is currently being restricted in some Muslim-majority countries, such as Egypt and Iran, it is not only permitted in Turkey but enjoying heightened popularity as part of the current Neo-Ottoman revival.[3] Where spiritual dance in Turkey is concerned, it forms a significant part not just of the worship of the Mevlevi Sufi order (the whirling dervishes), but also of Alevi-Bektaşi[4] rituals, both of which have even been enshrined in the UNESCO List of the Intangible Cultural Heritage of Humanity since 2008 and 2010 respectively.[5] These practices form part of the Islamic tradition of *samā*, meaning "listening," which is the belief that music, poetry and dance can offer spiritual insight.[6] This tradition ranges from the orthodox tradition of reciting the Quran with melodic improvisations to more radical understandings of dance, secular music and poetry offering alternative spiritual experiences outside of institutionalized religion.[7]

The enduring resonance of these dances in the Western imagination, which is undoubtedly part of their tourist appeal, is perhaps due to the way in which they seemingly confirm Orientalist expectations. However, the short stories "Libidoökonomie" (Libido Economy) and "Der Kranich auf dem Kiesel in der Pfütze" (The Crane on the Pebble in the Puddle) from the Turkish-German writer and visual artist Feridun Zaimoglu's short-story collection *Zwölf Gramm Glück* (Twelve Grams of Happiness, 2004) invite readers to think past the stereotypical associations and trivialization associated with these dances, as they act as starting points for discussions on how we understand the concept of identity and subjectivity in the postmodern age.[8] In "Libidoökonomie," the process of unveiling that takes place during a belly dance reveals no hidden identity, radically destabilizing the sovereign subject's understanding of itself based on knowledge and visibility,[9] and in "Der Kranich," a *semah* ritual (a whirling mystical folkdance) provides a means of accessing the divine beyond rational thought, overcoming identitarian divisions between Christianity and Islam.[10] Thus dance in Zaimoglu's postmodern writing serves to destabilize totalizing systems of thought, as opposed to the modernist view of dance as symbolizing the relations between binary opposites within a unified system.[11]

Many scholars have been guided by Edward Said's groundbreaking text *Orientalism* (1978) in their analyses of the Orient as a Western construct, created by academic writing, travel writing, literature, painting, etc., that positions the West as the Orient's superior binary opposite.[12] Whereas dervishes reinforce the idea that the Orient is a place of strange, mystical religiosities, belly dance, as Donnalee Dox states, fuels the "Orientalist fantasy of secluded, sensual women that in particular marked the East's alterity to European culture in the 19th century."[13] Together, the reception of these dances serves to position Turkey as the West's irrational and immoral symbolic Other, and their persistence into contemporary iconography reaffirms the widespread Western denial of Turkey's status as European and even of its "very possibility of development, transformation, [and] human movement."[14]

As a German writer and visual artist with a Turkish background, Zaimoglu (b. 1964 in Bolu) is implicated in the Orient-Occident binary in varying ways, and it forms a central theme in some of his publications, not least *Zwölf Gramm Glück*.[15] The collection clearly engages with this dichotomy, setting up such distinctions only to complicate and challenge them. For example, the stories of the collection are grouped into "Diesseits" (this side/world), set in Germany, and "Jenseits" (the other side/world), set ostensibly in Turkey, but perhaps also in the Maghreb. This division, together with the dual meaning of "Diesseits" and "Jenseits," plays with the mystical associations and the overgeneralization of the Orient. However, the titles alone demonstrate that mystical intensities permeate most of the stories, regardless of the half in which they are located. To name an example from the "Diesseits" stories, "Götzenliebe" (Idolatrous Love), whose title and plot resonate with the woman-worship of Sufism,[16] is a story with spiritual overtones about a relationship devoid of sexual passion. "Gottes Krieger" (God's Warrior), from the "Jenseits" half of the collection, involves a former terrorist's love affair with an older woman with mystical tendencies.[17]

The Orient-Occident binary has also affected the reception of Zaimoglu's work, be it the focus on the way in which he subverts Orientalist stereotypes,[18] or, by contrast, the criticisms of him for confirming them.[19] Meyda Yeğenoğlu rightly states in her 1998 monograph on Orientalist discussions of the Islamic veil, *Colonial Fantasies: Towards a Feminist Reading of Orientalism*, that it is important to bear in mind that the Orient only exists as a discursive construct: "the Orient is always-already articulated in a discursive field and . . . this articulation entails the materialization or incorporation of the Orient within such representations."[20] This point can be further extrapolated in the light of postmodern/poststructuralist critique to conclude that all representations of identities are discursive constructs. Thus, although literary texts can play their part in shaping how the Orient is imagined, it would be misguided to presume that literature's role is to represent more accurate identities beneath the false depictions. This would, in any case, merely continue the paradigm on which Orientalism is based. Rather than countering negative stereotypes with alternative identities, "Libioökonomie" and "Der Kranich" suggest that identities, be they stereotypes or not, are always a violent gesture, whereas the depictions of dances within these stories imply a more complex understanding of subjectivities in flux.[21]

In this regard, Margaret Littler's Deleuzian approach to Zaimoglu's writing moves beyond the view that it represents an identity, as she attempts to be more receptive to the affective power of his texts and how they disrupt majoritarian norms and expectations as "minor literature." Her reading method aims to defer understanding and interpretation in favor of a receptivity to literature as a destabilizing force that does not just present us with a known world, but increases our possibilities to think and feel.[22] It is my aim to build on Littler's reading of "Libidoökonomie" by analyzing both the way in which Orientalism plays a central role in the protagonist's responses to the destabilizing alterity of the other in the text, and also how attempts to fix and stabilize religious identities in "Der Kranich" are equally presented as a form of violence that militates against other spiritual experiences. The belly dance and *semah* ritual in these two stories are crucial in this regard, as it is during them that fixed relations between Self and Other (even a divine other) are challenged. These stories therefore move beyond modernist depictions of dance and dancers as dualistic symbolic representations, attending instead to post-representational ways of perceiving the other and, in turn, the self.

BELLY DANCE AND THE MALE GAZE IN "LIBIDOÖKONOMIE"

The opening sequence of "Libidoökonomie" is a vignette of a woman performing what appears to be a form of belly dance: "Lapislazuli ihre Augen, sie tanzt zwischen den Marmorsäulen, halb verdeckt, halb sichtbar. Die Kreisglieder ihrer Nippeskette auf den Hüften hüpfen im Rhytmus ihrer Sprünge, ihre Brüste nehmen die halben Drehungen auf und beben. Unlakiert ihre Fingernägel. Gelockt ihr Haar. Eine eurasische Venusfalle" (Her eyes lapis lazuli, she dances between the marble columns, half hidden, half visible. The links in her chain of trinkets hopping on her hips in the rhythm of her jumps, her breasts absorb her semi-gyrations and quake. Her fingernails unpolished. Her hair curled. A Eurasian Venus-trap) (39).[23] Although only a short sequence, there is a lot to examine here in terms of imagery and symbolism, much of which evokes an imagined, sensual Orient. The semi-precious stone lapis lazuli, the opening association of the unknown woman, is principally mined in Afghanistan, for example. The half-hidden dancer also draws upon widespread imagery of the inaccessible Oriental woman beyond the penetrative gaze of Western travelers. The emphasis on the movement of the highly eroticized areas of the hips, highlighted by a jangling chain, and breasts suggests the intricate and isolated movements and shimmies of belly dance, as does the focus on the dancer's hands. Her description as a "Eurasian Venus trap" leaves the subject of her ethnicity open and associates her seductive movements not only with the Roman goddess of love, but also with the carnivorous plant so named because it apparently reminded its discoverer of female genitalia. This last image can therefore be associated with danger and castration, hinting at a somewhat stereotypical Oriental *femme fatale*—one of many female love-interests in *Zwölf Gramm Glück*.

Indeed, all the collection's stories involve men's (often unsuccessful) pursuit of women, and the majority deal with the dichotomies of masculine/feminine, Occident/Orient and profane/sacred, which can be mapped onto one another in different ways. As Yeğenoğlu argues: "the representation of otherness is achieved simultaneously through sexual as well as cultural modes of differentiation. The Western acts of understanding the Orient and its women are not two distinct enterprises, but rather are interwoven aspects of the same gesture."[24] In the light of postmodern critique, the "universal subject" has shown itself to be Western, white, heterosexual and male, with woman being its quintessential Other. Men's understanding of women as their enigmatic Other is intensified by the inaccessible, veiled Oriental woman, "not only signifying the Oriental woman as mysterious and exotic but also signifying the Orient as feminine, always veiled, seductive, and dangerous."[25]

The opening scene tells us little about the actual dancer herself, but the way in which she is described by the first-person narrator implies that he is not only Orientalizing but also objectifying her with his gaze, in that he focuses on specific parts of her body rather than her face or, indeed, the whole person. Yet the power dynamics are not necessarily that straightforward here. The emphasis on the dancer's movement, her wobbling and bouncing body parts, and the way she remains at least partially out of sight arguably undermines the totalizing male gaze that seeks to know and possess her.[26] Moreover, that she also generates fear in the male protagonist, as he must see himself as the hapless fly in this metaphor, equally implies a more complex power dynamic than first meets the eye. Virginia Keft-Kennedy's feminist reappraisal of belly dance would suggest that this sense of danger stems from the male subject's perception of "the dancers' bodies as terrifying in their difference (female and non-Western) from his own dominant position as both male and Western."[27] A belly dancer's body is "seen as uncontrolled and uncontrollable. . . . Uncorseted, the spectacle of a woman's belly-dancing body posed a threat to the acceptable cultural norms of appropriate femininity."[28] Yet, depending on the context, belly dance remains ambivalent from a feminist perspective: "[t]he belly dancer produces a constant and complex slippage between the practice of belly dancing as a symbol of female empowerment on the one hand, and orientalist figurations of 'Eastern otherness' linked to colonialist discourse on the other."[29] In this regard, the narrator's male gaze is foregrounded constantly in "Libidoökonomie," as are his objectifying remarks that serve to emphasize his own position as subject. For instance, he generalizes female bookshop employees as "unnahbar, wie eine bessere Vorzimmerdame gekleidet, französisch anmutend, zum Anbeißen kühl und schön" (aloof, dressed like a glorified receptionist, seemingly French, cool and beautiful enough to eat) (41)[30]—one of the narrator's many objectifying remarks about women.

Directly after the opening dance scene discussed above, the protagonist is woken up by a telephone call, implying that the vignette was merely an erotic dream, or perhaps a memory. The first-person narrator does not know the caller's name, but it appears that their conversations, which have been going on for two weeks, are strictly regulated with calls at 9:24 in the morning and precisely twelve hours later in the evening. As in the opening dance scene, the call conjures up exotic imagery in the protagonist's mind: "Blütenfäden des Safrankrokus, frisch aus den Narben gezupft und über einer kleinen Flamme getrocknet, treiben im Wasser eines emaillierten Zubers. Langsam tauche ich eine Hand hinein, und langsam ziehe ich sie wieder hinaus, die Safranfäden haben sich in die Handlinien eingefügt und bilden ein magisches Skelett" (Threads of the saffron crocus, freshly plucked from their stigmas and dried over a small flame, float in the water of an enameled bathtub. I slowly submerge my hand into the water, and slowly pull it out again, the saffron threads have inserted themselves into the creases of my hand, forming a magical skeleton) (39–40). It could be argued that this image again constitutes an Orientalizing male fantasy, yet there is only vague, sensual imagery centered on his own hand here, and no objectifying description of the female body. The narrator's attempts to find out anything concrete about the caller, particularly with regard to her appearance, are frustrated as when he asks questions about her, she hangs up: "Fragen zu ihrer Person verstoßen gegen die Abmachung, doch ich möchte sie mir vorstellen können, Liebesinserenten bestehen auch auf die Einsendung von Ganzkörperfotos" (Questions about who she is go against our deal, but I wanted to be able to imagine her, lonely-hearts columns also insist that you send a full-body photo) (54–55).

The narrator is unfamiliar with the caller and his attempts to fix her as a known entity are unsuccessful, yet he tends to refer to her with Orientalist imagery, such as his nickname for her: the "anonyme Telefonterroristin" (anonymous telephone-terrorist) (40). This can be viewed as an attempt to impose order though familiar categories, as a coping mechanism to satisfy his own need for a stable identity, positioning her not just as mysterious, but as *essentially* mysterious. As Yeğenoğlu asserts, the binary construction of Orientalism not only serves to represent the Orient as a known, stable and inferior counterpart to the West, but also allows the Western subject to imagine themselves in a "sovereign, possessive, and unitary position," with any negative characteristics banished onto the Other.[31] Just as the narrator desires to know the anonymous caller, "the presumption of a hidden essence and truth behind the veil is the means by which both the Western/colonial and the masculine subject constitute their own identity."[32] Through analyzing European travel writing, Yeğenoğlu deduces that, in order to halt the decentering movement brought about by unknown nature of the Orient and its women, the very essence of the Orient is constructed as mysterious and deceptive.[33]

This relationship in the absence of the defining male gaze finds parallels with other stories in *Zwölf Gramm Glück* about the Islamic veil, such as "Gottesanrufung I" (Invocation of God I), in which the male protagonist is called upon by a friend to write love letters on behalf of his conservative female cousin. With similar words to the cousin of "Gottesanrufung I," the caller in "Libidoökonomie" complains of "die Unfreiheit, begehrt zu sein und die Blicke auf sich zu lenken" (the unfreedom of being desired and of attracting glances) (57)—the narrator, however, contends that the set-up is to allow the caller to control her libido (61), positioning the female as the one with the dangerous, uncontrollable desire, as is the customary patriarchal rationale for the Islamic veil. However, one key difference is that whereas the veil arguably reverses the privileged male position, allowing the woman to see and not be seen, the use of a telephone call, especially with the ban on personal questions, implies an altogether different way of relating to the other in the absence of both the gaze and of mutual understanding. Despite the caller's inability to see the narrator, there is still a sense of unease for him here, as implied by her nickname. This is arguably because she disrupts the narrator's sovereign subject position and plunges this astute businessman into a personal crisis, after which he drinks himself to sleep (61–62). In this regard, he is similar to depictions of the Western male when confronted with a veiled woman: "The apparently calm rationalist discipline of the European subject goes awry in the fantasies of penetration as well as in the topological excess of the veil."[34] In contrast to his relations with most women, the protagonist is more open to the unknown where his job as a second-hand bookseller is concerned and he is immersed in the forces and flows of capitalism: "Die Arbeit bringt es mit sich, daß ich mich herumtreibe und in Bewegung halte" (My work means that I am on the prowl and keep on the move) (48). In Littler's reading of the text she focuses on how Zaimoglu makes visible the forces that shape and permeate our world, mentioning how, where business is concerned, the narrator is not possessive and acknowledges his subordination to the uncontrollable currents of capitalism.[35] By contrast, when it comes to women, he attempts to fix them in his gaze and adopt a defining subject role.[36]

The lack of clarity surrounding the anonymous caller means that the narrator is unable to fully objectify her, and hence stabilize his own position as subject. Despite his lack of knowledge, he still falls in love with her, but as in "Gottesanrufung I," this is a love with "Spielregeln" [rules of the game] (58), and the narrator's frustrations are given chaste, religious connotations as he refers to himself as performing the role of her "Beichtvater" (father confessor) (60). The caller, by contrast, seems more comfortable with her lack of intimate and personal knowledge about the narrator and her own fluid subjectivity, which she likens to feeling like plasma: "Zähe Flüssigkeit, vom Ausfluß abgehalten von 'ner Zellwand" (doughy liquid, stopped from spilling out by a cell wall) (52). This less rigid understanding of subjectivity is also embodied by her dance at the end of the story, which, like the telephone calls, continues to frustrate any fixed Self-Other binary.

The bar in which they finally agree to meet is filled with singles and the narrator attempts to find his love-interest by looking women in the face while giving them the opportunity to look back at him. Most of them turn away, except for a "recht angejahrten Thailänderin—oder ist sie eine Taiwanesin?" (Thai woman who is no spring chicken—or is she Taiwanese?) (64), who he resolves to fall back on if the caller does not appear—again the overgeneralization of the Orient and its women is apparent here. He is then shoved onto the dancefloor, and a similar scene to the opening vignette unfolds, revealing the dancing woman to be the "telephone terrorist" all along:

> Und dann sehe ich sie, sie tanzt, halb verdeckt, halb sichtbar, zwischen den Marmorsäulen, eine Art eurasischen Stammestanz, ihr Haar peitscht ihren nackten Rücken, die Träger ihres weißen Tops sind an ihrem Nacken verknotet. Ihr Kettengürtel wird kaum von ihren schmalen Hüften gehalten. Sie spürt meinen Blick, dreht sich langsam tanzend um und schaut mich an, und ich wünsche, sie würde mich eine Ewigkeit ansehen. Ich kann mich nicht von der Stelle rühren.
>
> [And then I see her, dancing a kind of Eurasian tribal dance, half hidden, half visible, between the marble columns, her hair whipping her naked back, the straps of her white top are tied at the nape of her neck. Her chain-link belt is barely held by her narrow hips. She senses my gaze, turns slowly around still dancing and looks at me, and I wish that she would look at me for eternity. I can't move from the spot.] (65)

Again, there are echoes of belly dance here. The usual power dynamic has changed for the narrator, as it is he who is fixed by her gaze. The narrator, through whom the text is focalized, can initially only catch glimpses of the dancing woman and he and reader remain in the dark about who she is. No hidden identity is revealed and stabilized, and she remains unknown throughout the dance. As Keft-Kennedy argues, "the belly dancing body is marked as irregular, multiple, and changing," leading to a transformation in the spectator too.[37] This further resonates with Jacques Derrida's discussion of woman as a "non-identity" in his development of Friedrich Nietzsche's understanding of the feminine:

> Woman (truth) will not be pinned down. . . . That which will not be pinned down by truth is, in truth—*Feminine*. This should not, however, be hastily mistaken for a woman's feminini*ty*, for female sexuali*ty*, or for any other of those essentializing fetishes which might still tantalize the dogmatic philosopher, the impotent artist or the inexperienced seducer who has not yet escaped his foolish hopes of capture.[38]

Thus, whereas the narrator demonstrates a tendency evident in the modernist period to view dance as socially transgressive in its eroticism,[39] it has a more radically transformative potential here, presenting the possibility of a non-appropriative way of relating to the other.

Ultimately, however, the dance stops and, as Keft-Kennedy argues, once the belly dancer is stationary, she risks straightforward objectification: "it is the belly dancing body in motion—with its specific gestures and pelvic-oriented emphasis . . . which allows for a positive modification and subversion of dominant constructions of appropriate womanly behavior."[40] At this point, the dancer discloses her name, Nora, to the protagonist and the first hint of a seemingly coherent identity emerges.[41] However, the story ends before their relationship becomes "normal," subjectivities stabilize and the narrator can presume to know her and, by extension, himself in a binary construct. It opens out onto an unknown future, which, as Littler argues, is based on the negation of behavioral norms,[42] here with regard to sovereign subjectivity and how one relates to the other. Just as Zaimoglu's writing in "Libidoökonomie" makes the invisible forces of capitalism visible, it also shows the violent forces of the Self-Other binary, while also prolonging the moment of coexistence with the other before appropriation, understanding and any fixing of subjectivity can take place, for which the improvised and intricate movements of the belly dance serve as a fitting metaphor.

THE CRANE DANCE AND SPIRITUAL EXPERIENCE IN "DER KRANICH AUF DEM KIESEL IN DER PFÜTZE"

Like "Libiodoökonomie," "Der Kranich auf dem Kiesel in der Pfütze" is partly a story of heterosexual desire, here between a skeptical Muslim man, the narrator, and a Christian German woman, Saskia. It opens, however, not with a seductive dance but with a funeral procession under strange circumstances: a "Hexer" (warlock), dead for the second time, we are told, is being buried without prayer under a heap of rubbish, presided over by the "Priester" (priest) who had him killed. In the background, people engage in ritual self-flagellation. The narrator becomes implicated in the warlock's death because his friend Ben strangled his already dead corpse and so they escape to a Sufi monastery for safety, where the narrator embarks on a spiritual journey. Again, like many other stories from the collection, "Der Kranich" also features various references to the Occident-Orient dichotomy. For example, an Orientalist, racist view is embodied by Ben, who, with a reference to both religious difference and the colonial "civilizing mission," states: "Der Müll . . . der Müll, der Müll. Wir müssen euch missionieren, ihr braucht das" (The rubbish . . . the rubbish, the rubbish. We have to convert you, you need it) (171).

"Der Kranich" has been interpreted by Nimet Şeker as a meta-discourse on two forms of religiosity, orthodoxy and mysticism, with each embedded in their own traditional societal structures, but with the former being a collective and the latter an individualized identity.[43] Yet any references to actual Muslim identities in the text are obfuscated, as Zaimoglu repeatedly avoids using Islamic terms.[44] Given the setting and reference to martyrs, the self-flagellating can be viewed as a portrayal of the Day of Ashura (a Shi'ite festival of martyrdom, condemned as self-harm by some Muslim leaders) and by extension the "priest" must be an imam and the "warlock" perhaps a shaman. As Littler states, Zaimoglu "frustrate[s] any search for recognizable Muslim identities' in his writing."[45] Although various religious associations are blended and blurred in the story, it does not merely reproduce different Islamic identities that need to be researched and decoded by the reader. It also intimates a religious experience that falls outside the realms of knowledge and understanding, and hence outside of identity. Just as "Libidoökonomie" prolongs a destabilizing sense of encounter between a man and a woman and suggests that identity is something the self imposes on the other, in "Der Kranich" the encounter between a man and the divine is a similarly uncontrollable force that takes place during a dance and is distorted as more organized forms of religion attempt to control, mediate and label it. Indeed, the influence of the village's religious leaders, and that of the police who act as a secular variant of top-down authoritarianism, is criticized as the narrator laments: "längst habe ich aufgegeben, nach meinem eigenen Regeln zu leben" (I have long since given up living in accordance with my own rules) (160). This suggests a blanket rejection of those who enforce their will through institutionalized power, as the narrator is drawn toward other ideas of the sacred:

> Die alten Fundamente, von wenigen Sedimenten der Erde bedeckt und verhüllt, sind der wahre Boden under meinen Füßen. . . . Man weiß hier um den Wert des teuren Grundes und verletzt und tötet jeden Archäologen, der glaubt, eine amtliche Erlaubnis berechtigt ihn, eine Ruine auszugraben. Die Zeichen machen blind, unmöglich, die Signale auf ein erträgliches Mindestmaß zu filern. Unmöglich, über eine Verwendung außerhalb der Zeichen nachzudenken—alles Gelebte steht in den Mirakelbüchern der Vorväter, wer von diesem Leben abkommt, macht sich strafbar.

> [The old foundations, covered by a few layers of earth and hidden, are the true ground beneath my feet. . . . The worth of valuable ground is well known here and every archaeologist who believes that an official permit authorizes him to

> excavate a ruin is injured and killed. The signs blind you, it's impossible to filter the signals to a bearable minimum. Impossible to contemplate a use outside the signs—all that is lived can be found in the miraculous books of our forefathers. Whoever abandons this life invites punishment.] (160–161)

Here, as Şeker indicates, we can see a preference for alternative spiritualities that can be contrasted with stifling literalism of the organized religions,[46] while the archaeological metaphor hints that the traces of alternative forms of spirituality may be found in the past.

This is perhaps why the narrator is drawn to a heterodox Islamic order that shows characteristics of Sufism and Alevi-Bektaşism more specifically. Like the Sufis, Alevis priorities an inward, personal religiosity, to the point that they reject Sunni Islam's five pillars; for example, they shun the pilgrimage to Mecca (*hajj*) and favor an inner pilgrimage. As Ruth Mandel states: "This alternative value and worship system is seen as dangerously threatening to many Sunnis, to whom the Alevis represent a menacing, secret cabal, replete with mysterious beliefs and immoral rites."[47] In contrast to the bitter squabbles of the priest and warlock, the "Scharführer" (which can be translated as "squadron leader" and is used by Zaimoglu instead of "sheik") at the first monastery appears holy and wise, despite the Nazi connotations surrounding his title—"Scharführer" refers to a rank of the SS and the Sturm-Abteilung.[48] Although the cloister is cave-like, there are signs of modernity, such as the guard with one hand on his prayer beads and the other on his mobile phone (173). These prayer beads link the monastery to Sufism, as does the story of the nightingale and the rose, common tropes in Sufi poetry, that the narrator hears on his way there (169).[49]

The narrator's pilgrimage to another monastery further reinforces the Alevi-Bektaşi association, as he is sent with a heavy bag of stones on his back to deliver an envelope to a second "Scharführer" (176), a journey so arduous it almost kills him (176–179). Annemarie Schimmel states that it is through "constant purification and, in exchange, qualification with God's attributes" that the Sufi draws near to the divine,[50] and this difficult pilgrimage can be seen as such a form of purification. The protagonist wakes up dressed in a shroud (180), which can be regarded as a spiritual rebirth after the death of his former self. This type of initiation rite forms a link between Alevi-Bektaşism and shamanism, as Irene Markoff indicates:

> Another parallel includes "otherworldly" trance journeys bridging life and death during the initiation process of shamans that recall similar rites of passage experiences by uninitiated Alevi-Bektaşis who, led by a spiritual guide, symbolically "die before dying" (ölmeden önce ölmek) and are then reborn as

they follow the Sufi "path" (*yol*) . . . culminating with the immediate experience of God (*hakikat*).[51]

It is at the second monastery where the narrator meets the German Christian Saskia, who seems to be seeking a spiritual alternative to capitalism (185). That she is welcomed into the monastery demonstrates that it is not a closed religious group, like the organized religion of the priest, and perhaps also refers back to the coexistence of earlier spiritualities in Anatolia, when the boundaries between them were less defined. Indeed, although the Alevi community is now based on family lines, as the link to shamanism discussed above demonstrates, it can be regarded as syncretic. As Markoff states: "Considered from a Sunni perspective to be heterodox in their practices, the Alevis draw their worldview from Shiʿi Twelver Islam, Sufism (deriving from a close association with the Bektaşi order of dervishes), and pre-Islamic traditions tracing back to Central Asian shamanistic practices and beliefs."[52] The narrator and Saskia do not initially see eye to eye and he imagines a religious discussion with her, in which she says: "das Alte Testament, an das Mohammad Prophet die Offenbarung anschließt, sei überholt und der Blutdurst in Gottes Namen eine unsinnige Wut" (the Old Testament, to which the Prophet Muhammad added the revelation, is obsolete and the thirst for blood in God's name a none-sensical rage) (184). This fantasy suggests that he views doctrinal differences as a hindrance to their relationship, as, while highlighting common ground between Islam and Christianity, it nevertheless emphasizes that this is not normally viewed as "shared heritage," but as part of supersessionist claims; Muhammad is the "seal of the prophets," meaning the final one.

In this cloister, the second "Scharführer" also appears favorable to the priest as the former's status is not achieved through the abuse of power; Saskia informs the protagonist: "er hat so wenig Macht wie wir alle" (he has as little power as we all do) (185). Although he is still a religious leader of sorts, he is equal to the other worshippers, merely helping them on their spiritual path, rather than mediating God for them. It is here that dance again plays a pivotal role, as the "Scharführer" leads a *semah* ritual. *Semah* ceremonies constitute an embodied experience of the divine outside rational understanding, what Islam scholar (and writer of fiction) Navid Kermani refers to as its "aesthetic function," privileging affective experience, rather than linguistic meaning-making.[53] Popular amongst Sufi mystics, the idea of *samā,'* to which *semah* is both etymologically and conceptually related, drew the wrath of the orthodoxy and continues to be viewed by many as *haram* (forbidden) today:

> The mystics' practices, whose popular forms were part of the folk culture, were notoriously suspect to members of the orthodoxy. The founders of the four schools of legal thought in particular are infamous among mystics for their rejection of poetry, dance, music and excessively musical Quran recitation. . . . In their defence, the Sufis cited the innate ability of all living things to enjoy beautiful sounds . . . and the Prophet himself was portrayed as an enthusiastic music and poetry listener.[54]

There is, however, disagreement even amongst Sufis about the correct forms of *samā,'* with more conservative mystics rejecting some sheiks' use of drugs and erotic contemplation of beauty to commune with the divine.

The enigmatic title of the story gains some meaning at this point, as the whirling dance the group performs can be understood as the Alevi Crane Dance (*turnalar semahı*).[55] The rhythm (aided by a lack of commas) and consonance in the depiction of the dance resonate with the aesthetic dimension of the dance and its accompanying music:

> Der leise Bittgesang des Priesters erfaßt alle Kreise und alle Reihen des Kelchs, ich höre die Röcke der Frauen in der Drehung surren, zerklopfe zerkörne zermahle mich, zernage zermalme zernichte mich, die Männer kreisen, dass die Säume ihrer Hemden peitschen, und ich kreise mit offenen Augen, das ich Saskias Blick erhasche, zerreibe zereiße zerschlage mich, zerrütte zerschmeiße zerspalte mich, ihr Blick haftet kurz an meinen Augen, bis sie fortgeweht wird vom Schwung, mit meinen Atem rufe ich Dich, Herr, mit meinen Augen suche ich dich, Saskia, streife ertaste berühre mich, und die Silbe, tausend Male gehaucht, Gott, Tausend Male ersehnt, die Gottsilbe, unseren Kehlen entrungen, sammelt sich über unseren Häupten zum Licht, das ich nie gesehen in meinem Leben, ein Licht, daß wir niederknien, zertrenne zerrupfe zertrete mich, zerspelle zerspleiße zerstäube mich. Dann ist Stille.
>
> [The priest's quiet song of solicitation seizes all the circles and all the rows of the cup, I hear the women's skirts whirr as they turn, squash, crush, mash me to pieces, split shatter smash me to pieces, the men circle, the seams of their shirts whipping, and I circle with open eyes, so that I can catch Saskia's eye, trample tear grate me to pieces, beat blast break me to pieces, her gaze fixes briefly on my eyes until she is wafted away with the momentum, with my breath I call You, Lord, with my eyes I look for you, Saskia, brush, feel, touch me, and the syllable, whispered a thousand times, God, longed for a thousand times, the God-syllable, our throats wrung out, gathers itself above our heads towards the light that I had never before seen in my life, a light that made us kneel, gnaw splice sever me to pieces, burst grind shred me to pieces. Then there is silence.] (188–189)[56]

The various verbs beginning with the prefix *zer-* punctuate the flow, echoing how the dance itself is sometimes made up of two interwoven dances performed by men and women. Just as the aesthetic function of the *semah* ritual suggests an affective sense of the spiritual beyond exegesis and dogma, so Zaimoglu's rhythmic depiction of the dance also has an aesthetic dimension beyond its denotative, representational meaning.

The violent imagery of the dance can be linked to the so-called "annihilation of the self" (*fanāʾ*), the last stage on the Sufi path as the ego is extinguished and *unio mystica* can take place. This often has an erotic dimension, just as the spiritual and the sexual are conflated by the narrator as he longs for unity with both God and Saskia. Yet the story does not end with this open-ended moment of transcendence, but rather with the prospect of an interfaith relationship, a bond that does not result from a shared identity or doctrine, as the Crane Dance seemingly allows both to overcome religious divides. Here, Zaimoglu deploys Sufi and Alevi-Bektaşi tropes to suggest a form of spiritual experience with a genuine religious intensity that does not require any divisive ideology. This is due to the privileging of the aesthetic function over literalist interpretations that lead to doctrinal differences. At the very end, the last impression as the narrator departs from the cloister is physical, Saskia's eyelashes brushing his cheek (190), stressing the importance of an embodied experience of contact with both divine and human others as an alternative to more rational and appropriative forms of communication and understanding.

CONCLUSION: DANCE AND THE DECENTERED SUBJECT

That a female love-interest should provide access to the divine in "Der Kranich" also maps onto the idea that woman is man's unknowable Other, the central topic of "Libidoökonomie." Crucially, the moment of religious transcendence remains beyond representation, because it is unknowable, just as the telephone terrorist's identity is also unknowable. Women therefore somewhat stereotypically disrupt male sovereignty in these stories with transformative consequences. These disruptive moments are characterized by dance, as the types of dance most associated with Orientalist perceptions of Turkey are deployed to undermine fixed identities, problematizing any straightforward view of belly dance while rediscovering the radical potential of a lesser-known Alevi-Bektaşi ritual. Whereas the belly dance of the anonymous woman in "Libidoökonomie" frustrates the narrator's attempts to fix her identity, the Crane Dance of the second story suggests, on a similar level, a spirituality that is beyond rational thought, and hence beyond identity and representation. Both therefore undermine the stable identities that result from a binary relation with a fixed, known object, as both human and divine others ultimately resist rational understanding, explanation and control.

Both of these moments, the stage before Nora's identity can be fixed by the narrator and the other narrator's spiritual transcendence, are inevitably fleeting, and therefore lend themselves to the short-story format. In "Libidoökonomie," the plot can still move forward without much character development to flesh out identities. The story begins *in medias res* and ends abruptly before we can discover more about the mysterious Nora. In "Der Kranich," divine insight is similarly short-lived and takes place outside of the narrative. The dances too are also bound by time and spatial constraints, yet it is while they are taking place that non-rational and non-appropriative forms of relating to the other and to the divine come to the fore, and different experiences become possible as a decentered, postmodern subjectivity is glimpsed.

NOTES

1. After much public debate in Turkey, it was decided that confirming stereotypes by incorporating certain Orientalist tropes into Erener's performance would constitute a worthwhile trade-off if it made Turkey stand out from the other entries. For an in-depth discussion of how the Turkish media reported on the reception of their 2003 Eurovision entry in the context of Turkey's modernization process, see Thomas Solomon, "The Oriental Body on the European Stage: Producing Turkish Cultural Identity on the Margins of Europe," in *Empire of Song: Europe and Nation in the Eurovision Song Contest*, ed. Dafni Tragaki (Lanham, MD: Scarecrow Press, 2013), 173–201.

2. Dervishes are ubiquitous in tourist pamphlets and books, appearing, for example, on two different cover designs of the *Lonely Planet* guide to Turkey and as a cultural attraction on the Ministry of Culture and Tourism's official website. See Go Turkey Tourism, "Melevi Sema Ceremony in Turkey," 18 December 2018, https://www.goturkeytourism.com/things-to-do/mevlevi-sema-ceremony-unesco-turkey.html.

3. For a discussion of the status of belly dance in these countries, see Joanna Mansbridge, "Fantasies of Exposure: Belly Dancing, the Veil, and the Drag of History," *Journal of Popular Culture* 49, no. 1 (2016): 35–40.

4. Alevis follow the teachings of Haji Bektash Veli, whom they regard as a saint, and so there are strong links between Alevis and the Bektaşi Sufi order.

5. UNESCO, "Mevlevi Sema ceremony," accessed 12 December 2018. https://ich.unesco.org/en/RL/mevlevi-sema-ceremony-00100; UNESCO, "Semah, Alevi-Bektaşi ritual," accessed 12 December 2018. https://ich.unesco.org/en/RL/semah-alevi-bektasi-ritual-00384.

6. Such religious dances are mostly performed as "heritage" in museums and holiday resorts in today's Turkey, in part because the tradition was driven underground by Atatürk's secularization policies in the early days of the Republic, with restrictions only being significantly loosened in the 1990s.

7. Navid Kermani, *God is Beautiful: The Aesthetic Experience of the Quran*, trans. Tony Crawford (Malden: Polity, 2015), 299.

8. Although dance cannot be described as a dominant theme in Zaimoglu's oeuvre, it has been present in his work since the beginning. *Kanak Sprak: 24 Mißtöne vom Rande der Gesellschaft* (Kanak Speak: 24 Discordant Notes from the Edge of Society, 1995) includes a monologue by a break-dancer, Bayram: Feridun Zaimoglu, *Kanak Sprak: 24 Mißtöne vom Rande der Gesellschaft* (Berlin: Rotbuch, 2007), 39–42. In the short story "Gottes Krieger" (God's Warrior), also from *Zwölf Gramm Glück*, the protagonists participate in a whirling folkdance similar to that in "Der Kranich": Feridun Zaimoglu, *Zwölf Gramm Glück* (Cologne: Kiepenheuer & Witsch, 2008), 137–138 [Subsequent references in the body of the text]. In chapter 50 of *Siebentürmeviertel* (Seven Towers District, 2015), the protagonist is taught to dance by a gypsy: Feridun Zaimoglu, *Siebentürmeviertel* (Cologne: Kiepenheuer & Witsch, 2015), 478–484.

9. See Lucia Ruprecht's chapter in this volume for other postmodern instances of dance that serve to undermine the notion of the sovereign subject.

10. Whereas *semah* is the term used for mystical dance rituals in Turkey, the Arabic term *samā'* is broader, including recitation, music and poetry alongside dance as ways of accessing the divine.

11. See, for example, Margaret Harper's chapter in this volume.

12. In the German context, see Todd Kontje, *German Orientalisms* (Ann Arbor: Michigan University Press, 2004); Suzanne L. Marchand, *German Orientalism in the Age of Empire: Religion, Race, and Scholarship* (Cambridge: Cambridge University Press, 2010); and *Deploying Orientalism in Culture and History from Germany to Central and Eastern Europe*, ed. James Hodkinson, John Walker, Shaswati Mazumdar and Johannes Feichtinger (Rochester, NY: Camden House, 2013).

13. Donnalee Dox, "Dancing around Orientalism," *The Drama Review* 50, no. 4 (2006): 53.

14. Edward W. Said, *Orientalism* (London: Routledge, 1978), 208.

15. For example, his novel *Liebesbrand* (Fire of Love, 2006) blurs distinctions between Oriental and German Romantic tropes and the novel *Siebentürmeviertel* thematizes the Westernization program of the early Turkish Republic.

16. "The beloved is usually called an 'idol' in Persian poetry, worthy of worship, a sensual image of the divine": Annemarie Schimmel, *Mystical Dimensions of Islam* (Chapel Hill: University of North Carolina Press, 1975), 291.

17. Margaret Littler, "Intimacies Both Sacred and Profane: Islam in the Work of Emine Sevgi Özdamar, Zafer Şenocak, and Feridun Zaimoğlu," in *Encounters with Islam in German Literature and Culture*, ed. James Hodkinson and Jeff Morrison (Rochester, NY: Camden House, 2009), 221–235.

18. See Petra Fachinger, *Rewriting Germany from the Margins: "Other" German Literature of the 1980s and 1990s* (Montreal: McGill-Queen's University Press, 2001), 102; Sandra Hestermann, "The Turkish-German Diaspora and Multicultural German Identity: Hyphenated and Alternative Discourses of Identity in the Works of Zafer Şenocak and Feridun Zaimoğlu," in *Diaspora and Multiculturalism: Common Traditions and New Developments*, ed. Monika Fludernik (Amsterdam: Rodopi,

2003), 329–373; Frauke Matthes, "Of Kanaken and Gottes Krieger: Religion and Sexuality among Feridun Zaimoğlu's Young Muslim Men," in *Masculinities and German Culture*, ed. Sarah Colvin and Peter Davies (Rochester, NY: Camden House, 2008), 250–261.

19. See Liesbeth Minnaard, "Playing Kanak Identity: Feridun Zaimoglu's rebellious Performances," in *Das Verbindende der Kulturen / The Unifying Aspects of Cultures / Les points communs des cultures*, ed. Kurt Bartsch, Herbert Arlt, Donald G. Daviau and Gertrude Durusoy (Vienna: TRANS, 2004), http://www.inst.at/trans/15Nr/05_05/minnaard15.htm; Maria Stehle, *Ghetto Voices in Contemporary German Culture: Textscapes, Filmscapes, Soundscapes* (Rochester, NY: Camden House, 2012), 59.

20. Meyda Yeğenoğlu, *Colonial Fantasies: Towards a Feminist Reading of Orientalism* (Cambridge: Cambridge University Press, 1998), 20.

21. Various ironic clichés in *Zwölf Gramm Glück* demonstrate an acute awareness of Orientalist stereotypes, while implying that Zaimoglu does not view his role as simply "correcting" them. Indeed, with seemingly little concern for potentially affirming stereotypes about rural Anatolia, "Häute" (Skins), which won the prestigious Ingeborg Bachmann Jury-Prize in 2003 before being published in *Zwölf Gramm Glück*, depicts an unsettling image of village life as backward and threatening.

22. Margaret Littler, "Für eine kleine deutsch-türkische Literatur: Am Beispiel Feridun Zaimoglu," in *Traditionen, Herausforderungen und Perspektiven in der Germanistischen Lehre und Forschung: 90 Jahre Germanistik an der St.-Kliment-Ochridski-Universität Sofia: Akten der Jubiläumskonferenz der Fachrichtung Deutsche Philologie, 11–12. Oktober 2013*, ed. Emilia Denčeva and Maja Razbojnikova-Frateva (Sofia: University Press "St. Kliment Ochridski," 2015), 254–266.

23. All translations are my own, unless otherwise stated.

24. Yeğenoğlu, *Colonial Fantasies*, 26.

25. Ibid., 11.

26. This narrative technique echoes a similar cinematic one in Raja Amari's film *Satin rouge* (Red Satin, 2002). As Kaya Davies Hayon states: "Rather than constructing her heroine as a static object for (male) visual consumption, Amari focuses on Lilia's body in movement and highlights the pleasure and freedom her heroine experiences when she dances." Kaya Davies Hayon, "Resistance and reinvention: Representations of the belly dancing body in Raja Amari's *Satin rouge/Red Satin* (2002)," *Journal of African Cinemas* 8, no. 1 (2016): 38–39.

27. Virginia Keft-Kennedy, "'How does she do that?' Belly Dancing and the Horror of a Flexible Woman," *Women's Studies* 34, no. 3–4 (2005): 286.

28. Ibid., 287.

29. Ibid., 281.

30. The metaphor of consumption here resonates with the appropriative nature of such a subject-object binary.

31. Keft-Kennedy, "'How does she do that?'" 8.

32. Ibid., 11.

33. Yeğenoğlu, *Colonial Fantasies*, 56.

34. Ibid.

35. Littler, "Für eine kleine deutsch-türkische Literatur," 262.

36. Aside from the anonymous caller, it is only the prostitute, Vera, with whom his relationship is not based on knowledge and possession, perhaps because, as Littler argues, she too forms part of the world of capitalist exchange: Littler, "Für eine kleine deutsch-türkische Literatur," 262.

37. Keft-Kennedy, "'How does she do that?'" 284.

38. Jacques Derrida, *Spurs: Nietzsche's Styles / Éperons: Les Styles de Nietzsche*, trans. Barbara Harlow (Chicago: University of Chicago Press, 1978), 49, 55.

39. See Margaret Harper's chapter in this volume.

40. Keft-Kennedy, "'How does she do that?'" 295.

41. Although a name cannot provide conclusive evidence for a person's origins, the name "Nora" tentatively suggests that she is in fact a Western/Northern European. The name also establishes an intertextual link to Henrik Ibsen's 1879 play *The Doll's House*. Yet, whereas Ibsen's Nora dances the tarantella to break with bourgeois expectations and societal constraints, Zaimoglu's Nora attempts not only to subvert patriarchal norms, but also the appropriative nature of the Self-Other binary.

42. Littler, "Für eine kleine deutsch-türkische Literatur," 264.

43. Nimet Şeker, "'Dir biete ich mich an, zerstampfe zerfaser zerstreue mich': Islamische Mystik in Feridun Zaimoğlus Erzählung 'Der Kranich auf dem Kiesel in der Pfütze,'" In *Deutsch-türkische und türkische Literatur: Literaturwissenschaftliche und fachdidaktische Perspektiven*, ed. Michael Hofman and Inga Pohlmeier (Würzburg: Königshausen & Neumann, 2013), 21.

44. The use of Christian or Jewish terms for Islamic concepts is also common in other texts, such as *Kanak Sprak* and *Schwarze Jungfrauen* (Black Virgins, 2006).

45. Littler, "Intimacies Both Sacred and Profane," 223.

46. Ibid., 222–223.

47. Ruth Mandel, *Cosmopolitan Anxieties: Turkish Challenges to Citizenship and Belonging in Germany* (Durham and London: Duke University Press, 2008), 253.

48. This military terminology could hint at the close links between the Ottoman imperial guard, the Janissaries, and the Bektaşi order. That the monastery is called the "Wehrkloster" (Defensive Cloister) also has a marshal ring to it and even calls the Wehrmacht to mind, but could equally be linked to the defensive, secretive nature of Alevism.

49. Şeker, "'Dir biete ich mich an, zerstampfe zerfaser zerstreue mich,'" 30.

50. Schimmel, *Mystical Dimensions of Islam*, 134.

51. Irene Markoff, "Articulating Otherness in Alevi-Bektaşi Rituals and Ritual Space in a Transnational Perspective," in *Music, Sound, and Architecture in Islam*, ed. by Michael Frishkopf and Federico Spinetti (Austin: University of Texas Press, 2018), 88.

52. Ibid., 86.

53. Kermani, *God is Beautiful*, 326.

54. Ibid., 300–301.

55. To watch video footage of the dance, see UNESCO, "Semah, Alevi-Bektaşi ritual," November 3, 2010, https://www.youtube.com/watch?v=e2zsCoNnfg8 [The Crane Dance begins at 5:30].

56. The order of the groups of verbs differs in my translation in order to recreate the effect of repeated sounds in the original.

BIBLIOGRAPHY

Davies Hayon, Kaya. "Resistance and reinvention: Representations of the belly dancing body in Raja Amari's *Satin rouge/Red Satin* (2002)." *Journal of African Cinemas* 8, no. 1 (2016): 29–43.

Derrida, Jacques. *Spurs: Nietzsche's Styles / Éperons: Les Styles de Nietzsche*. Translated by Barbara Harlow. Chicago: University of Chicago Press, 1978.

Dox, Donnalee. "Dancing around Orientalism." *The Drama Review* 50, no. 4 (2006): 52–71.

Fachinger, Petra. *Rewriting Germany from the Margins: "Other" German Literature of the 1980s and 1990s*. Montreal: McGill-Queen's University Press, 2001.

Go Turkey Tourism. "Melevi Sema Ceremony in Turkey." Accessed 18 December 2018. https://www.goturkeytourism.com/things-to-do/mevlevi-sema-ceremony-unesco-turkey.html.

Hestermann, Sandra. "The Turkish-German Diaspora and Multicultural German Identity: Hyphenated and Alternative Discourses of Identity in the Works of Zafer Şenocak and Feridun Zaimoğlu." In *Diaspora and Multiculturalism: Common Traditions and New Developments*, edited by Monika Fludernik, 329–373. Amsterdam: Rodopi, 2003.

Hodkinson, James, John Walker, Shaswati Mazumdar, and Johannes Feichtinger (eds). *Deploying Orientalism in Culture and History from Germany to Central and Eastern Europe*. Rochester, NY: Camden House, 2013.

Keft-Kennedy, Virginia. "'How does she do that?' Belly Dancing and the Horror of a Flexible Woman." *Women's Studies* 34, no. 3–4 (2005): 279–300.

Kermani, Navid. *God is Beautiful: The Aesthetic Experience of the Quran*. Translated by Tony Crawford. Malden: Polity, 2015.

Kontje, Todd. *German Orientalisms*. Ann Arbor: Michigan University Press, 2004.

Littler, Margaret. "Für eine kleine deutsch-türkische Literatur: Am Beispiel Feridun Zaimoglu." In *Traditionen, Herausforderungen und Perspektiven in der Germanistischen Lehre und Forschung: 90 Jahre Germanistik an der St.-Kliment-Ochridski-Universität Sofia: Akten der Jubiläumskonferenz der Fachrichtung Deutsche Philologie*, 11–12. Oktober 2013, edited by Emilia Denčeva and Maja Razbojnikova-Frateva, 254–266. Sofia: University Press "St. Kliment Ochridski," 2015.

———. "Intimacies Both Sacred and Profane: Islam in the Work of Emine Sevgi Özdamar, Zafer Şenocak, and Feridun Zaimoğlu." In *Encounters with Islam in German Literature and Culture*, edited by James Hodkinson and Jeff Morrison, 221–235. Rochester, NY: Camden House, 2009.

Mandel, Ruth. *Cosmopolitan Anxieties: Turkish Challenges to Citizenship and Belonging in Germany*. Durham and London: Duke University Press, 2008.

Mansbridge, Joanna. "Fantasies of Exposure: Belly Dancing, the Veil, and the Drag of History." *Journal of Popular Culture* 49, no. 1 (2016): 29–56.

Marchand, Suzanne L. *German Orientalism in the Age of Empire: Religion, Race, and Scholarship*. Cambridge: Cambridge University Press, 2010.

Markoff, Irene. "Articulating Otherness in Alevi-Bektaşi Rituals and Ritual Space in a Transnational Perspective." In *Music, Sound, and Architecture in Islam*, edited by Michael Frishkopf and Federico Spinetti, 86–107. Austin: University of Texas Press, 2018.

Matthes, Frauke. "Of Kanaken and Gottes Krieger: Religion and Sexuality among Feridun Zaimoğlu's Young Muslim Men." In *Masculinities and German Culture*, edited by Sarah Colvin and Peter Davies, 250–261. Rochester, NY: Camden House, 2008.

Minnaard, Liesbeth. "Playing Kanak Identity: Feridun Zaimoglu's Rebellious Performances." In *Das Verbindende der Kulturen / The Unifying Aspects of Cultures / Les points communs des cultures*, edited by Kurt Bartsch, Herbert Arlt, Donald G. Daviau and Gertrude Durusoy. Vienna: TRANS, 2004. http://www.inst.at/trans/15Nr/05_05/minnaard15.htm.

Said, Edward W. *Orientalism*. London: Routledge, 1978.

Schimmel, Annemarie. *Mystical Dimensions of Islam*. Chapel Hill: University of North Carolina Press, 1975.

Şeker, Nimet. "'Dir biete ich mich an, zerstampfe zerfaser zerstreue mich': Islamische Mystik in Feridun Zaimoğlus Erzählung 'Der Kranich auf dem Kiesel in der Pfütze.'" In *Deutsch-türkische und türkische Literatur: Literaturwissenschaftliche und fachdidaktische Perspektiven*, edited by Michael Hofman and Inga Pohlmeier, 21–32. Würzburg: Königshausen & Neumann, 2013.

Solomon, Thomas. "The Oriental Body on the European Stage: Producing Turkish Cultural Identity on the Margins of Europe." In *Empire of Song: Europe and Nation in the Eurovision Song Contest*, edited by Dafni Tragaki, 173–210. Lanham, MD: Scarecrow Press, 2013.

Stehle, Maria. *Ghetto Voices in Contemporary German Culture: Textscapes, Filmscapes, Soundscapes*. Rochester, NY: Camden House, 2012.

UNESCO. "Mevlevi Sema Ceremony." Accessed 12 December 2018. https://ich.unesco.org/en/RL/mevlevi-sema-ceremony-00100.

———. "Semah, Alevi-Bektaşi Ritual." Accessed 12 December 2018. https://ich.unesco.org/en/RL/semah-alevi-bektasi-ritual-00384.

——— "Semah, Alevi-Bektaşi Ritual," 5 November 2010. https://www.youtube.com/watch?v=e2zsCoNnfg8.

Yeğenoğlu, Meyda. *Colonial Fantasies: Towards a Feminist Reading of Orientalism*. Cambridge: Cambridge University Press, 1998.

Zaimoglu, Feridun. *Kanak Sprak: 24 Mißtöne vom Rande der Gesellschaft*. Berlin: Rotbuch, 2007 [1995].

———. *Siebentürmeviertel*. Cologne: Kiepenheuer & Witsch, 2015.

———. *Zwölf Gramm Glück*. Cologne: Kiepenheuer & Witsch, 2008 [2004].

Chapter Thirteen

"Alive. Changing. New."

Impulses of the Jaques-Dalcroze Dance Institute on the Architecture of Ludwig Mies van der Rohe

Jan Frohburg and Tanja Poppelreuter

A NEW FORM OF ART

In June of 1913 at *Gartenstadt Hellerau* (Garden City Hellerau) a group of dance students of the Jaques-Dalcroze Institute performed Christoph Willibald Gluck's 1762 opera *Orpheus and Eurydice*.[1] In the opening scene, Orpheus sat on a raised platform, surrounded by mourners.

A wide set of steps connected the platform to the floor of the auditorium just a few feet below. Upstage, another set of stairs rose into obscurity. Dark blue curtains framed the scene, at once solemn and austere. Amor appeared, represented by a single shaft of intense light, and the opera unfolded. Accepting Amor's call, Orpheus climbed the stairs toward the mysterious light. The performance of *Orpheus' Descent into Hades* in the previous year had reversed this opening scene. Here, Orpheus climbed down from the highest point into ever-greater darkness, confronted by the Furies. Placed along the steps and platforms were dancers, their naked arms and legs swaying snake-like with the ebbs and flows of the music, creating constant waves of motion to be calmed only by Orpheus' song. The dancers' bodies and the atmosphere on stage were transformed by an ever-changing glow of bluish light. Both performances stimulated enthusiastic critiques: "It is a union of music, the plastic sense, and light, the like of which I have never seen," French poet and dramatist Paul Claudel enthusiastically reported, and the American writer Upton Sinclair recalled, "Men and women stood shouting their delight at the revelation of a new form of art."[2]

The dance performances at Hellerau marked a juncture in the evolution of modern arts practices that would, after the First World War, inform the

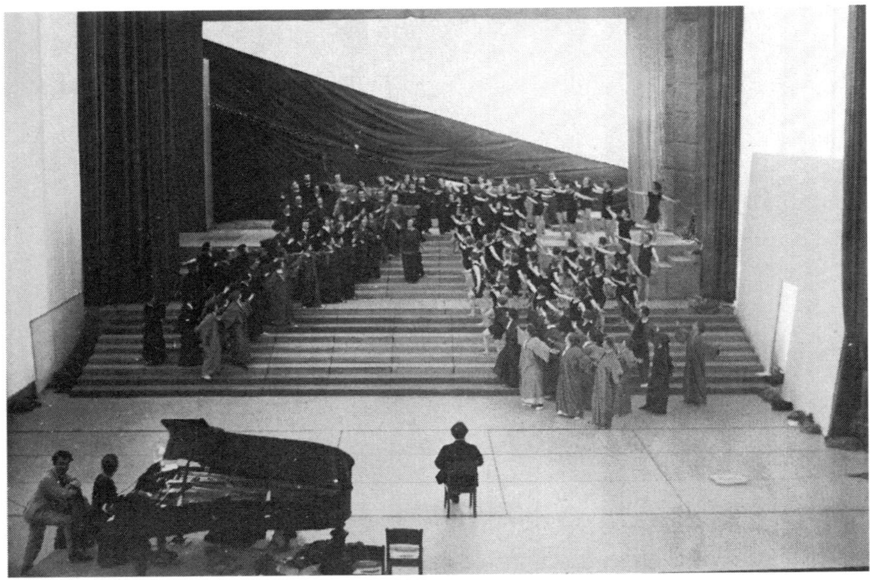

Figure 13.1. Émile Jaques-Dalcroze at a rehearsal of *Orpheus und Euridike*, 1912, at HELLERAU—European Centre for the Arts. Photograph by Dr med. Kurt Becker-Glauch. Used courtesy of HELLERAU—European Centre for the Arts, Dresden, Germany.

diverse cultural scene of the Weimar Republic. They were the realization of an innovative approach to dance performance and stage design and, at the same time, an inspirational moment with a lasting impact on modern architecture. In this chapter we explore the ways in which modern dance afforded an unprecedented freedom in movement and how this inspired architects to rethink the nature of architectural space.[3] We take as our example the work of architect Ludwig Mies van der Rohe not only because of his close connection to Hellerau but because of a distinct similarity in the theoretical frameworks that underpin both his and Jaques-Dalcroze's thinking.[4] Influenced by ideas—some of which we trace back to his encounters with modern dance at Hellerau—Mies envisioned the modern dweller, the subject of architecture, as less and less constrained by traditions and convention than previous generations had been. His architecture of the late 1920s reflected this emerging outlook: As the director of the 1927 *Werkbund* exhibition on housing as well as the chief planner of the experimental Weissenhof housing estate in Stuttgart, Mies was in a key position to redefine the idea of the modern dwelling. Furthermore, the open spaces and precious materials of his German Pavilion, designed for the 1929 International Exposition in Barcelona, represented the new national identity after the First World War. And no other residential design was more controversially discussed in the contemporary architectural press than the Tugendhat House, completed in 1930. Its open living spaces of the main floor, fully glazed along one façade and without conventional internal walls, made some critics wonder whether the house was intimidating or even habitable at all. To the inhabitants, however, the open space provided a unique sense of freedom that they described as uplifting and liberating.

Modern dance provided an important stimulus for introducing this "openness" and "freedom" into modern architecture, and a vital impulse came from the Jaques-Dalcroze Institute and its performances of *Orpheus and Eurydice*. Founded in 1910 within the Garden City Hellerau the Institute focused on the natural movement of the body and must be understood as the leading reform institution for dance in the early twentieth century. Artistic practice at Hellerau merged "the classical Greek model of a choreographed communion of art and life with sophisticated technologies capable of generating a multisensory, immersive spectacle of music, moving lights and bodies," as architectural historian Lutz Robbers found, and in this context "architecture functioned as an indeterminate space where the dissolution of the boundaries between stage and audience, work and life, spirit and body could be performed."[5] Dance education at Hellerau aimed at overcoming the rupture between emotion and intellect and taught movement that was unencumbered, for example, by the restrictive rules of classical ballet. By re-conceptualizing the unity of the arts—music, drama, architecture and dance—the Jaques-Dalcroze Institute became not only a common point of origin in the development of modern dance and modern architecture, but also a node in the philosophical debate regarding the reform of the arts in a rapidly modernizing world with the goal of enticing the senses and elevating the human spirit.

GARTENSTADT AND *LEBENSPHILOSOPHIE*

By the first decade of the twentieth century, reform movements started to react to a sense of loss and decay that had been sparked by widespread socioeconomic changes. They promoted the renewal of a traditional lifestyle that placed value on education and art, and they promoted urban reform, often in peripheral places away from metropolitan centers. Garden City Hellerau on the rural outskirts of Dresden was one of the earliest and most influential manifestations of this movement in Germany prior to the First World War. Established from 1906 onwards it realized ideas propagated by the *Deutscher Werkbund* (German Association of Craftsmen), a progressive organization devoted to economic renewal in German industry through the promotion of the applied arts. It was the first concrete manifestation in Germany of the English Garden City movement, a utopian vision of distributed settlements that would harmoniously bring together residences, industry and agriculture.

The Garden City movement resonated with aspirations of philanthropic German architects, artists, industrialists and publicists who shared a concern for the improvement of people's living environment. They conceived the Garden City project at Hellerau as a way to foster social equality, liberal and universal education, and a revival of unalienated art and labor.[6] The architects, patron and industrialists who founded Hellerau set out to find a balance between the destructive forces of capitalism and the often unsettling ideals of socialism and communism by providing a settlement where order was restored to lives jarred by modern civilization. In aiming at the organic unity of living and working, of culture and education, the Hellerau project drew on the ideas of a variegated and ambiguous movement known as *Lebensreform* (life reform), which in turn was based on *Lebensphilosophie*, a vitalist branch of philosophy that emerged after 1900.[7] Located within the broad scope of the interlinking sections of *Lebensphilosophie* was that of *Kulturkritik* (cultural criticism), an anti-modern movement that was critical of modernization, industrialization and urbanization.[8] Thought of as "a laboratory for a new humanity," Hellerau became the most comprehensive experiment in housing and urban planning, aesthetics and performing arts, and as such it was a tangible expression of *Lebensphilosophie* and *Kulturkritik*.[9]

RHYTHM AND EURHYTHMICS

Kulturkritik arose as a critical response to the mechanized production and the explosive growth of cities during the nineteenth century that had disrupted and changed traditional patterns of labor and leisure as well as art and agriculture. In his 1896 book *Work and Rhythm*, German economist Karl Bücher described modern civilization as afflicted by "arrhythmia," and he argued that the recovery of a lost "rhythm" would restore a healthy accord between citizens and society.[10] "Rhythm" became a leitmotif in German intellectual culture and beyond, understood as something that permeated and united psychological states and all aspects of physical existence: not as a static, compositional quality but rather dynamically, as a pulsating life force. The Hellerau project embraced Bücher's ideas and hoped to calm the growing dissonance between intellectual work and manual labor, thus quieting the unease that agitated German culture. The convergence on the abstract concept of "rhythm" was the reason why reform architecture sought to engage with dance in the first place.

These ideas fell on fertile soil at Hellerau as the ambition of this Garden City was not only to improve living conditions but also to reform the lifestyle of its inhabitants. Cultural activities of all kinds were central to the reform environment at Hellerau.[11] Music and dance were an integral part of its holistic concept. Eager to organize activities for music lovers and musicians and to provide musical education for children, starting as young as age six, the founders of Hellerau invited Swiss impresario Émile Jaques-Dalcroze to establish his dance institute at Hellerau in 1910.[12] Jaques-Dalcroze had developed an innovative (and controversial) method of teaching concepts of rhythm, structure and musical expression through instinctive yet regulated movements of the body by way of "rhythmic gymnastics," as he initially called it. Even at the time the term brought to mind "visions of rows of bloomer-clad girls swinging Indian clubs to the insistent throbbing of a nasal-voiced piano"—a common misconception.[13] Today widely known as Eurhythmics, the Jaques-Dalcroze method was conceived as a special training for musicians who were taught to translate musical composition into movement. Jaques-Dalcroze envisaged "a musical education in which the body itself played the role of intermediary between sound and thought and became the direct instrument of our feelings."[14] By engaging all the senses, the dancer gained both a physical awareness of music and a kinesthetic experience. The Jaques-Dalcroze method of musical education promised to reinstate "rhythm" and to restore harmony to individuals and their community.

The aspirations of Eurhythmics and those of the Garden City movement coalesced in the mutual desire for social and political renewal. Jaques-Dalcroze wanted to imbue dance in all its fleeting nature with the same presence and authority afforded to architecture, while architecture—*Baukunst*—in turn was to take its lesson from the performing arts. Jaques-Dalcroze hoped to create "a moral and aesthetic architecture identical to that of the buildings, to raise rhythm to the level of a social institution, and prepare the way for a new style . . . that may become the basis for a new society," and further "to harmonize, thanks to a special education, the village and its people."[15] Schmidt offered to build an Institute to Jaques-Dalcroze's exact specifications, to "replace the missing church."[16] Whereas the dance classes initially had taken place in Dresden and later in the factory buildings at Hellerau, the Institute's *Festspielhaus* finally opened in 1912.[17]

FESTSPIELHAUS AND AUDITORIUM

The *Festspielhaus* for the Jaques-Dalcroze Institute was at once house and temple, school and theatre, and it united actors and audience.[18] It included several classrooms or rehearsal spaces, changing and shower rooms, halls for small-scale exercises and an auditorium. To the rear, enclosed by an elegant pergola, was an area for open-air gymnastics. Characterized as "an amalgamation of Temple and Palaestra," it realized, in built form, the Greek-inspired reintegration of body and mind through dance.[19] The ideal of spiritual harmony was captured in the yin-yang symbol that was incorporated in the pediment above the entrance portico. The building for the Jaques-Dalcroze Institute was designed by Heinrich Tessenow.[20] Like all of his designs it was characterized by sobriety, restraint and "a virtual denial of architectural rhetoric."[21] The monumental appearance of the starkly geometric portico with its deep shadows and unusual proportions—small openings contrasted with tall columns and largely blank façades—was offset by a generous forecourt, symmetrically framed by modest houses. These were the lodgings for the female students of the Institute; only male students were allowed to take rooms in nearby houses.

A plain but impressive auditorium was at the heart of the Institute.[22] The space was free from all decorative detail. Its walls and ceiling were clad in fabric, creating a fully abstract space, immaterial even as the enclosing surfaces were all but dissolved in light. Conceived as an unobstructed and adaptable space it could accommodate an audience of close to six hundred, and about two hundred and fifty performers.[23] A pair of centrally located doors connected to adjacent foyers where performers and participants would mingle between acts before reentering the shared space of the auditorium. In a radical departure from the conventions of theatre design Tessenow and Jaques-Dalcroze omitted the proscenium arch, wings, flies, traps, act curtain and footlights. There were no physical barriers separating house and stage, and by giving an equal presence to actors and audience alike and thus creating a truly shared experience the Hellerau auditorium marked the transition from theatre to performance space.

RHYTHMIC SPACES

While Jaques-Dalcroze developed dance and movement and Tessenow provided the space for it, Swiss scenographer Adolphe Appia designed the stage that proved a pivotal link between architecture, dance and audience.[24] Appia and Jaques-Dalcroze had met in 1906 and recognized the importance of collaboration between the performance space and dance toward the renewal of both. Jaques-Dalcroze introduced Appia to his method of experiencing music through movement, while Appia introduced Jaques-Dalcroze to stage design. He provided, quite literally, the background to Jaques-Dalcroze's teaching and delivered a vision that reached far beyond music instruction. Sensitive to the influence of architecture on the theatrical event, it was Appia who had first proposed to define the space of the stage by unornamented, orthogonal surfaces and artful lighting. Initially, Appia had been drawn to Richard Wagner's ideal of the *Gesamtkunstwerk*, the consummate artwork that sought the union of music, drama, dance and even architecture. However, Appia soon became fundamentally critical of the "visual fraud" in Wagner's ungainly scenography, and believed that naturalistic representation constituted a psychological barrier between actor and spectator.[25] Instead, Appia wanted the audience to partake in the emotional process that was being acted out on stage, and he felt that the internal intensity of psychological states had to be "complemented by a strong, plastically expressive staging."[26] Appia was inspired by Jaques-Dalcroze's correlation of musical figures with specific physical gestures, and in the spring of 1909 he produced about twenty designs for what he called "rhythmic spaces" and offered them to Jaques-Dalcroze as settings for his exercises. Appia's drawings showed nuanced spaces created from archetypal elements. Their starkly geometric shapes were meant to offset the plasticity of the body and its fluid movements. Neither illustrating the action on stage nor representing psychological states, Appia granted autonomy to abstract form and atmospheric architecture.

Furthermore, Appia was discontent with a merely static approach to stage lighting, driven only by the need to illuminate the action. He identified with the idea of "creative light" as an artistic means to achieve "a living space for living beings."[27] The lighting in the auditorium, engineered by classically trained painter Alexander von Salzmann, was indeed one of the most innovative aspects of Hellerau's performance design.[28] Von Salzmann devised an ingenious (and costly) system of indirect steerable lighting that effectively transformed the entire auditorium into a constantly changing body of light.[29] Von Salzmann was interested in light that was "free-floating and agile" as well as "abstract and immediate"; he sought "not effect, but atmosphere" and created light that was at once "uniting" and "sounding."[30] Like daylight, the diffuse glow of the auditorium walls softened the contours and enhanced luminous colors, lending harmony to the stage. Projections of moving lights created a sensation of atmospheric density, and sparsely used spotlights supported the flow of action. Much like an actor, light became an integral part of the performance, thus shifting the emphasis from classical formula to engaged artwork. Arguably, the spatial impact of auditorium and stage designs heightened the emotional investment of the audience; it focused and channeled the spectators' attention and made them susceptible to enhanced aesthetic experiences.

A TURNING POINT IN THE ARTISTIC DEVELOPMENT OF THE EPOCH

The Hellerau performances, the stage the dancers occupied and the space they shared with the audience all challenged the conventions of theatricality at the time. Illusionism and representational aesthetics were left behind while new, performative concepts of art were established. Aware of their achievement, Appia confidently announced, "The *Raumstil* (spatial style) for bodily movements has been found."[31] The auditorium of the *Festspielhaus* was "a space that gathered all within it into an environment shaped almost entirely by light rather than substance" and, as art historian Kathleen James-Chakraborty argued, it played its architectural part in introducing the performing arts to a mass audience.[32] Overwriting the spatial as well as emotional divide between stage and house not only transformed the stage but also the audience. The *Festspielhaus* at Hellerau became the venue for few but highly acclaimed public performances during the school festivals. Over four thousand guests attended the festival performances of 1913, and media attention was immense, too.[33] This new kind of integrating stage and performance had an immediate impact on architects and their work. Belgian architect Henry van de Velde, for example, took inspiration for the design of the tripartite stage and the use of electric light for his 1914 *Werkbund Theater*.[34] Berlin's *Großes Schauspielhaus*, designed in 1919 by German architect Hans Poelzig in collaboration with director Max Reinhardt, was one of the great achievements of Expressionist architecture and thus contrasted with the aesthetic purity of elementary forms at Hellerau. However, the way the audience surrounded the stage echoed Tessenow's efforts to dissolve the separation between actors and spectators.[35]

Other connections were personal but no less significant. One student of Jaques-Dalcroze was Swiss musician Albert Jeanneret who passed his exam in 1911 and stayed on to teach. He was the older brother of Swiss architect Charles-Edouard Jeanneret, later prominently known as Le Corbusier.[36] The latter attended the performance of *Orpheus and Eurydice* and acknowledged the great performance space at the Institute as "a turning point in the artistic development of the epoch."[37] Later in his career, Le Corbusier introduced what he called *acoustique plastique* as a way to bridge the divide between rationalized construction and poetic yearning—an idea that can also be traced back to Hellerau.[38]

Whether Mies attended the performances in the summer of 1913 is not known. Yet his connection to Hellerau was equally strong and personal. Since 1910 Mies had frequently travelled to Hellerau to visit his future wife Ada Bruhn who studied dance at the Jaques-Dalcroze Institute at the time. Bruhn shared accommodations with two fellow students: Mary Wigman, soon to become a leading pioneer of expressive dance, and Erna Hoffmann, who later married art historian and psychiatrist Hans Prinzhorn.[39] A close friendship developed among this liberal group, and it is more than likely that Mies was familiar with the performances on the *Festspielhaus* stage, with the concept of Eurhythmics and the ideologies that informed the Hellerau project. Hellerau was for Mies, as for his contemporaries, the site of innovative stage performances, holistic social experiment and profound philosophical inquiry, all aiming for cultural and social renewal through the arts. Still under the impression of Hellerau, Mies began to develop his notion of *Baukunst* (art of building), which he formulated in writing and, most conclusively, in buildings such as the Barcelona Pavilion and the Tugendhat House throughout the 1920s.

BODY—SOUL—UNITY

At the core of Mies's idea of *Baukunst* stood the conviction that technological advancements must be considered as useful tools in the design and building process, yet at the same time Mies remained skeptical of the suggestion that technology was the main driver of progress and the principal solution for social problems. Mies was familiar with the then influential philosophy of Friedrich Nietzsche, and he had read Raoul Francé, a botanist and cultural philosopher, as well as the writings of Catholic architect Rudolf Schwarz and of Romano Guardini, a Catholic priest and intellectual. Reading Guardini and Schwarz aided Mies in clarifying a critical stance toward technology and reinforced his search for architecture's spiritual foundations.[40] After the First World War Mies explored questions such as what role technology should play in architecture and, more importantly, what kinds of spaces architecture should provide in support of the emerging modern civilization. It was Hans Prinzhorn, the acquaintance Mies had met in Hellerau, who provided him with a way of thinking about contemporary life and the development of mankind.[41] Prinzhorn's book *Body—Soul—Unity*, published in 1927, was a reassessment of traditional psychology and aimed to offer clarification about the sources of the "deep change of our entire perception of the human being."[42] Prinzhorn's critique of contemporary psychology echoed Mies's critique of contemporary architecture in that Prinzhorn, too, disapproved of a mechanical worldview according to which the soul could be studied separately from the body and that the natural sciences would be able to quantify and measure the essence of life.[43] Thus it may have aided Mies in his search toward understanding the modern dweller.

Firmly rooted within the realm of *Lebensphilosophie* and mainly based on Nietzsche's philosophy and Ludwig Klages' *Kulturkritik*, Prinzhorn understood the "Will" as the source of cultural decay.[44] In *Body—Soul—Unity* Prinzhorn explained that a tension between the mind (*Geist*) and life (*Leib-Seele*) was the cause for a broad variety of societal problems of the time. The

Will was part of the mind and was described as an invasive, unnatural force that replaced drives and instincts and that, in Klages' as well as in Prinzhorn's thinking, fostered a cultural condition that brought forth decadence and the many defects of the current age.[45] Klages emphasized the destructive character of the mind as it compromised peace, nature and life itself, and saw here the source for the ills brought about by industrialization and technology. Yet Prinzhorn proposed that a New Man was about to emerge. Free from societal conventions and the destructive forces that the Will had imposed on earlier generations, Prinzhorn's thesis "did certainly not apply to the needs and desires of the self-suffering and world-despairing coeval, but instead to still rare human beings who are confident about the world and in unison with the great rhythms of nature and all living entities."[46] Fostering the unity of body and soul—*life*—would free the human being from the destructive subordination to the invasive forces of the Will.

Mies was certainly familiar with Prinzhorn's fundamental critique of the Will, his understanding of the New Man and the concept of *Body—Soul—Unity.* Mies had collaborated with Prinzhorn on several occasions before and had invited Prinzhorn to share his ideas about mental health and creativity in *G—Material for Elemental Form-Creation*, an avant-garde design journal that Mies co-edited.[47] In return, Prinzhorn asked Mies to contribute the volume *Baukunst. Von der Höhle zum Hochhaus* (*Art of building. From the Cave to the High-rise*) tracing the art of building from cave to skyscraper. It was to be part of an ambitious series meant to provide a structured survey of how humans understood the world at the time: *Das Weltbild—Bücher des lebendigen Wissens* (*The Worldview—Books of the Living Knowledge*). Mies never delivered the promised manuscript but a lecture appears to have been written in relation to the book.[48] In this lecture of March 1926 Mies explained that architecture had to serve the spirit with the means of the time and he defined the "nature of building" as "the spatial execution of spiritual decisions." He further noted, "Nothing is more stupid than to assume that our will is adequate to change the situation under which we live, in this or that direction. Neither a populace nor an individual can attain its aim immediately. Only what lies in the direction of our life's goals can find fulfilment."[49] Mies shared Prinzhorn's suspicion of the Will as the demiurge of change, and both heralded the idea that life should unfold without constraints imposed by the Will. Prinzhorn offered an understanding of man that provided Mies with a clearer understanding of "our life's goals" and the New Man as the subject of modern architecture. Prinzhorn also provided Mies with a theoretical framework and an outlook that envisioned human beings not as corruptible by economics, religion or politics but instead living in accord with the rhythms of nature and all living entities.

THE NEW DWELLING AS AN INTELLECTUAL PROBLEM

Once the economic situation in Germany improved during the mid-1920s a widespread housing crisis had to be addressed, mainly through the construction of large-scale housing projects in urban centers. In parallel, social renewal as the objective of low-income housing was again widely discussed.[50] Architects started to analyze the basic requirements of living and searched for design solutions to accommodate subsistence dwelling (*Existenzminimum*). At times, these led to the conviction that mass housing may be utilized as a means of social engineering and apartments as tools toward changing undesirable behavior. Mies was familiar with this approach but responded critically to it. He rejected the notion that the basic needs of dwellers are quantifiable and that the housing problem should be concerned with satisfying physical needs alone. As the director of the 1927 *Werkbund* exhibition on housing and as the chief planner of the experimental Weissenhof housing estate in Stuttgart Mies asserted, "The problem of the New Dwelling is basically an intellectual problem and the fight for the New Dwelling only an element in the great fight for new ways of life."[51] As the architect of a block of twenty-seven apartments as part of the Weissenhof estate Mies developed moveable walls that allowed inhabitants to organize their apartments freely, rather than determining the floor plan and pursuing normative solutions. Mies's oppositional stance toward the rationalization of floor plans and housing units into types, that had informed his design for the Weissenhof apartments, also led him to search for a focus of his architectural thinking other than technology. As technology was to be a tool but not the sole purpose of architecture, the dweller and the social responsibility of the architect moved into the center of his deliberations.

During the 1920s Mies endeavored to demonstrate how the newly emerging lifestyle might be supported by architectural space in a spiritual way. The development of Mies's concept of *Baukunst* during that time was aided by Tessenow's abstract classicism and Appia's choreographic spaces, as architectural historian Claire Zimmerman explains, and their influence became evident in key buildings like the Weissenhof apartments and, subsequently, the Barcelona Pavilion and the Tugendhat House. The development of modern architecture before and after the First World War was characterized by close "affiliations between theatrical performance and architectural inhabitation," Zimmerman confirms, and she emphasizes that "Mies, more than any other architect of his day, integrated rhythmic movement into architectural planning."[52] The Barcelona Pavilion, designed to represent the new national identity of the Weimar Republic at the 1929 International Exposition, became the first instance for Mies to realize a new spatial concept that was at once unmistakably modern and rich in sensual experiences. Elevated onto a podium outlined by marble walls, visitors moved freely between the pavilion's various glass screens, its precious onyx wall, and the chrome-clad steel columns. Mies transposed choreographed movement through space into an architectural design, and by engaging ritual and performative practices he "also instilled a heightened self-consciousness in visitors to the building," Zimmerman observed.[53] Architectural historian Manfredo Tafuri was the first to link the pavilion to the stage at Hellerau, and he observed that within the space of the pavilion visitors are called upon to become dancers who create new meaning through the interaction of their bodies with light and space.[54]

SPACES FOR THE ELEVATED PERSONAL LIFE

Whereas the Barcelona Pavilion was designed as a temporary building only, it was the pavilion's conceptual twin, the Tugendhat House, completed in 1930, that allowed Mies to finally realize his concept of *Baukunst* as a spiritual endeavor in a permanent dwelling.

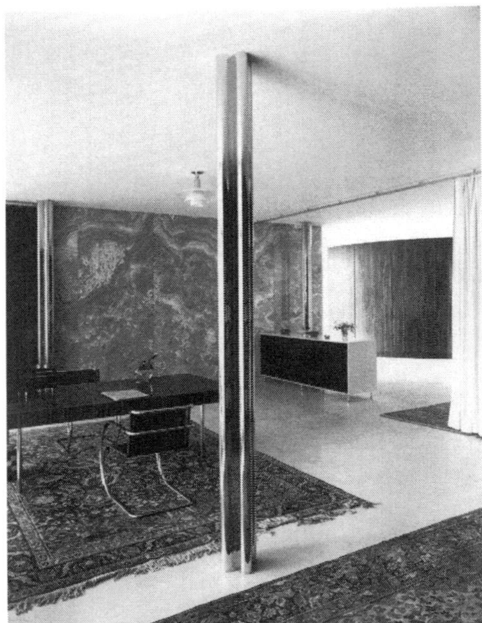

Figure 13.2. Ludwig Mies van der Rohe, Tugendhat House, Brno, 1929–1930, view of the main floor from the library toward the dining area. Photograph by Rudolf Sandalo Jr. Used courtesy of Brno City Museum, Brno, Czech Republic.

Mies's clients Grete and Fritz Tugendhat sought to depart from conventional notions of living and, according to architectural historian Detlef Mertins, "aspired to a freer, more noble, artistic and philosophical life than the traditional house could support."[55] Walter Riezler, a contemporary architectural critic, acknowledged the design as a demonstration of architecture that was not merely functional but also spiritually and intellectually conceived "for the elevated personal life."[56] However, the open living space in particular prompted other critics at the time to seriously question whether it was suitable for domestic life.[57] Justus Bier declared the house "unbearable to live in" and thought the expansive living space "dwarfed the individual lives."[58] Roger Ginsburger perceived the house as an intimidating piece of art that would not tolerate any changes by the inhabitants without suffering destruction.[59]

"I never sensed these rooms as displaying pathos, but rather as severe and great—but not in a sense that overwhelms but in one that liberates," responded Grete Tugendhat.[60] A sense of "rhythm" was evoked to highlight the exceptional architectural quality of this house, which in turn related back to the continued appreciation of "rhythm" as a term to capture positive life forces. In defending the Tugendhat House against its critics, German architect Ludwig Hilberseimer observed that its spatial qualities could only be fully appreciated through movement. "No photograph of this house can convey the right impression," Hilberseimer wrote, and he continued, "one has to move around in this house, its rhythm is like music."[61] It was, again, Grete Tugendhat who found that "the large room—precisely because of its rhythm—has a very particular tranquility, which a closed room could never have."[62] And Fritz Tugendhat emphasized that they "can feel free to an extent never experienced before."[63] Villa Tugendhat was attuned to self-assured and open-minded human beings. It was, as Mertins understood, a place where "a contemplative, if not philosophical life" could unfold.[64]

THE SHARED APPROPRIATION OF SPACE AND TIME THROUGH MOVEMENT

The changes in spatial arrangement in Mies's work during the late 1920s, from the Weissenhof apartment building to the Tugendhat House, exemplified a move away from providing conventionally preconfigured rooms toward adaptable dwellings that were spiritually charged and imbued with a sense of an emergent new lifestyle. Mies had come to comprehended "life" as the integral expression of body and soul, based on his understanding of Prinzhorn's work and by sharing a critical stance toward technological advancements fostered by rational considerations alone. Spatial openness and intellectual freedom had become the tenets of Mies's architecture, paired with the belief in human beings that were able to assert themselves confidently in a world that was driven not by the potentially destructive "Will" of the individual but by the "great rhythms of nature."[65] Expanding on his engagement with philosophical concepts, Mies rejected aesthetic speculation and formalist doctrines, and he came to define architecture as an essentially intellectual endeavor, as an evolving process. In aphoristic brevity he wrote, "Building art is the spatially apprehended will of the epoch. Alive. Changing. New."[66]

Prinzhorn's as well as Mies's thinking throughout the 1920s was informed by key aspects of *Kulturkritk* that had also been among the founding principles of the Garden City at Hellerau where art was meant to permeate into every aspect of life. The collaboration between Jaques-Dalcroze and Appia at Hellerau before the First World War signaled a turning point in theatre history. Yet its influence reached further still. The immediacy between dancer, space and audience that was achieved at Hellerau—combined with aspirations for social renewal and the creation of a renewed lifestyle that had been at the core of the Garden City concept at Hellerau—fostered a range of innovative artistic expressions. Jaques-Dalcroze's new concept in music education and Appia's reimagining of the stage suggested novel approaches that, in time and frequently at the hands of others, would establish the spatial arts on an entirely different basis. In the few years of its existence the Institute at Hellerau generated impulses that expanded from music education and dance into architecture, art and philosophy. Pioneering performance art and groundbreaking stage design helped to conceptualize the modern relationship between music, time, space and movement.

"Music torn from its isolation, the body coming into its own, plastic feeling brought to life, architectural ambience at the service of the body's proportions and movements," Appia summarized the achievements of dance at Hellerau.[67] Jaques-Dalcroze and Appia conceived of dance as a continuous experience across time and space. The idea of architecture as a spatial sequence, or as a succession of picture-like instances over time, was often credited to cinema whereas in fact it started with dance at Hellerau.[68] In their performances dancers bridged time-based art (*Zeitkunst*)—drama and music—and space-bound art (*Raumkunst*)—sculpture and architecture. These dance performances, so tightly intertwined with their stage settings, lead the way toward reconciling the physical and metaphysical dimensions also within architecture. By reaching beyond the idea of architecture's musical proportions and by adopting the concept of "rhythm" architecture was firmly established not only as present in space but as unfolding over time. Modern architecture and dance merged in a shared appropriation of space and time through movement.

NOTES

1. For details see Richard C. Beacham, "Appia, Jaques-Dalcroze, and Hellerau: Part Two: 'Poetry in Motion,'" *New Theatre Quarterly* 1, no. 3 (August 1985): 245–261.

2. Paul Claudel and Upton Sinclair quoted in Beacham, "Appia, Jaques-Dalcroze, and Hellerau: Part Two," 260, 258.

3. This text is an amalgamation of two papers presented at the International Conference "Connections in Motion: Dance in Irish and German Literature, Film and Culture," held in Limerick on 31 October and 1 November 2016: Jan Frohburg (Limerick) "Setting the Scene: Festspielhaus Hellerau," and Tanja Poppelreuter (Manchester) "Spaces for the Elevated Personal Life: Hans Prinzhorn and Mies van der Rohe." The latter also took into account outcomes of previous research, and developed relevant aspects of this further, e.g.: Tanja Poppelreuter, "Spaces for the elevated personal life: Ludwig Mies van der Rohe's concept of the dweller, 1926–1930," *The Journal of Architecture* 21, no. 2 (2016): 244–270, DOI: 10.1080/13602365.2016.1160946.

4. Ludwig Mies van der Rohe (1886–1969) was one of Germany's leading modern architects. He was Vice President of the *Werkbund* and the last director of the Bauhaus before emigrating to Chicago where he became director of the architecture program at IIT.

5. Lutz Robbers, "1912: Hellerau als 'Spielraum,'" in *Participation in Art and Architecture: Spaces of Participation and Occupation*, ed. Martino Stierli and Mechtild Widrich (London: I. B. Tauris, 2016), 198, 201. Robbers provides a highly detailed analysis that addresses issues closely related to the ones raised in this chapter.

6. Alongside a major furniture factory and several communal facilities, leading *Werkbund* architects designed Arts and Crafts-inspired houses; some four hundred houses were built in total, and by 1913 the Hellerau community had grown to almost two thousand residents. See Nils M. Schinker, *Die Gartenstadt Hellerau 1909–1945: Stadtbaukunst, Kleinwohnungsbau, Sozial- und Bodenreform* (Dresden: Sandstein Kommunikation, 2014) and Marco De Michelis, *Heinrich Tessenow 1876–1950: Das architektonische Gesamtwerk* (Stuttgart: Deutsche Verlags-Anstalt, 1991).

7. For a detailed definition of the complex term *Lebensphilosophie*, consult Nitzan Lebovic, "The Beauty and the Terror of Lebensphilosophie: Ludwig Klages, Walter Benjamin, and Alfred Baeumler," *South Central Review* 23, no. 1 (Spring 2006): 23–39, and Oliver A. I. Botar, "Defining Biocentrism," in *Biocentrism and Modernism*, ed. Oliver A. I. Botar and Isabel Wünsche (Farnham and Burlington: Ashgate, 2011), 15–45.

8. Poppelreuter, "Spaces for the elevated personal life."

9. Paul Claudel in an obituary for one of Hellerau's's founders, Wolf Dohrn, quoted in Nils M. Schinker, "Hellerau im Spannungsfeld sozialer und künstlerischer Reformansprüche des frühen 20. Jahrhunderts," in: *"Eine ganze Stadt müssen wir erbauen, eine ganze Stadt!" Die Künstlerkolonie Darmstadt auf der Mathildenhöhe,* Arbeitsheft 30 (Wiesbaden: Landesamt für Denkmalpflege, 2017), 135.

10. Karl Bücher, *Arbeit und Rhythmus* (Leipzig: Hirzel, 1896).

11. Already in 1906 Hellerau architect Theodor Fischer (1862–1938) formulated the ideal of a *Volkshaus*, describing it as "a house not to be inhabited by an individual or a family, but by all; not to study and to become wise, but rather simply happy; not to pray according to this or that belief, but rather to meditate and to live intimately. Therefore not a school, nor a museum, nor a church, nor a concert hall, nor an auditorium! . . . something of all of these and also something more." Theodor Fischer, quoted in Marco De Michelis and Vicki Bilenker, "Modernity and Reform, Heinrich Tessenow and the Institut Dalcroze at Hellerau," *Perspecta* 26 (1990): 150.

12. Émile Jaques-Dalcroze (Jakob Dalkes, 1865–1950) was born in Vienna where he studied music with Robert Fuchs and Anton Bruckner. Before coming to Hellerau, Jaques-Dalcroze taught harmony at the Conservatory in Geneva. He returned there after his Institute in Hellerau defaulted.

13. Margaret Naumburg, "The Dalcroze Idea: What Eurhythmics is and what it means," *The Outlook*, vol. 106 (17 January 1914), 127.

14. Émile Jaques-Dalcroze, quoted in De Michelis and Bilenker, "Modernity and Reform," 152.

15. Jaques-Dalcroze, letter to Wolf Dohrn, 1909, quoted in Ross Anderson, "Adolphe Appia and the Eurhythmic Promise of Hellerau," in *Bauhaus No. 8*, ed. Claudia Perren (Leipzig: Spector, 2016), 95 and Mary Elizabeth Tallon, "Appia's Theatre at Hellerau," *Theatre Journal* 36, no. 4 (December 1984): 496.

16. William Martin, quoted in Tallon, "Appia's Theatre at Hellerau," 496.

17. Despite all initial enthusiasm and political support, the building project had to overcome considerable resistance and uncertainties in its conception. Twice the allocated site was pushed further to the periphery of the garden city, and the design had to adapt. Yet within two years over three hundred students joined the Jaques-Dalcroze Institute, despite rather high fees, and in 1911 classes moved to the Institute's new building, then still under construction.

18. Alternately called *Festspielhaus* (festival hall) and *Bildungsanstalt* (academy), a precise English term for Jaques-Dalcroze's Institute is difficult to ascertain; a contemporary American article called it "College of Rhythm." Naumburg, "The Dalcroze Idea," 127.

19. Quoted in Richard C. Beacham, "Appia, Jaques-Dalcroze, and Hellerau: Part One: 'Music Made Visible,'" *New Theatre Quarterly* 1, no. 2 (May 1985): 163.

20. The buildings at Hellerau, including a number of radically simplified workers' houses, were among the first major commissions for Heinrich Tessenow (1876–1950) and set the tone for much of his later work.

21. Gerald Adler, "The German Reform Theatre: Heinrich Tessenow and Eurhythmic Performance Space at Dresden-Hellerau," in *Setting the Scene: Perspectives on Twentieth-Century Theatre Architecture*, ed. Alistair Fair (Abingdon: Routledge, 2015), 45.

22. The auditorium was twelve meters high, sixteen meters wide, and thirty-five meters long; a balcony above the entrance hall added another ten meters to the main auditorium space.

23. The raked banks of simple chairs were demountable and could be stored in a cavity underneath the auditorium floor. Once the seating was installed, that cavity was available as an orchestra pit.

24. Adolphe Appia (1862–1928) was a recluse, although he corresponded frequently with Jaques-Dalcroze, advising him on scenography and stage design. "Appia's theme was an action in relationship with an architecture," according to his obituary (Appia died young of a mental illness and alcohol). Jacques Copeau quoted in Tallon, "Appia's Theatre at Hellerau," 503.

25. Birgit Wiens, "Modular Settings and 'Creative Light': The Legacy of Adolphe Appia in the Digital Age," *International Journal of Performance Arts and Digital Media* 6, no.1 (2010): 28.

26. Adolphe Appia, quoted in Joseph L. Clarke, "How Not to Be 'Theatrical': Emile Jaques-Dalcroze, Adolphe Appia, Le Corbusier," *CENTER* 18 (2014): 108.

27. Adolphe Appia, quoted in Wiens, "Modular Settings and 'Creative Light,'" 35.

28. Alexander von Salzmann (1874–1934) must be credited with introducing lighting design to architecture well before the term *Lichtarchitektur* ("architecture of light") was coined by German engineer Joachim Teichmüller in 1926.

29. Some three thousand electric light bulbs, some colored, were installed behind translucent canvas screens, tightly stretched and impregnated with cedar oil. The light bulbs were wired to a central control panel, where a single operator could regulate intensity and distribution.

30. Alexander von Salzmann, "Licht Belichtung und Beleuchtung," in *Das Claudel-Programmbuch* (Hellerau: Hellerauer Verlag, 1913), 89, 90.

31. Appia quoted in Anderson, "Adolphe Appia," 99.

32. Kathleen James-Chakraborty, *German Architecture for a Mass Audience* (London: Routledge, 2000), 75.

33. Among the visitors in 1913 were Irish playwright George Bernard Shaw, the actor-director and theorist Harley Granville-Barker, the poets Rainer Maria Rilke and Franz Werfel as well as the painter Oskar Kokoschka, the theatre director and producer Max Reinhardt, the Russian actor and director Konstantin Stanislavski, and Serge Diaghilev, the artistic director of the infamous *Ballets Russes*. Many others made the pilgrimage to Hellerau, among them Ebenezer Howard, novelists Thomas Mann, Stefan Zweig and Upton Sinclair, painter Emil Nolde, art historians Heinrich Wölfflin, Wilhelm Worringer, Julius Meier-Graefe and architects Peter Behrens, Henry van de Velde, Hans Poelzig and Charles-Edouard Jeanneret. For an enthusiastic appreciation of the Hellerau experiment, see the introductory chapter "New Hellerau" in Harry Francis Mallgrave, *Architecture and Embodiment: The Implications of the New Sciences and Humanities for Design* (Abington and New York: Routledge, 2013), 1–8.

34. Katherine M. Kuenzli, "Architecture, Individualism, and Nation: Henry van de Velde's 1914 Werkbund Theater Building," *The Art Bulletin* 94, no. 2 (June 2012): 260.

35. Dorita Hannah, *Event-Space: Theatre Architecture and the Historical Avant-Garde* (New York: Routledge, 2019), 135.

36. In Hellerau, Albert Jeanneret (1886–1973) lived in the house Tessenow had designed for von Salzmann. His younger brother Charles-Edouard Jeanneret (1887–1965) was working with preeminent artist and architect Peter Behrens in Berlin at the time and came to visit. He was even offered to contribute as Tessenow's employee. In the end he declined and traveled instead. When Albert Jeanneret later returned to Paris and founded his own school of *plastique rhythmique*, Le Corbusier himself took a one-year course. He also published some of Albert Jeanneret's writings on Eurhythmics in his journal *L'Esprit Nouveau*.

37. Le Corbusier, quoted in Marco De Michelis, "Heinrich Tessenow: die Dresdner Jahre," *Academia.edu*, accessed 8 October 2016, PDF, 63.

38. For a more detailed discussion of Hellerau's influence on Le Corbusier, see Clarke, "How Not to Be 'Theatrical.'"

39. Mary Wigman (Karoline Sophie Marie Wiegmann, 1886–1973) developed groundbreaking choreographies in collaboration with Rudolf von Laban and new approaches to movement training and dance therapy. Through Wigman's student Erina Brady, who introduced modern dance to 1940s Dublin, the influence of Hellerau extended to Ireland. For details of the life of Mary Wigman, see Mary Anne Santos Newhall, *Mary Wigman* (Abington and New York: Routledge, 2009).

40. Mies took from Guardini's philosophy the notion that reality should be "artfully ordered," meaning that life should be secure on one hand but free to allow room for the unfolding of the spirit on the other hand so that, according to architectural historian Fritz Neumeyer, it would give "twentieth-century man the ordered, if contrasting, reality of both freedom and retreat, expansiveness and restraint." Fritz Neumeyer, *The Artless Word: Mies van der Rohe on the Building Art*, trans. Mark Jarzombek (London and Cambridge, MA: MIT Press, 1991), 200.

41. Before studying medicine in Freiburg, Hans Prinzhorn (1886–1933) had studied art history in Tübingen, concluding with a doctoral thesis on the aesthetics of German architect Gottfried Semper that led Prinzhorn to reject formalism and aestheticism. Prinzhorn's field-defining collection of artworks by psychiatric patients expanded the concept of art, and the related publication *Artistry of the Mentally Ill* (1922) was one of the first studies interested in the creative work of the mentally ill as a form of artistic expression. His investigations of the creative process caught the interest of artists and designers. Prinzhorn was invited to give guest lectures at the Bauhaus by Walter Gropius and Hannes Meyer as well as by Mies during their respective tenures as directors at the Bauhaus. The friendship between Prinzhorn and Mies lasted until Prinzhorn's death. For an outline of their friendship and professional collaboration, see Poppelreuter, "Spaces for the elevated personal life."

42. Hans Prinzhorn, *Leib—Seele—Einheit: Ein Kernproblem der neuen Psychologie* (Potsdam: Müller & Kiepenheuer, and Zürich: Orell Füssli, 1927), 13.

43. Prinzhorn, *Leib—Seele—Einheit*, 35.

44. Ludwig Klages, *Der Geist als Widersacher der Seele* (Bonn: Bouvier Verlag Herbert Grundmann, 1981).

45. Politically, Klages was an anti-Semite and Prinzhorn's philosophy, too, was situated in closer proximity to right-wing than left-wing politics between 1930 and 1932. Thomas Röske, "Hans Prinzhorn: ein 'Sinnender' in der Weimarer Republik,"

in *Wahn Welt Bild: Die Sammlung Prinzhorn*, ed. Kai Brodersen and Thomas Fuchs (Heidelberg: Universitäts-Gesellschaft, 2002), 34.

46. Prinzhorn, *Leib—Seele—Einheit*, 72.

47. Six issues of *G: Materialen zur Elementaren* Gestaltung [G: Materials for Elemental Form-Creation] were published between 1923 and 1926, with Hans Richter, Werner Graeff and Ludwig Mies van der Rohe as its main editors. Detlef Mertins and Michael W. Jennings, eds., *G: An Avant-Garde Journal of Art, Architecture, Design, and Film, 1923–1926* (Los Angeles: Getty Research Institute, 2010).

48. Neumeyer, *The Artless Word*, 197.

49. Ludwig Mies van der Rohe, "Lecture" [17 March 1926], in Neumeyer, *The Artless Word*, 252–256.

50. Tanja Poppelreuter, *Das Neue Bauen für den Neuen Men*schen (Hildesheim and Zurich: Olms, 2007).

51. Ludwig Mies van der Rohe, "Vorwort," in *Die Wohnung: Amtlicher Katalog der Werkbundausstellung* (Stuttgart: Tagblatt Buchdruckerei, 1927), 5.

52. Claire Zimmerman, *Photographic Architecture in the Twentieth Century* (Minneapolis: University of Minnesota Press, 2014), 76, 77.

53. Zimmerman, *Photographic Architecture*, 78.

54. Manfredo Tafuri, "The Stage as 'Virtual City': From Fuchs to the Totaltheater," in *Sphere and Labyrinth: Piranesi, architecture and the avant-garde*, trans. Pellegrino d'Aciero and Robert Connolly (London and Cambridge, MA: MIT Press, 1987), 111. See also Lutz Robbers, "Modern Architecture in the Age of Cinema: Mies van der Rohe and the Moving Image" (PhD diss., Princeton University, 2012), 246; and Zimmerman, *Photographic Architecture*, 76.

55. Detlef Mertins, *Mies* (London and New York: Phaidon, 2014), 180.

56. Walter Riezler, quoted in Mertins, *Mies*, 175.

57. Walter Riezler's enthusiastically positive appraisal of the house was countered by Justus Bier with the pointed question, "Can one live in the Tugendhat House?" A public debate in the influential architectural periodical *Die Form* ensued. This exchange between critics, supporters and clients is well documented and widely discussed, see for instance: Daniela Hammer-Tugendhat, Ivo Hammer and Wolf Tegethoff, ed. *Ludwig Mies van der Rohe: The Tugendhat House*. Basel: Birkhäuser, 2014; Mertins, *Mies*, 168–181; Dietrich Neumann, "'Can one live in the Tugendhat House?': A Sketch," *Wolkenkuckucksheim*, no. 32 (2012): 87–99.

58. Justus Bier, "Kann man im Haus Tugendhat wohnen?" *Die Form* 6, no. 10 (October 1931): 392.

59. Roger Ginsburger and Walter Riezler, "Zweckhaftigkeit und geistige Haltung," *Die Form* 6, no. 11 (November 1931): 433.

60. Grete Tugendhat [Letter to the editor], *Die Form* 6, no. 11 (November 1931): 438.

61. Ludwig Hilberseimer, "Nachwort zur Diskussion um das Haus Tugendhat," *Die Form* 6, no. 11 (November 1931): 438.

62. And further, "The rhythm of the large room is so strong that small changes are insignificant." Tugendhat [Letter to the editor], 438.

63. Fritz Tugendhat, “Kann man im Haus Tugendhat wohnen?” *Die Form* 6, no. 11 (November 1931): 437.

64. Mertins, *Mies*, 179.

65. Prinzhorn, *Leib—Seele—Einheit*, 72.

66. Mies van der Rohe, “Office Building,” *G,* no. 1 (July 1923), 3.

67. Adolphe Appia, quoted in Clarke, “How Not to Be ‘Theatrical,’” 111.

68. For the alleged influence of cinema on Mies’s architecture, see for instance Robbers, “Modern Architecture in the Age of Cinema;” and Lutz Robbers, “Filmkämpfer Mies,” in *Mies van der Rohe im Diskurs*, ed. Kerstin Plüm (Bielefeld: Transcript Verlag, 2014), 63–95.

BIBLIOGRAPHY

Adler, Gerald. “The German Reform Theatre: Heinrich Tessenow and Eurhythmic Performance Space at Dresden-Hellerau.” In *Setting the Scene: Perspectives on Twentieth-Century Theatre Architecture*, edited by Alistair Fair, 35–59. Abingdon: Routledge, 2015.

Anderson, Ross. “Adolphe Appia and the Eurhythmic Promise of Hellerau.” In *Bauhaus No. 8*, edited by Claudia Perren, 94–99. Leipzig: Spector, 2016.

Beacham, Richard C. “Appia, Jaques-Dalcroze, and Hellerau: Part One: ‘Music Made Visible.’” *New Theatre Quarterly* 1, no. 2 (May 1985): 154–164.

———. “Appia, Jaques-Dalcroze, and Hellerau: Part Two: ‘Poetry in Motion.’” *New Theatre Quarterly* 1, no. 3 (August 1985): 245–261.

Botar, Oliver A. I. “Defining Biocentrism.” In *Biocentrism and Modernism*, edited by Oliver A. I. Botar and Isabel Wünsche, 15–45. Farnham and Burlington: Ashgate, 2011.

Bücher, Karl. *Arbeit und Rhythmus*. Leipzig: Hirzel, 1896.

Clarke, Joseph L. “How Not to Be ‘Theatrical’: Emile Jaques-Dalcroze, Adolphe Appia, Le Corbusier.” *CENTER* 18 (2014): 102–113.

De Michelis, Marco. *Heinrich Tessenow 1876–1950: Das architektonische Gesamtwerk*. Stuttgart: Deutsche Verlags-Anstalt, 1991.

———. “Heinrich Tessenow: die Dresdner Jahre.” *Academia.edu*, accessed 8 October 2016, PDF, 52–67.

De Michelis, Marco, and Vicki Bilenker. “Modernity and Reform, Heinrich Tessenow and the Institut Dalcroze at Hellerau.” *Perspecta* 26 (1990): 143–170. DOI:10.2307/1567159.

Hannah, Dorita. *Event-Space: Theatre Architecture and the Historical Avant-Garde*. New York: Routledge, 2019.

James-Chakraborty, Kathleen. *German Architecture for a Mass Audience*. London: Routledge, 2000.

Klages, Ludwig. *Der Geist als Widersacher der Seele*. Bonn: Bouvier Verlag Herbert Grundmann, 1981 [3 vols. 1929, 1932].

Kuenzli, Katherine M. "Architecture, Individualism, and Nation: Henry van de Velde's 1914 Werkbund Theater Building." *The Art Bulletin* 94, no. 2 (June 2012): 251–273, DOI: 10.1080/00043079.2012.10786040.

Lebovic, Nitzan. "The Beauty and the Terror of Lebensphilosophie: Ludwig Klages, Walter Benjamin, and Alfred Baeumler." *South Central Review* 23, no. 1 (Spring 2006): 23–39.

Mallgrave, Harry Francis. *Architecture and Embodiment: The Implications of the New Sciences and Humanities for Design.* Abington and New York: Routledge, 2013.

Mertins, Detlef. *Mies*. London and New York: Phaidon, 2014.

Mertins, Detlef, and Michael W. Jennings, eds. *G: An Avant-Garde Journal of Art, Architecture, Design, and Film, 1923–1926.* Los Angeles: Getty Research Institute, 2010.

Müller, Ulrich. *Raum, Bewegung und Zeit im Werk von Walter Gropius und Ludwig Mies van der Rohe.* Berlin: Akademie Verlag, 2004.

Naumburg, Margaret. "The Dalcroze Idea: What Eurhythmics Is and What It Means." *The Outlook* 106 (17 January 1914): 127–131.

Neumeyer, Fritz. *The Artless Word: Mies van der Rohe on the Building Art*. Translated by Mark Jarzombek. London and Cambridge, MA: MIT Press, 1991.

Poppelreuter, Tanja. *Das Neue Bauen für den Neuen Menschen*. Hildesheim and Zurich: Olms, 2007.

———. "Spaces for the Elevated Personal Life: Ludwig Mies van der Rohe's Concept of the Dweller, 1926–1930." *The Journal of Architecture* 21, no. 2 (2016): 244–270, DOI: 10.1080/13602365.2016.1160946.

Prinzhorn, Hans. *Leib—Seele—Einheit: Ein Kernproblem der neuen Psychologie*. Potsdam: Müller & Kiepenheuer and Zurich, Orell Füssli, 1927.

Robbers, Lutz. "1912: Hellerau als 'Spielraum.'" In *Participation in Art and Architecture: Spaces of Participation and Occupation*, edited by Martino Stierli and Mechtild Widrich, 197–226. London: I. B. Tauris, 2016.

———. "Filmkämpfer Mies." In *Mies van der Rohe im Diskurs*, edited by Kerstin Plüm, 63–95. Bielefeld: Transcript Verlag, 2014. DOI: 10.14361/transcript.9783839423059.63.

———. "Modern Architecture in the Age of Cinema: Mies van der Rohe and the Moving Image." PhD dissertation, Princeton University, 2012.

Röske, Thomas. "Hans Prinzhorn: ein 'Sinnender' in der Weimarer Republik." In *Wahn Welt Bild: Die Sammlung Prinzhorn*, edited by Kai Brodersen and Thomas Fuchs, 31–40. Heidelberg: Universitäts-Gesellschaft, 2002.

Santos Newhall, Mary Anne. *Mary Wigman*. Abington and New York: Routledge, 2009.

Schinker, Nils M. *Die Gartenstadt Hellerau 1909–1945: Stadtbaukunst, Kleinwohnungsbau, Sozial- und Bodenreform*. Dresden: Sandstein Kommunikation, 2014.

———. "Hellerau im Spannungsfeld sozialer und künstlerischer Reformansprüche des frühen 20. Jahrhunderts." In *"Eine ganze Stadt müssen wir erbauen, eine ganze Stadt!": Die Künstlerkolonie Darmstadt auf der Mathildenhöhe,* Arbeitsheft 30, 135–144. Wiesbaden: Landesamt für Denkmalpflege, 2017.

Tafuri, Manfredo. "The Stage as 'Virtual City': From Fuchs to the Totaltheater." In *Sphere and Labyrinth: Piranesi, Architecture and the Avant-garde*. Translated by Pellegrino d'Aciero and Robert Connolly, 95–112. London and Cambridge, MA: MIT Press, 1987.

Tallon, Mary Elizabeth. "Appia's Theatre at Hellerau." *Theatre Journal* 36, no. 4 (December 1984): 495–504.

von Salzmann, Alexander. "Licht Belichtung und Beleuchtung." In *Das Claudel-Programmbuch*, 88–91. Hellerau: Hellerauer Verlag, 1913.

Wiens, Birgit. "Modular Settings and 'Creative Light': The Legacy of Adolphe Appia in the Digital Age." *International Journal of Performance Arts and Digital Media* 6, no.1 (2010): 25–39.

Zimmerman, Claire. *Photographic Architecture in the Twentieth Century*. Minneapolis: University of Minnesota Press, 2014.

Index

Page references for figures are italicized.

About the Contributors

Dr. **Finola Cronin** (Limerick) lectures in Drama Studies in the School of English, Drama, Film, and Creative Writing at UCD. She danced with Company Vivienne Newport (Frankfurt), Tanztheater Wuppertal (Pina Bausch), Raimund Hoghe (Germany/France), and most recently with Liz Roche Company (Dublin), and visual artist John Gerrard Austria/Ireland. Recent publications: *The Contemporary Irish Theatre and Performance Studies Reader* (with E. Jordan, Carysfort Press, 2016); "On Peregrine Collaborations: Cindy Cummings' Choreography of Triúr Ban: Woman, Disorientation, Displacement" in *Dance Matters* (eds. A. McGrath and E. Meehan, Palgrave Macmillan, 2018). A further publication on Pina Bausch is forthcoming (Palgrave Macmillan).

Irish-born **Marguerite Donlon** (Berlin) is a contemporary choreographer based in Berlin and Hagen, Germany. A former solo dancer with the English National Ballet and later with the Deutsche Oper Berlin (1990), she was appointed ballet director and choreographer at the Saarländisches Staatstheater from 2001 to 2013. She has created works worldwide for companies such as Nederlands Dans Theater 2, Stuttgart Ballet, Hubbard Street, Chicago, Rambert Dance, London, and Svetlanja Zacharova, Bolshoi, and been nominated for awards such as the "Prix Benois de la Danse" and the "Die Faust." Donlon was awarded the Medal of Merit in the Saarland (2007) and the Longford Civic Reception in honor of her distinguished career (2017). She is currently the ballet director and choreographer of Ballet Hagen, Germany, and Donlon Dance Collective Berlin.

Dr. **Sabine Egger** (Limerick) is Lecturer in German Studies at Mary Immaculate College and Joint Director of the Irish Centre for Transnational Studies. She has published widely on memory and questions of identity/alterity in German literature in the eighteenth to twenty-first centuries, including a monograph on Johannes Bobrowski's poetry (2009). Her current research focuses on space and movement across cultural and media boundaries in a European context. Recent publications include special issues of international journals (*ZiG; GiI*) on transit spaces in literature, film, and other media (co-edited with W. Bonner and E. Hess-Lüttich, 2016), articles on transit and borderland spaces in the work of contemporary authors such as Herta Müller or Lutz Seiler, and chapters on alterity in Theodor Fontane's *Effi Briest* and Thomas Mann's *Buddenbrooks* in the respective *Metzler Handbooks* (2018; 2019).

Dr. **Ruth Fleischmann** (Bielefeld) was born and educated in Cork and graduated from University College Cork in 1963. In 1968 she began to teach English at third level in Germany and from 1975 to 1980 taught at the University of Constantine in Algeria. From 1981 until she retired in 2007, she held a lectureship in the English Department of the University of Bielefeld in Germany and was Dean of Studies of her faculty. Her field of research is Irish Cultural Studies; she has published about forty articles and ten books.

Dr. **Catherine E. Foley** (Limerick) is Emeritus Senior Lecturer in Ethnochoreology at the Irish World Academy of Music and Dance, University of Limerick. She is Founding Chair Emerita of the international society Dance Research Forum Ireland, and Founding Director of the National Dance Archive of Ireland. Catherine is also the elected Chair of the Study Group on Ethnochoreology of the International Council for Traditional Music (ICTM) and is an elected member of the ICTM's Executive Board. Her research has been published in *Yearbook for Traditional Music*, *Dance Research Journal*, *Dance Research,* and *New Hibernia Review*. Her monographs include *Irish Traditional Step Dancing in North Kerry* (North Kerry Literary Trust, 2012) and *Step Dancing in Ireland: Culture and History* (Ashgate, 2013). Catherine's choreographies include *The Sionna Set Dance* (2007), and she has produced and performed in *Stór Damhsa* (2016), her solo step-dance DVD. Catherine is a dancer and musician.

Jan Frohburg (Limerick) is Lecturer in Architecture at the University of Limerick. A graduate of the Bauhaus University Weimar, he studied and taught architecture in Germany, Great Britain, Switzerland, and the United States. His main research interests include design education and the spatial expression of modernity, focusing on concepts characteristic to the work of Mies van der Rohe. Recently published articles include "Regarding Mies' courtyard houses" (2016), "The presence of art in Mies van der Rohe's houses" (2014), and "Ideas of freedom and nature in the work of Mies van der Rohe" (2012).

Margaret Mills Harper (Limerick) is Glucksman Professor in Contemporary Writing in English at the University of Limerick. She specializes in modern and contemporary Irish literature and the literature of the United States, especially poetry. She is the author of *The Aristocracy of Art: Joyce and Wolfe* (Louisiana State University Press, 1990) and *Wisdom of Two: The Spiritual and Literary Collaboration of George and W. B. Yeats* (Oxford University Press, 2006). She has co-edited four scholarly editions: two of the four volumes of *Yeats's* Vision *Papers* (1992 and 2001, with George Mills Harper), and both the 1925 and 1937 versions of Yeats's *A Vision* (2008 and 2015, with Catherine E. Paul). A former recipient of a fellowship from the National Endowment for the Humanities, she is also former Director of the Yeats International Summer School and former President of the International Yeats Society.

Dr. **Gisela Holfter** (Limerick) is Senior Lecturer in German and co-founder and Director of the Centre for Irish-German Studies, University of Limerick. Her research interests include German-Irish relations, German literature (nineteenth century to contemporary writing), exile studies, migration, and intercultural communication. She is a member of the PEN German-speaking Writers Abroad, has published many articles, and co-edited fifteen books, including *Wandern und Plaudern mit Fontane* (with G. Weiss-Sussex, Quintus 2019) *Ireland in the European Eye* (with B. Migge, Royal Irish Academy 2019), and *Exploring Connections between Ireland and the GDR* (with D. Byrnes and J. Conacher, WVT 2019). Her monographs include *Erlebnis Irland* (1996, WVT), *Heinrich Böll and Ireland* (CSP 2011, paperback 2012), and *An Irish Sanctuary: German-speaking Refugees in Ireland 1933–1945* (with H. Dickel, de Gruyter 2017, paperback 2018).

Susan Jones (Oxford) is Professor of English Literature and Fellow of St Hilda's College. She has published widely on Joseph Conrad, including *Conrad and Women* for Oxford University Press, nineteenth- and twentieth-century women's writing, the periodical press, and modernism. She continues to co-edit the Cambridge Edition of Conrad's novel *Chance* (1914). Formerly a soloist with the Scottish Ballet, Glasgow, she also writes on the history and aesthetics of dance. She is founder and director of Dance Scholarship Oxford (http://www.torch.ox.ac.uk/dansox) and author of *Literature, Modernism, and Dance* (Oxford University Press, 2013). She was awarded a Leverhulme Fellowship 2017–2018 to write on Samuel Beckett and choreography.

Dr. **Deirdre Mulrooney** (Dublin) is currently an inaugural UCD Arts and Humanities Creative Fellow. She is author of *Irish Moves: An Illustrated History of Dance and Physical Theatre in Ireland* (2006), and *Orientalism, Orientation, and the Nomadic Work of Pina Bausch* (2002), as well as several publications across the arts. A specialist in twentieth-century dance history in Ireland, her film documentaries *Dance Emergency* (TG4 Splanc!), and *1943—A Dance Odyssey* (RTÉ One) about Erina Brady have been screened at film festivals worldwide. Deirdre's most recent BAI-funded documentary on Lucia Joyce's modern dance career was broadcast on RTÉ Lyric FM in July 2019, and her short dance film "Lucia Joyce: Full Capacity," which premiered at Bloomsday Trieste 2019, is currently screening widely at Festivals. See www.deirdremulrooney.com.

Dr. **Tanja Poppelreuter** (Manchester) is Lecturer in the History and Theory of Architecture at the University of Salford, Manchester. Previously, she taught Art History at Auckland University, New Zealand, and at Ulster University, Belfast. Her research focuses on early twentieth-century architecture and émigré architects who fled the Nazi regime. Recent publications include *Glamour and Gloom: Modern Architecture of the 1930s in Belfast* (2017), "Architecture as Method of Self-Realization: The Belfast Architect Florence Fulton Hobson" (2017), "Spaces for the Elevated Personal Life: Ludwig Mies van der Rohe's Concept of the Dweller, 1926–1930" (2016), and "Before 1939: Émigré Architects to New Zealand 1933 to 1939" (2016).

Dr. **Siobhán Purcell**'s (Galway) research primarily focuses on representations of disability, impairment, and decadence in Irish literature. In 2016, she completed her PhD thesis on the subject of disability in Beckett's prose, poetry, and translations (1928–1945). This work was completed at NUI Galway and funded by the Irish Research Council. Her work has been published in *Samuel Beckett Today/Aujourd'hui*, *Breac*, *Dublin James Joyce Journal*, and the *James Joyce Literary Supplement.* She is currently expanding her research to include a number of Irish authors and has forthcoming articles on James Joyce, Samuel Beckett, Brian O'Nolan, and Lynda Radley.

Dr. **Lucia Ruprecht** (Cambridge) is a Fellow of Emmanuel College and an affiliated Lecturer at the Section of German and Dutch, University of Cambridge, UK. She has published widely on dance, literature, and film. She is author of *Gestural Imaginaries: Dance and Cultural Theory in the Early Twentieth Century* (Oxford University Press, 2019) and *Dances of the Self in Heinrich von Kleist, E. T. A. Hoffmann and Heinrich Heine* (Ashgate, 2006), edited *Towards an Ethics of Gesture* (special section of *Performance Philosophy*, 2017), and co-edited *New German Dance Studies* (University of Illinois Press, 2012), *Cultural Pleasure* (special issue of *German Life and Letters*, 2009), and *Performance and Performativity in German Cultural Studies* (Lang, 2003). Together with B. Brandl-Risi, she is preparing the *Handbuch Literatur & Performance* (de Gruyter, 2021).

Dr. **Joseph Twist** (Dublin) is a Lecturer in German Studies at University College Dublin. In broad terms, he is interested in the intersection of philosophy, religion, and literature. He focuses on the interaction between mystical and postmodern thought in the work of contemporary German authors of varying Muslim backgrounds, such as Navid Kermani, Emine Sevgi Özdamar, SAID, Zafer Şenocak, and Feridun Zaimoglu, analyzing the non-identitarian spirituality of their fiction and its transnational contexts. He has various publications in this field, including the book *Mystical Islam and Cosmopolitanism in Contemporary German Literature: Openness to Alterity* (Camden House, 2018).